TEXT AND TRUTH

REDEFINING BIBLICAL THEOLOGY

TEXT AND TRUTH

REDEFINING BIBLICAL THEOLOGY

Francis Watson

William B. Eerdmans Publishing Company
Grand Rapids, Michigan

Contents

PREFACE   vii

INTRODUCTION   1

PART ONE
STUDIES IN THEOLOGICAL HERMENEUTICS

1. The Gospels as Narrated History   33
   1. *Narrative and the Eclipse of History*   34
   2. *History and Difference*   37
   3. *History-Writing*   41
   4. *History and Tradition*   45
   5. *Events and Fiction*   54
   Notes   63

2. The Multiple Text and the Singular Gospel   71
   1. *The Singularity of the Gospel*   73
   2. *Mark as Parable*   78
   3. *The Glory of God in the Face of Christ*   82
   Notes   89

3. Literal Sense, Authorial Intention, Objective Interpretation:
   In Defence of Some Unfashionable Concepts   95
   1. *Writing as Communication*   98
   2. *Establishing the Literal Sense*   107
   Notes   124

4. Erasing the Text: Readings in Neo-Marcionism   127
    1. Schleiermacher   128
    2. Harnack   141
    3. Bultmann   153
    Notes   169

PART TWO
THE OLD TESTAMENT IN CHRISTOLOGICAL PERSPECTIVE

5. Old Testament Theology as a Christian Theological Enterprise   179
    1. Eichrodt   185
    2. Von Rad   197
    3. Childs   209
    Notes   219

6. Creation in the Beginning   225
    1. Creation as Foundation   227
    2. Creation in the Beginning and 'Natural Theology'   242
    Notes   267

7. In the Image of God   277
    1. Anthropology in Christological Perspective   279
    2. Image and Dominion   288
    Notes   300

8. Scripture in Dialogue: A Study in Early Christian
    Old Testament Interpretation   305
    1. From Athens to Jerusalem   310
    2. Torah as Divine Accommodation   313
    3. Prophecy and Proof   317
    4. The Old Testament and Christological Construction   320
    Notes   325

INDEX OF SCRIPTURAL TEXTS   331

INDEX OF SUBJECTS   339

INDEX OF NAMES   341

Preface

As redefined and practised in this book, 'biblical theology' is an inter-disciplinary approach to biblical interpretation which seeks to dismantle the barriers that at present separate biblical scholarship from Christian theology. Biblical theology is a theological, hermeneutical and exegetical discipline, and its hermeneutical and exegetical dimensions are placed at the disposal of its overriding theological concern.

In my previous book, *Text, Church and World* (Edinburgh: T. & T. Clark; Grand Rapids: Eerdmans, 1994), I began to outline and to practise a 'biblical interpretation in theological perspective', making extensive use of contemporary literary, canonical and feminist approaches to the biblical texts. A number of concerns have been raised by reviewers, who have questioned my criticisms of conventional historical-critical scholarship, the hermeneutical roles I assign to the canon and the church, and indeed the propriety of practising Christian theology at all in the modern, secular university. One reviewer suggested that I was 'in danger of swapping the exegetes' guild for that of the systematic theologians' – thereby missing the whole point of the book, which was to challenge precisely this structure of mutually-exclusive, self-contained 'guilds'. Another was dismayed to find that at one point a dis-tinction between 'believers' and 'non-believers' was drawn in what purported to be an 'academic' work. (It was not explained exactly how the academy is supposed to transcend this distinction.) Another reported that, as a non-believing biblical scholar, he felt excluded by my book. His response to this unfortunate experience was to reiterate his strident demand that Christian faith and theology should be excluded from academic discourse. Reactions such as these were only to be expected, and I do not find that there is anything in them that should cause me to rethink. Underlying most of them, it seems, is a basic inability to believe that Christian faith, in a more or less definite form, actually has a right to exist; that it still has a recognizable communal location; and that these facts have implications for the ways in which biblical interpretation is practised. Modern biblical scholarship has devised a variety of strategies for concealing, evading or denying the simple fact that Christian faith has its own *distinctive* reasons for concern with the Bible. To reassert this fact, and to draw from it implications about how biblical interpretation should be practised, is to break with the tacit consensus that this fact should on no account be mentioned. It is always tactless, impolite and risky to break with a consensus, but it is sometimes absolutely obligatory to do so.

The present book therefore attempts to clarify and elaborate the position outlined in the previous one. But both the subject-matter and the approach are somewhat different. The theological focus is, I think, sharper and more consistently maintained. The programmatic redefinition of 'biblical theology' is new, and so too is the technique of building up what I hope is still a coherent position by way of independent although mutually-reinforcing studies of particular topics. The range of topics covered is broader, and there is less emphasis on the interpretative possibilities opened up by contemporary non-historical modes of biblical interpretation. The complex relationship between text and truth is explored more thoroughly.

Of the many colleagues and friends who have been supportive of my work, I should like to mention in particular Alan Torrance and Iain Provan. Conversations with each of them, about systematic theology and Old Testament interpretation respectively, have left their mark at many points in this book.

FRANCIS WATSON
King's College, London

Introduction

For Christian faith, and therefore for Christian theology, truth is textually mediated. 'Truth' here is not any truth but the truth that the Word through whom all things were made is the Word who in Jesus Christ has become flesh. In this truth all other truth is comprehended. Yet there is for us no direct and immediate access to the Word made flesh; for this Word was uttered and this fleshly existence occurred in our own world but at a time and place that is not our own. This definitive divine Word was and is addressed to us, but, if the gap between its particular time and place and our own is to be bridged, then certain forms of mediation are necessary. The Spirit of truth bears witness to the grace and truth that are to be found in the enfleshed Word not directly but in and through the Christian community – in and through its preaching, its worship, its sacraments and its canonical texts. These texts are foundational to the life of the church, not on the legalistic and biblicistic grounds that they possess an inherent, absolute authority to which we are bound to submit, but on the grounds that in them we encounter the particular life upon which the communal life of the church is founded; the life that is the light not only of the church but also of the world. For that reason and in that sense, preaching, worship and sacraments must conform to these texts.

This textual mediation of truth does not imply that Jesus' first followers shared in an initial experience of non-textual immediacy whose textual embodiment is a necessary but secondary phenomenon. The Word made flesh is never encountered without textual mediation, for Jesus is only recognized as such on the basis of a prior textuality. Jesus is initially acknowledged as Christ and Lord because that which takes place in him is said to take place 'according to the scriptures'. In a circular relationship, the scriptures are reread in the light of what has taken place in Jesus in order that what has taken place in Jesus should be adequately understood as what it truly is, God's definitive self-disclosure and saving action. Without these prior writings – the 'Old Testament' – this understanding would be impossible. The life of Jesus does not take place in a text-free vacuum in which his followers are able to enjoy immediate experiences of the divine. Even on Easter Day, Jesus cannot be truly recognized unless it is understood that his death and resurrection are foreshadowed in the scriptures (Luke 24). The texts of both Testaments are necessary if the full scope of the truth that lies at their centre is to be grasped.[1]

If that is the case, then all Christian theology must be 'biblical theology' – not in the sense that it should consist in nothing but biblical exegesis but in the sense that the particular truth attested in the biblical texts must constitute its centre and foundation. If – as I shall argue – a specialized 'biblical theology' is needed that is not coextensive with Christian theology as a whole, this necessity can only be a pragmatic one. Consideration of the pragmatic necessity of such a project will clarify the nature of the project itself.

I

The pragmatic necessity for a specialized 'biblical theology' lies in the modern reconstruction of the theological curriculum. The Christian Bible is the object of study for three distinct communities of interpreters. Each community has its own relatively autonomous disciplinary structures. Each has developed an extensive and ever-expanding secondary literature, with its great names of past and present, its monograph series and its journals. Each offers programmes of graduate training and career possibilities, thereby securing its own future. Each promotes social interaction between its members, for example by way of conferences. Each lays claim to a relatively clearly-defined field, within which one encounters a complex network of subject-areas, traditions, methods and criteria, coexisting with one another in harmony, indifference, tension or antagonism, and constantly generating new patterns of alliance and alignment. Each, in other words, betrays the characteristic features of any modern 'academic discipline'. Interpretative communities condition their members to regard their disciplinary structures as normal and self-evident, and it therefore requires a conscious effort of the imagination to perceive the coexistence of three distinct communities of biblical interpreters as the anomaly that it actually is.

The first line of demarcation within the three communities differentiates 'biblical scholars' from 'theologians'. 'Biblical scholars' do not normally identify themselves as 'theologians', and 'theologians' do not normally identify themselves as 'biblical scholars'. In other words, biblical scholars define their own fields as essentially non-theological or pre-theological, and theologians ('systematic theologians', 'dogmaticians', or whatever) define their own field as lying outside the sphere of ('scholarly') biblical interpretation. Biblical scholars may have theological interests which impinge upon their work (although if so they may well be criticized for this); and theologians will inevitably have at least some interest in biblical interpretation. Yet disciplinary structures operate in such a way as to inhibit the pursuit of real competence in a field that has been defined in advance as lying outside one's own. Here, in one's own 'field', one strives to work to the highest possible professional standards; there, in someone else's 'field', one is an amateur, diffident about one's own abilities and over-dependent on the work of others.

The line of demarcation between 'biblical studies' and 'systematic theology' has normative force and does not represent a mere division of labour. It is true that some division of labour is necessary. The complexity of modern biblical interpretation requires some scholars to specialize in textual criticism, others in the synoptic gospels, others in the Pauline letters; and if even 'New Testament studies' (as currently understood and practised) is too large a field for any one individual to master in its entirety, the decision to limit this field to non-theological or pre-theological approaches might seem a wise precaution. Yet the line of demarcation was not established merely as a concession to human and scholarly finitude. If that were its significance, then there could be no objection in principle to scholars who chose to work on both sides of the boundary; this would simply be another example of the 'interdisciplinary' work which is an entirely acceptable aspect of scholarly endeavour. Biblical scholars may choose to work in quite different fields such as sociology or literary theory, in order to acquire new perspectives and insights to apply to the biblical texts. At this point, the existence of a disciplinary boundary is quite compatible with the decision to work with material acquired outside that boundary. This is not the case with theology, however: to bring theological – as opposed to sociological or literary – material within the disciplinary boundary would be to ignore the fact that at this point the disciplinary boundary has normative force. It does not merely represent a convenient division of labour; it claims the right to exercise a veto. Interdisciplinary work involving biblical studies and systematic theology is therefore a perilous and vulnerable activity whose legitimacy is open to serious doubt.

It might seem obvious that, since Christian theology must have an interest in biblical interpretation, theological concerns should have an acknowledged place within the field of biblical scholarship. Yet this is not at all the case. Theological concerns are, to be sure, not entirely absent, yet they are rarely identified as such; they lie half-concealed beneath a discourse that operates by non-theological criteria, and they cannot be subjected to explicitly theological development or critique. There are a number of interrelated reasons for this. First, the situation exactly mirrors the enforced privatization of religious commitment in modern western societies. Religious commitment is tolerated only in so far as it accepts its exclusion from the realm of properly public discourse: at this point the wider society has shaped the community of biblical scholars in its own image. Second, it is believed that theological concerns have an inevitable tendency to distort the autonomous processes of biblical exegesis – a prejudice so strong that to identify a theological motivation underlying an exegetical position is often held to be sufficient refutation. Third, there is an unwillingness to accept the existence and the significance of theology as a discipline in its own right. One of several roots of this unwillingness is, perversely, the popular Protestant insistence on *sola scriptura*. When one has the Bible, what need is there for the subtleties and sophistries of theology? In evangelical Christianity, the Bible is typically read with scant regard for the long and intricate dialogue with the Bible that is the history of Christian theology. Many (most?) Protestant biblical scholars are attracted to the field in the first place by an evangelical piety of this kind, and – whatever else is abandoned under the notoriously destructive impact of the so-called 'historical-critical method' – the abstraction of the biblical texts from their theological *Wirkungsgeschichte* is tenaciously maintained.

This attempt to exclude theology from the field of biblical interpretation has had a marked effect on the practice of theology itself. Theologians can hardly abandon all concern with the Bible, yet their relation to it has become indirect and second-hand. The field assigned to them is now post-biblical, and consists in the history of Christian doctrine from the Apologists to the present, understood in the light of and for the purpose of contemporary theological construction. Since this history is a history of dialogue with the biblical texts, a relation to biblical interpretation is retained; and direct appeal to biblical material is still practised. Yet the pervasive effect of the line of demarcation is seen in the theologian's characteristic assumption that, in drawing upon material from the Old or New Testament, he or she has entered someone else's professional domain. At home with Irenaeus, Schleiermacher and Barth, one is in danger of trespassing if one engages too freely in the interpretation of Isaiah, Paul or John. The biblical writings are no longer the intellectual property of the theologian. Where theologians accept biblical scholars' property-rights in this area, the fact that for Christian faith truth is textually mediated will be systematically distorted. The theologian will abstract truth from its concrete textual mediation, just as the biblical scholar has abstracted the texts from their truth-mediating function. Where this occurs, text and truth have fallen apart.

One line of demarcation divides biblical scholars from theologians; a second absolutizes the division of the Christian Bible into Old and New Testaments by assigning these collections to separate interpretative communities. Unlike the first, this second line of demarcation is not a site of inter-communal tension. The two interpretative communities have no difficulty acknowledging each other's right to exist, and dwell peacefully alongside one another in mutual indifference. The issues that move one discipline – the collapse of the pentateuchal documentary hypothesis, the 'new perspective on Paul' – will generally be ignored in the other. New Testament scholarship regards the Old Testament only as 'background' upon which one can often draw without much recourse to Old Testament scholarship: for the reuse of a text in the first century AD seems to have little to do with its 'original' setting in the eighth or the fifth century BC. Old Testament scholars have even less reason for interest in the affairs of the neighbouring discipline. The current tendency to rename their object of study as the 'Hebrew Bible' is the result not only of sensitivity to the presence of Jewish scholars in the field but also of a long-standing unease about the encroachment of 'anachronistic' Christian theological concerns and conceptuality. Unlike the 'Old Testament', the 'Hebrew Bible' is a complete and self-contained body of writings. Scholars of the 'Hebrew Bible' need the New Testament almost as little as New Testament scholars need the Koran; it lies beyond their normal field of vision. Even where the discipline of 'Old Testament theology' is practised and reflected on, the Old Testament is often considered in more or less complete isolation from its canonical place within Christian scripture. The separation and self-sufficiency of biblical scholarship's two interpretative communities ensure that serious and informed reflection on the relation between the Testaments is kept to a minimum. It is widely assumed that theological concerns of that sort – still taken seriously by scholars of the stature of Gerhard von Rad – have long since been superseded.[2]

It is tempting to suppose that this second line of demarcation is a less serious problem than the first – that the decision to limit biblical scholarship to non- or pre-theological approaches matters much more than the indifference of Old and New Testament scholars to one another's concerns. In reality, the second line of demarcation is simply an extension of the first. The notion of a dialectical unity between two bodies of writing, constituted as 'old' and 'new' by their relation to the foundational event that they together enclose and attest, only makes sense from a theological standpoint. Where theological concerns are marginalized, the two Testaments fall apart almost automatically. The Old Testament ceases to be Christian scripture at all, at least if the term 'Christian' implies a reference to Christ, and the New Testament's relation to the Old comes to seem hardly more significant than its relation to other elements in its 'background' such as the Dead Sea Scrolls. Where that is the case, however, the New Testament too has ceased to be Christian scripture. In their dialectical interdependence, Old and New Testaments stand or fall together.

The lines of demarcation between systematic theology and Old and New Testament scholarship represent more than a mere division of labour; they are ideologically motivated. They represent a collective decision of biblical scholarship that the biblical texts are to be construed as something other than Christian scripture. While this collective decision has not been universally and unproblematically accepted, it is nevertheless powerful enough to shape the interpretative practice of biblical scholars and theologians alike. 'Normal' biblical scholarship is founded upon this decision, and to reject the decision in practice as well as in principle is to be guilty of deviant behaviour. Needless to say, much of the work of modern biblical scholarship is of genuine theological value. There can be no question of a crude, one-sided rejection of 'the historical-critical method', as though the complexities of this issue could be dismissed with a mere gesture. Yet the limits imposed on the separated disciplines by the two lines of demarcation make it difficult for theological potential to be adequately exploited. In so far as the disciplinary boundaries hinder sustained attempts to interpret the biblical texts theologically, as Christian scripture, it does not seem exaggerated to claim that – from a theological standpoint – current interpretative paradigms *systematically distort* their object of investigation.

But perhaps this claim *is* exaggerated, representing an 'extreme' position which, whatever its possible insights, is ultimately too detached from the workings of 'normal' scholarship to understand its true rationale? Perhaps it is not theology as such but only a particular kind of theology that is (perhaps with good reason!) hindered by current interpretative paradigms? To criticize not only interpretative practice but also interpretative paradigms is to adopt a radical position which – like any other radicalism – may well prove untenable in the long run. Radicalisms of every kind have their characteristic illusions, one of which is the belief that to be a voice crying out in the wilderness is necessarily to be right. An initial scepticism in the face of the 'radical critique' is justified, for it is characteristic of this genre that partial insight is acquired at the cost of a blindness to realities that normal scholarship is right to take seriously. Radicalism tends to simplify, captivated by its own slogans. It inflates and absolutizes its claims. It seems condemned either to repeat them to the point of monotony or to moderate them in the concession that there are actually some very good reasons for scholarship's normal modes of operation. The radical is peculiarly exposed to the temptation to begin building a tower without first counting the cost. Radicalism can, however, minimize these dangers by remaining in dialogical relation to that which it criticizes. It must acknowledge its own dependence on and indeed its participation in the operation of normal scholarship. It must be attentive to nuance, open to counter-criticisms, and discriminating in its judgments. In its desire for clarity, it must not evade complexity.

This is all the more important in the light of the 'radical critiques' of normal biblical scholarship that are already in circulation. It has long been asserted, for example, that historical-critical scholarship is of little use to the preacher. In more contemporary idiom, it is said that this scholarship lays claim to an 'objectivity' and a 'value-free neutrality' that are impossible in principle and undesirable in practice. In its obsession with biblical authors and their historical circumstances, it ignores the rights of *readers* of the Bible, whose circumstances may well be very different. It is blind to the presence within the text both of multiple oppressions and of true liberating potential. It falsely believes that texts have only a single meaning. Its claim to universality masks the white, male, middle-class biases of most of its practitioners. Although these claims are not without an important moment of truth, constant repetition has hardened them into new hermeneutical dogmas that threaten to become just as restrictive as the old ones they seek to overthrow. Radical hermeneutics must learn to practise *self*-criticism, and that will mean, among other things, resisting the temptation to position itself outside and above that which it criticizes. It must learn to expose itself to counter-questioning. Is it really appropriate, for example, to understand 'historical-critical scholarship' as a single, monolithic entity, rather than as a plurality of interrelated and constantly-developing interpretative practices? Is the concept of 'objectivity' entirely lacking in significance and credibility? Is the biblical text rightly construed as mere raw material out of which its readers can construct whatever meanings they will? How far does *Angst* about whiteness, maleness and middle-classness, so typical of the middle-class intelligentsia, really promote anyone else's liberation? At point after point, the radical critique of conventional interpretative practice needs to be self-critically rethought – not in such a way as to abandon the undoubted hermeneutical gains of the last two decades or so but precisely in order to identify and consolidate their real significance.

To criticize current interpretative paradigms is to assume a 'radical' posture which must define itself in relation to other current radicalisms and which must practise a self-criticism born out of a dialogical relationship to existing interpretative practice. With that in mind, we return to the claim that the assigning of the biblical texts to three autonomous interpretative communities *systematically distorts* their subject-matter. The purpose of this claim is to establish a *model* of how biblical interpretation currently operates. A model is *only* a model. It is not the whole truth. It offers a partial access to the truth, the truth as viewed within a particular framework and for particular purposes; and it provides orientation for a particular interpretative practice. Thus, a model may coexist with other models. One model may be concerned with the effects of current disciplinary boundaries; another may be concerned with a state of affairs within a single discipline. One model (my own) speaks of the 'systematic distortion' arising from the lines of demarcation between disciplines; another may place the significant line of demarcation *within* the single discipline of Old or New Testament studies – between historical and literary approaches, for example, or between theologically-motivated and theologically-neutral modes of interpretation. No model should claim to offer a comprehensive description of reality, and each may retain its heuristic usefulness even where anomalies and complexities are detected of which it has taken no account. If, for example, it is pointed out that modern biblical scholarship again and again shows the unmistakable marks of scholars' theological commitments, that is true and significant; but it does not invalidate my own model, whose purpose is to highlight the *limits* to theological engagement with the biblical texts established by current disciplinary boundaries. That these limits exist is obvious, and the model does not draw attention to them for their own sake but in order to provide orientation for an interpretative practice that overcomes them, identifying and correcting the systematic distortions that they generate.

This interdisciplinary interpretative practice may appropriately be named *biblical theology*. This expression has been applied in the recent past to an approach that emphasizes both the ultimate coherence of the two Testaments and the theological dimension of the interpretative task. Biblical theology is *biblical*, that is, concerned with the whole Christian Bible; it is more than the sum of Old Testament theology and New Testament theology, understood as separate disciplines. Biblical theology is *theology*, where attempts are made to limit it to a purely descriptive capacity, it quickly becomes redundant and the expression passes out of use.[3] Biblical theology therefore entails the relativizing of both the lines of demarcation that I have analysed and criticized.[4] Whether and to what extent earlier forms of biblical theology were *successful* in carrying out such a programme is irrelevant at this point; for biblical theology must be redefined within a theological and hermeneutical situation very different from the one in which the 'biblical theology movement' once flourished, and it is not my intention to align the studies in this book with the earlier version of this discipline. Yet the criticisms that led to its demise must be taken into account here. A redefined biblical theology must be capable of answering these criticisms, which will otherwise simply be repeated (*mutatis mutandis*), as though they were unanswerable. We shall return to this subject in the third and final section of this introduction.

The next step, however, is to outline the content of the studies in biblical theology presented in this book.

II

The independent although interrelated studies that comprise the two parts of this book operate on both sides of the lines of demarcation we have identified: the line that distinguishes biblical scholarship from systematic theology (part 1: 'Studies in Theological Hermeneutics'), and the line that divides the interpretation of the Old Testament or Hebrew Bible from that of the New Testament (part 2: 'The Old Testament in Christological Perspective'). As we have seen, these lines are intended to be barriers, they do not mark a mere division of labour; and it is the purpose of these exercises in 'biblical theology' to challenge and to relativize these current disciplinary boundaries. Since the second line is an extension or an application of the first, the studies in the second part are no less explicitly theological than those of the first part. Negotiating the disciplinary boundaries requires constant hermeneutical vigilance, and a concern for theological hermeneutics is also evident at every point. The expression 'biblical theology' seems, however, more appropriate than 'theological hermeneutics' to the scope of this project as a whole. Theological reflection on the Christian Bible is everywhere present; hermeneutics is a crucially important element in this, but it is not the whole.

The first study, 'The Gospels as Narrated History', takes as its starting-point the dichotomy between historical-critical and narrative approaches to the study of the gospels. In the former case, the gospels function as historiographical texts only in so far as they are subjected to the various procedures characteristic of historical Jesus research, source criticism, form criticism and redaction criticism, in the course of which their narrative coherence is destroyed. Where, on the other hand, narrative coherence is preserved, the figure of Jesus is understood as immanent within the text and the question of extratextual reference is excluded. Both approaches share the assumption that historical reference and narrative form are incompatible.

The theological effect of these current paradigms for gospel interpretation is disastrous. The gospels cease to be gospel if they merely preserve scattered traces of a historical reality qualitatively different from its narrative rendering, or if they merely render an intratextual character whose extratextual existence is a matter of indifference. The tendency of these methods is towards a christological agnosticism or minimalism that wilfully overlooks the fact that, for Christian faith, Jesus – the real Jesus, as attested in the fourfold gospel record – is the Christ, in whom God reconciled the world to himself. It is true that, for a number of contemporary theologies, a christological agnosticism or minimalism of this kind is a matter of indifference or is even to be welcomed. Yet it is not clear that the methods and results of contemporary gospel scholarship are so decisive as to compel the abandonment of the central Christian truth-claim. On the contrary, the methods and therefore the results of this scholarship are fundamentally flawed. What is required is a more searching and less superficial account of the relationship between history and narrative, and at this point recent hermeneutical and historiographical theory offers some illuminating possibilities that could liberate gospel scholarship from its positivistic project of differentiating the so-called historical Jesus from the Christ of faith attested in the gospel narratives. The relationship between historical reality and historiographical narration is more complex and intricate than positivism supposes. When this is rightly grasped, there is no longer a problem in claiming that the evangelists practise a narration that is both theologically motivated and genuinely historiographical.

Despite its indifference to the extratextual reality of Jesus, the narrative-critical approach to the gospels at least has the merit of reasserting the integrity and irreducibility of the gospel narratives – an essential precondition for a theological interpretation that sees them as historiographical renderings of the uniquely and ultimately significant event of the Word become flesh. Narrative criticism is, however, vulnerable to a more radical literary theory according to which narrative withholds and subverts the determinate meaning that it appears to promise. In Frank Kermode's *The Genesis of Secrecy* (1979), the narrative of the Gospel of Mark is interpreted along these lines, and this has opened up the possibility of 'deconstructive' readings of biblical narrative that exploit the resources of contemporary literary theory far more effectively than conventional narrative criticism, with its relatively straightforward concerns with plot, characterization and so forth.[5] Radical literary theory finds in biblical narrative not a single sense but a multiplicity of voices, and it highlights this multiplicity in order to subvert the univocal meaning conventionally assigned to the text. The study of 'The Multiple Text and the Singular Gospel' offers an analysis of this approach, criticizing the attempt to convert an instance of the distinctive gospel genre into yet another exemplar of textual multiplicity and indeterminacy. As narration of the life, death and resurrection of Jesus, the Gospel of Mark is gospel only in so far as it communicates a determinate meaning: that Jesus, whose life, death and resurrection are narrated, is the Christ in whom God reconciles the world to himself. While theological interpretation must be attentive to the multiplicity of ways in which this basic truth-claim is rendered, it must oppose deconstructive readings of gospel texts in which the very concept of determinate meaning is rejected on principle.

Contemporary interest in the concept of textual indeterminacy is also expressed in the questionable view that meaning is determined by readers rather than by authors. Readers, it is said, are not isolated beings, they exist within 'interpretative communities' held together by agreed criteria as to what constitutes appropriate interpretative practice. Texts are therefore always read in the light of their readers' particular interests, and there can be no such thing as an interest-free, objective interpretation that merely reports the meaning of the text. If so, it follows that there can be no such thing as a privileged interpretative context; or, if there is, it is determined not by the nature of the text but by the claim that certain sociopolitical commitments are mandatory for the contemporary interpreter. On this view, the text is construed no longer as a communicative action but as an inert object, subject to interpretative criteria imposed on it from without.

In opposition to this one-sided reader-oriented hermeneutic, the study of 'Literal Sense, Authorial Intention, Objective Interpretation' offers a 'Defence of Some Unfashionable Concepts'. These unfashionable concepts are important not because a 'conservative' hermeneutic is inherently preferable to a 'radical' one but because the notion of the readerly creation of meaning is incompatible with the role of a particular set of texts as Christian scripture. This role requires the communication of determinate meaning to readers. Although the elaboration of that meaning will always be shaped by the context of its reception, it remains possible to argue that texts have a 'literal sense' dependent on 'authorial intention', and that their ambiguities may be contained (if not eliminated) by a set of 'objective', non-context-dependent interpretative procedures. The application of speech-act theory to writing enables us to understand writing as a mode of communication, indefinitely extended in time and space. A determinate communicative intention is embedded in the text; it is not to be found 'behind the text' in an authorial psychology or in an 'original' historical context. Interpretation *may* therefore concern itself with the appropriate reception of the communicative intention constituted by the text; and, if interpretation occurs within a communal context in which the text possesses some kind of normative significance, interpretation *must* concern itself with this issue. In so far as textual-critical and exegetical procedures make it possible to determine more precisely what a text does and does not *say*, they are indispensable for all interpretation, irrespective of its communal location. Yet, for a theologically-oriented interpretation of the biblical texts, it is crucially important to understand what is *said* in the context of an enduring communicative intention *to speak about something in order to bring about certain results*. Like any other communication, biblical communication is not utterance alone but *motivated* utterance, communicative *action* oriented – like all action – towards particular goals. Interpretation must therefore reflect on the conditions under which these textually-encoded communicative actions might continue to achieve their communicative goals.

In various ways, these first three studies in theological hermeneutics defend the claim that theological interpretation must be oriented towards the extratextual truth mediated through the biblical texts. To speak of the gospels as theologically-motivated historiographical narration is to assert their dependence on and mediation of a truth that precedes them and transcends them. This point also underlies the claim that the gospel narrative is, precisely, the narrative rendering of *gospel* – a determinate communication concerning the definitive divine self-disclosure. And if a determinate communication of God's self-disclosure in Jesus lies at the heart of the biblical texts, then the current emphasis on textual indeterminacy is theologically unacceptable in all its forms, whether it postulates an inherent instability in the texts themselves or hands over to readers responsibility for the construction of meaning. What these texts mediate is not the indeterminacy of the world or the self-image of their readers but the truth of God.

If these texts mediate the truth of God, then it must also be emphasized that the truth of God is textually mediated – in opposition to theologies that evade or downplay the irreducible textuality of Christian truth-claims. In 'Erasing the Text: Readings in Neo-Marcionism', I attempt to identify and analyse a variety of anti-textual, anti-scriptural strategies in the theologies of Schleiermacher, Harnack and Bultmann. Textuality is identified with the Jewish 'letter' and contrasted with the Christian emphasis on speech or 'the word'. The Old Testament is regarded as the paradigmatic form of 'the letter', and its authoritative status for the Christian community is denied. The formation of a new, Christian canonical collection is seen as a re-judaizing of Christian faith that can only obscure that which lies at its heart, the 'essence of Christianity'. In the case of Schleiermacher and Harnack, that 'essence of Christianity' is to be found in the speech in which Jesus communicates his own immediate experience of God, his perfect God-consciousness. In the case of Bultmann, it is to be found in the apostolic proclamation of Christ crucified as the radical divine challenge to all human self-sufficiency and self-assertion. In all three cases, it is acknowledged that traces of the all-important 'word' are to be found only in the New Testament texts. Yet (it is claimed) its textual embodiment is a mere accident; it must again be 'heard' as speech. The disparity between the textual form and the essential content of the biblical texts is resolved by a radical historical criticism, which strips away everything that is deemed to be 'secondary' – the term is used qualitatively and not only chronologically – in order to recover an utterance that is primary, original, unique and distinctive.

All three theologians identify textuality with a Jewishness alien to Christianity's true essence, and in subordinating textuality to an original speech they therefore offer purified theologies free from Jewish contamination. The fact that much of Bultmann's theology came into being in the context of the Third Reich makes the relationship between 'neo-Marcionism' and anti-Semitism especially urgent. And yet these theologies are perhaps best seen as stemming from a conflict internal to the Christian community about the mediation of Christian truth-claims. The 'neo-Marcionite' position is also a particularly clear instance of the tendency to subordinate 'writing' to 'speech' identified by Jacques Derrida in his *Grammatology* and elsewhere; but, rather than understanding this as a general hermeneutical problematic, it is more important to trace its specifically theological consequences and to oppose the erasure of textuality for distinctively theological reasons.[6]

These four studies in theological hermeneutics seek to establish a range of positive and negative criteria for a theologically-oriented biblical interpretation, a renewed practice of 'biblical theology'. It is not the role of hermeneutics to offer theologically-*neutral* insights into the process of interpretation, for example by pointing to a variety of ways in which a particular finding might be exploited theologically. The point is not to establish the legitimacy and possibility of *any* theological orientation within biblical interpretation, as though the task were merely one of methodological clarification. The point is to practise theology itself, in and with all the necessary methodological clarifications – and, more specifically, to practise a biblical theology primarily concerned to illuminate the convergence of the biblical texts around their single centre, while not neglecting the contemporary contexts within which illumination must occur. To practise theology is always to practise a particular theology. One cannot practise a theology-in-general in which one talks about theological choices without ever actually choosing. The discipline of theological hermeneutics is not mere prolegomena; it exists only *within* the sphere of biblical theology.

As we have seen, the disciplinary boundary that establishes the autonomy of biblical studies in relation to systematic theology has its correlate in a boundary dividing interpreters of the Old Testament or Hebrew Bible from interpreters of the New. If the object of biblical theology is the Christian Bible in its integrity, and if the two Testaments are constituted in dialectical interdependence by their relation to a single centre, then it is theologically unacceptable to construe the two Testaments as separate, self-contained collections of writings. From various other standpoints this construal may seem to make good pragmatic sense: historical-critical, literary and feminist approaches to biblical interpretation can operate with complete disregard for the question of the relationship between the two parts of the Christian canon. Whatever the value of these approaches, however, they cannot be allowed to dictate the terms on which Christian scripture can be used for theological purposes. In so far as they presuppose the self-sufficiency of each of the two canonical collections, Christian scripture is not the object of their study: for Christian scripture does not exist except in the form of the dialectical interdependence of two collections of writings. Biblical theology as a discipline must constantly bear this point in mind in all its necessary interaction with conventional Old and New Testament scholarship. In particular, as the title of part 2 of this book indicates, the Old Testament must be interpreted in consistently christological perspective. Biblical theology is not *christomonistic*, and there should be no arbitrary imposition of New Testament categories that undermine the distinctiveness of what the Old Testament has to say. Yet biblical theology must be *christocentric* if it wishes to reflect the fundamental structure of the Christian Bible.

The study of 'Old Testament Theology as a Christian Theological Enterprise', which opens part 2, reflects on the work of Eichrodt, von Rad and Childs as a contribution not so much to Old Testament scholarship as to Christian theology. All three scholars believe that the Old Testament has an essential contribution to make to Christian theology and understand Old Testament theology as the attempt to formalize that contribution. Old Testament theology can therefore be interpreted as a point at which Old Testament scholarship resists its own tendency towards self-enclosure and self-sufficiency and seeks to enter into dialogue with a Christian theology concerned with the interpretation of both Testaments in their relationship of dialectical interdependence.

From this standpoint, however, various problems come to light. Eichrodt's insistence on the centrality of the covenant for Old Testament theology has as its theological correlate the concept of an essentially ahistorical I–Thou relationship between God and the individual, frequently obscured by legalism but always available for rediscovery by the prophets and above all by Jesus. Continuity with certain of the concerns of the liberal Protestant tradition is obvious here, not least in the complete failure – despite good intentions – to do justice to the unique and ultimate significance that Christian faith ascribes to Jesus as the Christ. Childs' recent *Biblical Theology of the Old and New Testaments* (1992) unfortunately fails to live up to the promise of its title.[7] Although committed in theory to an understanding of the two Testaments as dialectically interdependent in their relation to a single centre, Childs is in practice so concerned to preserve the integrity of the Old Testament that its dialectical relationship to the New virtually disappears. In this model, the texts of Old and New Testaments lie as it were side by side, each possessing an 'authority' abstracted from its relationship to the central point of Christian scripture. In the background here is a Protestant biblicism according to which scriptural texts possess an inherent authority simply as scriptural texts, quite apart from their relation to any particular content. In the light of these theological failures, von Rad's achievement is all the more impressive, despite the vulnerability of many of its historical-critical foundations. Von Rad sees clearly the theological problem posed by the division of Christian scripture between two separate interpretative communities. He has an acute sense of the canonical shaping of the Christian Old Testament – its orientation towards the Christ-event – even without the benefit of Childs' canonical perspective; and his theory of a typological relationship between the Testaments remains suggestive, although it is now almost completely overlooked.

The study of 'Creation in the Beginning' reflects theologically on the fact that the biblical narrative begins with the beginning of all things in the creative action of God. Aristotle's claim that a properly integrated narrative has a beginning, a middle and an end evokes the question how the beginning of this narrative is to be understood in the light of its middle and its (still future) end; the question, in other words, how the doctrine of creation relates to christology and eschatology. Within biblical theology (the theology of the Bible), the world as divine creation constitutes the stable foundation for the unfolding narrative of salvation; this is the case in the Old Testament, and it remains so in the gospels. This interpretation of the biblical view may be contrasted with two alternative accounts that detach the biblical creation traditions from their narrative embodiment. According to the first account, all of God's activity is creative activity. God does not act creatively only 'in the beginning'; his ongoing, dynamic creative action draws the world of 'nature' and of humans towards its eschatological goal. The doctrine of creation must be rethought in the light of the anticipation of the eschaton in the resurrection of Jesus, which gives the whole of Christian theology an eschatological orientation. According to the second account, the biblical view of the world as creation is closely related to the project of a 'natural theology'; the Barthian assumption that biblical theology and natural theology are fundamentally opposed to one another is therefore false. Creation is an independent reality in its own right, and not only the 'beginning' of a single unfolding narrative of divine–human interaction. One may therefore speak of the world as God's creation and of God as creator of the world without reference to the God of Israel who is also the God and Father of our Lord Jesus Christ. In opposition to these two very different views, represented by Jürgen Moltmann and James Barr respectively, the concept of 'creation in the beginning' reasserts the particular role of the creation-narrative within the biblical narrative as a whole. The creation-narrative is *only* the beginning: the concept of creation cannot be detached from its narrative embodiment and converted into an eschatologically-oriented metanarrative. And the creation-narrative is *truly* the beginning – the beginning of a narrative which will also have a middle and an end, and not the product of a 'natural theology' that would detach it from its context within a narrative that reaches its centre in the event of the incarnation.

The chapter entitled 'In the Image of God' is a further attempt to interpret Old Testament conceptuality in the light of the christological centre of Christian scripture. Although the claim that humans are created in the image of God has traditionally played an important role in theological anthropology, this has often been interpreted in philosophical terms derived ultimately from Plato and Aristotle, according to whom it is the mind or reason that differentiates humans from the rest of the natural order and makes them god-like. The New Testament's identification of Jesus with the image of God indicates that the Genesis texts are to be interpreted along christological rather than philosophical lines. In Jesus is to be found the answer not only to the question who God is but also to the question who we are. The Genesis texts anticipate this answer by implying – with apparently naïve anthropomorphism – an analogy between Adam's begetting a son in his own image and likeness and God's creation of humans in his image and likeness (Gen. 5.1–3). As Seth resembles Adam, so Adam resembles God: God bears a form similar to the human one. In christological perspective, this view loses its naïvely anthropomorphic character and becomes an anticipation of the truth that God is 'like' the human Jesus and the human Jesus is 'like' God. In Johannine conceptuality, the Son's person and action are the one true likeness of the Father's person and action, and humans are created in the image of God in that they share Jesus' humanity. They are like God in that Jesus, a fellow-human, is like God.

In Genesis, human dominion over the creatures is closely related to creation in God's image, although the two ideas are not identical. In itself, the idea that humans rule over all creatures is almost as problematic as the idea that the human form resembles God's, and this should cause us to look more favourably at the apparently 'arbitrary' christological interpretation of Ps. 8 in Heb. 2, where human dominion over the creatures is interpreted in terms of Jesus' triumph over death. The psalm is read in the critical light of God's own answer, in Jesus, to the question 'what is man, that thou art mindful of him?' For biblical theology, the anthropological question requires a christological answer.

To read Old Testament texts in christological perspective is to revive a central concern of traditional Christian Old Testament interpretation, long suppressed by the hermeneutics of the Enlightenment. The final chapter, 'Scripture in Dialogue: A Study in Early Christian Old Testament Interpretation', offers a reading of Justin Martyr's *Dialogue with Trypho*, a text in which many of the characteristic emphases of classical Christian Old Testament interpretation are already evident: the subordination of Torah to prophecy, the Old Testament's christological goal as its sole unifying principle, its anticipatory disclosures of divine triunity. While Justin's exegesis is often indefensible in its literal form, its underlying theological and hermeneutical substructure still represents a possible and indeed a plausible construal of the Old Testament material. The assumption that the truth of the Christian gospel can be 'proved' by arguing from the fulfilment of prophecy turns out to be untenable, even on its own terms; and yet Justin does at least demonstrate that the claim that Christian faith in Jesus as the Christ is 'in accordance with the scriptures' is not an empty or arbitrary one. He thereby demonstrates, both to his Jewish dialogue-partner and to the followers of Marcion and Valentinus, the essential Jewishness of Christian faith. This Gentile Christian articulates not a 'parting of the ways' between Christian faith and Jewish tradition (the programme of Marcion and Valentinus) but a profound interpretative rupture *within* Jewish tradition. The Christian Old Testament is therefore Jewish scripture read as the semantic matrix of Christian faith.

These studies in theological hermeneutics and readings of the Old Testament in christological perspective are independent of one another, and can be read separately. They are each devoted to specialized questions of theology, hermeneutics and exegesis, and they do not outline any detailed programme for the practice of a future biblical theology. The only programme I have to offer is the proposal that theologically-oriented biblical interpretation should be an interdisciplinary activity, unconstrained by conventional disciplinary boundaries and critical of the distortions that these boundaries engender. The studies in this book merely apply this rather simple programme to various specialized issues. This somewhat *ad hoc* procedure seems to me the most fruitful and promising way to practise a contemporary 'biblical theology'. The time does not seem ripe for grand syntheses.

III

I am not aware of any close contemporary analogies to this programme for a renewed, interdisciplinary biblical theology – although the concerns it expresses are, in one form or another, widely felt, and the need for it seems to me to be obvious. There are, however, certain parallels between biblical theology as I wish to understand and practise it and an earlier biblical theology that flourished between about 1930 and 1960, before succumbing to increasingly strident criticism.[8]

This biblical theology also sought to practise a theologically-oriented biblical interpretation. It was capable of grasping the dialectical unity of the Christian Bible and the theological and hermeneutical significance of its christological centre. It saw the limitations of the 'purely historical' approach to biblical interpretation, and it was unimpressed by the anti-theological rhetoric that sometimes accompanies that approach. Believing that God was in Christ reconciling the world to himself, it tried to interpret the Bible in the light of that fact. It recognized the danger of imposing on the biblical material inappropriate models of the 'essence of religion' that ignored the primary fact of unique, particular divine self-disclosure. It did not accept that 'modern' views of history exempt us from the possibility and necessity of speaking about divine action in the historical sphere. It recognized that the distinctive content of Christian faith left its mark on biblical semantics. It knew that the Christian church is the privileged communal location for biblical interpretation. At these and other points, this biblical theology represented (at its best) not a mere passing trend but a genuine recovery of certain emphases that remain indispensable for Christian faith.

These emphases recur, in one form or another, in my own understanding and practice of biblical theology. That does not mean that I am merely attempting to revive an earlier biblical theology; it should already be clear from the outline in the previous section that the interdisciplinary biblical theology that I propose has a rather different scope from anything produced by the 'biblical theology movement'. Nevertheless, there are continuities and parallels. And this means that I must address the fact that, during the 1960s and early 1970s, the biblical theology of the preceding decades was (at least in Britain and north America) subjected to sharp criticism. The demise of the biblical theology movement is, after all, a well-known 'fact' of modern theological history. This demise was so skilfully engineered that 'biblical theology' has become, for both theologians and biblical scholars, a cautionary tale illustrating the folly of trying to practise theology and biblical interpretation simultaneously. The very expression 'biblical theology' has passed out of general theological usage, to such an extent that anyone whose theological education began after about 1975 will probably have little idea of what it once represented, only a few years previously.

I shall consider here the work of biblical theology's most significant and persistent critic, James Barr.[9] In a series of books and articles, beginning with *The Semantics of Biblical Language* (1961), Barr has ruthlessly criticized both the biblical theology of the previous theological generation and its potential successors. It is obvious that Barr scored a number of direct hits on the targets of his polemic, and a renewed biblical theology must take care not to repeat the mistakes that he correctly identified. Yet there are certain features of his polemical strategy that should cause one to question how much his critiques actually achieve. There is, first, a tendency to base sweeping criticisms on a very narrow foundation. An error is correctly identified: for example, certain works of biblical theology build far too much on the alleged distinction between the two New Testament words for time, *kairos* and *chronos*. This error is then said to be 'characteristic' not just of the two or three scholars identified but of biblical theology as a whole. It is not individuals but biblical theology itself that is at fault when its representatives go astray; the fact that the most important modern work on the New Testament and time – Oscar Cullmann's *Christ and Time* (1946) – explicitly rejects the *kairos/chronos* distinction is noted in a footnote but is not allowed to limit the scope of the polemic.[10] It is true that at certain points Barr does identify methodological errors that are, if not necessarily 'characteristic' or 'typical' of biblical theology, at least *common* – and therefore worth identifying, criticizing and avoiding. Here, however, a second aspect of Barr's polemical strategy comes to light. The criticism constantly presses towards the conclusion that the errors identified are not just common or even 'typical', but that they are somehow *foundational* to the whole enterprise of biblical theology, which therefore collapses as suddenly and dramatically as the house built on sand as soon as they are exposed. Biblical theology is not only imperfectly executed, it is fundamentally flawed; it is not even given the option of putting its house in order, for it is beyond redemption at least in its present form. It must go; or it must learn to moderate its excessive theological pretensions, re-marketing itself perhaps as a purely descriptive discipline.

I have already noted that there are continuities and parallels between my own attempts to redefine biblical theology and the earlier biblical theology attacked by Barr. The continuities and parallels derive from a common concern with the basic structure of Christian faith. Since it is very widely believed that the earlier biblical theology was overwhelmed by the sheer force and range of the criticisms it encountered, and since the potential critics of a contemporary biblical theology will no doubt avail themselves of the same previously effective weapons, a more detailed examination of some of these criticisms seems worthwhile.

In *The Semantics of Biblical Language*, Barr announces at the outset that the approaches to biblical language he intends to criticize are 'those very roughly associated with the movement for so-called "biblical theology"' (4–5). In particular, he is critical of the modern quest for the distinctive theological content of biblical *vocabulary*, exemplified by the many volumes of the Kittel-Friedrich *Theologisches Wörterbuch zum neuen Testament*. The tendency in such work, he argues, is to convert particular words, found in many different contexts and used in many different ways, into *concepts* which disclose something distinctive about the biblical view of reality. Vocabulary is used to reassert a particular form of biblical unity – for if words are understood as concepts, then different writers' use of the same words will represent major areas of agreement in their thinking. But all this is illegitimate: 'Theological thought of the type found in the NT has its characteristic linguistic expression not in the word individually but in the word-combination or sentence . . . The attempt to relate the individual word directly to the theological thought leads to the distortion of the semantic contribution made by words in contexts' (233). Biblical theology will be reluctant to accept this shift back from words and language to writers and their sentences, because this will again bring inner-biblical distinctions to the fore and so lead to 'the fragmentation of the Bible' (270): for to focus on usage is to become aware of the irreducible polysemy and fluidity of words in contexts. A further problem with the theologizing of biblical vocabulary arises from the need for the theological content discovered to be congenial to modern theological thought. In the case of the word *kairos*, for example, the linguistic fact that the meaning 'decisive moment' is weakened in later Greek will be played down: for 'the attractiveness to modern biblical theology of the *idea* of a time of decision, or of time as the area of God's work and decisive intervention, has led to a maximizing of the sense "critical, decisive time" for *kairos*, although the predominance of this sense belongs to the classical period . . .' (226). Theological interests have a natural tendency to distort the linguistic evidence.

There are, no doubt, 'dangers' in the approach to biblical theology which emphasizes the theological content of biblical vocabulary, and it is very likely that some contributors to the *Theologisches Wörterbuch* sometimes succumb to them. It is not clear, however, that the problems are anything like as fundamental as Barr wants them to be. In G. Delling's article on *kairos*, for example, it is true that the author is especially interested in New Testament occurrences where the word seems to mean 'fateful and decisive point', 'the specific and decisive point, especially as regards its content' (*TDNT* 3.459, 460).[11] He therefore gives a privileged status to those occurrences of the word that he takes to be theologically significant and deals more cursorily with theologically-neutral occurrences. But this is an entirely proper distinction in a work that purports to be a *theological* dictionary. When in John 7.6 Jesus announces that 'my time has not yet come', the word *kairos* is theologically significant in a way that it is not in the phrase 'At about that time' (Acts 12.1). It is not at all the case that words are isolated from their contexts in such an analysis: the occurrence of *kairos* in the statement 'my time has not yet come' can only be seen to be theologically significant by understanding this individual word in its immediate and broader Johannine contexts. The word *kairos* also occurs in other contexts where its theological significance appears to be similar or at least comparable; thus, in 1 Pet. 1.5, it is said that believers await a 'salvation ready to be revealed in the last time'. While *kairos* is used in John 7.6 to refer to the glorification of Jesus (his crucifixion/resurrection/ascension: cf. John 17.1) and in 1 Pet. 1.5 to refer to the parousia, *kairos* refers in both passages to a decisive, divinely-appointed moment in salvation-history, and it is therefore entirely appropriate to consider them together. It is just not true that Delling has taken the outmoded classical sense of *kairos* and imposed it on the New Testament texts because of some prior theological notion of the importance of 'decision'. The theologically-significant sense of the word is obtained precisely by reading it in its various contexts, distinguishing those that imply a more 'theological' sense from those that are more neutral. There are, naturally, points in the article where one might fault the exegesis or the method, but there is little here to justify a crusade against the very idea of a 'theological dictionary'.

For Barr, biblical theology's abuse of biblical words for time is so fundamental that he devotes an entire book to it (*Biblical Words for Time* [1962]). The crusade is resumed, and universal and fundamental significance is again ascribed to particular errors: 'The misuse of language in recent "biblical theology" is nowhere more evident than where the judgments of careful scholarship are . . . thrown aside because they do not fit the lexical-theological web woven by recent fashions' (40). Not surprisingly in view of its deservedly high reputation, Cullmann's *Christ and Time* comes in for particular criticism.[12] According to Cullmann, 'the characteristic thing about *kairos* is that it has to do with a definite *point of time* which has a fixed content' (*Christ and Time*, 39; italics original). Time is significant as the setting for the decisive, divinely-ordained events of a single unfolding *Heilsgeschichte*, and Cullmann is therefore interested especially in those occurrences of *kairos* which (like John 7.6 and 1 Pet. 1.5, quoted above) can be related to this point. Barr believes that he has discovered a fundamental flaw in Cullmann's position: there are a number of passages in which *kairos* does *not* mean 'a definite point of time which has a fixed content'. In Heb. 9.9, for example, we read that the 'the outer tent' is symbolic of 'the present age' (*ton kairon ton enestēkota*): *kairos* here refers to a period and not to a point of time. The existence of such counter-instances 'greatly weakens or entirely destroys the connection between [Cullmann's] theory of time and the facts of lexical usage in the New Testament' (50). Since 'the section on terminology is basic for much of what follows in Cullmann's book' (80), the argument of the whole book is in danger of collapsing. An initial linguistic error turns out to be a crucial weakness in the very foundation. Cullmann, like Kittel, is not to be relied upon: for theological arguments in danger of collapse should, like buildings, be abandoned as quickly as possible.

In his terminological chapter, Cullmann notes that 'the various expressions that refer to time' (*hēmera, hōra, kairos, chronos, aiōn, nun*, and so on) 'can also be used without special theological reference', a fact that 'becomes clear as one uses the lexicons' (*Christ and Time*, 39). He is therefore aware of the diversity of New Testament usage, but he is particularly interested in showing how 'this terminology expresses the distinctive quality of the Primitive Christian thinking concerning time' (39). It is *a priori* likely that early Christian christological and eschatological beliefs do entail a view of time that is at least relatively 'distinctive', and it is *a priori* equally likely that this distinctiveness will be apparent in at least some of the contexts where time-words are to be found. Those are the working hypotheses that Cullmann's book attempts to substantiate. The fact, acknowledged by Cullmann, that *kairos* does not *uniformly* and *necessarily* refer to decisive moments in salvation-history is entirely irrelevant to the success or otherwise of his argument; for, like the *Theologisches Wörterbuch*, he is concerned with what he takes to be theologically-significant rather than theologically-neutral uses of the term. Despite this, Barr claims that Cullmann's argument cannot tolerate the existence of any such exceptions: 'The whole case being argued is that the Bible has, and normally and constantly displays, a particular conception of time, which can be traced in its lexical stock and which forms an essential background or presupposition for the understanding of its theology. It is therefore naturally impossible to except any example of usage from full consideration on the grounds that it is "merely temporal" and not of theological significance' (*Biblical Words for Time*, 49). But the conclusion is a *non sequitur*: the claim that the New Testament has a distinctive understanding of time that is reflected in its use of time-words in no way entails the further claim that *every* occurrence of a time-word *must* express that distinctive understanding of time. The fact that the latter thesis is obviously untenable tells us nothing about the truth or falsehood of the former.

Cullmann is also heavily criticized in the context of Barr's attack on the contrast between 'Hebrew thought' and 'Greek thought'. (Cullmann does not appear to use the expression 'Hebrew thought' as equivalent to 'biblical thought': the imprecision of Barr's polemic is at odds with his stated concern for precision in matters of linguistic usage.) In his study of *Immortality of the Soul or Resurrection of the Dead?* (1956), Cullmann argues that the 'biblical' concept of resurrection is fundamentally different from the 'Greek' concept of immortality. It belongs, he claims, 'to the greatness of our Christian faith . . . that we do not begin from our personal desires but place our resurrection within the framework of a cosmic redemption and of a new creation of the universe' (9).[13] In the history of Christianity, however, '1 Corinthians 15 has been sacrificed for the *Phaedo*' (8); and this collective decision must now be reversed. Rather than attempting to demythologize the concept of resurrection or to bring it into line with the 'Greek' idea, 'we must recognize loyally that precisely those things which distinguish the Christian teaching from the Greek belief are at the heart of primitive Christianity' (8).

Barr finds in this last sentence 'something approaching a total and absolute incompatibility between Greek and biblical thought' (*Old and New in Interpretation* [1966], 46). He concedes that 'so long as we are working on the actual ideas, beliefs, philosophies, confessions, stories, and so on, i.e. on that which is expressed in the actual texts on one side or the other, there is no reason to doubt that very great differences will usually be found between Hebrew [*sic*] and Greek thought' (46–47). Yet, at the general level, 'no unitary contrast, no simple contrast, no contrast capable of being grasped within a single philosophical antithesis, could ever be given' (49). Cullmann, however, *is* 'working on . . . actual ideas [and] beliefs', as 'expressed in . . . actual texts' such as 1 Cor. 15 and the *Phaedo*; his contrast between 'the Christian teaching' and 'the Greek belief' refers *specifically* to the difference between the concepts of bodily resurrection and the immortality of the soul. Barr simply misreads and misrepresents him here. The result is that, although he concedes that 'very great differences will usually be found between Hebrew and Greek thought', he can nevertheless attack Cullmann for applying precisely this point to a particular instance, all the while conveying the impression that attempts to discover what is distinctive to the biblical texts within their original cultural contexts are deeply and fundamentally flawed. At times, trivial caricature masquerades as serious critique:

> The New Testament writers in general make no effort to deal with their problems by warning against the dangerous effects of Greek thought. St Paul, troubled by a difficult situation in the church at Corinth, never took pains to point out to his people that their troubles arose from a Greek way of thinking and that the adoption of Hebrew thought might heal their difficulties. (56)

To reply in the same vein, there is in 1 Cor. 1.18–25 a well-known passage in which Paul contrasts the folly of the cross, which is the true power and wisdom of God, with the wisdom sought by the *Greeks*. That Barr can overlook this passage is another indication of the casualness and inattention to detail that characterizes so much of his polemic. Of course, even if he were right and the New Testament did lack this passage, it would be inadmissible to oppose the contrasting of Greek and biblical conceptions on the grounds that this contrast is not explicitly thematized by the biblical writers.

This focus on Barr's polemical strategy suggests that there is little basis for his claim that 'biblical theology' as once practised was fundamentally and irretrievably flawed. If biblical theology collapsed, it did not do so because of the overwhelming force of its critics' arguments.

By the early 1970s, Barr could write that biblical theology, 'as a movement which aspired to domination within theology and which for a decade or two at least held some considerable initiative within it, must now be spoken of in the past tense' ('Trends and Prospects in Biblical Theology' [1974], 265–66). In place of this defunct movement, 'very radical questions are being asked afresh about the centrality and the decisive importance which were traditionally ascribed to the Bible and which seemed to be reasserted with some success in the post-war biblical revival' (*The Bible in the Modern World* [1973], 35). Radical opinion asks: '*Why the Bible?* Why should a group of ancient books have this dominant status? If a group of ancient books, then why *this* group of ancient books? And why in any case should anyone suppose that any objective external authority, in the shape of a group of books or any other shape at all, exists at all?' (36, italics original). Barr is deeply impressed by this new radicalism: it 'has brought us to a new stage of the discussion, which is likely to be stimulating and fruitful' (44). He does not necessarily agree with it, but he takes it to be a sign of the times that differences over issues such as 'cultural relativism' now seem 'entirely tolerable', that, 'unlike the men of an earlier age, one does not feel a pressure to confute, one does not feel that at all costs this error must be exposed and silenced' (51). On this view of theological radicalism, one can simply and conveniently classify different theologies by placing them at some point on a line that runs between the two extremes of 'radical' and 'conservative'. Barr's own sympathies lie at the 'radical' end of this line. Here, even if the arguments are flawed and one disagrees with them, 'one does not feel a pressure to confute'. As for the theologies at the other end of the line, however, it is clear that the pressure to confute, expose and silence is as strong as ever. Thus, having dealt with biblical theology in the 1960s, Barr now attempts to confute, expose and silence 'fundamentalism' (*Fundamentalism* [1977]), canonical criticism (*Holy Scripture: Canon, Authority, Criticism* [1983]) and 'Barthianism' (*Biblical Faith and Natural Theology* [1993]). In contrast to this inquisitorial zeal against 'conservative' theologies, Barr views the prospect of a continued 'radical questioning of the use of the Bible in the churches' with 'complete equanimity' (*The Bible in the Modern World*, 113). Indeed, he offers some radical questioning of his own – for example, when he 'questions' (i.e. rejects) the alignment of the Bible with concepts such as Word of God and revelation, concluding that 'if one wants to use Word-of-God type of language, the proper term for the Bible would be Word of Israel, Word of some leading early Christians' (120). While his critique of biblical theology must be considered on its own merits, it is worth noting that the impetus to criticize arises out of a theological commitment – not, perhaps, to any particular theology, but at least to a certain theological *style*. If one finds it 'stimulating and fruitful' to ask, with a certain radical flourish, 'why the Bible?', then one will obviously be unsympathetic to the aims and assumptions of biblical theology. But that does not mean that those aims and assumptions are self-contradictory or otherwise untenable. It simply means that one dislikes them.[14]

One final aspect of Barr's critique must be noted: biblical theology, he believes, is necessarily lacking in professionalism. If it is carried out by theologians, they will lack a rigorous professional training in the discipline of biblical exegesis. If it is carried out by biblical scholars, they will lack sufficient competence in matters of theology. In the old days theologians could use the Bible as they wished; but now 'the identification and understanding of the implied or underlying theology of historical and poetical books has become a highly technical process, in which the theologian is largely dependent on the expert biblical scholar' (*The Bible in the Modern World*, 90). Theologians should no longer imagine that they have direct access to the Bible. In compensation, they are given exclusive rights over their own field, into which biblical scholars should only venture with the greatest caution. In a study of 'The Theological Case against Biblical Theology' (1988), Barr argues that biblical scholars were at fault in incautiously aligning biblical theology with the theological stance of neo-orthodoxy. Biblical theology was therefore 'a partisan movement, lined up on one side of a series of disagreements that were really a matter for doctrinal theologians to discuss among themselves' (8). Theology, like exegesis, should be left to the professionals. Where this rule is disregarded, the result is likely to be an embarrassing impasse: 'What if biblical theology works out a biblical mode of thinking, which will provide the mental matrix for faith, but doctrinal theology says that it has to live in contact with modern philosophy and does not really want any scheme that will bypass that contact?' (11).

It is not impossible, however, that this 'biblical theology' might have the courage of its convictions and ask Barr's philosophically-minded 'doctrinal theology' how far a preoccupation with Kant, Nietzsche and Heidegger that precludes serious engagement with the biblical texts is theologically justified. What alternative theological basis has been discovered for this exclusive philosophical preoccupation? And if some answer is given to this question, biblical theology need not feel obliged to withdraw from the conversation forthwith, content to regard this as 'a matter for doctrinal theologians to discuss among themselves'. Conversely, a 'doctrinal theology' is imaginable in which 'contact with modern philosophy' is by no means incompatible with a concern for the right interpretation of biblical conceptuality. Is this 'doctrinal theology' obliged to accept that, as biblical interpretation is 'a highly technical process', it must simply subject itself to the guidance of 'the expert biblical scholar'? In both cases, there is much to be said for a less rigid and absolute conception of the disciplinary boundary. Where, on the other hand, there is an unquestioning trust in the appropriateness of this boundary, then criticism of a biblical theology that transgresses it will be no more than an automatic reflex.

Barr's criticisms of biblical theology are legion, and it has not been possible to address them all. Fortunately, a comprehensive response is unnecessary in the present context, where my intention has been to shed some light on the genesis of the mainly false belief that the earlier biblical theology collapsed under the weight of its own weaknesses and contradictions. If anything deserves to collapse under the weight of its own weaknesses and contradictions it is the hollow rhetoric of the theology of 'radical questioning', which Barr did so much to further in his polemics against biblical theology. There is, then, little or nothing in this piece of modern theological history to deter one from attempting to renew and to redefine biblical theology. There is no need to be apologetic in doing so, acknowledging the force of the earlier criticisms and promising that the new biblical theology will be quite unlike the old. As for the charge that biblical theology, old or new, is necessarily 'conservative' in character, this should be dismissed out of hand as the product of a projection into theology of the one-dimensional model of political allegiance as a line running from right to left. The question of the continuities and discontinuities between the new and the old biblical theologies is not a particularly important one; suffice it to say that there is a common concern with a theologically-oriented biblical interpretation that is in significant respects at odds with the main trend of modern biblical scholarship. Insights from the older biblical theology can be gratefully received, but more insights will probably be found elsewhere – especially, perhaps, in contemporary hermeneutics. A redefined, interdisciplinary biblical theology is not an attempt to turn the clock back thirty years to the point where its predecessor is said to have 'collapsed'. Yet some awareness of its achievements and the circumstances of its decline is presupposed in my own practice of a redefined biblical theology.

Is this a propitious time for a theological proposal of this kind? Does it have any future? The theological and exegetical disciplines are undergoing a process of fragmentation, under the impact of both increasing methodological pluralism and ever-narrower specialization. The 'expert biblical scholar', accomplished in analysing the theologies of individual biblical books yet quite incapable of any real theological construction, has no reason even to notice a proposal to rethink the boundaries of normal scholarly endeavour. Within the familiar framework, everything appears to be in good working order; monographs, commentaries and articles are written, and scholarship advances. Will a redefined biblical theology be of any more interest to systematic theologians? There appear to be so many more urgent demands on the theologian's attention than a call to reconsider the Bible. The Bible is, after all, someone else's professional domain. It is also an awkward and intractable book over which too much blood and ink have already been spilled; and its relation to many of the contemporary world's most cherished ethical and political projects is, to say the least, highly ambiguous.

It therefore seems *not* to be a propitious moment to propose a renewed biblical theology. Grounds for doing so are not to be found in the dictates of the contemporary theological *Zeitgeist*. This shadowy entity is, one might almost say, one of the principalities and powers against which a contemporary biblical theology must contend. Grounds for a renewed biblical theology are to be found in its subject-matter alone, in the peculiar relationship between text and truth. For Christian faith, and therefore for Christian theology too, Jesus is the truth, and as such also the way and the life. Faith is nothing other than the understanding and the perception of this fact. Its source is the Holy Spirit, who leads us into all truth – the truth that is identical with the being of Jesus, and not a spurious truth that lies beyond him. Yet the truth that Jesus is the truth is not perceived and grasped in unmediated form, through visions or a divine voice perhaps, but only by way of certain mediations: the Christian community, its preaching, its sacraments, its forms of life and, foundationally, its holy scriptures. Without this definitive textual attestation, the Jesus who is the truth would be a vague and uncertain memory, and the textual mediation of this truth is therefore not a fortunate or unfortunate accident but is integral to the truth itself. Jesus is the truth only in and through the textual mediation of this truth. He is, as it were, encompassed by textuality: preceded by writings that prepare his way before him, followed by the writings of those who cannot but speak of what they have seen and heard. A theology concerned with truth cannot evade this textuality. Since Christian faith proposes a comprehensive account of reality as a whole, theology must naturally be concerned with many things; but its various concerns will be fragmented and arbitrary if they are not held together by the textually-mediated truth that Jesus is the truth.

If this is the case, it is no exaggeration to claim that the disciplinary boundary that separates biblical interpretation and theology results in a systematic distortion of the subject-matter of Christian theology. It is the role of a redefined biblical theology to point this out – although not in a negative and polemical spirit, for Christian faith is concerned primarily

✓ and essentially with truth and only secondarily and incidentally with false-hood.

A biblical theology along these lines is, in my view, not only possible but also necessary.

NOTES

1. At this point, as Paul Ricoeur notes, 'biblical hermeneutics receives an important warning from philosophical hermeneutics: it must not be too quick to construct a theology of the Word that does not include, from the outset and as its very principle, the passage from speech to writing. This warning is by no means irrelevant, so great is the tendency for theology to raise the Word above Writing . . . The very originality of the [Christ] event requires that it be transmitted by means of an interpretation of preexisting significations already inscribed – available within the cultural community' ('Philosophical Hermeneutics and Biblical Hermeneutics', in *From Text to Action: Essays in Hermeneutics II*, ET London: Athlone Press, 1991, 89–101; 93, 94).

2. On this issue, and on von Rad in particular, see chapter 5.

3. Thus Krister Stendahl's well-known plea for a 'descriptive biblical theology', concerned with 'what the text meant' rather than 'what it means', is in fact a plea for a descriptive, non-theological *exegesis* ('Biblical Theology, Contemporary', in *The Interpreter's Dictionary of the Bible*, New York: Abingdon Press, 1961, vol. 1, 418–31).

4. Compare Gerhard Ebeling's definition of the task of biblical theology: 'In "biblical theology" the theologian who devotes himself specially to studying the connection between the Old and New Testaments has to give an account of his understanding of the Bible as a whole, i.e. above all of the theological problems that arise from inquiry into the inner unity of the Bible' ('The Meaning of "Biblical Theology"' [1955], in *Word and Faith*, ET London: SCM Press, 1963, 79–97; 96). The complexity of the hermeneutical problem means that the biblical theologian will be dependent on the discipline of systematic theology; biblical theology 'would then provide the compelling impulse towards close co-operation on the part of the various theological disciplines, from which the church historian also could not be omitted' (96). Rightly understood, biblical theology 'points back again to the unity of theology – not of course a unity achieved by abolishing the different disciplines, but a unity consisting in the right theological use of the different disciplines, each of which has its own peculiar task and yet is "theology" in the sense of participating in the scientific expression of the Word of God. This understanding of the unity of theology, in which the conversation is kept open between the historian and the systematic theologian because the historian, if he is to be a historian, must also be a systematic theologian, and the systematic theologian, if he is to be a systematic theologian, must also be a historian, seems to me to be peculiarly in keeping with the Reformers' understanding of theology' (96–97).

5. Frank Kermode, *The Genesis of Secrecy: On the Interpretation of Narrative*, Cambridge, Mass.: Harvard University Press, 1979. The distinction between the older literary criticism on which biblical scholarship has drawn and more recent literary theory is emphasized especially by Stephen D. Moore, in his *Literary Criticism and the Gospels: The Theoretical Challenge*, New Haven and London: Yale University Press, 1989.

6. J. Derrida, *Of Grammatology*, ET Baltimore: John Hopkins University Press, 1976; see also 'Edmond Jabès and the Question of the Book', in *Writing and Difference*, ET Chicago: University of Chicago Press, 1978, 64–78; 'Plato's Pharmacy', in *Dissemination*, ET Chicago: University of Chicago Press, 1981, 61–171. In its theological form, the speech/writing distinction tends to disparage writing for its deadness, its fixity, its purely legal authority – the opposite of Derrida's fluid, authorless writing endlessly disseminating non-authoritative meanings.

7. B. S. Childs, *Biblical Theology of the Old and New Testaments*, London: SCM Press, 1992.

8. For accounts of the biblical theology movement, see H. Graf Reventlow, *Problems of Biblical Theology in the Twentieth Century*, ET London: SCM Press, 1986; B. S. Childs, *Biblical Theology in Crisis*, Philadelphia: Westminster, 1970; J. D. Smart, *The Past, Present and Future of Biblical Theology*, Philadelphia: Westminster, 1979.

9. The following books and articles are cited in the text: *The Semantics of Biblical Language*, London: Oxford University Press, 1961; *Biblical Words for Time*, Studies in Biblical Theology 33, London: SCM Press, 1962; *Old and New in Interpretation*, London: SCM Press, 1966; *The Bible in the Modern World*, London: SCM Press, 1973; 'Trends and Prospects in Biblical Theology', *JTS* n.s. 25 (1974), 265–82; *Fundamentalism*, London: SCM Press, 1977; *Holy Scripture: Canon, Authority, Criticism*, Oxford: Clarendon Press, 1983; 'The Theological Case against Biblical Theology', in G. M. Tucker et al. (eds.), *Canon, Theology and Old Testament Interpretation: Essays in Honor of Brevard S. Childs*, Philadelphia: Fortress, 1988, 3–19; *Biblical Faith and Natural Theology*, Oxford: Clarendon Press, 1993.

10. J. Barr, *Biblical Words for Time*, 21n.

11. The reference is to the English translation of the Kittel–Friedrich *Wörterbuch*, the *Theological Dictionary of the New Testament*, ET Grand Rapids: Eerdmans, 1964–76.

12. O. Cullmann, *Christ and Time: The Primitive Christian Conception of Time and History*, ET London: SCM Press, 1951.

13. O. Cullmann, *Immortality of the Soul or Resurrection of the Dead? The Witness of the New Testament*, ET London: Epworth Press, 1958.

14. Barr's relationship to the 'radical' theology of the 1960s and 1970s is, however, a complex one. His use of its characteristic emphases is often cautious and tentative, and at some points his language is deliberately un-radical, indeed rather 'conservative' in tendency. Thus the Bible is said to be authoritative because 'being a Christian is not simply being a theist, believing that there is a deity; it is believing in a particular God who has manifested himself in a way that has some sort of unique and specific expression in the Bible' (*Explorations in Theology 7: The Scope and Authority of the Bible*, London: SCM Press, 1980, 52). The problem is that 'conservative' statements such as this one are neither developed much further nor integrated into any broader argument. James D. Smart's claim that Barr 'has always found it easier to expose the mistakes of others than to mark out constructively the path into the future that should be taken by biblical scholarship' is probably not unjust (*The Past, Present and Future of Biblical Theology*, 31).

PART ONE

Studies in
Theological Hermeneutics

Chapter 1

+ ⋅ ⋅ ≣◆≣ ⋅ ⋅

The Gospels as Narrated History

The four gospels are historical documents, in the sense that they preserve traces of past events, acts and utterances circumscribed by a particular set of spatio-temporal coordinates. They are also narratives: they tell a story with a beginning, a middle and an end related to one another in linear, teleological fashion. The gospels may therefore be studied as historical documents from which may be obtained various types of information about the origins of Christianity; or one may focus on the formal means by which the gospel narratives are constructed. But the term 'narrative' is too broad to constitute a single genre, since it encompasses material which may be oral or written, anecdote or epic, prose or poetry, history or fiction. The study of the gospels as narrative therefore cannot avoid the question what kind of narrative they are. There is no such thing as a narrative-in-general.

The history/fiction polarity is especially significant in this respect, as it is clear both that the gospel narratives express a fundamental historiographical intention, and that they nevertheless include fictive elements (however hard these may be to delimit). Priority should be ascribed to the historiographical function, since these texts reflect the general early Christian belief that authentic narration about Jesus is a *re*telling of that which has taken place prior to the act of narration. However much the telling may have developed a life of its own, the intention to refer to the prior reality of Jesus is omnipresent, and the fictionalizing tendency is therefore subordinate to the intended backward reference.

All this indicates the limitations of a narrative criticism that treats the gospels in abstraction from their intended function as historiographical testimony to the reality of Jesus as the Christ.[1] I shall argue here that it is possible to combine the orientations towards narrative and towards history by understanding the gospels as narrated history. This will require

33

an understanding of historiography and of historical research which diverges from the assumptions underlying current study of the gospels.

1. Narrative and the Eclipse of History

Narrative criticism has performed an invaluable service in its rediscovery of the gospels' narrativity; but in abstracting this narrativity from historiographical intention, it has tended to assimilate the gospel texts to purely fictional narratives which are not constrained by a direct external referent.[2] It is assumed that history and narrative must go their separate ways: for those with historical interests, various historical-critical strategies are available, while for those with a more literary orientation, ahistorical literary-critical analysis is a fruitful possibility. Unease about the fictive status that literary criticism assigns to the gospels is, in part, theologically motivated. As a character of fiction, Jesus is theologically uninteresting; for the Word became *flesh* and not text, even though the enfleshed Word is textually mediated. This theological criterion might be regarded as incommensurable with the secular criteria operative within narrative and historical criticisms; but I hope to show that it is possible to reflect on the historiographical intention of gospel narrative in a way that mediates between theological and secular concerns.

The ahistorical tendency of narrative criticism is a partly justified reaction against the perceived limitations of the standard historical approaches that dominate the modern study of the gospels. But the danger of an indiscriminate rejection of every attempt to look 'behind the text' is that the sphere of the historical will simply be abandoned, while the newly-rediscovered narratives are taken elsewhere. That might perhaps be appropriate if we knew these texts to be fictional. But if they are – in some sense, however attenuated or problematic – works of historiography, then it is clear that they intend to point to that which is external to them, a particular past which lies behind them and which they seek to mediate to their readers. The implied reader of these texts understands them not as an enclosed fictional world but as an imaginative rendering of a prior reality.

Thus the Gospel of Luke opens by locating itself within the manifold endeavour 'to compile a narrative of the events accomplished among us' (*anataxasthai diēgēsin peri tōn peplērophorēmenōn en hēmin pragmatōn*, Luke 1.1). A series of events has occurred, not in some far-distant time and place but 'among us' – in temporal and spatial proximity to the author and his first readers; and this series of events is evidently significant enough to have led 'many' (*polloi*) to attempt to render it in narrative form. The narrative that is to follow thus presents itself as a contribution to this collective effort: 'It seemed good to me also . . .' (1.3). The implied reader, represented by

Theophilus, is to read the narrative as a rendering of 'the events accomplished among us', prior to and external to the narrative, so as to acquire in this way a knowledge of 'the truth' (*asphaleia*) about them (1.4). To construct an implied reader who looks no further than the confines of the text is to overlook the historiographical genre within which this text so emphatically locates itself. Furthermore, the Lucan prologue implies a stratification comparable to the one employed in historical-critical research. At the first level, certain events have taken place 'among us'. Yet we do not have a direct and immediate knowledge of them. A second level is therefore required, in which knowledge of them is 'handed down [*paredosan*] to us by those who were from the beginning eyewitnesses [*autoptai*] and ministers of the word' (1.2). This handing-down of tradition is evidently oral, for the writing of narratives has not yet taken place, and the events concerned are therefore initially encountered through oral 'instruction' (cf. *katēchēthēs*, 1.4). The third level consists of a 'writing' intended to secure the tradition from the instability and fluidity to which its orality exposes it. Orality cannot give the firm knowledge of the truth that Theophilus requires: for although the main outlines are clear, divergences within traditions are quite evident. Indeed, writing itself does not guarantee stability. If there are many narratives extant, the reason must be that the events accomplished among us have been rendered in divergent ways, so that the fluidity of oral tradition reproduces itself in writing. Writing can only stabilize tradition if the writer is trustworthy – if his research has been patient, comprehensive and painstaking (cf. *anōthen pasin akribōs*, 1.3). Were the other writers lacking in these qualities? They wrote in accordance with what was handed down (*kathōs*, 1.2), and yet there are different degrees of faithfulness and insight, and the reader of these works will need to exercise a certain discrimination.[3] The implied reader of the Lucan narrative is therefore a critical reader who knows that the crucial events have been mediated by oral tradition and that a slippage can occur between the events and the tradition or writing which seeks to mediate them. Yet tradition and writing can maintain a sufficient degree of transparency to that about which they speak for knowledge of the truth to be attainable, and it is this attainable goal that critical discrimination serves.

The conclusion of the Gospel of John has a similar function to the Lucan prologue in asserting the historiographical credentials of this text. The narrative might have ended with Jesus' call to Peter to 'follow me' (John 21.19); Peter has focalized the narrative of John 21 up to this point (vv. 3, 7b, 11, 15–19), no doubt in anticipation of his forthcoming role in the period of Jesus' absence that will shortly begin. Yet the mysterious 'disciple whom Jesus loved' has been introduced again in v. 7 as recognizing the risen Lord on the lake-shore, and the narrative ends with an inconclusive dialogue between Jesus and Peter about what the future holds for this other disciple, who is introduced with a backward reference to his place at Jesus' breast at the last supper (vv. 20–22). Peter will glorify God in his martyrdom (v. 19). What of the beloved disciple? Will he perhaps survive until the parousia? At this point we suddenly leave the narrative and find ourselves in the sphere of 'the brothers', whose mistaken interpretation of Jesus' ambiguous words about the beloved disciple is corrected (v. 23). This disciple's special significance is not his relationship to the timing of the parousia; it is his role as witness and as writer of the text that is drawing to its close. 'This is the disciple who is bearing witness to these things, and who has written these things; and we know that his testimony is true' (v. 24). The text doubles back on itself, explaining the possibility of its own existence. Here we have a single *autoptēs*, in contrast to the plurality mentioned by Luke; and the two functions of oral testimony and writing, held apart by Luke, are here conjoined. The truthfulness of the written testimony is certified not by the author, as in Luke, but by an anonymous community of previous readers or hearers who 'know that his testimony is true'. In Luke, it is a matter of fact that other narratives about the events accomplished among us already exist, whereas, in John, it is the possibility of an unlimited number of such alternative narratives that is asserted: 'But there are also many other things which Jesus did; were every one of them to be written, I suppose that the world itself could not contain the books that would be written' (v. 25).[4] This imaginary threat of a deluge of writing also illustrates the artifice of historiography in general, which must always select a limited number of instances to represent the ungraspable manifold to which it points. This particular historiography wishes us to know not everything about Jesus but enough about Jesus: 'Jesus did many other signs in the presence of the disciples, which are not written in this book; but these are written, that you may believe that Jesus is the Christ, the Son of God, and that believing you may have life in his name' (20.30–31). It is the quality and not the quantity of knowledge about Jesus that is important. As in Luke, knowledge about Jesus is attained through the mediation of oral testimony and writing, and the implied reader is directed back down this chain of transmission to the historical reality in which the present narrative is grounded.

The reader implied by both John and Luke reads these texts in order to discover again that, outside and prior to these texts, Jesus is the Christ. The possibility of this discovery is dependent on their claim to be truthful to the prior reality they seek to render – the claim that, within the limits of necessary selectivity, the mediation of tradition, and a limited perspective, written history represents enacted history in a way that does not mislead. But it is one thing to identify the role these texts outline for their implied reader, quite another to show how a real reader might be able to fulfil that role. The gospels may represent themselves as works of historiography, but can one with integrity take this self-presentation at face value? Historical-critical research has problematized the gospels' historiographical claim at point after point, and a narrative criticism that disregards this claim might well be displaying a necessary prudence. The theological choice would then be between a historical Jesus qualitatively different from the protagonist of the gospel narratives, and the fictional Jesus of the narratives themselves.[5] But if this dichotomy is in fact the product of the interpretative paradigm out of which it emerges, and if this paradigm is questionable in important respects, then it may be possible to set the gospels' historiographic claim in a more sympathetic light. The result of this would certainly not be any proof of Christian belief in Jesus as the Christ; it would demonstrate at best that this belief is not a wholly unwarranted response to the texts. What is at issue is not the old question 'whether the gospels are historically reliable' but the more fundamental question of what historiography is and what it might mean to be 'historically reliable'.

2. History and Difference

Historical investigation aims to extract from the gospel texts as much information as possible about the life of Jesus and of the earliest Christians. Information is extracted not at random, but on the basis of a prior vertical structuring of the texts in layers or archaeological strata. Textual criticism is concerned with the uppermost stratum, its aim being the removal of the later accretions which partially conceal the authentic, original form of the textual object. With the object stabilized in this way, the next stage is to reconstruct the internal relationships of its four component parts, so as to establish a preliminary classification of the different traditions that they incorporate. This stratification of the textual object is the indispensable preliminary for investigation of the strata relating to the evangelist (redaction criticism), the history of tradition (form criticism), and Jesus himself (historical Jesus research). The excavation downward through the strata denotes a backward movement through time, and data relating to the earliest stage can only be obtained by way of the upper strata. Conventional historical research into the gospels normally presupposes this archaeological model whereby the object of investigation is prestructured.

There are obvious links between this model and the Lucan and Johannine reference to the mediation of tradition and writing between event and reader; to that extent, the model is actually closer to the world of the texts than a narrative criticism which disregards the texts' mediating role. And yet there is an equally obvious difference. In the gospels' self-presentation, the process of diachronic mediation takes place unproblematically, with the result that the narratives certify their own truthfulness. In the historical-critical model, however, the emphasis is not on diachronic continuities of tradition but on the synchronic study of the individual strata in relative isolation from one another. The gap between historical Jesus research and redaction criticism illustrates this tendency to assume the autonomy of the strata. To speak of 'the historical Jesus' is to assert a qualitative difference between the Jesus of historical reality and the Jesus of the Christian faith expressed and grounded in the canonical gospels. In the customary opposition between the Jesus of history and the Christ of faith, 'history' is taken to be synonymous with reality, whereas 'faith' is identified either with illusion or, at best, with an ungrounded non-rational conviction. There is therefore a qualitative difference between the stratum within which historical Jesus research operates and that in which redaction criticism identifies the faith and the theology of the evangelists. There is the real Jesus, and there are the Jesuses of Matthew, Mark, Luke and John.[6] The real Jesus is indeed to be found only within the gospel narratives, and yet he must be painstakingly reassembled from authentic fragments partially concealed in a mass of 'late' and therefore historically worthless material. This material becomes historically valuable again, however, as soon as we leave the question of the historical Jesus and ascend to the strata of early Christian tradition-history and the theology of the evangelists.

It is not immediately obvious why the conventional model emphasizes the synchronic autonomy of the individual strata, at the expense of organic diachronic development. The formidable difficulties of achieving clear demarcations between the strata are often recognized, yet renewed attempts at such demarcations continue unabated. Underlying this project appears to be a privileging of *difference*: redaction criticism, for example, seeks sharply-defined portrayals of the theologies of the individual evangelists, demarcated by their redactional activity both from one another and from the traditions they inherit. Do we detect here the influence of a basically individualistic and anti-ecclesial conception of the 'great theologian' as the one who is able to rise above the mediocrity of tradition so as to assert his own personal 'originality'? But the privileging of difference may also stem from a 'hermeneutic of suspicion' for which difference discloses untruth. The interpretative strategies this generates may be illustrated by comparing D. F. Strauss's characteristically 'modern' approach to a routine critical problem – the composite nature of the Sermon on the Mount – with Calvin's 'premodern' treatment of the same textual phenomena.[7]

Strauss notes the overlap and the differences between the Matthean Sermon on the Mount and the Lucan Sermon on the Plain, and his treatment of these texts arises out of his polemic against dated attempts at harmonization. Harmonization seeks 'to avoid the unpleasant admission that one of two inspired Evangelists must be in error'. Yet the supposition of error 'is inevitable if in relation to the same discourse one of them makes Jesus deliver it on the mountain, the other in the plain; the one sitting, the other standing; the one earlier, the other later; if either the one has made important omissions, or the other as important additions . . . The chronological divergencies, as well as the local, must be admitted, if we would abstain from fruitless efforts at conciliation' (*Life of Jesus Critically Examined*, Vol. I [1835], 335). Compelled by the evidence to admit that the teaching collected in the Sermon on the Mount was not in fact delivered on a single occasion, some claim that Matthew never intended to convey the impression that it was. Such critics are 'earnestly solicitous to avert from the Evangelist an imputation that might invalidate his claim to be considered an eye-witness', but 'it is with justice remarked in opposition to this, that when Matthew represents Jesus as ascending the mountain before he begins his discourse, and descending after its close, he obviously makes these two incidents the limits of a single address' (336). Strauss is here treating a typical example of the difference within similarity that characterizes the interrelation of the gospels, and his rhetorical strategies merit close attention.

Differences are, first, a sign of 'error': one or other evangelist must be wrong, or possibly both are. One naturally seeks to avoid this 'unpleasant admission', but intellectual integrity leaves one no choice. We must draw a firm line separating our own time from former times when a belief in divine inspiration led to all manner of improbable exegetical suggestions. Differences are, second, 'divergencies', and must be 'admitted' to be such if we are not to waste our time trying to salvage the battered reputation of the two evangelists. What if it is claimed that a degree of fictive activity (in this case, the compiling of the Sermon from various sources) is compatible with the evangelist's claim to communicate the truth? 'In opposition to this', a rigorous literalism points us back to the letter of the text in order to emphasize the unbridgeable gap between what the text actually says and what scholarship now knows to have been the case. The stratum of the historical Jesus is now distinguished from that of the evangelist, with the intention of stressing the non-coincidence between the real Jesus and the Matthean Jesus. These differences must be asserted in sharp opposition to the tendency to minimize them; that tendency is an anachronistic vestige of an older piety, and in combating it the author is fighting on behalf of modern truth against ancient error. 'If theologians regard this absence of presupposition from his work as unchristian, he regards the believing presuppositions of theirs as unscientific' (lii). The struggle is pursued into the narrowest recesses of the text, for this struggle is constitutive of this model of historical research. The establishing and exploiting of difference is the primary strategy in the struggle.

Yet Calvin too is clear that 'those who reckon Christ's assembly here [on the mount] to be a different one from that which is treated of in the sixth chapter of Luke, are swayed by an argument that is too weak and trifling – that Matthew tells how Christ spoke to his disciples on a mountain, while Luke appears to indicate that the sermon was given in the plain' (*Harmony of the Gospels*, I, 168). The difference should be allowed to stand, without complicated procedures for harmonization that lead to an obsession with trivia. Jesus probably addressed the disciples after choosing the twelve, as Luke but not Matthew asserts, but this is a point of little importance: 'I do not wish to be over-precise in matters of chronology, as I have observed how they are disregarded by the Spirit of God', who inspired these texts (168). A rationalistic doctrine of inspiration might insist that every least statement in holy scripture should be free from error, but empirical study of the texts leads Calvin to the opposite conclusion, that irreducible differences are a sign that the Holy Spirit is uninterested in arbitrarily-imposed standards of rational consistency. Matthew situates Jesus' teaching on a mountain, Luke on a plain, but what matters is the common purpose underlying the difference: 'Both evangelists had the intention of gathering into one single passage the chief headings of Christ's teaching, that had regard to the rule of godly and holy living . . . It should be enough for reverent and humble readers that here, before their eyes, they have set a short summary of the teaching of Christ, gathered from many and various discourses' (168). Theological integrity requires us to recognize that the gospels have been constructed out of various traditions and that the result is often irreducible difference in the presentation of very similar material; but this acknowledgment is not especially 'unpleasant' (as Strauss wishes it to be), it is not something that must be unwillingly 'admitted' as if under pressure, it does not contradict the doctrine of inspiration or impugn the credibility of the evangelists. Readers must be warned not to waste time over trivial matters that distract attention from Christ's 'rule of godly and holy living'.

Calvin in effect refutes the Straussian assumption that, for all participants in the discussion, difference will be subversive of Christian faith. Strauss envisages a spectrum, with Christian faith at one end and scientific historical research at the other. Christian faith will go to any lengths to explain away those phenomena identified by historical research which cast doubt on the strict historical veracity of the gospels, and the result is a power-struggle in which each side defines itself in opposition to the other. Historical research *is* resistance to the attempts of Christian faith to maintain a precise correspondence between text and reality, and every denial of this precise correspondence is therefore a proof of the scientific legitimacy of the historical research. Research *is dependent upon* the harmonizers of texts and reality, who constitute the counterpart against which it is able to measure its critical freedom. In defining itself, it needs what it will later call 'fundamentalism' as its other.[8] If Strauss, unlike Reimarus, still seems a remarkably 'modern' figure, it is because this model of historical research still lives on as a significant strand in the modern study of the gospels. The naïve assumption that the Sermon on the Mount is a transcript of Jesus' *ipsissima verba* serves as the necessary foil for the demonstration that redactional activity has been so extensive that the Sermon is really Matthew's more than it is Jesus'. Thus the strata of the evangelist and of the historical Jesus are not only distinguished (as they already are in Calvin) but separated, and each is made autonomous to such an extent that the evangelist's Jesus and the 'real', historical, Jesus simply subvert one another.

Rather than continuing to work within this interpretative paradigm, it may be possible to construct an alternative understanding of historical research which takes seriously both the gospels' historiographical claims and the critical problem of difference. This alternative approach would pose the fundamental question of what it is to engage in historiography or history-writing, and in doing so it would reject the positivistic assumption that historiography is a matter of ensuring that every assertion corresponds precisely to an empirical datum. As the following discussion will show, this alternative approach would be able to draw a range of insights from recent historiographical theory. Contemporary historiographical theory makes it possible to understand the gospels as *narrated history*, in a manner that combines the current 'literary' emphasis on the irreducibility of the gospels' narrativity with the conventional 'historical' concern for the relationship between text and reality. It will be necessary to show that the question of the relationship between a historiographical text and historical reality is more problematic than a naïve view of history-writing as 'pure description' would suggest.

3. History-Writing

In his book *History/Writing* (1988),[9] Albert Cook identifies a fundamental tension in the practice of all historiography:

> History writing is a form of literature; it could be said that it began as such. But it carries, in its very conception, an especially sharp angle on what it designates. It lays claim, both rhetorically and actually, to a validity of correspondence to the public processes of the real world. (1)

We must therefore

keep in view the two seemingly contradictory constraints on historiography, the validity that in one form or another the theorists of historical explanation single out for discussion, and the 'rhetoric' analyzed by recent writers who stress the literary structure of historiography. (1)

Historical discourse's assumption of a subordinate relationship to a prior historical reality precludes a purely literary or rhetorical analysis which abstracts from the intention to speak truthfully about the past.[10] On the other hand, the susceptibility of historical discourse to literary and rhetorical analysis indicates that to see it as pure repetition of 'how it actually was' is inadequate.

Literary works are concerned with the creation of orderly structures out of the raw material offered by language, experience and tradition. A similar activity of imaginative synthesis occurs in historiography. As Lionel Gossman remarks in connection with Gibbon, 'It is for the sake of the "order and perspicuity" of the narrative ... that the historian carries out a rigorous selection among the chaotic and obscure materials that press upon him' (Cook, 3). Events are identified and selected not in isolation, as in a mere chronicle, but in their interrelatedness, and particular attention may be paid to the causal links between an event and earlier events. Yet, as in the literary work, order is never fully realized: for 'the patterns of causation, since they are never total, will not effectually work when applied to the plethora of happenings in the human past' (7). Details may be amassed which resist incorporation into a single narrative line. Thus Herodotus begins by identifying one man as the 'cause' (*aitia*) of the events to be narrated; but 'this one man, Croesus, will very soon get buried in the complexities of a narrative to which his own career is necessarily contributory but also necessarily not fully commensurate' (7). Partially-realized order is, paradoxically, both imposed by the historian and implied in the data. Historical reality is not merely a chaos of random happening, but the patterns it appears to offer to historical comprehension may later be falsified or relativized by the discernment of different patterns arising out of a different selection of material.

One implication of this emphasis on history as writing is that criteria for distinguishing 'real' history from other modes of discourse are diversified, so that the bounds of actual and possible historiographical practice are extended. Thus, modern historians have tended to agree with the criteria that led Thucydides to criticize predecessors such as Herodotus for including legendary material in their work. Yet 'the modern concern for a purified professional historiography will overlook the historiographic element in such admixtures, classifying them oversimply as fiction, when actually they may be performing the historiographic task of organizing data around a central question about the past much more probingly than many an additive chronicler will have done' (15). The difficulty of the history/fiction distinction is compounded by the fact that fictions too 'refer to the real world, for all the imposed patterns of their arbitrary structures' (9); history and fiction thus share an orientation towards the real world without which both would be unintelligible.[11]

The same diversity is to be seen if we consider not the material available to the historian but the historian's attitude towards this material. Tacitus' decision to write of the reigns of the early emperors 'without indignation or partisanship' (*sine ira et studio*) may seem to make him a model of the 'impartiality' so often commended to the historian. Cook sees here 'a neutrality that has a Stoic cast', although without formal adherence to a Stoic world-view; he also suggests that 'Stoicism would become particularly attractive under the conditions that Tacitus depicts' (95–96). An attitude of *apatheia* and resignation to the providential ordering of the world would then be a strategic response to the moral and political chaos depicted in Tacitus' narrative, and the repudiation of *ira* and *studium* would be a defensive measure intended to enable narrator and readers to accept the unacceptable about their own common history. But if impartiality is seen as a culturally-conditioned, strategic response to a set of intractable problems, then it can no longer be seen as an imperative binding on all historians at all times. If *ira* and *studium* are likely to have their blind spots, the same is true of the gesture that repudiates them.

Diversification of the criteria of historical judgment makes it possible to accept the historiographical credentials of texts that fail to meet the criteria of modern historical research.[12] It is arbitrary to apply these criteria in such a way as to 'deny not only a historiographic purpose but also a historio-graphic result to the biblical narrative about the successive events in the collective life of the Hebrews from the Exodus, or even earlier, to the destruction of the First Temple' (139). The historiographic *purpose* is clear enough: it is evident in the fact that here one cannot 'invoke the "suspension of disbelief"' one brings to a fictive work, because the rhetorical thrust of this text declares it not to be fiction' (140). But does Old Testament narrative as a whole achieve a historiographic *result*? It is true that 'the writer puts at the center of his narrative an active agent, God, whose presence cannot be established by the canons of evidence that the modern historian uses' (139). Yet historical narration often implicitly or explicitly alludes to large supra-empirical entities which are supposed to guarantee the coherence of apparently heterogeneous events on the surface of history – Zeus, Fate, Destiny, the Idea, Progress or the Class Struggle, for example. The historiographical status of texts that express a belief in one or other of these universal ordering principles may be accepted even by those who do not share this particular belief. There is therefore no reason to deny historiographical status to the narrative of Yahweh's dealings with Israel.

Correspondingly, the New Testament is dependent upon the early Christian construal of history and its unique focal point:

> Every section of the New Testament sets out its presentation so that it is all sited in history and dependent on a historical sequence. The establishment of the authority for a new church and its doctrines is communicated through, and made dependent upon, events in historical sequence that have been singled out and organized. Thus the sense and senses of the New Testament are derived from a temporal sequence of public import; they satisfy a definition of history. (159)

Gospel narrative is to be understood as primarily historical rather than biographical:

> It differs from 'aretology' – the tale of a supernatural wonder-worker – by its stated, constant bearing on historical developments. This biographical centering, the presence of miracles and other untestable events, and the heavy doctrinal emphasis, all tend to obscure the preponderant historical focus of the New Testament, which is at the same time so obvious as to be taken quietly for granted. (159–60)

Although the distinction between biography and history is hard to draw precisely, the point is that New Testament narrative sets the particular figure of Jesus in the context of the history of Israel, itself seen as the key to the history of the world. Its universal horizon is seen especially clearly in the supplementing of the gospel narrative by the Book of Acts, which arises out of the general early Christian sense that the end of the gospel narratives marks not only a conclusion but also a definitive beginning within the history of the world.[13]

According to Cook, a vast and heterogeneous body of writing, including not only Thucydides and Gibbon but also the gospels, is unified by its historiographical intentionality, its orientation towards the writing of a past related to the present by way of a temporal continuum. Unfortunately, much of Cook's discussion of biblical narrative is confined to the literary plane, which means that there is no acknowledgment of the diversity of narrative material in the Old and the New Testament. If the term 'historiography' is to be stretched to accommodate most if not all of this material, it would be necessary to reflect on the variety of relationships to prior historical reality presupposed by this material. The story of Jacob's victorious struggle with the angel of Yahweh is not historiography in the same sense as the narrative material about the last days of the kingdom of Judah in the Book of Jeremiah. The suggestion made in connection with Herodotus that even legendary material may fulfil a genuine historiographical role is unfortunately left undeveloped. In addition, the problem of reference is treated as though it were simply a function of the text's rhetoric: the intention to refer is treated in abstraction from the question of the successful performance of the act of reference, and this tends to align Cook with theorists such as Hayden White who emphasize the literary affiliations of historiography at the expense of its orientation towards prior historical reality.

We are not entitled to solve the problem of reference merely by rhetorical analysis. Yet Cook's argument remains valuable for its underlying claim that criteria for assessing putatively historical narratives require diversification if the complexities of history-writing are to be allowed their full weight.

4. History and Tradition

The central preoccupation of Hans-Georg Gadamer's *Truth and Method* (1960) is a view of classic literary texts (and other art-works) as bearers of truth, over against a historical approach which, in relocating them within their circumstances of origin, systematically marginalizes their enduring truth-claim.[14] For Gadamer, the truth of the classic text comes to light in the process of conversation or dialogue that constitutes the act of interpretation. It is wrong to imagine that the interpreter's own preconceptions can and should be set aside, in accordance with the ideal of 'historical objectivity'; on the contrary, preconceptions are made explicit as the horizons of interpreter and text encounter one another, seeking – as in any conversation – consensus about the subject-matter (*die Sache*). While consensus will not be easily achieved, it is made possible by the fact that text and interpreter are not alien to one another but participate in a continuum of tradition already shaped in part by the classic status accorded to the text. Although the important second section of *Truth and Method* is supposedly concerned with 'the extension of the question of truth to understanding in the humanities', the issue of an appropriate historiography never quite comes into focus; for Gadamer's preoccupation with 'the alien control of historical studies' over the *Geisteswissenschaften* (303) causes him to overlook the fact that 'history' too is a *Geisteswissenchaft*.[15] Yet it is possible to extend Gadamer's insights into the sphere of historiographical theory, and to show how this might help to rehabilitate the historiographical claim of the gospels. In order to do so, we must clarify further that 'modern' understanding of historiography that has made the gospels' claim seem so questionable.

Gadamer illustrates the historicist thesis that he opposes with a remark from Wilhelm Dilthey's obituary of a former colleague: 'He was', says Dilthey, 'a modern man, and the world of our forebears was no longer the home of his spirit and his heart, but his historical object.' According to Gadamer, this indicates that Dilthey 'saw scientific knowledge as involving the dissolution of the connection with life: the establishing of a distance from its own history, which alone makes it possible for that history to become an object' (8). To understand an object 'purely historically' presupposes an alienation from the truth-claim made by that object. This is especially clear in the use of history in the Enlightenment's critique of the biblical texts, and Gadamer cites Spinoza's *Tractatus theologico-politicus* (1670) as an early example of this: here, 'the necessity of the historical interpretation "in the spirit of the writer" follows ... from the hieroglyphic and incomprehensible nature of the contents' (159).[16] Strauss's approach to the gospels also illustrates this Enlightenment strategy of deploying historical methods in the service of the criticism of religion. But for Dilthey this disillusioning discovery of the otherness of that which tradition has handed down to us must be succeeded by a reappropriation of tradition by way of an empathetic understanding of the historical life in which it originated. The hermeneutic of empathy influences the modern study of the gospels alongside Straussian critique, and since Gadamer points towards an alternative to both it is worth identifying its main features.

Dilthey's attempts to provide a philosophical grounding for the historical research of the *Geisteswissenschaften* led him to conceive the project of a 'Critique of Historical Reason', which was never completed. In a preliminary study, Dilthey grounds the possibility of historical understanding in our general human 'understanding of other persons and their life-expressions'.[17] For Dilthey, historical understanding entails a dialectical relationship between otherness and empathy. In one sense, the past is alien to us; to make it the object of historical research implies that we are no longer at home in the world of our predecessors. Yet if the past were entirely alien, we would not be able to understand it at all; inherited texts and traditions would be indecipherable. In ordinary life, we understand other people in so far as we are able to trace their 'life-expressions' (utterances or actions) back into the mental life in which they originate; empathetic understanding is possible because of our own mental life, that is, on the basis of a shared life.[18] In historical understanding, the otherness which critique brings to light is preceded by the reality of a shared life which enables us to penetrate the otherness of the past and so to enlarge the scope of our own mental and intellectual life.

Inherited religious traditions offer a paradigmatic case of this dialectic of otherness and empathy. Critique has left its indelible mark, for Dilthey writes: 'The possibility of experiencing religious states in one's own life is narrowly limited for me as for most of my contemporaries.' Thus, if I read the letters and writings of Luther, I must conclude that the eruptive power expressed here is 'beyond the possibility of direct experience for a man of our time'.

Nevertheless, 'I can re-live it' (160): *Nacherleben* offers a substitute for direct *Erlebnis*. Through historical study of Luther's texts, there is disclosed

> a religious world in him and his companions of the first period of the Reformation which widens our horizon of the possibilities of human existence. Only in this way do they become accessible to us. Thus the inner-directed man can experience many other existences in his imagination. Limited by circumstances, he can yet glimpse alien beauty in the world and areas of life beyond his reach. Put generally: man, tied and limited by the reality of life is liberated not only by art . . . but also by historical understanding. (161)

History, like art and travel, broadens the mind. Historical study is an exercise of the imagination through which the vanished world of the past is restored to life, not so much for its own sake as for ours: to enable us to suspend the world of our immediate, everyday experience and to indwell the recreated historical world, where what is alienatingly strange is mingled inextricably with what is poignantly familiar. There is here a double fictive movement: the recreation of the past *as if* it were still present, and the personal engagement with that past *as if* one were truly at home there. This imaginative possibility of fictively indwelling the past is a major motivation for the laborious work of historical recreation, and it presupposes the enduring value of that lost but recreatable world and of the human beings who inhabited it.[19] Long-dead people can seem to impose on us the ethical or quasi-ethical duty not to allow them to pass wholly into oblivion. The critical rejection of certain of the claims that reach us from the past is in part an anti-historical gesture that seeks to ensure the autonomous reality of the present, but it may also prepare the way for an appropriate indwelling of the past. Critique and empathy belong together; empathetic recreation moderates and mollifies the harshness of critique, but the critical moment is nevertheless indispensable. Real historical study can arise only on the near side of the breach created by critique, for the tendency otherwise will be to assimilate the past to the present in the ahistorical fashion of a medieval painting in which biblical characters are portrayed in contemporary clothing. The fictive, *as-if* character of historical understanding assumes as its non-fictive counterpart that *in reality* we indwell a present that is discontinuous with the lost world of the past.

Applied to the gospels, this historical hermeneutic enables a partial imaginative overcoming of the distance engendered by Straussian critique. The critique makes it possible to resist the assumption of these texts' continuing normative status, but the labour of historical recreation is not motivated solely by this negative, polemical factor. In historical study, we enter imaginatively into the recreated intellectual and social world of the first Christians. Jesus himself – the historical Jesus – becomes our quasi-contemporary as we enter his world, and the same is true for Paul, the evangelists and the anonymous bearers of tradition who have left behind them innumerable traces of their activity. This is a *quasi*-contemporaneity in the twofold sense that we indwell the past only fictively and that the past we fictively indwell is not a past *an sich* but our own representation created out of the traces left behind by the real past. The possibility of different, perhaps incompatible, representations of the same past further underlines the fictive character of historical understanding.

This seductive hermeneutic of empathy stems from a one-sided and ultimately impoverished understanding of both the present and the past. The present is impoverished in that it represents a narrowness and a restriction which, as Dilthey puts it, needs historical understanding so as to open up 'a wide range of possibilities which do not exist within the limitations of [one's] real life'. Left to itself on the near side of criticism's breach with the past, life must create for itself a surrogate wealth out of the traces left behind by the life of the past. In his essay 'On the Uses and Disadvantages of History for Life' (1874), Nietzsche makes this point with characteristic directness:[20]

> We moderns have nothing whatever of our own; only by replenishing and cramming ourselves with the ages, customs, arts, philosophies, religions, discoveries of others do we become anything worthy of notice, that is to say, walking encyclopaedias, which is what an ancient Greek transported into our own time would perhaps take us for. (79)

> Historical culture is indeed a kind of inborn grey-hairedness, and those who bear its mark from childhood must instinctively believe in the *old age of mankind*: to age, however, there pertains an appropriately senile occupation, that of looking back, of reckoning up, of closing accounts, of seeking consolation through remembering what has been, in short historical culture. (101)

Historical culture stems from and perpetuates the impoverishment of the present, which seeks through historical knowledge a surrogate life elsewhere, in the past. But the past too is impoverished by the historical quest, for its ongoing energies are systematically immobilized:

> A religion, for example, which is intended to be transformed into historical knowledge under the hegemony of pure historical justice, a religion which is intended to be understood through and through as an object of science and learning, will, when this process is at an end, also be found to have been destroyed. (95)

> Recent theology . . . seems to have entered into partnership with history out of pure innocence, and even now it refuses to see that, probably much against its will, it has thereby placed itself in the service of the Voltairean *écrasez*. (96)

Nietzsche believes that historical investigation destroys Christianity because it exposes so much pious although productive illusion. Yet the real problem of the historical approach is not its exposure of illusions but its immobilizing of the past. In the music of Mozart and Beethoven, for example, the greatness of the past is borne into the present by a living, moving tradition; but here too we see this greatness 'already engulfed by all the learned dust of biography and compelled by the torture-instruments of historical criticism to answer a thousand impertinent questions' (97). This historical criticism is not interested in the enduring presence of the past, but is concerned only to return classic works to their circumstances of origin. 'Classic' or 'canonical' status means precisely that a work cannot be wholly explained by reference to its circumstances of origin, and the historical approach must therefore overlook or deny the movement from the past into the present that drew its attention to the work in the first place. Turning its attention to certain works and not others precisely because of their classic or canonical status, the historical approach proceeds by abstracting these works from their historical effects or – in Gadamer's terminology – their *Wirkungsgeschichte*.

There is a danger here that the historical emphasis on the pastness of the past will be countered by an assertion of the presence of the past that denies that pastness remains pastness within this present.[21] To hear the music of Mozart or Beethoven is to be in the presence not of a pure simultaneity but of a living past identifiable as that of the late eighteenth or early nineteenth century. The endurance of classic or canonical texts such as the gospels does not erase the historical moment of their origin. It is integral to classic status that works should be broadly locatable in historical terms, and it is therefore not the case that to ask a historical question is immediately to have committed a transgression against the work in its classic form. Gadamer develops the concept of 'occasionality' (*Okkasionalität*) in order to account for this aspect of the classic work. The work's reference to particularities of person, time and place is especially clear in the case of the portrait, where 'occasionality' is obviously 'part of what the work is saying and is not something forced on it by its interpreter' (*Truth and Method,* 127–28). This example represents a 'particular case of the general relationship appropriate to the being of the work of art: namely, to experience from the "occasion" of its coming-to-presentation a continued determination of its significance' (130). In abstracting the occasion from the ongoing significance that bears the occasion with it, the historical approach is evading 'the basic question whether one accepts the claim to meaning that the work makes', regarding it instead as 'an historical document that one merely consults' (129).[22]

'Classic' or 'canonical' status means that a work is borne along into a future of indefinite duration by a communally-authoritative tradition which has found in the work a claim to normative significance. To be located within communally-authoritative traditions is a mark of our human finitude or 'thrownness' (*Geworfenheit*), which precludes the arrogance of the 'objective standpoint' outside history. Yet our present is determined not only by the past but by an openness towards the future which gives a relative freedom to determine how the truth-claim perceived in normative works is now to be understood and appropriated. There can therefore be no single, definitive interpretation: 'We would regard the canonisation of a particular interpretation, e.g. in a gramophone recording conducted by the composer . . . , as a failure to understand the actual task of interpretation' (107). Rather,

> the real meaning of a text, as it speaks to the interpreter, does not depend on the contingencies of the author and whom he originally wrote for. It certainly is not identical with them, for it is always partly determined by the historical situation of the interpreter and hence by the totality of the objective course of history. (263)

But the historical distance between the work's origin and the interpreter is not an empty, alienating space:

> The important thing is to recognise the distance in time as a positive and productive possibility of understanding. It is not a yawning abyss, but is filled with the continuity of custom and tradition, in the light of which all that is handed down presents itself to us. (265)

The handing-down occurs within a particular communal context, and the classics of one community may be unknown or unappreciated in another.

If the gospels are regarded as canonical, communally-authoritative texts, then there can be no question of confining these texts to an immobilized past into which one enters through the fictive activity of the empathetic imagination. As classic texts, they bear with them a truth-claim, and the primary task of interpretation is to come to terms with that truth-claim in a context which will always be different from past contexts in which the truth-claim has been heard, to struggle with the difficulties that it may pose, and to bring to light its disclosive possibilities for the present. In this case, the truth-claim relates to particularities of person, time and place that lie outside and prior to the texts themselves. While one might ascribe to these texts a significance that is 'more than merely historiographical' (whatever that might mean), this must not imply that they are in fact 'less than' or 'other than' historiographical texts, for it is in the guise of an account of what has taken place that they present themselves.

Yet this application of Gadamer's hermeneutic to the gospels needs to be supplemented. On its own, it might seem to appeal to a communally-authoritative location in order to protect the gospels from the critical questioning that is carried on elsewhere. But the sphere of the church and its proclamation is not hermetically sealed against the rest of the world, and to confine the significance of the gospels within narrow communal limits would betray the universality of their truth-claim. We must search for a conceptuality which mediates between the ecclesial and the non-ecclesial spheres, and show how an understanding of the gospels as historiography neither assumes nor precludes acceptance of the basic Christian truth-claim that Jesus is the Christ.[23]

The equivalent in the historical realm to the 'classic' text or art-work is the 'historic' event, the event that marks an enduring turning-point in a historical process and that generates its own *Wirkungsgeschichte* out of which it is constantly interpreted and reinterpreted.[24] Thus the 'historic' event has a foundational quality, constituting a relatively new start (in so far as history permits this); a 'histori*cal*' event, on the other hand, is one that flows out of antecedent events and into subsequent events without any suggestion of qualitative newness. If, reverting to now-dated terminology, we describe the life of Jesus and its reception by the early Christians as 'the Christ-event', then it is obvious that this constitutes a 'historic event' of extraordinary proportions. According to Gadamer, it is clear that 'the nature of historicity [*Geschichtlichkeit*] became conscious to the human mind only with the Christian religion and its emphasis on the absolute moment of the saving action of God' (481). Is this 'historic event' therefore absolutely and not just relatively unique? But it is unnecessary to claim on general historical grounds that this 'historic event' is any more significant than the foundational events of other major religious traditions. In any case, significant for whom? How would one compare the significance of the Christ-event with, say, the 'discovery' of America or the French Revolution? And who is to decide what constellation of particulars counts as a 'historic event'? Despite its indeterminacy, however, the category of the historic event is firmly established in our perception of history, and it is applied indiscriminately to 'world-events' of the kind mentioned above and to more limited events which are 'historic' within a particular communal context.

How does an event come to be regarded as 'historic'? It does not enter the world with this predicate already attached. Even if an event appears to contemporaries to constitute a historic event in the making, the foundational nature of the historic event means that contemporaries can only guess at its significance; for this will depend on the new future that it generates and will therefore only be discerned retrospectively. The event now known as 'the collapse of Communism' in Eastern Europe and the former Soviet Union appears to us to be a good candidate for 'historic' status, but we will have only a very imperfect understanding of its significance until the nature of the new futures it opens up becomes clearer. Temporal distance from the event is therefore necessary in order for its significance to emerge, and this emergence will take place both through subsequent events and in the manifold discourse in which various interrelated social groupings negotiate a range of interpretative options which structure the ways in which that significance comes to speech. Temporal distance may also clarify the nature of the event by filtering out early misconceptions and false expectations, elements in the complex event that seemed important to contemporaries but which proved to be short-lived in their effects. As seen retrospectively, the main outline of the event on which its historic status depends has become clear, and much of the heterogeneity that attends present occurrence has been dispelled. No 'final meaning' will be accessible, for there is no absolute position of retrospection short of the eschaton, yet the process of tradition or *Wirkungsgeschichte* will nevertheless have generated one or more relatively stable, communally-normative interpretations of the event in which its historic status is put into speech and handed down to posterity.[25]

This analysis has a number of applications to our understanding of the gospels as historiography.

(1) The historic event is identified as such only in retrospect. Only retrospectively do the heterogeneity and contingency that attend the unfolding of Jesus' life-history assume the stable outlines of 'the Christ-event', an event believed to be of ultimate and universal significance. The retrospective character of this interpretation is not a sign that an arbitrary meaning has been imposed on an event whose reality was quite different; for the reality of the present is never available to that present, and the present must always look to the future for the disclosure of the truth about itself. The canonical, communally-normative interpretation of Jesus' life-history as the Christ-event is therefore dependent on temporal distance and on the development of tradition within its communal context. The gospels are individually and as a collection indications of successive moments in the stabilization of that tradition.

(2) What is the 'history' that is written in the gospels? This history-writing includes an indeterminate number of 'historical events' (including 'speech-events') that occurred in the course of Jesus' life, but this succession of events is recounted only within the context of the historic 'Christ-event' that the completed life constituted for the communal tradition it generated, which looked back to it as its own foundation. The gospels write not a chronicle of occurrences in Jesus' life but the Christ-event which that life had become within the communal interpretative process, and they are

therefore history-writing in the sense that they write the historic event that the life of Jesus was retrospectively seen to be. Of course, they assume that historic significance is inherent to Jesus' life and not merely imposed afterwards. But the retrospective significance of any historic event is always inherent to it, for that which is inherent to it is not only its bare empirical presence but also its openness to the future of its effects in the realm of action and of discourse. It should therefore be uncontroversial, and not a matter of a decision for or against Christian faith, that the history the gospels write is that of the Christ-event. What is at issue is not the so-called 'historicity' of this or that element in the gospels' story but the question whether the Christ-event truly possesses the transcendent grounding that is claimed for it, or whether its historic status remains within the bounds of immanence.

(3) In this history-writing, the evangelists' past and present are inextricably intertwined. The evangelists render neither an inert, immobilized past, nor a purely present address in historical disguise. The past that is rendered is a past that lives and remains effective in the present, for it is the past of the Christ-event whose historic status secures it against a 'merely historical' immobility. The present in which the past is rendered is not self-sufficient but lives out of that living past. As history-writing, the gospels are books about the past; as the writing of that which is historic, they are books about their own present and future, which are the present and future of this past. Past, present and future are not distinct from one another, as though the evangelists were concerned with each in turn. The past, present and future are the past, present and future of a single historic event which it possesses through the *Wirkungsgeschichte* it generates. The gospels claim a transcendental grounding for this unity, in the fact that 'Jesus Christ is the same yesterday, today, and for ever' (Heb. 13.8). 'Lo, I am with you always, till the end of the age' (Matt. 28.20): from the standpoint of the text, a single past, present and future presence is announced. Without this transcendent grounding, the single past, present and future of the Christ-event would belong entirely within the limits of immanence. But it remains possible, even without reference to the question of transcendent grounding, to criticize a mode of interpretation which stratifies the past of the historical Jesus, the past of the early church and the present of the evangelist in static, inert layers. The historic event is a dynamic entity in which past, present and future are interdependent.

(4) What is the relation between the historic event and the writing of this event? Writing is not extraneous to the event, but belongs to its very nature.

Writing stabilizes and preserves – not absolutely, since interpretations will differ, but relatively in that the boundaries within which interpretation will occur are now firmly marked out. But the historic event is precisely the event that is stabilized and preserved within the *Wirkungsgeschichte* that it generates, and writing is therefore integral to its historic status. Permanence can of course be achieved by other means: for example, through institutional control over a tradition that remains oral, or through representations such as paintings or monuments. Yet, in a literate culture, writing is perhaps the most effective way of securing the stability that historic status requires. We may therefore say that the Christ-event demands its own writing in the form of the gospels. This non-contingent relationship between event and writing further underlines the fact that the gospels are historiographical texts which should be interpreted as such.

5. Events and Fiction

In his three-volume *Time and Narrative* (1983–85; ET 1984–88),[26] Paul Ricoeur argues that philosophical thinking about time finds itself entangled in insoluble perplexities on account of the radical elusiveness of its object. Ricoeur summons Augustine as his first witness: 'What then is time? I know well enough what it is, provided that nobody asks me; but if I am asked what it is and try to explain, I am baffled' (*Confessions*, xi.14). In particular, Ricoeur explores the dichotomy between a phenomenological account of time, anticipated by Augustine and associated especially with Husserl and Heidegger, and the physical account developed by Aristotle, with its emphasis on the link between time and movement through space; Kant is seen as a second great representative of a 'physical' approach, even though time is here a form of intuition. Ricoeur takes it for granted that a physical account of time cannot explain the human experience of living in time, but he also argues that the phenomenological starting-point in experience cannot fulfil its totalizing ambitions and that the time of the natural order cannot be generated out of the ego. This 'aporia' remains insoluble if one remains within the philosophical tradition, for the true mediation between phenomenological and physical time is the humanized time of narrative, whether fictional or historical.[27] Narration is the human *activity* in which human meanings are projected upon time, and fictional as well as historiographical texts therefore give a privileged access to the reality of time.

This argument is, in effect, an assertion of the need for a hermeneutical philosophy that approaches reality by the indirect route of interpreting texts, rather than assuming any more direct access.[28] The texts that are here interpreted are historiographical as well as literary, and Ricoeur is able to draw literary and historiographical theory into dialogue with one another in constructing his 'solution' to the philosophical failure. Indeed, the chief value of Ricoeur's work lies in its mediating role. In itself, his philosophical argument shows signs of artifice – for example, in its distribution of 'negative' and 'positive' roles to philosophy and narrative respectively. Thus, Augustine's philosophical reflections on time are removed from their narrative and theological contexts within the *Confessions*, and compelled to testify to a purely philosophical aporia. Selected 'tales about time' – Woolf's *Mrs Dalloway*, Mann's *Magic Mountain*, Proust's *A la recherche du temps perdu* – are presented as a somewhat informal 'solution' to the failure of phenomenological accounts of time, with the result that possible links between philosophical and literary texts (Husserl and Proust, for example) remain unexplored. In the end, the individual moves Ricoeur makes in constructing his hypothesis about time and narrative are perhaps of more interest than the hypothesis itself.[29]

(*i*) *Emplotment*

For our purposes, it is Ricoeur's treatment of historiographical theory that is most significant. As he says, his inclusion of historiography within his field of vision fills 'a serious lacuna in the studies currently dealing with narrativity' (II, 156). Ricoeur does not share the formalistic prejudice against reference that unites the new-critical, structuralist and poststructuralist traditions in literary studies, and that has also marked literary approaches to the gospels. There can be no question here of marginalizing reference by regarding historiography as a mode of fiction. Yet Ricoeur's general thesis requires points of contact as well as contrast between historiographical and fictional narration, and the main point of contact is to be seen in the imaginative activity of emplotment that underlies both. The Aristotelian definition views plot as a teleological synthesis of disparate elements comprising beginning, middle and end. *Mimesis* of reality occurs through the mediation of *muthos* (plot), and the aim is therefore not a copy or replica of an original: 'Imitating or representing is a mimetic activity inasmuch as it produces something, namely, the organization of events by emplotment' (I, 34). The raw material for emplotment is derived from experience, but emplotment itself is not: for beginning, middle and end 'are not features of some real action but the effects of the ordering of the poem' (I, 39).[30]

Ricoeur wishes to extend concepts drawn from Aristotle's analysis of tragedy to the entire realm of fictional and historiographical narration. Historical and fictional works must select an appropriate beginning, also supplying background information about action preceding that beginning. The teleological drive towards resolution of the conflicts that arise out of this beginning is usually stronger in fiction than in historiography, where the 'sense of an ending' is weaker. Yet a historiography entirely lacking in teleology would not possess adequate criteria for selecting events out of the broad stream of heterogeneous occurrence. Events are events precisely because they are retrospectively seen to open up a future that is different from what would have been the case without them; as in fiction, an occurrence is constituted as an event by its contribution to the plot. The synthesis of heterogeneous particulars that creates the plot is an act of the imagination, determined in historiography not only by surviving traces of the past but also by the historian's point of view and delimitation of his or her subject-matter. Even where the same time and place are under consideration, an occurrence which constitutes a major 'event' in one emplotment may hardly register at all in another. Thus, despite their radically different modes of referring to prior reality, fiction and historiography share an organization through emplotment. This exposes the inadequacy of the empiricist or positivist understanding of the event as a physical occurrence which an observer would be able to verify through the evidence of the senses.

It would be straightforward enough to show that the gospels are emplotted narratives, with a teleologically-interrelated beginning, middle and end. Unusually, the end towards which the narratives move juxtaposes the conventions of tragedy and comedy, as the protagonist is successively both the victim of and the victor over the powers ranged against him – a possibility grounded in a transcendent character who appears only indirectly but from whom the action of this drama ultimately derives. Yet, if historiographical as well as fictional narrative is emplotted, then the characteristically 'literary' focus on the emplotment of the gospels need not proceed by assimilating these texts to fictional texts. There are indeed significant points of contact, which make the relationship of the gospels to fictional texts a fruitful area of investigation. But some if not all of these points of contact would be common both to fictional texts and to historiographical writing, and they therefore do not indicate a basically fictive intentionality rather than a historiographic one. Historiographical as well as fictional plots can be tragic, or comic, or both: for 'history borrows from literature' so as to enable us 'to see a given series of events *as* tragic, *as* comic, and so on . . . What is surprising is that this interlacing of fiction and history in no way undercuts the project of standing-for belonging to history, but instead helps to realize it' (III, 186–87). To point out the 'interlacing of fiction and history' is to imply a major weakness in contemporary study of the gospels, which assumes that fiction and history are simple opposites. On that view, the gospels may be studied *either* as historical sources *or* as fictive narratives; the assumption that their narrativity entails a basically fictive intentionality concedes the sphere of the historical to positivistic methods and presuppositions inherited from the nineteenth century. Ricoeur enables us to conceive of a historiography enriched by fiction and not subverted by it.[31]

(ii) Causal explanations

Ricoeur identifies two points in modern historiography where the relation between history and narrative has been 'eclipsed': the French *Annales*-school, with its interest in *longue durée* and *mentalités* and its tendency to see the 'events' studied by traditional historiography as epiphenomenal; and the attempt to extend into historiography the epistemology of English-speaking analytic philosophy (I, 95–120). To illustrate the latter, Ricoeur discusses Karl Hempel's article on 'The Function of General Laws in History' (1942), which defends the thesis that 'general laws have quite analogous functions in history and in the natural sciences' (quoted, I, 112). As Ricoeur comments, the historical event was here 'divested of its narrative status and . . . subsumed under a general concept of event that included all physical events and every noteworthy occurrence' (I, 112). On this view, the antecedents of any event, natural or historical, are to be understood as its *causes* in a sense strict enough to make it possible to predict that 'every time an event of type C occurs at a certain place and time, an event of the specific type E will occur at a place and time related to those of the first event'. It follows that 'the unique character of any event . . . is a myth which must be put beyond the horizon of science' (I, 113).

Underlying the general conception of historical uniqueness that is opposed here is probably the Christian understanding of the uniqueness of the Christ-event. From Spinoza onwards, attempts to extend a strict view of causality from the natural into the historical realm have functioned as an attack on the Christian claim that a particular set of events is qualitatively unique. Before tracing Ricoeur's account of critical responses to the natural-scientific reduction of historiography, it is worth bringing into play a more theologically-oriented account of the nature/history relationship, that of Ernst Troeltsch. I shall refer in particular to his *The Absoluteness of Christianity and the History of Religions* (1911[2]), with this single issue in mind.[32]

For Troeltsch, there can be no question of a strict reduction of history to quasi-natural laws, in the manner advocated by Hempel. On the contrary, the modern idea of history has 'gained recognition as a way of thinking independent of . . . the natural sciences, the more it has demonstrated that it is the matrix out of which all world views take shape' (45–46). The chief concern of history 'is with the individual and unique', which stem 'from an inner movement of life that cannot be reduced to a prior cause' (63). At one point, however, the realms of history and of the natural sciences run in parallel to one another. Like the sciences in the natural sphere, historical investigation seeks a comprehensive and totalizing understanding of all phenomena in the human sphere: 'The modern idea of history is a dynamic principle for attaining a comprehensive view of everything human' (45). One result of this is that the Christian claim that a certain set of events is *absolutely* unique becomes untenable. The modern view of history has led to

> the incorporation of Christianity as one individual phenomenon into the current of the other great individual phenomena that history has brought forth ... The apologetic wall of division, the wall of external and internal miracles, has slowly been broken down by this idea of history ... With this, however, there no longer exists any means by which one may isolate Christianity from the rest of history and then, on the basis of this isolation and its formal signs, define it as an absolute norm. (48)

The drive to incorporate what purports to be absolutely unique into an all-encompassing historical interconnectedness betrays the influence of the natural sciences, as the example of Darwinism indicates. The closeness of the natural and the historical spheres is also suggested by Troeltsch's use of the polarity of 'supernatural' and 'natural' in characterizing orthodox belief in Christian uniqueness and absoluteness. Despite the insistence on the distinctive reality of human historical existence, the omnipresent causality of the natural sciences lies just beneath the surface of Troeltsch's language. Ricoeur's account of the rejection of Hempel's version of the reduction of history to nature may therefore expose the limitations of Troeltsch's position.

Ricoeur traces the process in which proponents of Hempel's thesis were forced to modify its claims to such an extent that it lost all explanatory power. More significant, however, is the work of William Dray (1957), W. B. Gallie (1968) and others, according to whom historians' causal explanations are qualitatively different from those found in the natural sciences, since their intention is to incorporate historical events into a narrative context (I, 121–74).[33] The broad shift to which such work belongs may be characterized by referring to Wittgenstein's *Philosophical Investigations* (1953), which both symbolizes and influences the trend away from totalizing interpretations of reality on the basis of 'modern scientific thought', in recognition of the heterogeneity of language-games or social contexts within which some kind of 'access to reality' is asserted. There is no single entity, 'causality', which can be used to unlock the mysteries of reality as a whole; only a number of different contexts in which we employ various types of causal language.[34] In the historical realm, causal or quasi-causal explanations of historical phenomena are often given; but 'it is unlikely that we shall find any *logical* features according to which all historical explanations can be grasped together as historical. For the explanations found in history books are a logically miscellaneous lot' (W. Dray, quoted in *Time and Narrative*, I, 122). As Ricoeur summarizes Dray's position,

> Historians, in fact and legitimately, do use expressions of the form 'X is the cause of Y' . . . They use them in fact with numerous variations on 'cause': produces, leads to, sets in motion (or their contraries: prevented, omits, stops). They use them legitimately by assuming the explanatory force of a cause . . . The underlying thesis is that the *polysemy* of the word 'cause' is no more an obstacle to the rule-governed usage of this term than is that of the term 'explain' . . . The problem is to regulate this polysemy, not to conclude that the term must be rejected. (I, 125)

The rejection of polysemy and the quest for univocity stems from a now-questionable belief in the openness of all reality to the unifying gaze of the scientifically-trained observer.

The abandonment of this ideology makes it possible to reintegrate events into narrative. According to W. B. Gallie, 'whatever explanations a work of history contains must be assessed in relation to the narrative form from which they arise and whose development they subserve' (quoted in *Time and Narrative*, I, 149). Historical explanations enable a reader to follow the course of a historical narrative. Ricoeur summarizes:

> [T]he reading of . . . historians' stories derives from our competence to follow stories. We follow them from one end to the other, and we follow them in light of the issue promised or glimpsed through the succession of contingent events . . . Correlatively, the theme of these stories is worth being recounted and their narratives are worth following, because this theme is superimposed on interests that are our own as human beings. (I, 152)

> One result of this primacy of the concept of followability is that the explanations, for which historians borrow laws from the sciences to which they link their discipline, have no other effect than to allow us better to follow the story, when our vision of its interconnections is obscured or when our capacity to accept the author's vision is carried to the breaking point. (I, 154)

The polarizing of history and fiction has obscured the extent to which the historian must share the novelist's ability to make a story followable, plausible and acceptable.

In opposition to the tendency to subject history to a single, quasi-natural system of causation, two important points have emerged. First, it has been argued that in historiography causal explanation is heterogeneous. This would challenge the Troeltschian thesis of the universal interconnectedness characteristic of the historical sphere, which is obviously intended to integrate the phenomenon of Christianity into its environment without remainder, in accordance with the programme of the history-of-religion school. The alternative account does not start from an *a priori* position labelled 'the modern view of history'; it begins instead from the heterogeneous causal explanations that are actually found in texts regarded as historiographical, and it will conclude from this heterogeneity only that no explanation is likely to be exhaustive. Like other historiographical texts, the gospels too offer causal explanations. There are explanations of individual actions; the women fled from the tomb and kept silent, '*for* they were afraid' (Mark 16.8). But there are also much more far-reaching causal explanations. Jesus' ministry as a whole is strange enough to require an explanation, and the explanation offered grounds this piece of immanent reality in transcendence; Jesus acts as he does *because of* the uniqueness of his relationship to God, which is that of the beloved son to his father (Mark 1.11). Explanations in historiographical writing do not compel assent, but there is no normative principle of explanation which would permit one to rule out in advance a historiographical explanation in terms of transcendence.

Second, this heterogeneity of historical explanations casts the historian in the role of the story-teller who must make a true story followable and persuasive for its hearers or readers. The explanation offered will therefore be determined by the story-teller's judgments as to the types of explanation necessary to make the story followable and persuasive *for this particular audience*. Story-teller and projected audience will share a set of implicit conventions about the points in the narrative where telling needs to be supplemented by explaining, and about the type of assertion that counts as an explanation. A contemporary biographer may project an audience which shares his or her own faith in the explanatory power of psychoanalytic theory; yet there may well be actual readers of the resulting work for whom this type of explanation is wildly implausible. A historical explanation may facilitate the followability and plausibility of the story for some but hinder it for others, for whom it seems to raise greater problems than the problem it attempts to solve. The gospels are not the only historiographical texts whose explanatory conventions seem implausible to sceptical and suspicious readers; on the contrary, the absence of universal explanatory conventions means that any conceivable historiographical text will have to reckon with sceptical and suspicious readers.

(*iii*) *The tremendum*

If there is an 'interweaving of history and fiction' in historiographical emplotment and explanation, one might ask at what point fictivity begins to undermine historical narration rather than to enable it. Granted that fiction too has its own modes of referring to reality, and granted that the relationship between history-writing and historical reality is not straight-forward, the fact remains that 'the historian's constructions have the ambition of being reconstructions, more or less fitting with what one day was "real"' (*Time and Narrative*, III, 100).[35] Ricoeur adds: 'Everything takes place as though historians knew themselves to be bound by a debt to people from earlier times', and it is not clear how that debt could be paid off by narrating the quasi-events characteristic of fiction. When, for example, Matthew tells of the opening of the tombs and the resurrection of the saints at the moment of Jesus' death (Matt. 27.52–53), it is not obvious how this narrated event could be a reconstruction of 'what one day was "real"'. In narrating this event, and in seeking to authenticate it by the refer-ence to the 'many' who witnessed these strange corporeal apparitions, is Matthew simply demonstrating his credulity? Is his text only 'historiography' if we confine ourselves to the referential claim internal to the text, and refuse to admit the question of the success of a particular act of reference?

Ricoeur discovers a special case of 'the fictionalizing of history' in the narration of 'epoch-making' events which 'draw their specific meaning from their capacity to found or reinforce the community's consciousness of its identity' (III, 187). If 'the *tremendum fascinosum* constitutes the emotional core of our experience of the Sacred, the meaning of the Sacred remains an ineradicable dimension of historical meaning' (III, 187). But this *tremendum* is also a *tremendum horrendum*, a manifestation of the anti-divine or demonic at a place such as Auschwitz. Here events cannot be integrated into the normal flow of happening; they radically individuate themselves, they are 'uniquely unique' (III, 188). Explanation connects, horror isolates, 'and yet this latent conflict must not lead to a ruinous dichotomy between a history that would dissolve the event in explanation and a purely emotional retort that would dispense us from thinking the unthinkable' (III, 188). But what has this to do with fiction? The answer is that 'individuation by means of the horrible . . . would be blind feeling . . . without the intuitiveness of fiction. Fiction gives eyes to the horrified narrator' (III, 188). The only appropriate response to the inexplicable is to narrate the stories of the victims.

But in what sense would this narration be fictional? One might narrate the stories of the victims in a biographical mode that conformed to the historiographical ambition to reconstruct 'what one day was "real"'. Would such a narration convey the historical 'reality' at a deeper ontological level than a historical account of the ideological, technological and bureaucratic factors that 'caused' the event of the 'negative revelation' or 'Anti-Sinai' (III, 188)? Or would it create the ultimately misleading impression that the event consists only of the sum of individual tragedies? Fictional narration might conceivably penetrate more deeply into the event. Primo Levi's *Moments of Reprieve* (1981) is, in terms of genre, a collection of short stories, as its original Italian title, *Lilit e altri racconti,* indicates; the stories draw upon the author's experiences in Auschwitz.[36] In the preface from which the phrase 'moments of reprieve' is drawn, the author asserts the historical veracity underlying the fictional artifice of his stories; and yet the context of this assertion is a psychological analysis of his own motivation for writing which only marginally affects the way in which the stories are read.[37] Stories of individual encounters in which there occurred 'moments of reprieve' from horror do not merely point back to individual, datable moments; the reader is untroubled by the fact that the fictive 'short story' genre prevents historical verification. The reason for this is that 'moments of reprieve' refers us not to isolated, datable, verifiable events but to a possibility which, when actualized, denied to the *tremendum horrendum* the total dehumanization it sought to enact. One might speak of this denial as an event; but this would be an event inaccessible to 'normal' historical verification and open only to a fictional rendering of possibilities in stories fulfilling a representative function in relation to the real.

  Ricoeur discerns a link between metaphor and narrative which may help to clarify this point. Metaphorical reference, he claims, 'consists in the fact that the effacement of descriptive reference – an effacement that, as a first approximation, makes language refer to itself – is revealed to be, in a second approximation, the negative condition for freeing a more radical power of reference to those aspects of our being-in-the-world that cannot be talked about directly' (I, 80). The same is true of fictional narrative. Here, the aorist tenses characteristic of historical narration cannot be relied upon as direct reconstructions of the real; and yet it is a common experience of readers of these texts that reality seems to come to expression here almost more powerfully than anywhere else – an experience that cannot be reduced to an effect of the text's rhetoric, however much this is a factor that must also be taken into account.[38] In the case of Primo Levi's stories, however, the reality indirectly expressed through the fictive form cannot adequately be subsumed within the category of 'aspects of our being-in-the-world that cannot be talked about directly'. The stories do not point to 'moments of reprieve' as an aspect of a general being-in-the-world: even as fictions, they are entirely bound to a particular historical event and would be meaningless without the reader's background knowledge of that event.[39] It is the nature of this overwhelming, irruptive, incomprehensible event that these stories seek to penetrate, guided by a concern with the subsidiary event of 'moments of reprieve' within the catastrophic event itself. Through their representative function, these fictions therefore manifest a historiographical intentionality which is actualized precisely by their fictivity. This would remain true even if the author had deliberately flouted conventions of narrative realism is order to achieve a more 'mythical' effect. Fiction can depict 'limit-experiences' by exploring 'the borderline between story and myth' (III, 271), and where these limit-experiences are historically particular rather than universally human myth too can serve a historiographical function.

If there is a *tremendum horrendum* – a 'negative revelation', an 'Anti-Sinai' (III, 188) – there is also a *tremendum fascinosum*, a revelatory event which founds the community's consciousness of its identity (III, 187). This event too will be a historically-particular 'limit-experience', the truth of which cannot adequately be disclosed by normal procedures of historical verification. The resources of fiction, bequeathed by the traditions in which the evangelist stands, will be needed if the community-founding event is to be written. The primary reference of the more 'fictive' elements of the narration is indeterminable, but this does not hinder its historiographical function; for what is important is the secondary, indirect, quasi-metaphorical reference to the historically-particular limit-experience that occurs by way of the negation of the primary reference. In such a context, legendary narratives can fulfil an indispensable historiographical role.

NOTES

1. Narrative criticism operates on the basis of a disjunction between meaning and reference most clearly proposed by Hans Frei. In opposition to the modern identification of meaning with 'ostensive' or 'ideal' reference, Frei argues that meaning should emerge 'solely as a function of the narrative itself' (*The Eclipse of Biblical Narrative: A Study in Eighteenth and Nineteenth Century Hermeneutics*, New Haven and London: Yale University Press, 1974, 35). In a lecture dating from 1987, Frei continues to contrast 'the literal reading or meaning of the New Testament stories about Jesus', about which there can be broad consensus, with the intractable (and secondary) issue of 'the reality status' of the Jesus of the gospels, the 'extratextual reference' of the text (in *Types of Christian Theology* [ed. G. Hunsinger and W. C. Placher], New Haven and London: Yale University Press, 1992, 143). As we shall see in connection with the Lucan prologue and the Johannine epilogue, it is precisely the literal meaning of these texts that compels the reader to take seriously their extratextual reference.

2. Responding to this objection, Mark Allan Powell accepts that 'the Gospels are not works of fiction but intend to convey historical truth', but adds: 'To the extent that the genres of novel and gospel share a narrative form . . ., both are subject to narrative analysis' (*What is Narrative Criticism?*, Minneapolis: Fortress, 1990, 94). The 'narrative analysis' Powell has in mind is concerned only with a text's internal workings, and will therefore analyse nonfictional texts *as if* they were fictional.

3. Why does Luke write when many have written already? 'The answer is, that although he spares the others who had written before him, he does not altogether approve

their work' (J. Calvin, *A Harmony of the Gospels*, Vol. I, Edinburgh: St Andrew Press, 1972, 2).

4. Michael Edwards sees here a reply to the complaint in Eccl. 12.12 about the curse of endless writing: for John, 'the potential infinity of books is a function of the infinite Word' ('The World Could Not Contain the Books', in M. Warner [ed.], *The Bible as Rhetoric: Studies in Biblical Persuasion and Credibility*, London and New York: Routledge, 1990, 179–88; 186–87).

5. This dichotomy would be a contemporary form of the old Straussian dilemma of 'the Jesus of history' and 'the Christ of faith'. My own argument might be seen as a restatement of Martin Kähler's rejection of the distinction between 'the so-called historical Jesus' and 'the historic, biblical Christ' (D. F. Strauss, *Der Christus des Glaubens und der Jesus der Geschichte: Eine Kritik des Schleiermacher'schen Lebens Jesu*, Berlin, 1865 [ET Philadelphia: Fortress, 1977]; M. Kähler, *Der sogennante historische Jesus und der geschichtliche, biblische Christus*, Leipzig, 1892[1] [ET Philadelphia: Fortress, 1964]).

6. Thus Paula Fredriksen distinguishes 'Images of Jesus in the Gospels and Paul' from the 'Historical Image of Jesus', located in 'the World of Judaism' (*From Jesus to Christ: The Origins of the New Testament Images of Jesus*, New Haven and London: Yale University Press, 1988, ch. 3, 6). The gospels represent 'a self-conscious Christian tradition that deliberately distanced itself from the historical Jewish context in which Jesus had lived and died' (vii). There is no teleological development from Jesus to the gospels, for the images of Jesus found in the latter 'were the independent creations of their respective communities' (xi).

7. D. F. Strauss, *The Life of Jesus Critically Examined*, ET London: Chapman, 1846, repr. Philadelphia: Fortress, 1972; J. Calvin, *A Harmony of the Gospels*, I.

8. James Barr identifies in conservative biblical scholarship a 'maximal conservatism' which, committed to a strong view of 'biblical authority', advocates broadly conservative results without recourse to a rationalistically-conceived principle of 'inerrancy' (*Fundamentalism*, London: SCM Press, 1977, 85–89). Might there also be a 'maximal anti-conservatism', expressed not only in superficial phenomena such as late datings but also in at least some of the basic concepts and paradigms with which biblical scholars work?

9. A. Cook, *History/Writing: The Theory and Practice of History in Antiquity and Modern Times*, Cambridge: Cambridge University Press, 1988.

10. Cook has in mind work such as Hayden White's *Metahistory* (Baltimore: Johns Hopkins University Press, 1973), where concepts drawn from literary criticism are employed in order to locate historiographical works in the space of narrative fiction. In the case of emplotment, for example, a historian 'is forced to emplot the whole set of stories making up his narrative in one comprehensive or *archetypal* story form' (White, 8), such as romance, tragedy, comedy or satire – a typology derived from Northrop Frye's *Anatomy of Criticism*. The literary-critical perspective leads to the marginalizing of the question of the relationship to the real which is normally supposed to distinguish historiographical from fictional texts. My own analysis is based on work that explores the interrelatedness of 'referential' and 'literary' dimensions of historiography.

11. Are such references to 'the real world' vestiges of a naïve empiricism untenable in the light of the poststructuralist universalizing of 'textuality'? On that view, the world to which historiographical texts 'refer' is merely that of their own production; to speak about the past would then be to speak about the present in the guise of speaking about the past. If 'the subjects responsible for scientific discourse are . . . determined in their situation, their function, their perceptive capacity, and their practical possibilities by

conditions that dominate and even overwhelm them' (Michel Foucault, *The Order of Things: An Archaeology of the Human Sciences*, ET London and New York: Tavistock/Routledge, 1970, xiv), then historians construct the past they write out of the resources of their own present, to which their works stand as monuments. One might, for example, uncover the late eighteenth-century *episteme* which is the matrix of Gibbon's *Decline and Fall of the Roman Empire*, and this might involve suspending the question of adequacy to the 'event' that is recounted. But the methodological decision to limit the field of enquiry does not imply an epistemological claim about the inaccessibility of the real (in this case the past). Foucault implicitly acknowledges this when he defines his 'archaeology' as seeking to expose 'the epistemological field, the *episteme* in which knowledge, envisaged apart from all criteria having reference to its rational value or to its objective forms, grounds its positivity and thereby manifests a history which is not that of its growing perfection, but rather that of its conditions of possibility' (xxii). To consider an instance of discourse *apart from* those criteria that might seek to determine its rational value is not to deny that a different enquiry (more interested in, say, the third century than in the eighteenth) might legitimately employ such criteria. Foucault's own work is, of course, a writing of history.

12. The phrase 'the criteria of modern historical research' is itself question-begging: 'Whether "history" is considered simply as "the past", the documentary record of this past, or the body of reliable information about the past established by professional historians, there is no such thing as a distinctively "historical" method by which to study this "history". Indeed, the history of historical studies displays ample evidence of the necessity of importing conceptual models, analytical methods, and representational strategies from other disciplines . . .' (H. White, 'New Historicism: A Comment', in H. Aram Veeser [ed.], *The New Historicism*, London: Routledge, 1989, 293–302; 295).

13. Within biblical studies, recognition of the historiographical dimension of the gospels is still hindered by the view that 'in the relating of past history they proclaim who he is, not who he was' (G. Bornkamm, *Jesus of Nazareth*, ET London: Hodder & Stoughton, 1960, 17). The historiographical dimension is at the same time acknowledged ('past history' is indeed related) and undermined ('who he is' is different from 'who he was'). For criticism of this approach, see Eugene E. Lemcio, *The Past of Jesus in the Gospels*, Cambridge: Cambridge University Press, 1991.

14. Quotations are taken from the English translation of the second edition, London: Sheed & Ward, 1975.

15. Gadamer's critique of historical reason fails to reflect on the possibility that historical study, rightly understood, might fulfil a positive ancillary role within the interpretative conversation between present and past. Within theology, the legacy of this dichotomy between truth and history has been a failure to engage the historical-critical tradition in critical dialogue about the nature and significance of historical study. Polemic against the notions of 'objectivity' or 'authorial intention' is no substitute for such a dialogue.

16. In chapter 7 of the *Tractatus theologico-politicus* (ET New York: Dover, 1951), to which Gadamer refers, Spinoza advocates the historical investigation of 'the environment of all the prophetic books extant; that is, the life, the conduct, and the studies of the author of each book, who he was, what was the occasion and the epoch of his writing, whom did he write for, and in what language' (103). The aim is to enable us to distinguish 'precepts which are eternal' from 'those which served only a temporary purpose' (103). Thus, 'we seek first for that which is most universal and serves for the basis and foundation of all Scripture, a doctrine, in fact, that is commended by all the prophets as eternal and

as most profitable to all men; for example, that God is one, and that he is omnipotent, that he alone should be worshipped, that he has a care for all men, and that he especially loves those who adore him and love their neighbour as themselves, &c.' (104). In this characteristic product of the early Enlightenment, scripture continues to bear witness to the eternal; but the category of the transitory – illustrated for Christians by superseded elements in the Mosaic Law – is extended through historical investigation so as to cover more and more material.

17. Text in Kurt Mueller-Vollmer (ed.), *The Hermeneutics Reader: Texts of the German Tradition from the Enlightenment to the Present*, Oxford: Blackwell, 1986, 152–64.

18. As Dilthey states elsewhere: 'Every word, every sentence . . . , every political deed is intelligible because the people who expressed themselves through them and those who understand them have something in common' (quoted by Anthony Thiselton, *New Horizons in Hermeneutics*, London: Marshall Pickering, 1992, 249).

19. Werner Jeanrond rightly notes that for Dilthey 'the task of understanding finally aims at an understanding of persons, though through their works' (*Theological Hermeneutics: Development and Significance*, London: Macmillan, 1991, 52).

20. F. Nietzsche, *Untimely Meditations*, ET Cambridge: Cambridge University Press, 1983, 57–123.

21. This danger is also evident in Nietzsche's view of art and religion as the 'unhistorical and suprahistorical' remedy to the disease of 'history': 'With the word "the unhistorical" I designate the art and power of *forgetting* and of enclosing oneself within a bounded *horizon*; I call "suprahistorical" the powers which lead the eye away from becoming towards that which bestows upon existence the character of the eternal and stable, towards *art* and *religion*' (120). Art and religion protect life from a self-absolutizing science: 'The unhistorical and the suprahistorical are the natural antidotes to the stifling of life by the historical, by the malady of history' (121). 'Life' recovers its vitality when we encounter the eternal, through its mediations, in a pure, pastless presence.

22. Gadamer's concept of *Okkasionalität* is of greater significance than he himself allows. If the 'truth' attested by the work is permanently marked by its occasion of origin, then an interpretation that engages with the work's 'claim to meaning' would always have to take that occasion into account – at least in certain respects.

23. Despite this relative abstraction from the basic Christian truth-claim, the quest for a mediating conceptuality would derive from faith seeking a communicable understanding of the universality of the truth-claim. This approach to the gospel story is therefore more appropriate *theologically* than a narrative theology for which the context of the gospel story is an enclosed Christian community. This restriction is seemingly implied in Stanley Hauerwas' claim that 'the primary social task of the church is to be itself – that is, a people who have been formed by a story that provides them with the skills for negotiating the danger of this existence, trusting in God's promise of redemption' (*A Community of Character: Toward a Constructive Christian Social Ethic*, Notre Dame: University of Notre Dame Press, 1981, 10). The sharp church/world polarity threatens to undermine the outward-directedness of the church's story, manifested especially in the call to universal mission that belongs to the events of resurrection, ascension and Pentecost.

24. David Tracy extends Gadamer's category of the 'classic' to include the Christ-event as well as texts and art-works: thus, 'the event and person of Jesus Christ' *is* 'the Christian classic' (*The Analogical Imagination: Christian Theology and the Culture of Pluralism*, London: SCM Press, 1981, 248). Against this, the shift to the category of the 'historic' emphasizes that the classic biblical texts bear witness to prior realities in the

public, profane, fallen and everyday sphere of human sociohistorical life; they do not belong to a pure intratextual world from which human persons are excluded. More promising is the analogy Paul Ricoeur draws between texts and actions ('The Model of the Text: Meaningful Action Considered as a Text', in John B. Thompson [ed.], *Hermeneutics and the Human Sciences*, Cambridge: Cambridge University Press, 1981, 197–221). Like a text, 'a meaningful action is an action the *importance* of which goes "beyond" its *relevance* to its initial situation' (207). Like a text, human action is addressed to an unlimited range of possible 'readers' (208), and 'the meaning of the event' is therefore 'the sense of its forthcoming interpretations' (209).

25. The inaccessibility of the 'final meaning' does not necessarily lead to relativism, for a provisional meaning is still concerned to differentiate truth from falsehood and so may be said to anticipate the final meaning. 'Every assertion of meaning rests upon a fore-conception of the final future, in the light of which the true meaning of every individual event first becomes expressible in a valid way' (W. Pannenberg, *Basic Questions in Theology*, Vol. 2, London: SCM Press, 1971, 62). 'Every historian is in the role of the last historian. Hermeneutic discussion of the inexhaustibility of the horizon of meaning and the new interpretations of future generations remains empty: it has no consequences for the historian's task . . . It is precisely the openness of history . . . that permits the hypothetical anticipation of history as a whole without which the retrospective interpretation of the parts would not be forthcoming' (J. Habermas, *On the Logic of the Social Sciences* [1967], ET Cambridge: Polity Press, 1988, 160, 161). Pannenberg and Habermas both trace these insights back to Hegel. For discussion of Pannenberg's hermeneutics of history, see A. Thiselton, *New Horizons in Hermeneutics*, 331–38.

26. Paul Ricoeur, *Time and Narrative*, 3 vols., ET Chicago: The University of Chicago Press, 1984–88. For an introduction to this work, see Kevin J. Vanhoozer, *Biblical Narrative in the Philosophy of Paul Ricoeur: A Study in Hermeneutics and Theology*, Cambridge: Cambridge University Press, 1990, 90–104.

27. Compare Frank Kermode's definition of plot as 'an organization that humanizes time by giving it form' (*The Sense of an Ending: Studies in the Theory of Fiction*, Oxford: Oxford University Press, 1967, 45; this work is frequently cited by Ricoeur).

28. For this point, see Ricoeur's essay on 'Existence and Hermeneutics', in *The Conflict of Interpretations: Essays in Hermeneutics* (ed. D. Ihde), Evanston: Northwestern University Press, 1974, 3–24, esp. 6–11.

29. It is arguable that the function of Ricoeur's hypothesis about time and narrative is primarily to orient and structure the complex three-way conversation between historiographical theory, literary theory and phenomenology. The privileging of narrative recalls the privileging of the unscientific, unmasterable language of symbol, myth and metaphor in Ricoeur's earlier work, but in *Time and Narrative* the late Heideggerian ontology underlying much of this earlier work has receded. According to that ontology, 'language is less spoken *by* men than spoken *to* men', since 'men are born at the heart of language within the light of the Logos "which illuminates each man who enters the world"' (*Conflict of Interpretations*, 319). The task of hermeneutics is therefore to open up the 'second immediacy' or 'second naïveté' (298) in which language again occurs as revelatory event, 'beyond the wastelands of critical thought' (288). In *Time and Narrative*, however, this ontology is either absent altogether or, at best, present only in the quite different form of the thesis that narrative uniquely discloses the nature of *time* (rather than of 'Being'). This difference does not necessarily represent a departure from the earlier position. It might indicate that Ricoeur sees a fundamental difference between the disclosive possibilities of narrative on the one hand and of religious symbols and poetry on the

other. Narrative discloses partial aspects of the multifarious, unmasterable phenomenon of time; religious symbols and poetry direct us towards the totality of Being that underlies all phenomena.

30. However, Ricoeur rejects the one-sided view that narrative gives consonance to an inherently dissonant temporality: 'So long as we place the consonance on the side of the narrative and the dissonance on the side of temporality in a unilateral fashion . . . , we miss the properly dialectical character of their relationship' (*Time and Narrative*, I, 72).

31. In his book on Ricoeur, Kevin Vanhoozer contrasts the philosopher's possible understanding of Christ as 'a symbol of our desire to be free' with the theologian's question 'how the symbol is rooted in the historical witness of the apostles' (*Biblical Narrative*, 128). If 'what is ultimately at stake when I read Scripture is *me* and my subjectivity', then 'what becomes of "objectivity" and the "realism of the event of history"?' (139). Vanhoozer has rightly noted the problem that arises if elements of Ricoeur's general hermeneutics are applied to the gospels (see below, note 35). Yet two points might be made in response: (1) Reflecting on the biblical concept of 'testimony', Ricoeur concludes that testimony directs us back to 'events, acts and persons that attest that the unjustifiable is overcome here and now' and that 'can reopen the path toward originary affirmation' (*Essays in Biblical Interpretation* [ed. Lewis B. Mudge], London: SPCK, 1981, 111). Such language shows that Ricoeur is capable of recognizing the significance for Christian scripture of unique, foundational events. (2) In addressing the relationship between historical and fictional narration, *Time and Narrative* makes it possible to re-conceive the gospels as historiography in a way that answers Vanhoozer's concerns about 'objectivity'. Ricoeur does not discuss the gospels in this work, and it is hard to see how he can be accused here of 'foist[ing] a poetics of the modern novel onto biblical narrative' (Vanhoozer, 218).

32. ET London: SCM Press, 1972.

33. W. H. Dray, *Laws and Explanations in History*, London: Oxford University Press, 1957; W. B. Gallie, *Philosophy and the Historical Understanding*, New York: Schocken Books, 1968.

34. On this specific topic Wittgenstein writes: 'The insidious thing about the causal point of view is that it leads us to say: "Of course, it had to happen like that." Whereas we ought to think: it may have happened *like that* – and also in many other ways' (*Culture and Value*, ET Chicago: University of Chicago Press, 1980, 37e). 'The causal point of view' represents the tendency of the natural sciences and historicism to eliminate contingency in the name of a deterministic monism. One way of carrying out Wittgenstein's recommendation of a pluralistic, open-ended understanding of occurrence is to emphasize the diversity of language-games in which causal language is used.

35. Ricoeur's emphasis on the importance of first-order reference in historical narration points to the limitations of his earlier tendency to subordinate what lies 'behind the text' to the 'world unfolded in front of it' (*Hermeneutics and the Human Sciences*, 93). The context of this antithesis is a shift in the balance of power between the author (emphasized by the 'romantic hermeneutics' of Schleiermacher and Dilthey) and the reader: hermeneutics culminates not in empathetic penetration into authorial psychology but in self-understanding 'in front of the text'. The disadvantage of this conceptuality is that it appears to place out of bounds *everything* that precedes the text, irrespective of the genre of the text. Ricoeur has redressed this imbalance in his study of 'Threefold *Mimesis*' in *Time and Narrative*, I, 52–87.

36. Primo Levi, *Moments of Reprieve* (1981), ET London: Abacus, 1986.

37. *Moments of Reprieve*, 9–11.

38. Metaphor and (fictional) narrative both belong to the category of 'poetic' language (understanding 'poetic' in a broad sense), which 'suspend[s] the reference of ordinary language and release[s] a second order reference . . .' (*Hermeneutics and the Human Sciences*, 93). The same point can therefore be made about 'fictional discourse': 'It is precisely in so far as fictional discourse "suspends" its first order referential function that it releases a second order reference, where the world is manifested no longer as the totality of manipulable objects but as the horizon of our life and our project, in short as *Lebenswelt*, as being-in-the-world' (112).

39. This 'background knowledge' could be understood as belonging to our own being-in-the-world (*In-der-Welt-sein*), in which case Ricoeur's Heideggerian language would be acceptable. In itself the language implies a fundamental ontology 'beneath' the level of historical particularity; but the concept of 'thrownness' (*Geworfenheit*) could be used to mediate between ontology and historical particularity.

Chapter 2

— ⋈⋄⋈ —

The Multiple Text and the Singular Gospel

Interpretation is never-ending. A text may have been intensively studied for centuries, but there is no danger that what can be said about it will be exhausted. On the contrary, far from inhibiting new interpretations by filling up all the available space, prior interpretations are precisely what enable interpretative work to continue. We are dependent on our predecessors, whether continuing to build where they left off or demolishing their work so as to begin anew. It is, however, puzzling that finite texts appear to be open to infinite interpretation. It is true that a great deal of interpretative activity consists only in repeating what has already been said. Interpretation occurs within traditions, and repetition – with variations – is integral to tradition. Yet interpreters believe themselves to be like householders who bring forth from their treasure things new as well as old. Interpretation occurs in the expectation that, at certain points, one will be able to say what has not previously been said.

There are various ways in which one might resolve the conundrum of the infinite interpretability of the finite text. Previous interpretations may be rejected as misinterpretations. Divergent interpretations may be traced back to varying interpretative paradigms, each the product of a particular context. Such solutions as these are compatible with the view that a text has or may have a single, literal sense, a thread to guide one through the labyrinthine complexities of interpretation. It may not be possible to isolate the 'single sense' of the text as a whole, or to state it in definitive form, or to eliminate its ambiguities and complexities; but the notion of the 'single sense', for all its difficulties, is valuable in preserving the insight that the text as a communicative act ultimately intends one thing and not another. Any act of communication is directed towards a particular addressee, upon whom it intends a particular effect; and this directedness is inherent in the communication itself. Where the communication takes the form of a written text, its directedness may still be perceptible even if the identity of the intended addressee is not explicitly specified. A written communication may have as precise a performative intention as a spoken one, and in both cases that intention will exist not in the privacy of an authorial mind but in the communication itself. This directedness may be identified with the text's literal sense.[1]

Interpretation may respond to a text's directedness in various ways. The interpreter may see him- or herself as representing the text's intended addressee, reporting to its readers what it is saying to 'us'. (Different reports may vary considerably.) Or the addressee might be construed as a third party – consisting perhaps of those readers who were contemporary with the long-dead author – and a 'historical' account of the text would be the result. Or the issue of the text's directedness might be marginalized and other questions pursued, in accordance with the interests of the particular interpreter. Interpretative plurality stems in part from these differing relationships between interpreter and text, and is compatible with the view that the text represents an intentional communicative action. There is, however, an alternative explanation of interpretative plurality, and that is to trace it back to a *radical indeterminacy within the text itself.* On this view, a text in which one voice seems to speak is in fact inhabited by many voices; its name is legion. This would exclude any simple account of the directedness of a text – unless it be argued that it is directed towards precisely that addressee who is able to grasp its indeterminacy and open-endedness.

Typically, this open-endedness is evaluated positively. In his study of *The Classic* (1975), Frank Kermode argues that 'the coexistence in a single text of a plurality of significances' is a criterion for classic status (133).[2] It is readers who bestow classic status, and 'the only works we value enough to call classic are those which . . . are complex and indeterminate enough to allow us our necessary pluralities' (121). The modern classic in particular must be 'carefully unauthoritative, open to multiple interpretations because the modern world is so' (108). A world with many meanings is correlated with the many meanings of the (fictional) text; the single sense is the product of an order imposed on text or world by our desire for coherence and transparency, and as such it is a fiction rather than a reproduction of any prior reality in text or world. Modern classics may highlight our problematic situation by wilfully frustrating our normal means of sense-making, and in accustoming us to multiplicity they also make it possible to reread older classics with new eyes, as we recognize the indeterminacies upon which these supposedly substantial entities are in fact founded. On Kermode's view of reading, we are promised a fourfold pleasure. There is, first, the pleasure of the play of the text which in its to-and-fro movement teasingly withholds the prize of the single sense, the truth transparent to reality itself, offering instead multiple possibilities without truth or falsehood. Second, there is the pleasure of patterns of consonance created by author and reader in full awareness of their fictive status. Third, there is the pleasure of the fit between text and world: for the world too is multiple and without final truth or falsehood, and the text can therefore be said to be world-disclosive.[3] And fourth, there is the pleasure of allowing this textually-mediated world-disclosure to expose the various dogmatisms and metanarratives as the oppressive idols that they actually are.

It is this general theory of the classic, or something like it, that Kermode brings to his reading of the Gospel of Mark in a slightly later work, *The Genesis of Secrecy* (1979). Kermode is interested not only in indeterminacy *in* Mark but also in the explicit thematizing of this indeterminacy *by* Mark: Mark is therefore a narrative about the indeterminacy of narrative.[4] Bypassing the literal or 'carnal' meaning of the text, Kermode is interested in exploiting a 'spiritual' or non-obvious meaning opened up by Mark's theory of parable (Mark 4.11–12). According to this theory, the purpose of the parables is to conceal the truth from outsiders; it transpires in the course of the narrative that the insiders (the disciples) are also outsiders; and the whole narrative may therefore be seen as a parable which excludes disciples and readers alike from its innermost heart and only permits them to play on its obscure surface. The singular gospel is converted into a multiple text.

From the standpoint of Christian faith and theology, it is clear that this reading of Mark is untenable. The Word-made-flesh comes as light, not as darkness; he does not bring a world without truth or falsehood, but comes into a world of falsehood as the way, the truth and the life. Yet Kermode's powerful and lucid interpretation must be taken seriously – not least because its thoroughgoing relativism is so immediately plausible and attractive within the ironic, sceptical ethos of postmodernity. Theologies imbued with this ethos already proliferate, and Kermode's book is therefore not just an individual performance but one symptom among many of the critical situation in which theology and biblical interpretation currently find themselves.

1. The Singularity of the Gospel

Why should the Gospel of Mark not be read as a multiple, opaque text, as recommended by postmodern homiletics? The answer is that, if it is indeed *gospel*, it cannot be multiple or opaque. The effect of gospel is to expel the legion of discordant voices that destroy the integrity of the self, and to leave the hearer or reader clothed and in his or her right mind.

The claim that gospel cannot be multiple or opaque is not only a statement of faith; it is also a statement about genre. The Gospel of Mark is gospel, not parable. For Kermode, parable is dark and enigmatic, luring its hearers or readers into its labyrinthine ways with the promise of enlightenment, yet ensuring that they never reach the central shrine that they seek. Mark as a whole is a witness 'to the enigmatic and exclusive character of narrative, to its property of banishing the interpreters from its secret places' (34–35). But gospel has little in common with these esoteric procedures: 'By the open statement of the truth we commend ourselves to every person's conscience, in the sight of God. And even if our gospel is veiled, it is veiled only to those who are perishing . . . It is the God who said, "Let light shine in darkness" who has shone in our hearts to give the light of the knowledge of the glory of God in the face of Jesus Christ' (2 Cor. 4.2–3, 6). It is the human heart and not the gospel that is dark and veiled; but 'when one turns to the Lord, the veil is removed', in the freedom bestowed by the Spirit of the Lord (2 Cor. 3.16–17). As gospel, the Gospel of Mark proclaims not darkness but the shining of the light: 'Is a lamp brought in to be put under a bushel, or under a bed, and not on a stand? For there is nothing hidden, except to be made manifest; nor is anything secret, except to come to light' (Mark 4.21–22). It may be possible to deconstruct these oppositions of gospel and parable, light and darkness, arguing that the light is founded upon precisely the darkness that it strives to exclude; but before we watch Kermode performing this deconstruction, the claim that the Gospel of Mark is *gospel* must be further elaborated.

According to the manuscript tradition, the title of this text is *euaggelion kata Markon*. This is occasionally expanded (*to kata Markon hagion euaggelion*) or contracted (*kata Markon*), but the meaning remains the same: that there is a single gospel, that it may take written form, and that the present text is one among a number of varied renderings of this gospel in written form.[5] In agreement with this usage, Irenaeus tells us that, as the living creatures in Ezekiel's vision have four faces, so the gospel is fourfold, *tetramorphon*. But because each face of the gospel is complete in itself, the individual texts can be referred to as 'gospels'. Irenaeus can speak within a few lines both of 'the gospel' and of 'the gospels': God 'has given us the gospel under four aspects, but bound together by one Spirit', and he has done so in the form of 'gospels' which 'cannot be either more or fewer in number than they actually are' (*adv.haer.* iii.11.8).[6] This plural form develops naturally out of the earlier singular usage, and is acceptable so long as the absolute priority of the singular usage is acknowledged; but the singular usage already serves to identify the written text as gospel. While it may be that the original manuscript of the 'Gospel according to Mark' did not bear this title, the fact remains that for all its known readers its genre was that of gospel (*euaggelion kata . . .*). They may or may not have been aware of connections with other, secular genres – the Graeco-Roman *bios* or *vita*, for example – but they do not assign to this text any such title as *peri tou biou Iēsou*, they can think of it only as *euaggelion.*[7] Although it does not exhaust the gospel message (it is limited by the *kata Markon*), this text actualizes the proclamation upon which its readers' communal life is founded.

If the book is entitled *euaggelion kata Markon*, then its opening words, *archē tou euaggeliou Iēsou Christou huiou theou*, clearly include a reference to the text itself.[8] The gospel has a 'beginning', and this suggests that it here takes the form of a narrative. Its content is 'Jesus Christ, Son of God', and the narrative will therefore give an account of the person who bears that name and identity. Since the gospel is a true story, 'the beginning' refers us not only to the text but also to the history that the text narrates: a history that began when 'John came baptizing in the desert and preaching a baptism of repentance for the forgiveness of sins' (1.4). In addition to its primary reference to the written text, *euaggelion* also refers to oral proclamation. This proclamation has its beginning in the preaching of John the Baptist, who proclaims Jesus Christ in advance as the written gospel does in retrospect: 'After me there comes one stronger than me . . .' (1.7–8).[9] The *euaggelion* is here proclaimed by God's appointed *aggelos* (1.2). For all their differences, narrative and prophecy are at one in their focus on a particular person, and both are therefore a form of gospel. The gospel narrative begins with the beginning of the gospel proclamation. And this is a real beginning, not a starting-point chosen at random; for it is foretold in an earlier prophetic utterance which announces in advance the proclamation in the wilderness of the coming of the Lord (1.2–3). The past to which this gospel relates is twofold: the past of Jesus' life, death and resurrection, and the past that prepared the way for this complex event. John the Baptizer stands on the boundary between these two pasts.

The gospel of Jesus Christ, Son of God, is also proclaimed by Jesus himself: 'After John was arrested, Jesus came into Galilee, preaching the gospel of God and saying, "The time is fulfilled and the kingdom of God is at hand: repent and believe the gospel"' (1.14–15). Is the gospel of Jesus Christ, proclaimed by Mark, identical to the gospel of God proclaimed by Jesus? Jesus preaches the kingdom of God, the early church preaches Jesus; the proclaimer becomes the proclaimed. Yet there is no real difference or tension here, but rather a further sign of the diversity of expression generated by the one gospel. Only if 'kingdom of God' referred to some reality apart from Jesus would there be a conflict; but that is not the case. Jesus' proclamation of the kingdom is a proclamation about the present moment and its unique significance. 'The time is fulfilled and the kingdom of God is at hand': the present in which Jesus' ministry unfolds is the time of fulfilment spoken of by the prophets Isaiah and John, and it is also a present open to a future represented as 'the kingdom of God'. This future is the future of *this* present, the present of Jesus' ministry, and it is therefore the future of Jesus Christ, the Son of man who is to die, to be raised and to return in power and glory. The evangelist does not need to specify in any more detail the content of Jesus' preaching of the gospel, for his entire text is an exegesis of Jesus' proclamation.[10]

On the basis of Marcan usage, it is misleading to claim that the gospel is a narrative. The gospel *is* Jesus Christ, Son of God, a person whose human existence is understood as a divine act. It can take the form of John's prophetic utterance about the imminent future, Jesus' announcement of a fulfilled and open present, and Mark's narrative about a living past which is the ground of his own present and future. Since the gospel is a proclamation about a person, it is possible for it to take narrative form. Yet narrative is dispensable: 'God was in Christ reconciling the world to himself' is the gospel, but it is not narrative – at least if narrative is defined in terms of sequence and causality.[11] The elaboration of this statement would naturally entail elements of narrative, but narrative as such cannot adequately represent the realities of God, Christ, reconciliation and world. Gospel as a genre comprehends both spoken and written utterances which may or may not take narrative form, and this diversity finds its unity in the common reference to a person. 'Just as there is no more than one Christ, so there is and can be no more than one gospel' (Luther, *LW*35.118). Thus Jesus can speak of the possibility of losing one's life 'for my sake and the gospel's' (Mark 8.35), implying the strictest identity between his own person and the gospel proclamation.

Thus far, Marcan usage of the term *euaggelion* has emphasized the particularity of its content. The gospel speaks of a single person, and without that person there is no gospel. In its other three Marcan occurrences, however, *euaggelion* emphasizes the universal significance of this particularity. Before the end comes, 'the gospel must first be preached to all nations' (13.10). The gospel preached to all nations will include the story of Jesus' anointing by a woman: for 'wherever the gospel is preached in the whole world, what she has done will be told in memory of her' (14.9). The primary agents of this worldwide proclamation are to be the disciples themselves, according to the Longer Ending: for Jesus commands them, 'Go into all the world and preach the gospel to the whole creation' (16.15). Thus, at least in its longer form, the gospel that begins with a proclamation in the desert and in Galilee ends with a worldwide proclamation which the

Lord confirmed by the signs that attended it (16.20). The gospel events are accompanied from the first by the gospel message; and the message is the authoritative disclosure of the significance of the events, which is to be found in the unique identity of the person at the heart of the events. The authoritative interpretation is no subsequent addition to an initially self-contained set of events: for proclamation is integral to the events themselves. Yet proclamation continues, whereas the gospel events reach a provisional conclusion when 'the Lord Jesus, after he had spoken to them, was taken up into heaven, and sat down at the right hand of God' (16.19). Indeed, it is at this point that proclamation comes into its own, for the whole story from beginning to end can now be told and the universal and ultimate significance of the person of whom it speaks can now be grasped. Only now can the gospel of Jesus Christ be preached to all nations; earlier, the confession that Jesus is the Christ had to be kept strictly secret (8.29–30). This drive from secrecy into openness takes place in accordance with the principle that 'there is nothing hidden except to be made manifest' (4.22). The Gospel according to Mark is itself an integral part of this ongoing process of disclosure.[12]

Universal proclamation implies universal accessibility. There can be no universal proclamation of a dark saying which withholds its innermost meaning from its hearers. The preaching of the gospel is light, not darkness. The gospel narrative does not seek to inform us about the nature of narrative in general; it is an instantiation of the gospel of Jesus Christ, addressed to all people without exception by virtue of his unique significance as the incarnate Son of God who lived, died and was raised. As a reader, one can place oneself in the position of an addressee of this message, or one can at least observe that the text does indeed define its intended addressee in these terms. In either case, the genre of this text as gospel is acknowledged; and in the first case, it is this recognition of genre that will control interpretation.

But this may seem too bland and literal-minded a reading of Mark. It takes Mark seriously at precisely the points that modernity finds most problematic. It assumes that the role of addressee of the Marcan text is still open and available to an interpreter and to the community that he or she represents. Perhaps it is only possible to place oneself in this role through a series of repressions and exclusions that drastically restrict one's understanding of the world as well as one's ability to read Mark's text? This text may be much less straightforward than the simple identification with 'gospel' would suggest. It is, perhaps, devious, disjointed and divided; in it, the darkness of parable subverts the false clarity of gospel. Views of this kind are commonplace today, and I shall show, by way of a fuller analysis of Kermode's *Genesis of Secrecy*, that they are essentially gnostic in tendency.[13]

2. Mark as Parable

Alone with the disciples, Jesus explains why he teaches in parables: 'To you has been given the secret of the kingdom of God, but for those outside everything is in parables, so that seeing they may indeed see but not perceive, and hearing they may indeed hear and not understand; lest they should turn again, and be forgiven' (4.11–12). Kermode finds here a statement about interpretation in general: that it is founded upon a distinction between insiders and outsiders. Outsiders have to make do with the literal or carnal sense of the text; their reading is superficial, and they miss the point. Insiders are dissatisfied with the carnal sense, and strive to penetrate more deeply into the text in search of its secret meanings. 'Insiders can hope to achieve correct interpretations, though their hope may be frequently, perhaps always, disappointed: whereas those outside cannot. There is seeing and hearing, which are what naïve listeners and readers do; and there is perceiving and understanding, which are in principle reserved to an elect' (3). However, the elect do not agree with each other: 'Carnal readings are much the same. Spiritual readings are all different' (9) – perhaps because each of them selects a particular focus, which is 'chosen at the expense of others, and is bound to ignore much of the information offered by the text' (12).

Parables are told not because of a prior blindness and deafness (Matthew's view) but *in order to bring about* blindness and deafness. Their role is to conceal, not to reveal. Kermode is critical of the tradition of parable-interpretation represented by Jülicher, Dodd and Jeremias, which rejects the Marcan parable-theory and insists that Jesus told straightforward, lifelike stories to help his hearers to understand his message. On the contrary, a parable is a riddle: thus – although a different word is used – the disciples contrast Jesus' plain speech with his enigmatic parabolic utterances (John 16.29, *paroimia*; cf. 16.25; 10.6). Even the impression that parabolic enigmas exclude some but not others turns out to be false. Mark's parable-theory is still more radical: parables exclude insiders as well as outsiders. Thus the disciples too are addressed as outsiders: 'Do you not yet perceive or understand? Are your hearts hardened? Having eyes do you not see, and having ears do you not hear? And do you not remember?' (Mark 8.17–18). Mark's parable-theory can be understood as referring not just to parables but to narrative in general. If it seems counter-intuitive to us that 'all narratives are essentially dark, despite the momentary radiance that attends divination' (45), it would not have surprised older interpreters, who in their use of allegorical interpretation assume the scriptural texts' 'inexhaustible hermeneutic potential' (44).[14]

A particular instance of this narrative's exclusion of insiders may be found in the puzzling reference to the young man in a linen garment who fled naked from the scene of Jesus' arrest (14.51–52). Various ingenious explanations of this passage have been offered by professional interpreters: one can trace a possible Old Testament background, one can find here the figure of the evangelist himself making an appearance in his own story. What interests Kermode is not the problem itself but the interpreters' longing to solve it, their inability to allow a possibly insoluble enigma to stand as such. Drawing a parallel with scholarly exegesis of comparable enigmas in Joyce's *Ulysses*, Kermode notes that our whole practice of reading is founded on the expectation of narrative coherence. We are all united in the conviction 'that somehow, in some occult fashion, if we could only detect it, everything will be found to hang together . . . We are all fulfillment men, *pleromatists*; we all seek the center that will allow the senses to rest, at any rate for one interpreter, at any rate for one moment' (72). But what if the text eludes our desire, resisting our explanatory schemata and reasserting its otherness? Do we really control the text, or does it escape our grasp as the young man in the garden evaded his would-be captors?[15]

As pleromatists, we desire the text to be transparent to reality – historical reality, or, failing that, any other kind. Interpretation seeks to pin the text to the world. The gospels' history-likeness is 'the consequence of an extraordinary rhetorical feat' (113) which still makes it 'exceedingly difficult to treat them as stories, as texts totally lacking transparency on event' (121). The apparent plausibility of parts of these accounts is, however, beside the point, for 'to seem plausible is the aim of a great deal of fiction' (112). Indeed, interpreters have plausible fictions of their own: all of us too easily 'slip back into the old comfortable fictions of transparency, the single sense, the truth' (123). Yet these *are* fictions, and texts have their own ways of exposing them as such; interpreters must accept that the opacity of narrative precludes definitive interpretation and dooms them to inevitable disappointment. Hope is 'a symptom of the interpreter's disease' (127), and the continual production of interpretations is a sign that the desire to understand and to interpret rightly is incurable. This situation is at least preferable to a resignation that would bring reading and interpretation to a standstill: 'The desires of interpreters are good because without them the world and the text are tacitly declared to be impossible; perhaps they are, but we must live as if the case were otherwise' (126). In Kermode's final chapter, 'The Unfollowable World', the text becomes an emblem of the world itself, and a bitter-sweet scepticism has the last word:

> World and book, it may be, are hopelessly plural, endlessly disappointing; we stand alone before them, aware of their arbitrariness and impenetrability,

knowing that they may be narratives only because of our impudent intervention, and susceptible of interpretation only by our hermetic tricks. Hot
for secrets, our only conversation may be with guardians who know less and
see less than we can; and our sole hope and pleasure is in the perception of a
momentary radiance, before the door of disappointment is finally shut on us.
(145)

The Gospel of Mark, so puzzling in its opacity, turns out to be world-disclosive
after all: the opaque narrative is a parable of an opaque world. The radiance
of gospel has been subverted by the darkness of parable.[16]

In all this, a gnosticizing tendency is perceptible. There is said to be a
carnal and a spiritual interpretation, the province of outsiders and insiders
respectively. Classical Christian biblical interpretation has rarely taken any
such form. The 'carnal' or rather the literal sense has normally been held in
high esteem, so much so that one needs to justify diverging from it by
appealing to some special factor such as anthropomorphism. Spiritual and
allegorical senses have not usually been the preserve of an elect group: there
is nothing in Augustine's much-cited interpretation of the parable of the
Good Samaritan that lies beyond the capacity of the ordinary Christian.
Allegorical interpretation was generally employed for homiletic and devotional
purposes. It is the gnostic community and not the Christian one that
distinguishes the spirituality of its being and its reading from the carnality of
the vulgar.

Similarly gnostic is the practice of a reading that can conjure up dazzling
new structures out of a few miscellaneous pieces of text, while disregarding
the whole of which they are part. Irenaeus illustrates this procedure with a
parable of his own. A skilful artist has created an image of a king out of
precious jewels. Incomprehensibly, someone takes this apart and rearranges
the jewels in the poorly-executed likeness of a dog or fox, claiming that this
botched production is the original kingly image and so deceiving the ignorant
who know no better. Gnostics 'assemble their views from non-scriptural
sources, and . . . try to weave ropes of sand, speciously adapting to their
personal opinions the parables of the Lord, the sayings of the prophets, and
the words of the apostles . . . In doing so, they disregard the order and
connection of the Scriptures, and so far as possible dismember and destroy
the truth' (*adv.haer.* i.8.1). In the Gospel of Mark, a skilful artist has created
an image of a king. Contemplating this image is the only good reason for
reading this text. But the image has been dismantled, and from some of the
detached fragments a new image has been fabricated. Mark is now a parable
of the impenetrability of narrative, and as such it discloses an equally
impenetrable world; Mark dutifully underwrites modern or postmodern
scepticism about truth-claims, religious or otherwise. Non-scriptural texts

by Kafka and Joyce try to accustom Mark to this unfamiliar role; but it remains unmistakably *Kermode's* Mark that spins its tales of opacity and alienation – a fictive construction which cannot bear too close a comparison with the original.

For the gnostic, the sacred text discloses a world that is 'unfollowable', 'hopelessly plural', 'endlessly disappointing' (145). The world is not the secure home we had expected it to be, although we conceal this from ourselves by believing our own stories about it. Truth does not find its dwelling-place here. It is perceptible at best only in momentary radiances, glimpsed out of the corner of an eye. The world's plurality is a sign of its origination out of confusion and mixture; and this is really a non-origin, not a true beginning – for true beginnings are found only in stories. That the world is not our home is also an assertion about ourselves: we are not at home in the world. In finding ourselves endlessly disappointed by the world, we discover our own transcendence of the world. In the world we do not find what we were looking for, the pearl of great price that is also our own true being. But we have not fallen so far from our true being as to be comfortably at home in the world. In our disappointment, we already have, in some measure, that which we seek. The world as *kenoma* becomes a mirror in which we read our own awareness of this absence and thus our own participation in *pleroma*. Yet the world is endlessly deceitful. It invites the interpretation by which we would make it our home, finding ourselves at one with it in the depths that lie beneath its enigmatic surface. It makes us believe that it contains the *pleroma* we seek, and that if we do not cease from exploration this prize will be ours. Thus it evokes our fictions, and even acquiesces in them for a while, as if our quest for truth had been successful – before allowing its plurality to play upon them, to dissolve their foundations and to expose their groundlessness. If we succumb to the world's seductions, we will lose our way, deceived by one or other of the fake images of *pleroma* erected by previous victims of its stratagems. But, as the shepherd found the lost sheep and the woman her lost coin, so we can be recalled from our lostness by the voice of our true being, which makes us *aware* of the incorrigible plurality of the world and thus of our own transcendence of it.

In one sense it is true that this gnostic gospel originates, at least in part, from the canonical texts, although the texts themselves have no intention of promoting gnostic mythologizing. The canonical gospels proclaim the gospel: that the light shines in the darkness and that the darkness has not overcome it. This gospel founds the life of a community, in which it is given institutional expression, and it is in this institutional context that the truth is taught: that the light shining in the darkness is Jesus Christ, the Word made flesh. The social space in which the community finds itself is not, however, a vacuum.

It has its own ideas and traditions about truth and falsehood, light and darkness, and the fact that it holds itself aloof from the community indicates that it has no intention of subordinating its existing truth to ecclesial truth. In face of the challenge of ecclesial truth, a counter-truth must be developed, partly out of existing resources and partly on the ground marked out by ecclesial truth itself. This counter-truth may represent ecclesial truth either as untruth or as half-truth. To represent ecclesial truth as *untruth* is quickly done, requiring no very close acquaintance with it: for belief in the Word-made-flesh is a *skandalon* that flies in the face of existing plausibility-structures, and resources for resisting it lie close at hand. But if ecclesial truth is conceived as *half-truth*, it must be engaged at a deeper level. The texts to which it appeals must be carefully read – but read against the grain. Their status as sacred scripture must be acknowledged – alongside the very different texts to which the broader culture accords canonical status. They must be understood as disclosing the truth about the world – a truth that subverts ecclesial truth. On this construal, ecclesial truth is no longer a threat. Its problem lies in its narrowness, its literal-mindedness, its lack of imagination and creativity. Where possible, its devotees must be persuaded to transcend the harsh confines of their partial truth, and helped to a richer apprehension of the breadths and depths of existence. There thus emerges a gnostic truth dependent on ecclesial truth and constituted by resistance to it as half-truth. Fragments of ecclesial truth will be found in it, but none of them will remain the same; for they now belong to an image very different from the original.[17]

3. The Glory of God in the Face of Christ

Much of Kermode's book might plausibly be seen as a midrash not on Mark but on a parable in Kafka's *The Trial.* A man comes to the temple to consult the Law. To his surprise, the doorkeeper persistently refuses to admit him, although he waits patiently at the door year after year. He engages the doorkeeper in conversation, and tries unsuccessfully to bribe him. As the man lies dying, a strange radiance streams forth from the door. He asks the doorkeeper why no one else has come seeking admittance, and is told: 'This door was intended only for you. Now I am going to shut it.' Kermode finds here a parable about interpretation: longing to penetrate to the innermost heart of a text, the interpreter is mysteriously kept outside, although there are intimations that he or she belongs within. Kafka rather than Mark inspires the concluding sentence of *The Genesis of Secrecy*: 'Hot for secrets, our only conversation may be with guardians who know less and see less than we can; and our sole hope and pleasure is in the perception of a momentary radiance, before the door of disappointment is finally shut on us' (145). But Mark too knows of a momentary radiance, on the mount of transfiguration (Mark 9.2–13). Is the interpreter doomed to exclusion and disappointment here as well?

We begin by reflecting on the theological genesis of the transfiguration story. At the heart of the gospel is the person of Jesus Christ. But if the gospel concerns 'Jesus Christ, Son of God' (Mark 1.1), then we must add that at the heart of the gospel lies not simply an individual person but a relationship: Jesus Christ in relation to God, the Father disclosed as in mutually-constitutive relation to his Son. In its narrated form, the gospel would not remain gospel if it confined itself to a Jesus constituted solely by his human relationships – with the inhabitants of Nazareth, with John, the disciples, the crowds, the Pharisees and so on. As a genuinely human figure, the person of Jesus is indeed constituted by his relationships with other humans, but if that is the whole truth of his person then he is confined within the sphere of immanence and possesses only the relative significance of any other historical figure. A life of Jesus that rendered its subject with the most scrupulous attention to the historical facts would not be gospel, for it would omit precisely the factor that gives the life of Jesus its ultimate and universal significance – Jesus' relation to his Father.[18] But this creates a problem for the narrator: how is the relationship of Father and Son to be represented within the narrative? Old Testament precedents (especially in the books of Genesis and Exodus) indicate that the divine–human relationship can be rendered in narrative form – but only at the cost of appearing to turn God into one agent among others. The God who is the Father of Jesus Christ cannot be one agent among others, for his action is not a reaction to contingent circumstances; it is grounded in the love which is his own being, and it is universal in its scope. It is only the relation between Father and Son which can establish and ground the truth of the gospel narrative, and some means must be found of acknowledging this within the narrative itself. If, in the baptism and transfiguration narratives, Mark's solutions to this difficulty take the form of 'legendary' material, then 'legend' (if that is really an appropriate term) must be understood in relation to the reality it intends, the mutually-constitutive relationship of Father and Son. A rationalism which believes that reality is what you get when you subtract legend loses everything here.[19]

Jesus took three chosen disciples 'up a high mountain apart by themselves; and he was transfigured before them, and his garments became glistening, intensely white, as no fuller on earth could bleach them' (Mark 9.2–3). Here the 'myth of transparency' becomes truth. This is a place apart from other places, a sanctuary, the 'shrine of the single sense' in which a disclosure occurs of the ultimate truth of Jesus' being, the key to the real significance of his life. His glory already indicates a relation to God far transcending normal worldly possibilities (as the naïve remark about bleaching indicates), but the nature of that relation is not yet clear. Moses too had been transfigured – although only his face shone, not his garments (Exod. 34.29–35). Angels may appear in glory and communicate something of their own radiance to others (Dan. 10.4–8). Jesus' glory on the mount of transfiguration does not in itself convey the truth of his identity.

Nor does the appearance of Elijah and Moses bring any immediate clarification. They speak with Jesus, but we and the disciples do not over-hear the conversation. In this context, the appearance of Elijah should be related to the belief of the scribes 'that first Elijah must come' (Mark 9.11): the Elijah who appears on the mount of transfiguration is an eschatological figure. Moses' appearance too must be related to his role elsewhere in the Marcan narrative. He it is to whom both Jesus and his opponents appeal when debating the enduring foundations of the covenant relation between God and Israel (Mark 7.10; 10.3–4; 12.26). Moses belongs to the begin-ning, Elijah to the end; between them they span the whole history of the covenant. Thus, in the text from Malachi to which Mark 9.11 alludes, the prophet points back to Moses and forward to Elijah: 'Remember the law of my servant Moses, the statutes and ordinances that I commanded him at Horeb for all Israel. Behold, I will send you Elijah the prophet before the great and terrible day of the Lord comes' (Mal. 4.4–5). The fact that Moses and Elijah converse with the transfigured Jesus suggests that he too has a significant part to play in the outworking of the history of the covenant, and Peter's odd proposal to accommodate them in tents has the effect of placing all three figures – Jesus, Moses, Elijah – on an equal footing. But it is not yet clear what Jesus' role is within the salvation-history marked out by his two conversation-partners. Nor is it clear why they make this unique personal appearance.

The moment of disclosure occurs as the voice speaks out of the cloud: 'This is my beloved Son; listen to him' (9.7). At this point Moses and Elijah vanish: 'Looking around they no longer saw anyone with them but Jesus only' (9.8). It is strange and unexpected that the divine voice has nothing to say about Moses and Elijah, and this silence together with their unexplained presence and sudden disappearance is surely significant. They are, as it were, eclipsed by the transfigured Jesus himself. 'What once had glory has come to have no glory at all, because of the glory that surpasses it' (2 Cor. 3.10). Jesus alone is the centre, the substance and the goal of the divine–human relationship.[20] There can be no question of assigning him an important role alongside other important roles, or even of regarding him as first among equals. Moses and Elijah are not his equals; he is qualitatively different from them. The divine voice does not admonish the disciples to listen to the word of God in the mouths of his three servants gathered on the mountain, Jesus, Moses and Elijah – each seated perhaps in one of Peter's rather absurd tents. Jesus' word is not one word among many. The disciples are to listen to him alone and exclusively; only when they have learned to do that can they understand the true significance of Moses, Elijah and the whole history of Israel as a preparing of the way of the Lord.[21]

The disciples are to listen exclusively to Jesus because he alone is God's beloved Son. This is the truth of which the divine radiance of the transfigured Jesus is the sign. It is not a truth among other truths about Jesus – such as that he came from Nazareth, or that he was baptized by John; for flesh and blood can reveal such truths as these, or confirm them through historical investigation, but only the Father in heaven can reveal Jesus as 'my beloved Son' (cf. Matt. 16.17). 'No one knows the Son except the Father' (Matt. 11.27): this is a truth that remains in the hand of the Father and is not subject to the weighing up of probabilities and the arguments for and against that attend ordinary human truth-claims. Normally, to assess a truth-claim is to consider it in relation to what is already known to be the case, employing the informal rules for such procedures established by local convention. Existing truth and existing criteria for truth retain a certain precedence over proposed new truth. But if new truth is qualitatively different from all other truths, existing truth and criteria can make nothing of it. Thus, in this case, new truth can be revealed by God alone, and this revelation takes the form of personal address to the disciples.[22] When the divine voice announced God's beloved Son, '*we heard* this voice borne from heaven, for we were with him on the holy mountain' (2 Pet. 1.18). This hearing was no mere overhearing, for the voice was meant for Peter, James and John, and its words were addressed to them.

The revelation is of an identity, and that identity takes the form of a relationship. Jesus' sonship is not a unique status or possession belonging to him as an abstract individual; it is a relationship, and Jesus can never be abstracted from that relationship. He is God's beloved Son because God is his beloved Father; and God is Father in so far as he is constituted Father through his relationship to his Son. Thus the revelation on the mount of transfiguration does not simply disclose information that would otherwise have been inaccessible. In revealing his own Son, God reveals *himself* as Father of the Son; and this is one revelation rather than two, the revelation of God as Father and Son. God's identity is inseparable from Jesus', and the revelation of Jesus' identity is the definitive and unsurpassable revelation of God. As so often, Johannine theology makes explicit what is implicit in synoptic narrative. 'He who sees me sees him who sent me' (John 12.45):

and the reason is that truly to 'see' Jesus is to see him in his identity as the Son of the Father, and at the same time to see God's identity as the Father of the Son. The glory manifested by the Word made flesh is not his own personal attribute as an abstract individual but 'glory as of the only Son from the Father' (John 1.14).[23]

The mount of transfiguration, at the centre of the Marcan narrative, is a vantage-point from which the whole of the narrative, before and after, can be understood. The light of the transfigured Jesus illuminates the whole of his story, from beginning to end. In relation to the beginning, the voice from heaven confirms the divine address to Jesus himself at his baptism: 'You are my beloved Son; with you I am well-pleased' (Mark 1.11). At the beginning, Jesus' self-knowledge is intended for himself alone. The concealment of his identity is confirmed when the unclean spirits that cry out, 'You are the Son of God', are silenced (3.11–12). Now, at the centre of the narrative, it becomes clear that this concealment is only provisional. 'You are . . .' becomes 'This is . . .': knowledge of Jesus' identity is granted to others. The disclosure is from God alone, and by narrating this disclosure the narrative acknowledges its own inability adequately to render Jesus' identity in narrative form. The identity of Jesus cannot be read off the surface of the text. His words and his actions are ambiguous in themselves. They excite astonishment and wonder, they cause Jesus to be held in the highest regard as the Baptist *redivivus*, as Elijah, or as one of the prophets of old (6.14–15; 8.27–28), but they do not in themselves enable a recognition of Jesus as the Son of God or of God as the Father of Jesus. History – even a history conforming closely to that which is narrated by Mark – has no such inherent disclosive power, and neither does the narration of that history. For this reason, the theme of the disciples' blindness (cf. 8.14–21) does not indicate an animosity towards the twelve, a homiletic intention, or a preoccupation with the paradoxes of interpretation. The disciples are blind because, however close their acquaintance with the person and ministry of Jesus, this is not yet a knowledge of his identity as constituted within the divine identity. Only God – and not history or narrative – can reveal God's own identity. Only retrospectively, from the vantage-point of the mount of transfiguration, can Jesus' words and actions be rightly understood as the words and actions appropriate to his identity as God's beloved Son. At this point, the promise is fulfilled that 'To you has been given the secret of the kingdom of God' (4.11). On the mountain the disciples see what they had previously not seen, that 'the kingdom of God has come with power' (9.1).

The divine glory and the divine voice therefore disclose the truth hitherto concealed, and by removing the veil from the words and actions of Jesus they make it possible to understand them retrospectively in their previously concealed testimony to the truth. Although the truth of Jesus' identity cannot be directly read out of the history of his ministry, this does not mean that this history is irrelevant to his identity and might equally well have taken a quite different form. If Jesus' identity should not be abstracted from his relationship as Son to the Father, neither should it be abstracted from his history. If the divine voice at Jesus' baptism indicates that the Father–Son relationship precedes the history, the history that follows is still the history of that relationship. The Jesus who heals Peter's mother-in-law, who argues with scribes and Pharisees and who teaches in parables acts and speaks as the beloved Son with whom the Father is well pleased. But this identity, known to him alone, is not yet known to the other participants in his story; for God has not yet made himself known to them.

The significance of Jesus' history for his identity as the beloved Son of the Father is still clearer if the conclusion and goal of that history is understood from the vantage-point of the mount of transfiguration. The disciples are to keep silent about what they have seen, 'until the Son of man should have risen from the dead'. The divine voice has disclosed that the Son of man who is to die and to rise is the Son of God; and the dying and rising of the Son of man are the historical goal of the Father–Son relationship here disclosed. Although the relationship precedes and grounds the history, it requires the completion of the history if it is to be adequately understood. The disciples have received the disclosure, but only after the resurrection will they be enabled to appropriate it and to proclaim it; and their enablement will proceed from the fulfilment at Pentecost of the promise that the one stronger than John will baptize with the Holy Spirit (1.7–8; Acts 1.4–5). At present, on their way down the mountain, they are full of uncertainties and in no position to proclaim: they question what the rising of the dead means, and they find it difficult to correlate the appearance of Elijah with traditional belief about his eschatological role (Mark 9.10–11). According to Jesus, the scribes have scriptural warrant for their teaching that Elijah will come: thus, 'Elijah does come first, to restore all things' (v. 12a). But it is also written that the Son of man 'should suffer many things and be treated with contempt' (v. 12b). How are the two scriptural traditions compatible? As at the transfiguration Jesus eclipses Elijah and is the only one whom the disciples are to 'hear', so it must be in the interpretation of holy scripture: God wills and scripture teaches that God's definitive act of salvation is to take place through the dying and rising of the Son of man, and the scriptural testimony regarding Elijah must therefore be subordinated to this: 'I tell you that Elijah has come, and they did to him whatever they pleased, as it is written of him' (v. 13). The dying and rising of the Son of man must occupy the centre, and it is this complex event that henceforth constitutes the goal of the Marcan narrative. Thus, in the dialogue between Jesus and the disciples that occurs on the way down the mountain, the significance of what has taken place is shown to relate in part to that which still lies in the future. The now-disclosed relationship of Jesus to the Father has a history that has yet to be fulfilled.[24]

This theological exegesis makes possible a response to the hermeneutical question from which we started. According to postmodern hermeneutics, interpreters can expect only 'the perception of a momentary radiance, before the door of disappointment is finally shut on us' (*Genesis of Secrecy*, 145). 'No one, however special his viewpoint, can get past all those doorkeepers into the shrine of the single sense': that is the disappointing reality of interpretation, from which we all too easily 'slip back into the old comfortable fictions of transparency, the single sense, the truth' (123). On the mount of transfiguration, there occurs a momentary radiance, and there are witnesses to behold it who are also interpreters: in due course, they will tell of what they have seen, when they have learned to understand it rightly. The mountain is a shrine in which the divine glory is manifest and in which opacity gives way to transparency. In this shrine there is disclosed the single sense of the otherwise ambiguous story of the ministry, death and resurrection of Jesus of Nazareth: that this story is grounded in the identity of Jesus as the Father's beloved Son, and that the history it relates is the history of that relationship. Although the radiance is momentary, its power to illumine the story that precedes and follows it is enduring, and it is for this reason alone – and not because they have experienced some isolated marvel – that its eyewitnesses and first interpreters will eventually have to recount what they have seen. As they do so, preaching the gospel to the whole creation, the Father's disclosure of Jesus as his beloved Son is reactualized; to the extent that this occurs, the gospel is not only preached but also believed.

This suggests that the interpreter's 'disappointment' is contingent rather than necessary. Disappointment may occur, perhaps repeatedly, but it is not an inevitable fate; Peter, James and John, and those who believed through their word, do not appear to have been disappointed. Disappointment finds in the Marcan narrative a dark labyrinth in which one encounters at best only momentary and perhaps delusive glimmers of light. From this standpoint, Mark is parable not gospel, multiple not single, fabrication not truth. In order to refute this radical misreading, Mark offers a parable, not to darken but to illuminate: 'Is a lamp brought in to be put under a bushel, or under a bed, and not on a stand?' (4.21). To place the lamp under a bushel, delighting in the fascinating play of shadows that this produces, is simply to misuse it. The purpose of a gospel is to give light – by bearing witness to the light that shines in the darkness, which the darkness did not overcome.

NOTES

1. The concept of 'directedness' is derived from A. C. Thiselton's hermeneutical application of speech-act theory (*New Horizons in Hermeneutics: The Theory and Practice of Transforming Biblical Reading*, HarperCollins: London, 1992, 597–602).

2. Frank Kermode, *The Classic: Literary Images of Permanence and Change*, Cambridge, Mass.: Harvard University Press, 1983².

3. This notion of a 'fit' between multiple text and multiple world should be distinguished from the view that contrasts fictive *order* with chaotic reality. Thus Kermode can also speak of a fictive plot as 'an organization that humanizes time by giving it form', bringing order into a chaotic world without end or beginning (*The Sense of an Ending: Studies in the Theory of Fiction*, Oxford: Oxford University Press, 1967, 45). In the modern era a transition has occurred 'from a literature which assumed that it was imitating an order to a literature which assumes that it has to create an order' (167).

4. Frank Kermode, *The Genesis of Secrecy: On the Interpretation of Narrative*, Cambridge, Mass.: Harvard University Press, 1979.

5. See Martin Hengel's study of 'The Titles of the Gospels and the Gospel of Mark', in his *Studies in the Gospel of Mark*, London: SCM Press, 1985, 64–84. Hengel argues (against Harnack and Zahn) that the short form *kata* ... is an abbreviation of the earlier *euaggelion kata* ..., and that the titles precede the compilation of the fourfold canonical collection. The uniformity of the titles in the earliest period indicates that they 'go back to the time of the final redaction and first circulation of the Gospels themselves': for 'circulation of anonymous works without a title would of necessity have led to a multiplicity of titles' (82). The use of *euaggelion* in the titles probably derives from Mark 1.1, from which it was transferred to other canonical and non-canonical texts (82–83).

6. The translation is taken from *The Ante-Nicene Fathers*, vol. I, repr. Grand Rapids: Eerdmans, 1975.

7. This point tells against David Aune's claim that the gospels 'constitute a *subtype* of Greco-Roman biography' (*The New Testament in its Literary Environment*, Cambridge: James Clarke, 1987, 46, italics original). The title *euaggelion kata* ... indicates that, for their readers, the gospels did not constitute a 'sub-type' of an existing genre but a new genre. This would of course not be a *creatio ex nihilo*: the gospels may employ many of the conventions of the Hellenistic *bios*, without erasing the difference implied by the substitution of *euaggelion* for *bios* in their titles.

8. The title, added no doubt on the basis of 1.1 (see note 5 above), subsequently affects the reading of 1.1. According to M. D. Hooker, Mark's 'first readers would have understood him to be referring to a message ... not to a particular literary form' (*The Gospel according to St Mark*, London: A. & C. Black, 1991, 33). But the universally-accepted title is itself evidence as to how Mark's 'first readers' understood Mark 1.1. As regards the text-critical problem, *huiou [tou] theou* was part of the text of Mark for almost all its ancient readers, and this fact makes it appropriate to retain it – quite apart from the question of what the evangelist originally wrote.

9. In 1.1, *euaggelion Iēsou Christou* is to be understood as an objective genitive. If the reference is to Jesus' own preaching (as in 1.14), it is difficult to understand why the scriptural quotation (vv. 2–3) refers to the preaching of his forerunner.

10. 'It is in [Jesus'] words and works and person that the kingdom has come. In fact, we may actually go so far as to say that the kingdom of God *is* Jesus and that he *is* the

kingdom . . . The kingdom has both come and is still to come, because Jesus has come and is to come again' (C. E. B. Cranfield, *The Gospel according to St Mark*, Cambridge: Cambridge University Press, 1955, 66).

11. Compare Kierkegaard's view: 'Even if the contemporary generation had not left anything behind except these words, "We have believed that in such and such a year the god appeared in the humble form of a servant, lived and taught among us, and then died" – this is more than enough' (*Philosophical Fragments*, Kierkegaard's Writings VII, ET Princeton: Princeton University Press, 1985, 104). Kierkegaard's more-than-adequate rendering of the gospel hardly constitutes a 'narrative'.

12. Brevard Childs points out that 'the longer ending consists of a catena of passages taken from the other three canonical Gospels', and argues that it was added in order to integrate Mark into the fourfold collection: 'The canonical Mark has thus been fashioned in such a way as to harmonize with the other three' (*The New Testament as Canon: An Introduction*, London: SCM Press, 1984, 94, 95). But to speak of 'the canonical Mark' ignores the fact that Mark also functioned as a canonical text in forms that lacked this ending. The important issue is not whether the commentator regards 16.1–8 or 16.9–20 as the conclusion of the gospel, but whether (if the former option is taken) Mark is treated as 'an idiosyncratic witness in open conflict with the other three' (95 – an approach that Childs rightly criticizes). My own argument shows that, at least at certain points, the Longer Ending is appropriate to the Gospel of Mark itself.

13. Approaches such as this apply to Mark a set of deconstructive strategies which can in principle be applied to any text. The intention is to identify the hierarchies and privileged terms on which a text is founded, and to demonstrate the instability of the fundamental gesture of exclusion. Traditional theology is said to be 'logocentric' in the sense that it 'is scarcely conceivable apart from some use of contrast terms along the line of "lower" and "higher", "world" and "spirit", "darkness" and "light"' (W. Lowe, *Theology and Difference: The Wound of Reason*, Bloomington and Indianapolis: Indiana University Press, 1993, 17). It seems that 'any theology which takes deconstruction seriously . . . must identify and expel from its vocabulary the entire lexicon of terms which serve the metaphysics of presence'; the irony that this would be to re-enact the gesture of exclusion which is supposedly undone 'is precisely where deconstruction intends to place us . . . Deconstruction makes us suspicious of a whole network of terms *and* it makes us aware that the network is, in effect, without end, so that *all* of our language is affected' (17). Granted that Marcan antitheses such as light and darkness, gospel and parable, inside and outside *can* be deconstructed, and granted that new antitheses will be established in the process, it remains unclear what it is that *motivates* the ironic, self-entangling act of deconstruction.

14. In contrast to Kermode's esotericism, Mary-Ann Tolbert argues that Mark is to be understood as popular literature, 'the perfect medium for religious edification *because of its broad accessibility and appeal*' (*Sowing the Gospel: Mark's World in Literary-Historical Perspective*, Minneapolis: Fortress, 1989, 71, my italics). The omniscient narrative voice establishes 'a thoroughly unified point of view' which 'produces a very straightforward and clear narrative', devoid of ambiguity (98). As regards 4.10–12, 'the parables, like Jesus' healing and preaching ministry in general, do not force people outside or pull people inside; they simply reveal the type of ground already present' (160–61).

15. I owe this use of the young man as an image of the Marcan text to Stephen Moore. Referring to the old hypothesis that the young man is Mark himself, Moore converts him into Mark the text and his would-be captors into exegetes. 'Denuding, undressing, exposing, unveiling: these are the prurient gestures of scholarship in search of truth.' Yet

what is exposed is only the truth about scholarship itself, 'the truth that criticism is a fantasy of violent possession . . .' (*Mark and Luke in Poststructuralist Perspectives: Jesus Begins to Write*, New Haven and London: Yale University Press, 1992, 32–33, 36).

16. Compare J. D. Crossan's interpretation of parable as the opposite of myth: myth 'creates reconciliation for irreconcilables', whereas parable 'creates irreconciliation where before there was reconciliation' (*The Dark Interval: Towards a Theology of Story*, Sonoma: Eagle Books, 1988[2], 38). We are to distinguish between 'mythical religion, a religion that gives one the final word about "reality" and thereby excludes the authentic experience of mystery, and parabolic religion, a religion that continually and deliberately subverts final words about "reality" and thereby introduces the possibility of transcendence' (105). For a similar understanding of 'parable', see Mark C. Taylor, *Deconstructing Theology*, Chico: Scholars Press, 1982, 120–21.

17. Don Cupitt evokes a perspective of this kind in his *Radicals and the Future of the Church* (London: SCM Press, 1989). 'Our entire culture has depended on the doctrine that God is the ultimate Master of all meaning . . . He ensures that his church gets the truth and thereafter remains infallibly or indefectibly in the truth' (11). But a contemporary understanding of language indicates that 'there is no Meaning out there and no Truth out there' (11), and that 'both the *parousia* and the *arché*, the absolute End and the absolute Beginning, thus seem to be mythical notions' (12). Faced with this 'endless undecidability', post-orthodox Christians must make something of their own out of the resources provided by scripture and liturgy, myth and symbol: for 'this mighty flowing river of signs does not have just one true pre-established Meaning, out-there. It gets a meaning as it comes to life in me' (13). Naturally, all this 'makes the very notion of a single publicly-established, authoritative, permanent and compulsory orthodoxy impossible either in society at large or in the church in particular' (15).

18. For Jesus as for us, 'to be a creature is to be constituted, to be made what one is, by and in a network of relationships', both 'horizontal' and 'vertical' – that is, both with the world and other humans, and with God (C. E. Gunton, *Christ and Creation*, Carlisle: Paternoster, 1992, 37; for the horizontal/vertical distinction, see also A. E. McFadyen, *The Call to Personhood: A Christian Theory of the Individual in Social Relationships*, Cambridge: Cambridge University Press, 1990, 18–24). Yet there is something distinctive about Jesus' relationships. In the case of the horizontal dimension, the New Testament portrays him 'as being in a relationship that must be called redemptive'. In the case of the vertical dimension, 'he is related in particular ways to God the Father', although 'without prejudice to his Jewish humanness' (*Christ and Creation*, 47). The two dimensions must be brought together: it is in so far as he is related in particular ways to the Father, and in so far as this is recognized, that his relationships with others may be said to be redemptive. His redemptive activity is grounded in his person.

19. In this analysis I assume that the evangelist intends a theologically-oriented history-writing even (or especially) in his use of apparently legendary material; and that, from the standpoint of Christian faith, the act of reference to Jesus is here accomplished in a way basically appropriate to its true object. These assumptions contrast with the historical-critical conclusion that Mark's story of Jesus 'had little to do with the historical Jesus, much, however, with the recent history of the Jesus movement to which Mark belonged' – a history characterized by 'a failure to reform the diaspora synagogues' resulting in 'withdrawal into a sectarian mentality and enclave' (Burton Mack, *A Myth of Innocence: Mark and Christian Origins*, Philadelphia: Fortress, 1988, 355). While it is obvious that the evangelist's 'situation' must have influenced his presentation of his material, it is improbable that this situation is retrievable from a text which purports to speak of

something else, and questionable whether the attempt to retrieve it need be of any significance for interpretation. The difference between Mack's Jesus and Mark's Jesus arises out of a distinction between the laudable inclusiveness of the former and the objectionable exclusiveness of the latter (347): 'The Markan legacy is a myth of innocence that separates those who belong to the righteous kingdom within from those without' – a legacy that continues to exercise a baneful influence on US foreign policy (372). Such statements make it clear that a 'radical' historical-critical posture is as inseparable from the interpreter's world-view as is a Christian-theological reading such as the one presented here.

20. 'St. Peter in his halting, frightened utterances equates the three celestial figures, Moses, Elijah, and the Lord . . . But the heavenly voice corrects his error; "this (person only), he is my unique *Son*; hear ye *him*". Henceforth the Lord alone is to claim their allegiance' (R. H. Lightfoot, *The Gospel Message of Mark*, Oxford: Clarendon Press, 1950, 43).

21. This interpretation of the divine address in terms of the significance of Jesus as the goal of salvation-history suggests that the command, 'Hear him', does not relate exclusively to Jesus' announcement of his imminent death (the view of Ched Myers, *Binding the Strong Man: A Political Reading of Mark's Story of Jesus*, Maryknoll: Orbis, 1988, 249–51). For Myers, this passage together with Mark 8.34–9.1 is rooted in Danielic apocalyptic myth: the purpose is to give us eyes to see 'the apocalyptic moment of the cross as the "glory of the Human One"' (249). For the reader/disciple as for Jesus, 'to be vindicated in the "Danielic" courtroom is to be condemned in the Jewish/Roman one, and vice versa' (249). This identification of cross and glory has the effect of suppressing the christological focus of the transfiguration narrative; compare Myers' implausible claim that in 8.27–38 the confessional question is simply 'eclipsed' by the question of political praxis (238). In fact, the question of praxis only arises *on the basis* of the christological confession: the 'Son of man' suffers and is raised as the one who is already 'the Christ', God's 'beloved Son'.

22. Compare Bonhoeffer's distinction between the questions *how?* and *who?* 'An unknown object can become known when it is possible to place it in an already existing classification' (*Christology*, ET Glasgow: Collins, 1978, 29). But what if there appears a Counter-Logos in the form of a person, declaring himself to be the way, the truth and the life? 'When the Counter-Logos appears in history . . . as Word become flesh, there is no longer any possibility of assimilating him into the existing order of the human logos. The only real question which now remains is: "Who are you? . . ." This is the question with which christology is concerned. Christ is the Counter-Logos. Classification is no longer a possibility, because the existence of this Logos spells the end of the human logos. Only the question, "Who are you?" will do . . . Not, "How are you possible?", that is the godless question, the serpent's question, but "Who are you?"' (30).

23. 'Knowledge of God the Father and knowledge of Jesus Christ the incarnate Son of the Father arise in us together, not one without the other. We do not know the Father apart from the Son, for there is no Father but the Father of the Son. Nor do we know any Son of God apart from the Father, for there is no Son of God but the Son of the Father' (T. F. Torrance, *The Mediation of Christ*, Edinburgh: T. & T. Clark, 1992², 55).

24. In this presentation I have attempted to fuse two approaches to identity designated by Hans Frei as 'intention-action description' and 'description of the ascriptive subject' (in *Theology and Narrative: Selected Essays* [ed. G. Hunsinger and W. C. Placher], New York and Oxford: Oxford University Press, 1993, 62, 64). According to the first model, 'a person's identity is constituted (not simply illustrated) by that intention which he carries

into action' (63). This may be applied to Jesus: 'In his general intention to enact, in obedience to God, the good of men on their behalf, and at the crucial juncture in his specific resolve to do so if necessary in this terrifying way [the reference is to the decision taken in Gethsemane] – and in the event in which this intention and resolve were enacted – Jesus was most of all himself in the description of the Gospels. This was his identity' (57). According to the second model, 'the intender-actor knows himself to be anterior and subsequent to each intention-action in a way that he does not know that he is anterior and subsequent to himself' (65). This view of the self is 'more elusive and indirect than that of the intention-action description which holds firmly to the self as publicly enacted' (66). For Frei, 'ascriptive subject description' occurs in the resurrection narratives, where 'Jesus is declared to manifest himself as who he is, the one who as the unsubstitutable human being, Jesus of Nazareth, is not a myth but the presence of God and savior of men' (74). Frei tends to accord privileged status to his intention-action model, and he is excessively cautious about ascribing an identity to Jesus that is 'anterior and subsequent to each intention-action', in other words, that grounds the narrative of Jesus' life, death and resurrection in his relation as Son to the Father.

Chapter 3

Literal Sense, Authorial Intention, Objective Interpretation: In Defence of Some Unfashionable Concepts

In recent years, a new paradigm for biblical interpretation has begun to take shape and to establish itself. In addition to the newer interpretative *practices* – of, for example, literary, feminist and canonical approaches – a theoretical framework is proposed that is capable of accommodating these new practices while not excluding the more conventional approaches associated with the historical-critical tradition. The fact that the main elements of the proposed new framework are now familiar is an indication of its relative success:

(1) It is said that we must now abandon the dogma of the single sense of the biblical texts, characterized by an emphasis on verbal meaning, authorial intention and historical circumstances of origin. No text has a single meaning, fixed for all time; that view derives from ideas of 'objectivity' or 'value-free neutrality' that must now be recognized as untenable, and indeed as ideologically conditioned.

(2) It is said that meaning is determined not by authors but by readers, located within their respective contexts or interpretative communities. Interpretation is therefore necessarily pluralistic. Any claim to present a normative, definitive interpretation would simply express the will-to-power of one interpretative community over all others.

(3) It is said that this new pluralism has the advantage of comprehensiveness. In particular, explicitly religious or theological interpretative practices need no longer be excluded, since the 'value-free neutrality' that

the exclusion was intended to protect has ceased to seem desirable or plausible. If all readings are committed readings, then theological readings are no less but also no more legitimate than any others. Theological readings must, however, learn not to 'absolutize' themselves, and must acknowledge the right of different readers to pursue different interests.[1]

These points could be expressed in slightly different ways, and further points could be added. Yet, in its various forms, the proposal as a whole is now a familiar minority position within biblical scholarship. Its critique of the privileging of historical-critical scholarship has been at least partially successful, to the extent that interpreters must now either find ways of accommodating themselves to the new situation or adopt a defensive posture as guardians of traditional scholarly values. Unlike the old, the new paradigm is interdisciplinary in orientation, and it can claim a particular affinity with those trends in the wider culture that have led to talk of a *postmodern* era: an era in which, following the collapse of the totalizing metanarratives of modernity, truth is local, style is substance, meanings are fluid, and even natural scientists are story-tellers.

Yet there are difficulties in the assumption that a certain set of practices and beliefs can be clearly identified as 'postmodern' and demarcated from that which is merely 'modern' or (in the case of theology, perhaps) 'pre-modern'. Such schematizations can be heuristically useful, but they mislead when they are naïvely taken to reflect an authoritative self-revelation of the contemporary *Zeitgeist*. Rather than analysing the new paradigm for biblical interpretation as a phenomenon of the so-called 'postmodern condition', it seems preferable to understand its three major proposals as responses to local difficulties encountered in the act of biblical interpretation. In each case, a genuine and valuable hermeneutical *insight* is converted into a more questionable hermeneutical *dogma*. The insight that 'meaning' is more than the transference of a given content from the mind of the author to the mind of the reader is incorporated into a radical hermeneutic that proclaims the death of the author and the openness of texts to an unlimited plurality of readings. The insight that textual interpretation takes place within particular communal contexts is converted into the dogma that autonomous readers and reading-communities create their own meaning out of inert textual raw material. The insight that different approaches to interpretation can further the interpretative task, rather than hindering it, becomes the dogma that all interpretations can lay claim to equal 'legitimacy' and 'validity'. In each case, a hermeneutical breakthrough has occurred that makes possible a significant expansion in the range of interpretative practice; and in each case this hermeneutical breakthrough is subjected to a premature dogmatization for the sake of a clear demarcation of the new in relation to the old. In this black-and-white world, the new can only be successfully marketed if its relation to the old can be summed up in a few simple slogans. Thus, in the new order, the reader is in fashion and the author out of fashion; author and reader are supposedly engaged in a struggle for control of the text, and the possibility of an alternative, less conflictual understanding of the author/ text/reader relationship is systematically excluded – despite the overwhelming *prima facie* plausibility of the assumption that to read a text is to construe it as the product of some kind of communicative intention. In the new order, terms such as 'objectivity' can only be used pejoratively or ironically. They are, it now appears, simply weapons in the struggle of élite groups to maintain their ideological legitimacy and to silence the voice of the marginalized. It is therefore difficult to raise the question whether all readers, 'marginalized', 'élite' or whoever, might have an interest in whatever is meant by the term 'objectivity'.

Criticism of these contemporary hermeneutical dogmas is not motivated by hostility towards dogmas in general – that is, towards relatively stable and clearly-defined positions which an interpretative community believes that it must maintain in order to preserve its identity. While it would be possible to argue that a dogmatizing postmodernism is self-contradictory, since postmodernism dissolves the concept of stability that necessarily under- pins all dogmas, that is not the intention here. The current hermeneutical dogmas are to be rejected *because they conflict with the dogmas held to be foundational to orthodox Christian faith, and because, in the light of that conflict, certain inherent problems and implausibilities rapidly come to light.* If, in a situation of *laissez-faire* interpretative pluralism, such a claim seems redolent of a distinctly 'pre-modern' theological authoritarianism, that is unfortunate but it cannot be helped. A Christian faith concerned to retain its own coherence cannot for a moment accept that the biblical texts (individually and as a whole) lack a single, determinate meaning, that their meanings are created by their readers, or that theological interpretations must see themselves as non-privileged participants in an open-ended, pluralistic conversation. Such a hermeneutic assumes that these texts are like any other 'classic' texts: self-contained artefacts, handed down to us through the somewhat haphazard processes of tradition, bearing with them a cultural authority that has now lost much of its normative force, yet challenging the interpreter to help ensure that they will at least remain readable and continue to be read. While certain parallels may be drawn between the general phenomenon of the classic and Christian holy scripture, they break down at the crucial point – which is that Christian scripture bears witness, in many and various ways, to the decisive series of events in which God is held to have uniquely disclosed himself, and to the pattern of life shaped in response to that self-disclosure. If some such testimony is – objectively – at the heart of holy scripture, and if this testimony has not yet ceased to find adherence, then a hermeneutical dogma that overlooks this will seem at best a dangerous half-truth.

In this study, I shall criticize, on hermeneutical and theological grounds, the main elements in the 'postmodern' paradigm for biblical interpretation: opposition to the notion of the single, literal sense; the readerly construction of meaning; and the theological relativism entailed by the commitment to pluralism. It will be necessary to clarify and to defend the concepts of the literal sense, authorial intention and objective interpretation.

1. Writing as Communication

(i) Writing speech-acts

Writing, like speaking, is a communicative action. It is an *action*, carried out by human agency; it does not just happen, nor does it simply exist without any relation to its origin. It would be as odd to characterize writing as the occurrence of certain shapes in more or less regular patterns as it would be to characterize speech as the occurrence of certain more or less regular patterns of sound. Like speech, writing bears within it an essential reference to its origin in human action, and without this it cannot be understood. Writing is a technology that makes possible the extension of a particular speech-act in time and space; or rather, writing *is* that speech-act (or quasi-speech-act) which intends a context beyond the range of the human voice. It is a *communicative* action in the sense that it is an action directed, in the first instance, not towards some aspect of the non-human environment but towards other humans. All human interaction includes a communicative component, even in the absence of speech or writing: thus, the various kinds of intentional physical contact between humans constitute a parallel (although much more limited) semiotic system to that of language itself. Yet speech (together with its extension in writing) is more comprehensive than other semiotic systems and may appropriately be seen as the paradigmatic instance of the category of communicative action. Spoken communication presupposes (1) a shared medium of communication (or 'code'); (2) certain forms of proximity between speaker and hearer – (a) physical, (b) relational, and (c) institutional; (3) a state of affairs which is (or is held by the speaker to be) of common concern to speaker and hearer, at least at the moment of utterance; (4) an intention, embodied in the communication itself, to evoke from the hearer (a) an understanding of what is said, resulting in (b) the appropriate response to the state of affairs to which the communication explicitly and/or implicitly refers (the acknowledgment of a truth, the fulfilment of a command), and

(c) an accompanying recognition of the communication as an intentional action rooted in a relationship between persons; (5) the possibility of further communicative *inter*action or conversation, opened up by the initial speech-act.[2]

Where communicative action takes the form of the speech-act or quasi-speech-act of writing, certain modifications of this pattern will occur:

(1) A secondary code (writing) is superimposed upon the primary one (speech): writing presupposes in its addressee a double competence, as speaker and as reader. To read is to convert certain conventional marks back into speech, and writing is therefore entirely dependent upon speech. While it is true that certain conventions (of vocabulary, syntax and so on) are especially characteristic of written forms of language, this does not mean that writing is independent of speech; for oral speech too will deploy particular conventions in particular contexts. Corresponding to the multiplicity of (oral and written) speech-act situations is a multiplicity of 'local' conventions or sub-codes tailored to those situations. The sub-code that enables one to write a personal letter is of a piece with the sub-code that enables one to make a telephone call. Written communication makes use of the comprehensive code of the linguistic system as a whole, the secondary code of the system of written marks, and the sub-code that constitutes its particular genre.

(2a) Writing does not preclude physical proximity; in certain circumstances, one can speak from a prepared text, and one can also equip one's hearers with the text, or a summary of it, as an aid to comprehension and concentration. Yet, although writing *can* function in these ways, its more characteristic function is as an instrument for extending the range of a speech-act beyond the confines of physical proximity.

(2b) As regards relational proximity, writing may be no less directed towards a specific individual than an oral speech-act. It is, however, characteristic of many forms of writing (or 'genres') that the addressee is specified less precisely than in most oral speech-acts. Writing in many genres ('published' writing) must compete in the market-place like other products, and the relation between author and reader is therefore in part a relation between producer and consumer, and might seem to be characterized precisely by the absence of the personal relationship integral to oral speech-acts. Yet that which is here 'consumed' retains its character as a communicative action, in which the reader freely adopts the role of addressee of the authorial message. There is here at least an analogy to –

or simulacrum of – the face-to-face encounter characteristic of oral speech-acts.

(2c) Writing may be as closely bound to particular institutional contexts as are oral speech-acts. Even in 'published' writing, where the identity of the addressee is not precisely specified, the text may be directed towards an intended reader with a clear institutional profile. In such cases, a text will be addressed not to a reader who is wholly anonymous and unknown to the author, but to one whose institutional context is similar enough to the author's to make communication possible and worthwhile. Thus the scope of the communicative action embodied in a philosophical or scriptural text is dependent on an institutional continuum (educational, ecclesial, or whatever) which functions as the comprehensive context within which author, text and readers are comprised. This institutional continuum is characterized by the phenomenon of 'tradition': author and intended readers are conscious of participating in a tradition which mediates the historical and/or geographical distance that separates them and brings them into a certain proximity to one another.

(3) If oral speech-acts presuppose a state of affairs that is a matter of shared concern, the same is true of their written equivalents. For *A* to write to *B* about *x* is simply an extension of *A*'s *speaking* to *B* about *x*. This extension does, however, bring about certain modifications. Where *A speaks* to *B* about *x*, *A* does so on the assumption that *B* needs to receive this communication about *x*. In other words, the initiative lies entirely with the speaker, and the hearer may receive his or her communication involuntarily or even unwillingly. Where *A writes* to *B* about *x*, however, the initiative is more evenly distributed between author and reader. One chooses to read or not to read; one does not read involuntarily or against one's will. In the case of 'published' works whose addressee is not precisely identified, one can be said to *volunteer* for the role of addressee of the communicative action embodied in the text one takes up to read. (An approximate oral equivalent would be voluntary attendance at a public lecture.) Yet one does not choose to read just any text; one volunteers for the role of addressee of some texts but not others because one has acquired a range of interests and aptitudes which makes one a suitably qualified candidate for the role of addressee of some texts but not of others. (In relation to texts one chooses not to read, one may be either under-qualified or over-qualified.) We are interested in what *A* has to say about *x*; we recognize in *x* an object of shared concern, and we believe that *A* is or may be a person competent to communicate with us concerning *x* in accordance with the conventions of a particular genre. The shared concern with *x* may be variously

motivated: author and reader may be at one in a concern with the entertainment-value to be found in x (as in the case of popular fiction), or the x in question may consist in certain kinds of 'serious' scientific, philosophical or religious truths.

(4) Communicative actions seek to produce (a) an understanding that will issue (b) in an appropriate response (acceptance of a truth-claim, granting a request), and (c) in a simultaneous recognition of what is said as an act of intentional communication. (This last clause excludes a behaviourist understanding of a speech-act situation purely in terms of stimulus and response.)

(4a) Writing, like speech, must be *understood* if it is to fulfil its communicative intention. To understand is to experience in connection with each successive sentence a gradually-dawning moment of transparency in which the relation of the words to their subject-matter and to the unfolding strategy of their speaker or writer becomes clear. Where transparency is the norm it will hardly be noticed, and the appropriateness of this metaphor (and its converse, opacity) is best illustrated by the experience of listening to an address or reading a text in a language with which one is relatively unfamiliar. Here, each sentence evokes both the hope of disclosure and the threat of disappointment. The successive words may open out onto the subject-matter intended by the speaker or writer, or they may remain distressingly opaque, locked doors rather than windows. Indeed, whatever the language, communicative acts of speech or writing always run the risk of failure. They may be imperfectly or ambiguously executed, or their addressee may fail to grasp the codes that govern them, resulting perhaps in damaging *mis*-understanding – for example, as an utterance intended ironically is taken at face value. One undertakes communicative actions at one's own risk; and the danger of communicative actions miscarrying is more acute in writing than in speech, partly because the author lacks the speaker's opportunities to identify and correct misunderstandings, and partly because the distances of space and time that writing can traverse increase the scope for communicative breakdown.

(4b) In analysing what is intended or aimed at in a speech-act, it seems possible to distinguish the passive or receptive moment of understanding from the active moment of response. Thus, the actual response may be quite different to that which was intended without understanding being in any way impaired: one may understand a request but refuse to grant it. As in the case of understanding, the writer may be at a certain disadvantage to the speaker in securing the desired response; the increased range of writing may be correlated with a decrease in efficacy. Yet, in adopting the role of the addressee of a written text, one exposes oneself to the author's attempts, embodied in the text, to do something to the addressee: to convince, exhort, warn, inform, amuse, sensitize or inspire, and by such means to modify both thought and practice. Authors and their texts have designs upon their readers, and readers are aware of that fact. As in the case of oral speech-acts, these designs may be more or less precise and explicit or vague and diffuse.

(4c) Where A speaks to B about x, what B receives is not a communication about x that might have come from anywhere (but happens to have come from A) but a communication that is, distinctively, A's communication. To understand and to respond to the communication is therefore not only to understand and respond to what is said about x but to understand and respond to A. Communication is an irreducibly *interpersonal* event, although the significance of the personal element will vary in accordance with the nature of the communication. In the case of a printed text, the appearance on the cover of the author's name (A) as well as the title (x) is an indication that to read is to enter into a personal or quasi-personal relationship with the author, who is 'known' in and through his or her communicative action, embodied in the text. The fact that the same authorial name may appear on a number of different books is a promise that the reader can get to know an author better if he or she so wishes, and particular authorial names may engender feelings of intense affection, loyalty and indebtedness in their readers.

(5) An oral speech-act can initiate various forms of communicative interaction. For example, the addressee may ask for (and is normally entitled to receive) clarification of any aspect of the initial utterance, by way of locutions such as 'do you mean that . . . ?', 'what did you mean by . . . ?', or 'are you sure that . . . ?' In contrast, the author will normally be absent from the reception of the written communication and will therefore be unavailable to answer questions. The extendedness of writing in space and time makes most authors more or less inaccessible, and, where a text is deemed significant enough for answers to questions of meaning and truth to be important, a surrogate for the absent author is installed in the form of the *interpreter*. Consulting an interpreter rather than an author has a number of advantages. First, the interpreter may well be closer to the reader in space and time than the author is; and, if so, he or she will understand what 'lies behind' certain questions much better than the author would have done. Second, the interpreter may possess a specialized knowledge that the author lacks or lacked,

making it possible to contextualize particular utterances in ways beyond the scope of the author. Third, since the need for interpretation only really arises in the case of texts that have been received as 'classics' or as 'canonical', the interpreter possesses a broader perspective on the text than does the author. On the other hand, some interpretative practices may be seen as attempts to limit the damage done to the text by the irreparable loss of the author. The author would have been able to tell us which of two or more variant readings represents the original text, which of the various possible senses of an ambiguous phrase was intended, and when, where and why the text was written.

If, as I have argued, the category of the speech-act can be extended to include written communications, then current hostility to the concepts of determinate meaning and authorial intention is unjustified. To be understood at all, a series of words must be construed as a communicative action which intends a determinate meaning together with its particular illocutionary and perlocutionary force.[3] This point may be further elaborated with the help of a biblical example.

(ii) Understanding Mark

A text may be taken to constitute a single communicative action, but it nevertheless comprises a number of interconnected but distinct communicative actions in the form of its individual sentences (which may be defined as its minimal units of meaning). Mark 1.9 may serve as a randomly-selected sentence for analysis: 'In those days Jesus came from Nazareth in Galilee and was baptized by John in the Jordan.' What takes place when a sentence such as this is 'understood'?

'In those days': that is, in this context, during the time of John the Baptizer's activity. The author here employs, and expects the reader to understand, the convention that a valid reference to the past need not include a precise statement of chronology. What matters is the temporal proximity of John and Jesus, and to try to fix the exact scope of 'those days' or the exact moment during this period when 'Jesus came from Nazareth' would indicate a partial breakdown of the author's communicative intention, which requires recognition of the conventions he employs. Another convention relates to the use here of proper names. To understand this sentence, the reader must be familiar with the convention that persons (here, John and Jesus), settlements (Nazareth), administrative regions (Galilee) and natural features (the Jordan) may be assigned proper names as a mark of their distinctiveness and their uniqueness. John and Jesus are both messengers of God, but John is John and not Jesus and Jesus is Jesus and not John. Nazareth and Capernaum may both be towns or villages, but they will be thought of in their distinctiveness so long as their proper names are employed. At this point the author is considerably more precise than in his initial chronological reference. Salvation itself depends on the correct understanding of the proper name 'Jesus', and one way of clarifying its significance is to relate it to other proper names that are to be found in its proximity. The reader must therefore be familiar with the conventions that determine the use of proper names. As regards the verbs, it is said that Jesus 'came' from Nazareth and that he was 'baptized' in the Jordan by John. The convention that human actions are to be regarded as motivated unless there are clear indications to the contrary leads the reader to understand the author as meaning that Jesus came from Nazareth *in order* to be baptized by John in the Jordan. Despite the apparent open-endedness of the words, the text does not in fact leave open the possibility that Jesus left Nazareth for some quite other reason, and that, on reaching the Jordan and seeing what was happening, he made a sudden decision to submit to baptism. The text can only mean that Jesus left Nazareth *with the intention* of getting himself baptized by John. As a communicative action, this text therefore presupposes knowledge of a range of linguistic conventions; and, in so far as its author's confidence in the linguistic competence of his readers is justified and mistakes are avoided, the single, literal meaning of the text will be correctly understood.

On this view, the 'meaning' of a text is irreducibly *verbal*: it is bound to the words, the conventions that govern their usage, and the specific intentions expressed in their use. Verbal meaning is not to be confused with contextual significance.[4] It might be argued (although not very plausibly) that the original 'significance' of the author's decision to begin his account of Jesus' ministry with this reference to his baptism lay in his intention of opposing an anti-sacramental group in his own community, who appealed to the Pauline claim that 'Christ did not send me to baptize but to preach the gospel' (1 Cor. 1.17) to justify discontinuing the practice of baptism. On this hypothesis, the evangelist's argument would be that, if even Jesus submitted to baptism, how much more should we? Let us suppose that, in writing as he did, Mark really did intend this intervention in a current controversy. Even if he did, verbal meaning would still have priority: until we have ascertained that, according to this text, Jesus came from Nazareth and was baptized by John, we cannot ask what its significance might have been in the context of the (hypothetical) baptism-controversy. In addition, an initial contextual significance is bound to disappear when the context changes. Verbal meaning is not so ephemeral: the text can never 'mean' anything other than that Jesus came from Nazareth and was baptized by John, whatever the context in which it is being read and whatever its possible significance within that context. Readers can only *receive* meaning, they cannot *create* it.[5]

An initial 'contextual significance' is relevant for interpretation only if it leaves its explicit mark on the wording of the text. In the Marcan example, the verbal meaning stands at a certain distance from any particular contextual significance (its subject is Jesus and not the so-called 'Marcan community'). The absence of an explicit reference to current circumstances already prepares the way for the dissociation of verbal meaning and initial contextual significance which, *ex hypothesi*, occurred at an early stage in the reception of the Marcan text. While it might be said (again, *ex hypothesi*) that Mark 'intended' his words to be taken as an intervention in a current controversy, it can also be said that Mark 'intended' the distance that he has in fact set between his statement and the current controversy by omitting any explicit reference to it, and that he therefore 'intended' his statement to be capable of communicating its verbal meaning in contexts where the baptism-controversy is no longer a live issue. This situation may be contrasted with the explicit indication in 1 Cor. 15.12 that Paul 'intended' his discussion of the resurrection of the dead as an intervention in a current controversy: 'If Christ is preached as raised from the dead, how can some of you say that there is no resurrection of the dead?' The initial contextual significance here remains permanently embedded in the text, it is comprised within the 'verbal meaning' of this text; but this very fact confirms the interpretative priority of verbal meaning over an (actual or hypothetical) initial contextual significance.[6]

The programme of reconstructing an original *Sitz im Leben* as an inter-pretative matrix for a text may stem from the sense that the verbal meaning alone is too 'obvious' to be interesting. It is in extracting non-obvious meanings out of apparently straightforward texts that interpreters can best demonstrate their own virtuosity. But they may also demonstrate their complete failure to comprehend the illocutionary and perlocutionary aspects of a text, read without any virtuosity and in accordance with its literal, verbal meaning. If we ask what Mark is *doing* in writing as he does, the initial answer is that he is *informing* or *reminding* his readers of something (that Jesus came from Nazareth and was baptized in the Jordan by John). The acts of informing and reminding are subject to the criterion of significance: one does not inform or remind one's addressee of just anything at all, but of that which one takes to be significant within the context of utterance. In this case, the significance of this act of informing or reminding lies in its broader context within the speech-act of *beginning a story*, governed as it is by conventions about the introduction of major characters, the providing of background information, and so on. Yet this story is not just one story among many, it is 'the gospel of Jesus Christ the Son of God' (Mark 1.1). What Mark is *doing* is not simply telling a story but *proclaiming the gospel.* (He is rightly described as an 'evangelist', and his book is rightly described as a 'gospel', that is, as one of a number of renderings of the single gospel.) The perlocutionary effect intended in the speech-act of proclaiming the gospel is the creation or confirmation of faith in Jesus Christ, the Son of God (cf. Mark 16.15–16), and to achieve this effect it is necessary (although not sufficient) to inform or remind one's addressees how they are to identify the bearer of the name 'Jesus Christ', who is to be the object of their faith. Correct identification is inseparable from faith itself; only faith correctly identifies Jesus Christ. It is not the case that Jesus can be correctly identified on the basis of an 'objective' biographical narrative, and that one then considers whether or not to believe in him. If Jesus *is* the Son of God, then the narrative that enables us to identify him must tell us not of an abstract 'Jesus of Nazareth' but of 'Jesus Christ the Son of God'. The sentence in which Jesus is first introduced into the narrative informs or reminds us that he came from Nazareth and was baptized by John in the Jordan, and what we learn here is already indispensable for faith: that the 'Son of God' is a human figure limited by the contingencies of a particular time and place, and that he is not too proud to share in a popular religious movement inspired by a revivalist preacher who practised baptism as a mark of repentance and confession.

The speech-act of proclaiming the gospel, with the intention of creating or confirming faith, presupposes – like any other speech-act – an institutional context. The evangelist is not called to a purely individual task: for God's gifts, that 'some should be apostles, some prophets, some evangelists', are given to individuals on behalf of and within the *church* (Eph. 4.11–12). As we have seen, a speech-act may through writing be indefinitely extended in space and time, so long as the institutional context that gives it its force is maintained. Mark's illocutionary act of proclaiming the gospel in writing may therefore be said to remain in force so long as there is an institutional context in which the intended perlocutionary effect of his speech-act continues to be felt. Where an institutional context changes so fundamentally that a text's intended perlocutionary effect ceases to operate, interpreters have the freedom to assess its continuing significance and interest as they will (provided they grasp its verbal meaning). Yet to claim such a freedom in the case of the Gospel of Mark would be an aggressive action directed against the life of the community in which the intended illocutionary and perlocutionary force of this canonical text remains intact. Understood in this light, it can be said that true 'significance' is to be found *in the single, verbal meaning itself,* that is, in its enduring illocutionary and perlocutionary force. The notion of a secondary, ephemeral 'contextual significance' is therefore dependent on and subordinate to the primary, universal significance this text claims by virtue of its role as 'gospel'.

2. Establishing the Literal Sense

(*i*) *Verbal meaning*

The notion that texts have a single, literal, verbal meaning ascribes a certain stability and solidity to the phenomenon of the text.[7] Yet the biblical texts have circulated and continue to circulate in a number of translations, each of them the work of specialists in the biblical languages, but constantly disagreeing with one another not just about matters of idiom but about the meaning itself. (If differences of idiom are always also differences of meaning, then the problem becomes still more acute.) Study of the texts in the original languages is no solution to this problem, since in many cases it will simply clarify *why* the translations differ so much from one another, disclosing the extent to which substantive differences between the translations are grounded in the problems posed by the 'originals'. Textual criticism and exegesis seek to restore the original text and its verbal meaning, yet the persistence of difference of opinion – publicly manifested in the form of the difference between the various translations – casts doubt on the stability both of the verbal meaning and of the text itself. It is not much comfort to be told that there was once a stable text with a stable meaning.

To illustrate this problem, we may consider a text from Ps. 42, which in its Masoretic form runs as follows: *'ēlleh 'ezkᵉrah wᵉeshpᵉkah 'ālay naphshî kî 'eᶜᵉbōr bassāk 'eddaddēm 'ad-bêth 'ᵉlōhîm bᵉqôl rinnah wᵉtôdah hāmôn ḥôgēg* (v. 5 MT). The first five words are rendered by RV as 'These things I remember, and pour out my soul within me'. The conjunction *kî* might be rendered as 'that' (or equivalent), in which case it introduces a clause stating the content of what is remembered. If, on the other hand, it is translated as 'for', then 'These things I remember' will refer back to the previous verse, where the psalmist recounts that 'my tears have been my food day and night, while people say to me continually, "Where is your God?"' A decision on this question is linked to the translation of *'eᶜᵉbōr* (from *ᶜbr*: 'pass over, pass through, go'). The Hebrew imperfect often has a future sense: 'These things I remember, and pour out my soul within me; for I shall go . . .' But it can also express habitual or continuous action in the past, in which case the meaning of *kî 'eᶜᵉbōr* would be 'that I used to go . . .'. The following phrase, *bassāk*, is obscure. Ignoring the vocalization, the noun *sk* may be related to the verb *swk*, which can mean 'enclose'. Thus in Ps. 76.3 (MT) it is said that 'his [God's] abode [*skw*] is in Salem, and his dwelling-place in Zion'. If that is the meaning, *kî 'eᶜᵉbōr bassāk* would mean ' . . . that I used to go [or, for I shall go] to the abode . . .', i.e. the temple. But the preposition *bᵉ* (in *bassāk*) would more naturally mean 'in' or 'with' rather than 'to', and an alternative would be to understand *sk* as a corruption of *sd*, 'assembly, company, throng'.

(The letter *daleth* is easily confused with a final *kaph*; and although *sd* is normally found in the form *swd*, Gen. 49.6 gives a precedent for the omission of the letter *waw*.) The psalmist will go/used to go to the abode/with the throng: there are already at least four possible translations. As for the next word, *'eddaddēm*, minor adjustments to the pointing would make this a first person singular Piel imperfect from the verb *ddh*, 'lead slowly, walk slowly' (cf. Isa. 38.15), together with a third person plural suffix: 'I led them slowly' (i.e. in procession?) would make good sense in the light of the sequel (*'ad-bêth 'elōhîm*, 'to the house of God'). Alternatively, one might follow the minority of Hebrew manuscripts which read *'drm* rather than *'ddm*, a plural from *'dyr*, 'noble, majestic' (cf. LXX, on which see below). On this reading, the psalmist speaks of going 'in the company of the noble to the house of God'. The remainder of the verse is more straightforward: *beqôl rinnah wetôdah hāmôn hôgēg* may be translated '. . . with the voice of joy and praise, a multitude keeping festival'. But *hāmôn* can mean 'sound' as well as 'multitude', and LXX's *ēchou heortazontōn* ('of the sound of those keeping festival') implies a Hebrew text reading *hôgegîm* ('those keeping festival') rather than MT's *hôgēg* ('keeping festival').

LXX translates *kî 'ee'bōr* as *hoti dieleusomai* ('because I will pass through'), taking the Hebrew imperfect as future in sense. Its equivalent for the Masoretes' *bassāk 'eddaddēm* is *en topō skēnēs thaumastēs* ('in [the] place of [the] wonderful tent'), *topos skēnēs* presumably paraphrasing *sk* ('abode') and *thaumastēs* perhaps representing some form of *'dyr* ('majestic, noble'), although not the plural form *'drm* attested in some Hebrew manuscripts. The LXX interpretation of this verse was faithfully transmitted to western Christendom through the Vulgate, with the central clause expressing a hope rather than the memory referred to at the beginning of the verse: *quoniam transibo in locum tabernaculi admirabilis, usque ad domum Dei* ('for I shall pass into the place of the wonderful tent, even to the house of God'). The only difference is that the LXX's use of the dative (*en topō*) is replaced by an accusative ('I shall pass *into* the wonderful tent'), which clarifies an otherwise obscure sense by deviating further from the Hebrew.

We thus have (at least) the following range of possible translations: 'These things I remember, and pour out my soul within me: [1] for I will go/for I used to go/how I used to go [2] to the abode of the noble ones/to the wonderful abode/with the assembly of the nobles/with the assembly, and I led them   to the house of God, with the voice of joy and praise, [3] a multitude keeping festival/the sound of those who keep festival'. The question is whether a text such as this (of which there are many in both Testaments) can possibly still fit the pattern of a speech-act whose verbal meaning and illocutionary and perlocutionary force remain basically intact, stabilized in the act of writing.

Here are nine English versions of this passage (Ps. 42.4 in the EVV, except for BCP and ASB [Ps. 42.4–5]; MT Ps. 42.5, LXX and Vg Ps. 41.5):[8]

> Now when I think thereon, I pour out my soul by myself: for I went with the multitude and brought them forth into the house of God, in the voice of praise and thanksgiving, among such as keep holy-day. (Coverdale/BCP)

> When I remember these things, I pour out my soul in me: for I had gone with the multitude, I went with them to the house of God, with the voice of joy and praise, with a multitude that kept holyday. (AV)

> These things I remember, and pour out my soul within me, how I went with the throng, and led them to the house of God, with the voice of joy and praise, a multitude keeping holyday. (RV)

> These things I remember, as I pour out my soul: how I went with the throng, and led them in procession to the house of God, with glad shouts and songs of thanksgiving, a multitude keeping festival. (RSV/NRSV)

> I remember, and my heart melts within me: I am on my way to the wonderful Tent, to the house of God, among cries of joy and praise and an exultant throng. (JB)

> As I pour out my soul in distress, I call to mind how I marched in the ranks of the great to the house of God, among exultant shouts of praise, the clamour of the pilgrims. (NEB)

> My heart breaks when I remember the past, when I went with the crowds to the house of God and led them as they walked along, a happy crowd, singing and shouting praise to God. (GNB)

> These things I remember as I pour out my soul: how I used to go with the multitude, leading the procession to the house of God, with shouts of joy and thanksgiving among the festive throng. (NIV)

> As I pour out my soul by myself I remember this: how I went to the house of the Mighty One, into the temple of God, to the shouts and songs of thanksgiving: a multitude keeping high festival. (ASB)

(1) Coverdale and AV render *kî* as 'for', following the Vulgate's *quoniam*, but in rendering the Hebrew imperfect with an English past tense rather than a future ('for I went', 'for I had gone') they part company with the Vulgate – and also with Luther's *denn ich wollte gerne hingehen* ('for I would gladly go . . .'), which perhaps takes *'eʿᵉbōr* as equivalent to the cohortative. In replacing 'for' with 'how', RV links the *kî*-clause with 'These things I remember' at the start of the verse. RV's 'how I went' is followed with minor variations (NEB, 'how I marched'; GNB, 'when I went') by the other versions, with the exception of JB's eccentric 'I remember . . . : I am on my way'. RSV, NEB, NIV and ASB reinforce the link between 'These things I remember' and 'how I went' by substituting an *as*-clause for RV's rendering of the intermediate words ('*as* I pour out . . .' rather than '*and* pour out').

(2) The Vulgate's *in locum tabernaculi admirabilis* (based on LXX's *en topō skēnēs thaumastēs*) is closely followed by JB ('to the wonderful Tent'). ASB too retains *sk* ('abode') and the emendation of MT's *'eddaddēm* to some form of *'dyr* ('majestic', cf. *thaumastos, admirabilis*), but it understands the phrase in strict parallel to *bêth 'elōhîm* in the following phrase (' . . . to the house of the Mighty One, into the temple of God'). Otherwise the versions accept Coverdale's 'with the multitude' (based perhaps on Luther's *mit dem Haufen*), and thus the emendation of *sk* to *sd*. Coverdale's 'and brought them forth' rests on a (Protestant) preference for MT over the Vulgate, and it is followed by AV ('I went with them'), RV ('and led them'), RSV ('and led them in procession') and NIV ('leading the procession'). NEB agrees with JB and ASB in taking *'eddaddēm* to be a corruption of *'dyr*, but finds here a reference not to the 'wonderful Tent' (JB) or the 'house of the Mighty One' (ASB) but to the psalmist's fellow-pilgrims ('in the ranks of the great') – following the minority of Hebrew manuscripts that read *'drm* rather than *'ddm*.

(3) At the end of the verse, LXX's *ēchou heortazontōn* and the Vulgate's *sonus epulantis* seem to be based on a Hebrew text reading *hᵃmôn ḥôgᵉgîm* ('the sound of those keeping festival') rather than MT's *hāmôn ḥôgēg* ('a multitude keeping festival'). Coverdale's 'among such as keep holy-day' betrays the influence of Luther's *unter dem Haufen derer, die da feiern* in its preference for the MT over the Vulgate and in its insertion of 'among'. AV's 'with a multitude that kept holyday' restores the noun suppressed by Coverdale's 'such', but is otherwise similar. Most modern versions abandon the attempt to coordinate this clause more precisely with the preceding one by inserting 'among' or 'with', but the older preference for MT here is retained. NEB's 'the clamour of the pilgrims' is the one exception: the LXX reading is preferred to MT on the grounds that this gives the phrase a slightly better sense in its context.

These difficulties may suggest that, in this case as in countless others, a stable text with a stable meaning is unattainable. Indeed, each of the translations might be seen as an act of bad faith. Each tacitly promises its readers that it faithfully renders the original text, without deviation, addition or subtraction, and that it is therefore an adequate substitute for the original. Each presents the façade of a stable text with a stable meaning; and yet this turns out to be an illusion when the various renderings are compared and contrasted with one another and when their differences are traced back to the deficiencies and ambiguities of the original (or rather, of the late Hebrew text that is itself a substitute for the lost original). Are these translations merely houses built on sand, outwardly stable yet with exceedingly shaky foundations? Are their readers aware of the extent to which decisions have been taken not because the evidence clearly points in one direction rather than another, but because decisions *must* be taken if the work of translation is ever to be completed? Translations conspire to conceal uncertainties. The selected difficulties that may be acknowledged in marginal notes are merely the tip of the iceberg. Rather than concealing uncertainties and differences, however, might one not choose to celebrate them? If meanings are fruitful and multiply, why should this be regarded as a misfortune?

If such a position seems attractive, one reason for this is postmodernity's fascination with the difference and the dissemination of meanings that are said to be at work within even the most stable-seeming structures. In particular, a biblical text in which nothing is fixed and in which everything opens up infinite interpretative possibilities would enable the interpreter to subvert and to erode the much-resented stabilities, dualities, hierarchies and orthodoxies that are so characteristic of Christian faith. If, however, one registers a conscientious objection to participating in postmodern games of this kind, then the case against textual stability becomes much less persuasive.

To begin with, the hypothesis of radical instability overlooks the fact that translators and interpreters may have good reasons for preferring one possibility to another. In the case of Ps. 42.4, RV's rendering of *kî 'e'ʿbōr* as 'how I went' is surely an improvement on LXX's future tense, Coverdale's 'for I went', and AV's 'for I had gone'.[9] Of these translations, RV alone links the *kî*-clause to 'These things I remember . . .', thus creating a poignant contrast between a present in which 'my tears have been my food day and night' (v. 3) and a remembered past of participation in the temple worship. It thereby characterizes the psalmist's present condition as one of *exile*, thus accounting for the use of the word 'again' when the psalmist expresses his confidence that 'I shall *again* praise him' (vv. 5, 11). There is in the context no other plausible referent for 'These things I remember', for the preceding verses have been speaking not of remembered but of *present* experience. It is therefore understandable that the more recent translations (with the partial exception only of JB) follow RV at this point, rightly recognizing that it makes better exegetical sense than LXX's future tense. That does not make it *impossible* that the psalmist intended the sense offered by LXX. One may have 'good reasons' for preferring one interpretative possibility to another even if they do not amount to an absolute 'proof'.

Similarly, there are good reasons for emending *sk* ('abode, dwelling-place') to *sd* ('throng, company'). An emendation either of this or of the following word (*'ddm*) is almost unavoidable, for if one translates *kî 'e'ʿbōr bassāk* as

'how I used to go to the dwelling-place', then the third plural suffix in '*ddm*
('I led *them* in procession') will lack an antecedent. Emending '*ddm* to some
form of '*dyr* does not seem plausible, however. LXX's *en topō skēnēs thaumastēs*
does not represent any likely Hebrew idiom, and JB's similar rendering is
obviously a translation of the Vulgate rather than the Masoretic text. ASB's
'house of the Mighty One' requires a more substantial emendation (of '*ddm*
to '*dyr*) than that of *sk* to *sd*. To read *ky* '*'br bsd* ('how I went with the
throng') enables one to give the preposition *bᵉ* a sense within its normal
range, and it harmonizes well with the conclusion of the verse, with its
emphasis on the communal nature of the temple-worship that the psalmist
recalls. Once again, these reasons for preferring the reading of RV, RSV and
NIV do not amount to a proof, but they are 'good reasons' nevertheless.

Discussion of this kind is integral to any interpretative practice that takes
seriously the problems of verbal meaning. It is of course possible to opt out
of such discussion, regarding it as yet another instance of a neurotic obsession
with stability and celebrating instead the merits of diversity and difference.
Yet to place all translations on the same level and to celebrate their diversity
is simply to declare that one has no interest in the arts of translation and
interpretation. From the standpoint of translation itself, diversity is *constituted*
by the concern for verbal meaning. Diversity exists because translators have
believed that some renderings of the Hebrew are better than others, and
because they have rejected the conservative view that older translations such
as the Septuagint, the Vulgate or the Authorized Version possess an authority
of their own apart from their relation to the Hebrew and Greek originals. To
dissent from an authoritative translation is not to concede that the text itself
is unstable and that its meanings are many. It is to recognize that, although
all translations are approximations, some approximations capture the single
sense of the text much more accurately than others, and that progress and
improvement are therefore possible.

At the root of the willingness to dissent from received translations is the
hypothesis of authorial intention. In considering the appropriate rendering
of a phrase such as *kî ᵉᵉbōr*, one should not mechanically translate 'for I shall
go', on the grounds that 'for' is often an appropriate rendering of *kî* and that
the Hebrew imperfect usually has a future sense (compare LXX and the
Vulgate here). That would be to consider the words in isolation from an
authorial intention, which is to be understood not as some subjective
occurrence lying behind the text but as the principle of the text's intelligibility.
To construe a series of marks as a series of words is already (in normal
circumstances) to assume that these words are combined with the intention
of communicating an intelligible meaning; and if the words objectively
embody an intention to communicate, then that intention can only be that

of the author.[10] In writing *kî 'e'bōr*, the author of Ps. 42 probably wished to communicate a sense approximating to 'how I went' rather than 'for I shall go'; for the whole verse, within its context, becomes more intelligible and transparent if the former rendering is preferred to the latter. To disregard authorial intention would be to refuse to strive for intelligibility and to allow the text to fall into relative or complete opacity and thus to lose the communicative function without which it is nothing. Intelligibility may sometimes necessitate certain interventions by the interpreter, as in the case of the minor emendations that render the unintelligible *bassāk 'eddaddēm* intelligible as '. . . with the throng, I led them'. In such an intervention, it is assumed that unintelligibility arises out of the loss of an initial intelligibility in the process of transmission, and that it is the duty of translators to attempt to restore this initial intelligibility. Even if an alien sense is unknowingly imposed on the text, its intelligibility will make it a better representative of the lost sense than any over-scrupulous attempt to preserve the opacity of the received text.

Decisions about the meaning of words can be said to appeal to 'objective' criteria. The truism that there is no such thing as 'absolute objectivity' is much less significant and interesting than the fact that there is an 'objectivity' which is indispensable for all textual interpretation. It is indispensable for three main reasons:

(1) The concept of objectivity implies a relative freedom from particular, local interests. The question whether to give *kî 'e'bōr* a past or a future sense may be distinguished from the subsequent question how best to render this phrase in the language of the translator's own linguistic community. (Thus the modern English translations are mainly agreed about the sense despite differences of wording.) It cannot be said that interpreters' decisions on this point are determined by contingent criteria operative within their own local interpretative communities – as though one rendering met the needs of Greek-speaking Alexandrian Jews in about the third century BC, whereas the other is more attuned to the interests of English-speaking readers of the nineteenth and twentieth centuries AD. Nor can it be said that the two renderings reflect the ideologies through which certain élite groups (to which the translators no doubt belonged) sought to maintain their hold on social and political power. The two competing renderings of *kî 'e'bōr* derive simply from a difference of opinion about the meaning of the Hebrew phrase in its context. Contingent communal factors may certainly be reflected even in minor decisions about translation, and they may sometimes be highly significant – for translation is always also a political act. Yet, in the present case, both translations of *kî 'e'bōr* appear to be primarily motivated by the concern to

render the Hebrew words as accurately as possible, and (from their own standpoint) they must be judged solely by their success or failure in this endeavour. To understand them as characteristic products of different interpretative communities would be to overlook their common interest in the accurate rendering of a sacred text.

(2) The concept of objectivity implies that some of the questions which interpreters ask about texts have a single right answer, and that this answer remains right (and other proposed answers remain wrong) in all circumstances. Whether *kî ʾeʿbōr* has a past or a future sense appears to be one such question. Might the author have meant both? In pressing the choice between the two, are we giving expression to a typically western and androcentric yearning for clarity and resistance to opacity? But the linguistic feature in question – the co-determination of meaning by context – is not specific to western languages: words that, in themselves, might bear two or more different meanings can nevertheless bear a single meaning, to the exclusion of any others, in the context of a particular communicative action. The reduction of ambiguity and the avoidance of misunderstanding are hardly a distinctively western concern; indeed, that view is itself the product of a typically western idealizing of the non-western 'Other'. While some texts may deliberately exploit the possibility of ambiguity, this does not seem to be characteristic of the poetry of the psalter. In any case, the suggestion that both possible senses are intended would merely constitute a third option alongside the preferences for the past or for the future renderings. In confirming the assumption that there is a right answer to the question, and that the other answers are inadequate, this suggestion would *assume* the concept of objectivity rather than subverting it.

(3) The concept of objectivity implies the existence of criteria which enable interpreters to assess the relative merits of the various proposed solutions to a problem. In advocating a particular solution to the exclusion of others, one appeals to criteria which structure both the positive and the negative dimensions of one's argument; and one appeals to these criteria not just because they happen to be accepted in one's own local interpretative community but because they are the normative rules for participation in the discussion. It is impossible to specify in advance exactly what these rules are, or how they are to be applied. Like driving a car or playing the piano, translation and interpretation are rule-governed activities in which one learns and internalizes the rules and their application in an 'apprenticeship' consisting of instruction, imitation and practice, and not by theoretical reflection. Yet it is possible to observe the operation of the rules or criteria by reflecting on what takes place in interpretative practice. For example, to assign a past sense

to *kî 'eʿbōr* requires one to show (*i*) that this falls within the semantic range of the Hebrew imperfect (clear parallels would have to be produced); (*ii*) that this increases the transparency of the sentence in which the phrase is embedded; (*iii*) that the meaning proposed for the sentence as a whole is consistent with the wider context; (*iv*) that alternative proposals fail to meet these criteria. Applying these general criteria necessitates further criteria which enable one to determine what counts as transparency or as consistency with the wider context. There is no need to pursue this identification of criteria any further, for they are encoded in the *practice* of interpretation – just as the rules for negotiating a sharp bend in the road or a Bach fugue are encoded in certain learned practices and need not be exhaustively identified through theoretical reflection. In each case, the criteria allow some scope for individual performance. No single negotiation of a bend, fugue or text will be exactly like any other, and, within a certain range, it is not always possible or necessary to show that one such performance is any better or worse than another. Yet this scope for individual performance does not make the criteria for determining whether these activities are done well or badly any less objective. In all three cases, it is easy to imagine circumstances in which it is beyond dispute that a particular performance has been incompetently executed – where, in other words, the rules for correct performance have been flouted. To ascribe these rules to 'social convention' and to deny that they possess 'objective status' would only be justified if one had in mind contexts in which the same activities were carried out in accordance with a quite different set of rules, and if one wished to assert the equal validity of the different performing styles. In the absence of any plausible alternative set of rules for determining the meaning of a sentence in the Hebrew psalter, an 'objective' interpretation will be one that operates within the space opened up by the existing rules.[11]

(*ii*) *Illocutionary and perlocutionary force*

The hypothesis of the determinacy of verbal meaning requires an understanding of authorial intention as the presupposition of a text's intelligibility, and implies as its consequence the necessity of an objective interpretative practice. However, establishing the verbal meaning of a text is a necessary but not a sufficient condition for establishing its literal sense. The literal sense is the sense intended by the author in so far as this authorial intention is objectively embodied in the words of the text. But the intention embodied in a communicative action goes beyond the expression of a series of words bearing a certain meaning, as if for its own sake. What is intended in communicative action is that determinate meaning should be the vehicle of illocutionary and perlocutionary force.[12] In speaking, one is acting so as to bring about a particular effect, for utterance is not an end in itself but intends a response on the part of the one addressed. Like the translator, the addressee of an utterance must decode the meaning of the words; there can be no appropriate response without comprehension. And yet the converse is also true: for comprehension is only the means to the true end of communicative action, which is responsive action. The author intends not only a meaning but also an action, directed towards another, which aims to evoke a response. An adequate interpretation of the literal sense of a text will seek to explain not only what the author is *saying* but also what he or she is *doing*.

There are, perhaps, residual uncertainties in our understanding of Ps. 42.4, and the question is whether and how far these impair the psalm's capacity to embody effective communicative action. The uncertainties may be seen as an instance of the residual opacity of all but the simplest of speech-acts. Where a speech-act takes place and succeeds in evoking comprehension and the intended response, that need not entail complete transparency or total comprehension. Whether the fault lies in the execution of the utterance, its reception, or both, even successful communicative action is often attended by a degree of opacity. Confronted by a border guard speaking a language I do not understand, I conclude, correctly, that he is performing the speech-act of requesting or commanding me to produce my passport: and, in this case, the success of the speech-act is compatible with an almost complete failure to comprehend the verbal meaning of the words that are uttered. In the case of the psalm text, communication is not seriously impaired by the difficulties in establishing the text and its verbal meaning. The psalmist remembers the joy of participating in communal worship at the temple during the festivals, and contrasts this joyful past with the sorrow of exile in the present. He may or may not have led the worshippers in procession (RSV), and he may or may not have spoken of 'marching in the ranks of the great' (NEB), but such problems do no more than introduce a slight opacity into a picture that remains basically clear. If the reference is to the future rather than the past (LXX, Vulgate), that would make more of a difference. Yet, even on this view, this verse would still be rooted in memory, projected into the future in the form of hope. There would still be a contrast between the ideal of being at home in the house of the Lord and the reality of being apart from him. The hope that 'I shall again praise him' (v. 5) implies that the idealized past and future are identified with each other. It therefore cannot be said that the communicative action embodied in this text is severely impaired even by its traditional Greek and Latin forms.

In composing this psalm, the psalmist is not simply giving expression to his innermost feelings about the harshness of exile and its contrast with a life lived in the vicinity of the house of the Lord. On that view the text functions as a mirror, reflecting the psalmist's experience back to him; this poetry is seen as a communing with self for the sake of self, and the intrusion of the reader into this private place is left unaccounted for. However obvious such a view may seem, it ignores the fact that as communicative action writing is normally directed towards others, with the intention of conveying a communicable, public meaning that evokes a definite response. This text is intended for *use*. In its use of the first person singular, it invites its readers to step inside it, using it as a means of articulating, shaping and interpreting their own experience of the tension between a tear-filled present, in which the question 'Where is your God?' is inescapable, and the remembered and hoped-for reality of true worship, in which the joyful, definitive answer to that question lies concealed. The memory is the source not only of the hope but also of the present tension. Were it not for that memory, one might settle in 'the land of Jordan and of Hermon' (v. 6) and make it one's home, no longer subjecting oneself to the distress of thirst for a God whose absence is so obvious that the frivolous, the malicious and the serious-minded alike constantly bring it to one's attention (vv. 1–3). The psalm does not require readers whose experience exactly matches that of its author: they need no more have had any first-hand experience of worship in the Jerusalem temple than they are obliged to dwell in the land of Jordan and of Hermon. But, if the psalm is to be used properly (if it is to reach its intended goal as a communicative action), then its readers must be capable of discovering in their own experience a tension analogous to that of which and out of which the psalmist speaks. Only so will the psalm serve to articulate, shape and interpret their experience; it cannot bestow on that experience anything that is not already latent within it. Indeed, as a scriptural text among other scriptural texts, this is a text for repeated use, and its readers will not normally be encountering it for the first time. It gives poignant expression to a tension already familiar to readers whose understanding of self and world is mediated by the scriptural texts. It does not conjure up a previously unheard-of interpretation of experience, as if out of nowhere. It offers no radical novelty, for it is primarily intended for the use of readers who so indwell the tradition in which it stands that it comes naturally to them to accept its rendering of experience as true and persuasive.

Speech-acts require an institutional context if they are to achieve their intended effect; to make a promise or to issue a command presupposes a complex set of prior conditions and relationships. If speech-acts are embodied in written texts, their intended illocutionary and perlocutionary force as communicative actions requires institutional continuities extended through the space and time that they traverse. The possibility of adopting the role of the intended addressee of Ps. 42 is grounded not only in the text itself but also in the reality of institutional continuities that guarantee the identity of the God referred to in this psalm with the God who is still the object of worship. A Canaanite text expressing a longing for communion with Baal could no longer achieve its communicative intention, however attractive and moving it might be as a poem. As a communicative action, such a poem would presuppose a community bound together by a set of practices, roles, material objects, beliefs and stories relating to the god Baal. Its intended addressees would be members of that community, and with the disappearance of the community the poem's intended communicative role would be brought to an end. As an intentional communicative action, its effects lie irretrievably in the past. It is a symptom of this situation that the text itself disappears from circulation and can only be recovered by archaeologists and scholars who read it – against its intention – as a communication of information relating to the society in which it was produced. Within the modern, scholarly interpretative community devoted to the study of the ancient Near East, the recovered text will once again be valued, and with the help of other ancient artefacts and of modern analytical techniques it may even be possible to imagine 'what it must have felt like' to utter this text as a devout worshipper of Baal. However, that does not mean that the poem's intended effect is revived. As an intentional communicative action, the poem remains as dead as ever, and painstaking study of its corpse can bring about only an imaginary reanimation. The poem intends to incite its readers to the worship of Baal, and the new readers it has acquired for itself will have no intention of complying.[13]

In contrast, Ps. 42 is not a corpse – the empty shell of a communicative action whose illocutionary and perlocutionary force expired along with the institutional matrix that enabled and sustained it. It does not require any special 'faith perspective' to make this point – only a recognition that this text is still in communal and individual use and that the communicative intention embodied in it is therefore still operative. The common assumption that current usage of a psalm (or any other scriptural text) is somehow detached from an 'original' communicative intention, understood as confined to the author's immediate historical context, is untenable. It misunderstands authorial intention as a purely psychological event that precedes and constrains the words, exerting a continuing influence on the text from the outside. Against this view, authorial intention is to be seen as primarily embodied in the words the author wrote – in their verbal meaning together with their illocutionary and perlocutionary force. It is true that speech-acts do indeed presuppose a particular, determinate context. But it is integral to written communicative actions that their effect may be indefinitely extended in space and in time, and that the scope of this effect is largely beyond the control of the author. If the relative permanence of the written communicative action subjects it to the contingencies of an open future, then that is what is intended in the act of writing itself. In writing as he does, the author of this psalm intends a communicative action whose full scope lies beyond his knowledge or control. His communicative action occurs on the basis of certain institutional conditions, and he writes in the awareness that the extension of these institutional conditions in time and space may serve to extend the scope of his communicative action. Indeed, other psalms express a certain confidence in their own survival into the distant future: 'Let this be recorded for a generation yet to come, so that a people yet unborn may praise the Lord' (Ps. 102.18). Yet it is not necessary for an orientation towards an open future to be explicitly acknowledged, for this is implicit in the act of writing itself.

(iii) The relation to the centre

A significant extension of the scope of a written communication will often occur only as the text is coordinated with other texts, so that there gradually emerges a 'canonical' collection of writings set aside for various normative roles in, for example, educational and liturgical practices. In some cases, the canonical context serves not only to extend the scope of a written communication but also to impose certain restrictions on the communicative intention embodied in it. The significance of this point may be illustrated by contrasting the continuing effectiveness of the communicative action embodied in Ps. 42 with the restrictions that the Christian canon imposes on the communicative action embodied in Ps. 137.

There are obvious parallels between the two psalms. Like Ps. 42, Ps. 137 is written out of the bitter experience of exile and the loss of the holy place:

> By the waters of Babylon, there we sat down and wept, when we remembered Zion. On the willows there we hung up our lyres. For there our captors required of us songs, and our tormentors mirth, saying, 'Sing us one of the songs of Zion!' How shall we sing the Lord's song in a foreign land? If I forget you, O Jerusalem, let my right hand wither! Let my tongue cleave to the roof of my mouth, if I do not remember you, if I do not set Jerusalem above my highest joy! Remember, O Lord, against the Edomites the day of Jerusalem, how they said, 'Rase it! Rase it!' (Ps. 137.1–7)

The author of Ps. 42 also weeps, is subjected to taunts, and remembers Zion (Ps. 42.3–4). Ps. 137 depicts the tension between remembered past and present experience in particularly sharp and concrete form. The specification of time and place (the exile in Babylon following the destruction of Jerusalem) gives the experience that is rendered here a precise and exclusive focus that is absent in Ps. 42, where (despite the reference to 'the land of Jordan and of

Hermon') experience is rendered in terms general enough to be open to a variety of applications. Ps. 137 is more concerned than Ps. 42 to communicate a *particular* experience. It functions as an urgent, intense appeal not to forget Jerusalem, even though return to Jerusalem is beyond the bounds of present possibilities. It does not counsel the exiles, as Jeremiah did, to 'build houses and live in them', to 'plant gardens and eat their produce' and 'to seek the welfare of the city where I [the Lord] have sent you into exile . . . , for in its welfare you will find your welfare' (Jer. 29.6–7). Babylon is, simply, the enemy:

> O daughter of Babylon, you devastator! Happy shall he be who requites you with what you have done to us! Happy shall he be who takes your little ones and dashes them against the rock! (Ps. 137.8–9)

Unlike Ps. 42, this text does not express the hope that 'I shall again praise him, my help and my God' (Ps. 42.5–6, 11). It expresses instead a prayer for vengeance, directed first against the Edomites because of their unbrotherly conduct but above all against Babylon herself. The violated order of the world will only be restored when the children of Babylon are subjected to the same outrages as their fathers have perpetrated against Jewish children.

The question is whether and to what extent this text can continue to fulfil its role as an intentional communicative action. The particularity of its setting is not in itself a difficulty. Although, unlike Ps. 42, it speaks on the basis of a highly specific experience, its illocutionary force lies in its urgent appeal not to forget Jerusalem; its intended reader is therefore familiar with the pressures of a pagan environment and the temptation of amnesia, which he or she is exhorted to resist at all costs. For Christian readers, the elaboration of the Babylon/Jerusalem contrast in Rev. 14–22 serves to extend the scope of the earlier text, as does the description of the Christian life as 'exile' in 1 Pet. 1.1, 17; 2.11. But for the same Christian readers, the conclusion of the psalm presents a difficulty. The urgent imperative not to forget Jerusalem is followed by a blessing on those who perpetrate frightful acts of violence on the children of Jerusalem's enemies. The implied reader is expected to acquiesce in this judgment, and the text may therefore be said to perform the speech-act of inciting hatred – hatred of a particularly intense and extreme kind.

There are no general ethical or pragmatic criteria which could determine that this speech-act is inappropriate. The writer's hostility towards the children of Babylon is not unmotivated but originates in actual atrocities committed against Jewish children. If, perhaps with this psalm in mind, survivors of Auschwitz expressed the desire that their tormentors' children should suffer the treatment that their fathers inflicted on Jewish children, the proper response might be to keep silence rather than to deliver a lecture on the importance of forgiveness. In an extreme situation such as this, and as part of the holy scripture of the Jewish community, Ps. 137 as a whole might still enact its communicative intention in the most direct manner.

In its context within Christian scripture, however, that could never be the case. Christian victims of oppression could never legitimately appropriate this psalm in its entirety, however extreme their sufferings; and its use in Christian liturgical contexts can in no circumstances be justified.[14] Although the psalm as a whole belongs to Christian scripture, it is not permitted to enact its total communicative intention: for all communicative actions embodied in holy scripture are subject to the criteria established by the speech-act that lies at the centre of Christian scripture, the life, death and resurrection of Jesus as the enfleshment and the enactment of the divine Word. In this case, the relevant criteria are derived in the first instance from passages such as the following:

> You have heard that it was said, 'You shall love your neighbour and hate your enemy'. But I say to you, Love your enemies and pray for those who persecute you, so that you may be sons of your Father who is in heaven . . . (Matt. 5.43–45a)

> And he sent messengers ahead of him, who went and entered a village of the Samaritans, to make ready for him; but the people would not receive him, because his face was set toward Jerusalem. And when his disciples James and John saw it, they said, 'Lord, do you want us to bid fire come down from heaven and consume them [as Elijah did]?' But he turned and rebuked them [and he said, 'You do not know what manner of spirit you are of; for the Son of man came not to destroy human lives but to save them]'. (Luke 9.52–55)

> And when they came to the place which is called The Skull, there they crucified him, and the criminals one on the right and one on the left. And Jesus said, 'Father, forgive them; for they know not what they do.' (Luke 23.33–34)

> God shows his love for us in that while we were yet sinners Christ died for us . . . If while we were enemies we were reconciled to God by the death of his Son, much more, now that we are reconciled, shall we be saved by his life. (Rom. 5.8,10)

These passages are cited in order to show that, within the context of Christian scripture and the Christian community, Ps. 137 as a whole is not permitted to exercise one of its intended perlocutionary functions, which is to incite hatred (deserved hatred) of one's enemies. It is not the case that New Testament texts possess any inherent hermeneutical privilege in relation to the Old Testament; for the New Testament texts are significant only by virtue of their witness to the possibility of an alternative practice in relation to one's enemies, rooted in the practice of Jesus as embodying God's love for his enemies. There may be many other cases where, on the basis of criteria derived from the centre of holy scripture, texts from the Old Testament speak more adequately than texts from the New. There may also be many cases where criteria derived from the centre can lay claim to Old Testament support. These criteria are not intended to deny the particularity of the Old Testament witness to the divine–human relationship, nor do they rule out the possibility that passages such as Ps. 137.8–9 retain a positive role of some kind. The point is simply to assert that Christian scripture is not a random assortment of texts but that it has a particular shape, characterized above all by the enclosure of a normative centre by the two distinct canonical collections, and that this must affect the literal interpretation of individual scriptural texts of both Testaments.[15]

In contrast to Ps. 137, Ps. 42 retains its intended illocutionary and perlocutionary force in its context within Christian scripture, where it serves to articulate and to interpret Christian experiences of 'exile' from the presence of God. Here too, however, theological interpretation must uncover the connections with the centre. When, in Gethsemane, Jesus says, 'My soul is very sorrowful, even unto death' (Matt. 26.38, Mark 14.34), he appears to be alluding to this psalm (*perilupos estin hē psuchē mou*, compare *hina ti perilupos ei, psuchē*; [Pss. 41.6, 12, 42.5 LXX]). In addressing God even in Gethsemane as 'my Father' (Matt. 26.39) or as 'Abba, Father' (Mark 14.36), Jesus in his distress recalls past experiences grounded in the joyful reality of God's being as his Father and his own being as God's Son (cf. Matt. 11.25–27), and he longs to recover that joy through the removal of the bitter cup of exile. In declaring his willingness to drink the cup given him by his Father, Jesus expresses his confidence that beyond the sorrowful night of exile there lies the joyful day when hope in God will be vindicated. 'I shall again praise him, my help and my God' (Ps. 42.5–6) – that is, on Easter Day, when 'the stone which the builders rejected' will become 'the head of the corner' (Ps. 118.23; Matt. 21.42). After the distress of Gethsemane, Jesus must descend still lower, into the chaotic darkness of Golgotha, where, again echoing the psalmist, he cries, 'My God, my God, why have you forsaken me?' (Ps. 22.1; Matt. 27.46). Only by way of this darkness can he fulfil the promise that 'I will tell of thy name to my brothers and sisters, in the midst of the congregation I will praise thee' (Ps. 22.22; Heb. 2.11–12). His Easter joy is not his alone: when he praises the one who is his help and his God he does so in the midst of the congregation of his disciples. Their souls too have been sorrowful, and their sorrow is turned into joy as his sorrow is turned into joy: 'When a woman is in travail she has sorrow, because her hour has come; but when she is delivered of the child, she no longer remembers the anguish, for joy that a child is born into the world. So you have sorrow now, but I will see you

again and your hearts will rejoice, and no one will take your joy from you'
(John 16.21–22). The disciples' experience follows the pattern of Jesus', but
the pattern itself is anticipated in the psalmists' rendering of their experience
of the God of Israel in terms of sorrow preceding joy. Thus it becomes clear
on Easter Day that not only the law and the prophets but also the psalms
speak of how 'the Christ should suffer and on the third day rise from the
dead' (Luke 24.44–45).

The rendering in Ps. 42 of the sorrow of exile and the hope of future joy
should therefore be seen as anticipating the events of death and resurrection
that lie at the heart of holy scripture. And yet the psalm retains its own particularity. It does not speak directly – let alone exclusively – of the experience
of Jesus, although as part of the scriptural matrix of Jesus' experience it does
provide resources on which he and his followers can draw as they seek to
grasp the full scope of the events of death and resurrection that lie at the
centre. Jesus' experience of Gethsemane, Golgotha and Easter Day is uniquely
his own. It is not reducible to the experience rendered in the psalm, any
more than the experience rendered in the psalm is reducible to the experience
of Jesus. The centre does not engulf or overwhelm the scriptural texts that
bear witness to it, but allows them to bear their witness from a position at a
certain distance from the centre which is uniquely and irreducibly their own.

The implications for theological hermeneutics of these extended discussions
of particular texts may be summarized as follows:

(1) The *literal sense* of the biblical texts comprises (*i*) verbal meaning,
(*ii*) illocutionary and perlocutionary force, and (*iii*) the relation to the centre.
As communicative actions, the texts seek to convey a meaning in order to
evoke a particular response. To concern oneself with the literal sense is
therefore to reflect on 'application' as well as verbal meaning, for without
this dimension the texts are no longer understood as communicative actions.
The criteria by which scriptural communicative actions are assessed derive
from God's definitive communicative action in the incarnation of the Word.

(2) To grasp the verbal meaning and the illocutionary and perlocutionary
force of a text is to understand the *authorial intention* embodied in it. Authorial
intention is the principle of a text's intelligibility, and cannot be detached
from the text itself. The capacity of writing to extend the scope of a speech-
act in space and time precludes an understanding of authorial intention purely
in terms of the author's immediate historical context.

(3) A text's verbal meaning, illocutionary and perlocutionary force, and
relation to the centre precede and transcend the additional meanings or

significances it may acquire as it is read in different communal contexts. *Objective interpretation* concerns itself with the primary and determinate aspects of a text's existence. While local, contextual concerns will often and rightly leave their mark on interpretative practice, they should not deprive the text of its proper vocation, which is to represent, in frail human language, a divine communicative action which does not arise from among ourselves but addresses us from without.

NOTES

1. For typical expressions of one or more of these positions, see W. Brueggemann, *The Bible and Postmodern Imagination: Texts under Negotiation*, London: SCM Press, 1993, 1–25; D. J. A. Clines, 'Possibilities and Priorities of Biblical Interpretation in an International Perspective', *Biblical Interpretation* I (1993), 67–87; G. Phillips, 'Exegesis as Critical Praxis: Reclaiming History and Text from a Postmodern Perspective', *Semeia* 51 (1990), 7–50; E. Schüssler Fiorenza, 'The Ethics of Biblical Interpretation: Decentering Biblical Scholarship', *JBL* 107 (1988), 3–17.

2. This discussion of writing as a speech-act is indebted to J. L. Austin, *How to do Things with Words*, Oxford: Clarendon Press, 1975²; John R. Searle, *Speech Acts: An Essay in the Philosophy of Language*, Cambridge: Cambridge University Press, 1969; Mary Louise Pratt, *Towards a Speech Act Theory of Literary Discourse*, Bloomington: Indiana University Press, 1977; Jürgen Habermas, *The Philosophical Discourse of Modernity*, ET Cambridge: Polity Press, 1985, esp. ch. XI; and Anthony C. Thiselton, *New Horizons in Hermeneutics: The Theory and Practice of Transforming Biblical Reading*, London: Marshall Pickering, 1992, esp. chs. VIII, XV–XVI. In the context of biblical scholarship, Thiselton's emphasis on the importance of speech-act theory in countering the hermeneutics of indeterminacy is especially significant.

3. The terminology is J. L. Austin's. To perform a 'locutionary act' is to utter 'a certain sentence with a certain sense and reference' (*How to do Things with Words*, 109). In doing so, we also perform an 'illocutionary act', an act that occurs *in* (*il-*) the act of locution – e.g. asking or answering a question; giving information, an assurance or a warning; announcing a verdict or an intention (98). We also perform a 'perlocutionary act': we intend, *by means of* (*per-*) the locutionary and illocutionary act, to bring about some effect – e.g. convincing, persuading, deterring, surprising or misleading (109).

4. This distinction between an unchanging 'meaning' and shifting, contextual 'significance' is derived from E. D. Hirsch, *Validity in Interpretation*, New Haven and London: Yale University Press, 1967, 6–10. One problem with this terminology is that to claim that 'meaning' becomes 'significant' only within certain contexts is to overlook the possibility that meaning may be inherently and therefore transcontextually significant.

5. Once they have received meaning, readers may engage in various creative activities: they may draw implications from it, apply it to their own circumstances, formulate counter-arguments or questions, link it to what is said elsewhere, and so on. Conventions governing the practice of formal 'interpretation' may permit interpreters to engage in these and many other activities, all of which presuppose the primacy and the stability of verbal meaning.

6. The historical-critical tendency to conflate the literal sense with an alleged 'original meaning' is rightly criticized by Brevard Childs: 'Because of the preoccupation of exegesis with origins, the literal sense dissolves before the hypothetical reconstructions of the original situations on whose recovery correct interpretation allegedly depends. Instead of achieving a new level of objectivity by restricting the primary sense of the text to its literal meaning, the plain sense has become the captive of countless speculative theories of historical and literary reconstruction' ('The Sensus Literalis of Scripture: An Ancient and Modern Problem', in H. Donner, R. Hanhart, R. Smend [eds.], *Beiträge zur Alttestamentlichen Theologie* [FS for W. Zimmerli], Göttingen: Vandenhoeck & Ruprecht, 1977, 80–93; 90–91).

7. 'Verbal meaning' may be defined as 'whatever someone has willed to convey by a particular sequence of linguistic signs and which can be conveyed (shared) by means of those linguistic signs' (E. D. Hirsch, *Validity in Interpretation*, 31). 'Verbal meaning' refers in the first instance to sentences rather than to complete texts.

8. Abbreviations: EVV = English versions; MT = Masoretic Text (R. Kittel [ed.], *Biblia Hebraica*, Stuttgart: Württembergische Bibelanstalt, 1973[16], from which some of the textual information discussed here is drawn); LXX = Septuagint; Vg = Vulgate; BCP = Book of Common Prayer (1662), incorporating Miles Coverdale's translation of the psalms (1535); AV = Authorized Version (King James Version, 1611); RV = Revised Version (1881–85); RSV/NRSV = Revised Standard Version/New Revised Standard Version (1952/1989); JB = Jerusalem Bible (1966); NEB = New English Bible (1970); GNB = Good News Bible (1976); NIV = New International Version (1978); ASB = Alternative Service Book: Services authorized for use in the Church of England in conjunction with The Book of Common Prayer (1980).

9. Numerous examples of the use of the Hebrew imperfect 'to express actions, &c., which were *repeated* in the past' are given in E. Kautzsch (ed.), *Gesenius' Hebrew Grammar*, ET Oxford: Clarendon Press, 1910[2], §107e. 'How I used to go' would perhaps be slightly more accurate than 'how I went'.

10. As P. D. Juhl argues, 'There is a logical connection between statements about the meaning of a literary work and statements about the author's intention such that a statement about the meaning of a work *is* a statement about the author's intention' (*Interpretation: An Essay in the Philosophy of Literary Criticism*, Princeton: Princeton University Press, 1980, 12).

11. Hans Frei argues that literal or 'plain' readings are 'warranted by their agreement with a religious community's rules for reading its sacred text' ('The "Literal Reading" of Biblical Narrative in the Christian Tradition: Does It Stretch or Will It Break?', in his *Theology and Narrative: Selected Essays*, eds. G. Hunsinger and W. C. Placher, New York and Oxford: Oxford University Press, 1993, 117–52; 144). According to Frei, there is in Christian tradition a broad consensus over the 'rules' that the gospel narratives are irreducibly about Jesus and cannot be allegorized into referring to anything else (a tendency which Frei detects in the work of Paul Ricoeur and David Tracy), and that Old and New Testaments must be read as a unity (144–45). The question is where such rules come from. Are they authoritative for the community because the texts themselves require to be understood along these lines, or are they authoritative because the community has 'arbitrarily' decided to read the text in certain ways and to exclude other readings that might appear to be equally plausible in themselves? The relationship between the literal sense and biblical translation suggests that, here at least, the first alternative must be preferred to the second; and the problem for Frei would then be that the rules for correct translation are not specific to the Christian community.

12. For the meaning of these terms, see note 3.

13. In current conditions, however, it is conceivable that attempts might be made to revive the communicative intention embodied in a Canaanite text addressed not to the masculine Baal but to Asherah, the Canaanite mother-goddess.

14. In the liturgical use of this psalm, vv. 7–9 are designated as optional in the Church of England's unofficial Prayer Book of 1927–28, the *Shorter Prayer Book* (1946) and the *Alternative Service Book* (1980).

15. The metaphor of the centre is derived from Karl Barth, *Church Dogmatics* III/1, ET Edinburgh: T. & T. Clark, 1958, 24. It is unfortunate that canonical approaches to biblical interpretation, pioneered by Brevard Childs, James A. Sanders and others, do not take adequate account of this feature of the Christian Bible.

Chapter 4

***

Erasing the Text:
Readings in Neo-Marcionism

The prefix *neo-* denotes a particular mode of recourse to the past. It presupposes fundamental, irreversible change, a breach between now and then that precludes continuity and repetition. But it also presupposes an openness of the present towards the past and of the past towards the present, such that, in this new present, an old constellation of ideas and strategies (an *-ism* associated with a proper name, perhaps) is released from its confinement to a past historical era in order to fulfil new roles in the new present. It is, however, the present that determines, structures and limits those roles. The present does not remain defenceless in the face of incursions from the past. Its openness to the past takes the form of a mesh that allows through only what is required for present usage, and many of the original interconnections are simply disregarded. *Neo-* denotes an occurrence that remains firmly rooted in the present.

In the history of Christian theology, the name of Marcion represents a simple, well-known combination of ideas which the church deemed to be unacceptable. The occurrence of a 'neo-Marcionism' would not entail the mere repetition of those ideas, for at some points the church's arguments against Marcion have proved so successful that reversion to Marcion's original positions is difficult, if not impossible. There could be a 'neo-Marcionism' without the hypothesis that there are two Gods, the creator who is just and the redeemer who is good, since a dualism of *this* kind has not proved an enduring problem for Christian theology. What *has* been an enduring problem is the associated hypothesis that the Old Testament is not to be regarded as part of Christian scripture; and it has been a problem because, whether in ancient or modern forms, it gives radical expression to a more widespread Christian unease about the status and function of the Old Testament.

In the modern period, the Marcionite hypothesis has been asserted by Schleiermacher, Harnack and Bultmann (among others), and it is with their work that the present study is concerned.[1] Their names are not linked with Marcion's for merely polemical purposes: to associate a modern theological proposal with the name of an ancient heretic or heresy need not be simply a gesture of rejection but can fulfil a genuine heuristic function. In this instance, the formulation 'neo-Marcionism' is used with reference to a particular hypothesis: that the erasure of scriptural texts from both Testaments is motivated by a desire for immediate encounter that seeks to dissolve all forms of textual mediation. Textuality is identified with Jewishness, the letter that kills by corrupting the original purity of the gospel; and neo-Marcionism proposes to cleanse theology and church from the defilement of the Jewish letter. While such a proposal, put forward by German theologians, is now ideologically unfashionable in this form, the challenge of neo-Marcionite theologies can be met not by emphatic assertions about the 'Jewish roots' of Christian faith but by analysing and criticizing the quest for immediacy that dispenses with the Jewish letter. Christian faith cannot dispense with writing. Its reliance on written, scriptural texts is not accidental but of its essence.

1. Schleiermacher

In a recent study of the relationship between Schleiermacher and Calvin, Brian Gerrish has pointed to certain structural similarities between the 1559 edition of Calvin's *Institutes* and Schleiermacher's *Glaubenslehre* (1821–22; 1830–31[2]).[2] Both works offer an account of Christian faith as a whole; both take as their starting-point a general anthropological tendency towards *pietas* or *Frömmigkeit* in relation to the divine origin of all being (*Inst.* 1.1–3; *Gl.* §§3–6); and both argue that this original relationship has been obscured by sin and that we become aware of it only through being redeemed (*Inst.* 1.6.2, 4, 2.6.1; *Gl.* §§32.1, 3, 62.3). It is all the more striking, then, that the two works differ so sharply in the location and content they assign to the doctrine of holy scripture.

For Calvin, the doctrine of scripture forms the turning-point of book 1, 'The Knowledge of God the Creator'. Having learned that (according to the chapter headings) the knowledge of God, 'naturally implanted in the minds of men' (1.3), is 'either smothered or corrupted, partly by ignorance, partly by malice' (1.4), and that we now lack the eyes to see that the knowledge of God also 'shines forth in the fashioning of the universe and the continuing government of it' (1.5), we discover that scripture is the divinely-appointed remedy for our condition. 'Scripture is needed as guide and teacher for anyone who would come to God the Creator' (1.6), a scripture whose credibility is 'confirmed by the witness of the Spirit' (1.7) and additionally supported by 'sufficient firm proofs' of a historical kind (1.8). In a well-known image: 'Just as old or bleary-eyed men and those with weak vision, if you thrust before them a most beautiful volume, even if they recognize it to be some sort of writing, yet can scarcely construe two words, but with the aid of spectacles will begin to read distinctly; so Scripture, gathering up the otherwise confused knowledge of God in our minds, having dispersed our dullness, clearly shows us the true God' (1.6.1). The text that can only be read with the assistance of spectacles bifurcates into a dual text, world and scripture, in which the latter serves as the authorial and therefore authoritative commentary on the former and thus provides us with the spectacles that can make the world legible to us. Yet the sceptical question remains as to how we know that what is perceived through scriptural spectacles is indeed the truth. Perhaps those technologies which purport to make our sensory experience more reliable merely perpetuate the errors into which the senses have led us? Rational argument·can be of some assistance in refuting sceptical questioning of this kind, but for Calvin (unlike Descartes) it is insufficient. If we are asked for rational proof 'that Moses and the prophets spoke divinely', the answer is that 'the testimony of the Spirit is more excellent than all reason. For as God alone is a fit witness of himself in his Word, so also the Word will not find acceptance in men's hearts before it is sealed by the inward testimony of the Spirit. The same Spirit, therefore, who has spoken through the mouths of the prophets must penetrate into our hearts to persuade us that they faithfully proclaimed what had been divinely commanded' (1.7.4). God has ordained that the certainty of Word and of Spirit should be inseparably joined, and those enthusiasts are to be rejected 'who, with great haughtiness exalting the teaching office of the Spirit, despise all reading and laugh at the simplicity of those who, as they express it, still follow the dead and killing letter' (1.9.1). The enthusiasts who appeal to the Spirit apart from the Word could in principle be the same people as the sceptics who question the divine origin of the utterances of Moses and the prophets. Scepticism about scripture's capacity to serve as spectacles that make the world legible can take the form of critical questions about the origins of scripture. Thus there are sceptics who ask, 'Who assures us that the books that we read under the names of Moses and the prophets were written by them?', even daring to question 'whether there ever was a Moses' (1.8.9). Rational argument can help to refute such people, but only the testimony of the Spirit can bring conviction.

Schleiermacher's doctrine of scripture presupposes the victory of the sceptical and enthusiastic tendencies that Calvin already identified over against his own attempts to hold together Word, Spirit and Reason.[3] A crucial precondition for the abandonment of classical Protestant doctrines of scripture

is a shift in the social location of the 'sceptical' position. As represented by
the English Deists, for example, it is still a peripheral, oppositional position
that parades its own radicality by attacking the claims of established churches.
Its often crude, unsystematic form makes it vulnerable to counter-attack
from a scholarship that deploys the resources of learning to defend moderate,
reasonable and orthodox positions. The shift occurred in the world of the
German universities during the second half of the eighteenth century: the
resources of learning were increasingly deployed in the service of non-orthodox
positions, which thereby attracted to themselves not only the inevitable
controversy but also the prestige of *Wissenschaft*. Schleiermacher's theology
occurs at precisely the historical moment when the irreversibility of this shift
has become clear. As he argues in the second of his open letters to G. C. F.
Lücke (1829), historical science has made every fixed point fluid: 'Do you
know what the final verdict will be about the Pentateuch and the Old
Testament canon? Do you hope that the traditional views of the messianic
prophecies and indeed of types will be found credible by those who have
come to a sound and lively view of historical matters? I cannot believe it'
(65).[4] We can expect changes in our views of New Testament texts too. It is
inevitable that 'the previously scattered comments about the character of the
Gospel of John' will eventually be 'presented in the proper form of a critical
hypothesis' (66). 'And should we not also come back to the doubt that earlier
prevailed in the church about several of the epistles?' It is clear what the
future holds in store: 'It will become increasingly difficult to adhere to the
principle that everything in Scripture is divine teaching, and so it will be
hard to determine which texts are Holy Scriptures and what distinguishes
them from all others' (67). Schleiermacher, however, is able to observe this
dissolution of the previously firm outlines of holy scripture with complete
equanimity; for, in parallel to the transformation of the sceptical tradition
into historical science, it became possible for the 'enthusiastic' appeal to the
Spirit apart from the Word to evade the censures of orthodoxy and rationalism
and to move from the periphery of culture into the centre. Thus, as the
orator and prophet of *Über die Religion: Reden an die Gebildeten unter ihren
Verächtern* (1799[1]), Schleiermacher proclaims that the reality (*die Sache*) of
religion can only be immediately experienced: 'Of all that I praise and feel
[*fühle*] as its work, hardly anything may be found in holy books' (15/9).[5]
Ignoring the complaints of the 'theologians of the letter [*Buchstabentheologen*]'
(29/17), who seek to restore 'the fallen walls of their Jewish Zion and its
Gothic pillars' (4/3), we must discover the essence of religion in personal
experience: the spirit of religion 'reveals itself in the unique way in which it
moves the spirit, merges or rather dispenses with all normal functions of the
human soul, and dissolves all activity into a wondering contemplation of the

Infinite [*ein staunendes Anschauen des Unendlichen*]' (26/15–16). The extension of the Pauline disparagement of 'the letter' to holy scripture as a whole, resulting in the pejorative identification of a scriptural Christianity as 'Jewish', is characteristic of the rhetoric of the period. The Enlightenment's incorporation of the sceptical tradition within its historical-critical research creates space for the Romantic celebration of the liberation of the spirit from the letter.[6]

It is therefore unsurprising that, even in the more ecclesial setting of the *Glaubenslehre*, the doctrine of scripture has lost its traditional position near the beginning of Protestant dogmatics and is now to be found nearer the end; for Christian faith is to be developed in a form that is, so far as possible, independent of the vicissitudes of historical research. In place of the endless variations found in the *Speeches*, the essence of religion is now given a single, precise definition that underlies all that is to come. As the second of the *Speeches* had already argued, it is a modification of feeling, a basic human faculty distinct from knowing and doing, and therefore independent of metaphysics and ethics (*Gl.* §3): it is the feeling of absolute dependence (*das schlechthinige Abhängigkeitsgefühl*), which is a consciousness of being in relation to God (§4) and which comes to its supreme expression in Christian faith (§§7–14). Here, the feeling of absolute dependence takes the particular form of the experience of redemption, which occurs as we are drawn into the perfect God-consciousness of the Redeemer, recognizing our attempts at independent existence as sinful and finding the power of the Redeemer's perfect dependence on God effective in our own relation to God. The sinlessness of the Redeemer is a deduction from the experience of redemption. In developing the christological heart of the 'Explication of the facts of the religious self-consciousness, as they are determined by the antithesis of sin and grace', which occupies about two-thirds of this work, Schleiermacher cannot avoid having recourse to scripture, and especially to the gospels; for redemption is communicated not by way of mysterious, supernatural influences but quite naturally, through the 'picture' of the Redeemer contained in the gospels and encountered within the life and proclamation of the church (§§88.2, 105.1). It is notable, however, that even here Schleiermacher reduces the written Word to an almost invisible medium through which the power of the Redeemer's sinless life continues to 'flow' to us from him (§100.1). That power derives from God's presence in him, and it extends even to us as, within the Christian community, we are drawn into Jesus' experience of God. For this to happen, it is necessary for us to know who Jesus is, and this can only occur on the basis of holy scripture. But, although that is Schleiermacher's view, he lays all the emphasis on the continuing power of God's act and is virtually silent about the textual mediation of this divine

power. In order to fulfil its indispensable positive role as the medium of
God's continuing redemptive activity, the text must efface itself and become
transparent to the figure of the Redeemer. In much of Schleiermacher's text,
it preserves only a tenuous existence.

The New Testament text suddenly becomes solid again on the numerous
occasions when Schleiermacher subjects the gospel 'picture' of Jesus to
criticism. In these contexts, its particularities are simply sacrificed in order
that it should speak, over and over again, of a single, monotonous, all-
consuming concern: the communication of Jesus' sinless, perfect experience
of God. Thus, it is claimed that the stories of the virgin birth are not attested
outside the Matthean and Lucan infancy narratives, that they conflict with
the gospel genealogies and with John, and that they are theologically
misleading and unnecessary for belief in Jesus as the Redeemer (§97.2). The
sinlessness of the Redeemer is incompatible with the temptation narratives,
so they too must be jettisoned (§98.1). In the case of miracle-stories, 'our
attention is directed away from the individual, more physical miracles to the
general spiritual miracle', that is, the person and work of the Redeemer
(§103.4). The accounts of Jesus' death are of value only in so far as they
confirm the perfection of his blessedness, which was unperturbed even by
the test of extreme suffering. The notion that on the cross he 'willingly gave
up even his blessedness, and experienced, even if only for moments, real
misery' is a 'caricature' resting on a 'magical' conception of redemption
(§101.4): thus, in a later text, Schleiermacher asserts that the Gethsemane
narrative and the cry of God-forsakenness are not to be understood literally
(*Life of Jesus*, 396, 423).[7] Jesus' resurrection, ascension and prediction of his
return are declared to be inessential to the doctrine of his person (*Gl.* §99),
in yet another reductive application of the methodological principle that
'nothing concerning him can be set up as real doctrine unless it is connected
with his redeeming causality and can be traced to the original impression
made by his existence' (§29.3). Thus, 'the disciples recognized in him the
Son of God without having the faintest premonition of his resurrection and
ascension, and we too may say the same of ourselves' (§99.1). Only in the
case of Jesus' teaching do we encounter a particular element in the gospel
picture that is *essential* to his redemptive activity. The source of his teaching
was 'the absolutely original revelation of God in him', its aim 'the assumption
of men into his fellowship' (§103.2); specific Johannine sayings are cited in
which Christ speaks of his perfect fulfilment of the divine will (cf. John 4.31;
5.19, 30; 6.38) and of its goal, that we too should fulfil the divine will ever
more perfectly (cf. John 15.2, 5, 8, 11; §104.3). By means of such utterances,
Christ's God-consciousness is both expressed and communicated; for
Schleiermacher, they indicate that the modern tendency to contrast the

proclaimer with the proclaimed is entirely mistaken (§103.2).[8] Yet even Jesus' teaching must be subjected to the usual reduction: for it expresses what is essential only 'so far as it is connected with his self-presentation, for it was only by the proclamation of his peculiar dignity that men could really be invited to enter into the fellowship offered them' (§103.2).

The consistency with which Schleiermacher is willing to sacrifice the particularities of the gospel texts to his single christological idea is in its own way just as ruthless as the *Kaltblütigkeit* of which D. F. Strauss boasted in the preface to the first volume of his *Life of Jesus Critically Examined* (1835).[9] In terms of Schleiermacher's hermeneutical theory, it shows the precarious status of the reciprocal relationship between parts and whole asserted in the doctrine of the hermeneutical circle: the claim that 'each part can be understood only out of the whole to which it belongs, *and vice versa*' (*Hermeneutics* [1819], 113; my italics) can easily be replaced by the non-reciprocal claim that 'within each given text, its parts can only be understood in terms of the whole' (115).[10] The apparently trivial, casual omission of 'and vice versa' may be seen as a symptom of a basic tension within Romantic thought in general. The tendency to celebrate the dynamic, dialectical relationship between parts and whole, on the grounds that individuality is genuinely preserved in this dialectic alone and not in any abstract separateness, is crossed by a counter-tendency to dissolve the parts back into that prior whole out of which they emerge.[11] In its treatment of the gospels, Schleiermacher's christology might be seen as a remarkably pure instance of the counter-tendency. On the other hand, for Schleiermacher the synoptic gospels do not really constitute wholes. In his critical study of the Gospel of Luke (1817; ET 1825), he argues that the synoptic tradition consisted originally of 'many circumstantial memorials of detached incidents' (10), and that the gospels are therefore to be seen as collections of these originally separate fragments of oral or written tradition.[12] As a note of 1833 puts it, the synoptics 'are unified only in the sense that the authors tried to collect all the details' (*Hermeneutics*, 227). In the circumstances, therefore, there is no unified 'whole' to which the parts can be related. The situation is different in the case of the single eyewitness text, the Gospel of John, which gives us unique access to Jesus' self-consciousness. This text is superior to the synoptic gospels, and Schleiermacher vigorously defends its authenticity.[13]

One might therefore draw on another aspect of Schleiermacher's hermeneutical theory in order to shed light on his treatment of the gospels, the distinction between 'grammatical' and 'psychological' interpretation. This distinction arises out of the fact that 'understanding a speech always involves two moments: to understand what is said in the context of the language with its possibilities, and to understand it as a fact in the thinking of the speaker'

(*Hermeneutics*, 98). Although the two sides of interpretation should never be entirely separated, one will in interpretative practice always be closer to the one or the other. Texts that do not purport to express the inner life of an author will require a predominantly grammatical interpretation; but 'highly individualized and minimally commonplace' texts require something more than that (102). In such cases, interpreters should 'identify themselves as much as possible with the moments of creativity and conception which break into the fabric of the author's everyday life like higher inspirations' (204), desiring to 'reconstruct the creative act that begins with the generation of thoughts which captivate the author' (192) and so to attain 'an immediate comprehension of the author as an individual' (150). In the case of the synoptic gospels, a 'grammatical' – or rather, a 'grammatical-historical' – interpretation is appropriate (212–13); and this is undertaken by the emerging critical tradition in which Schleiermacher himself participated. In the case of the Gospel of John, however, it is insufficient: for, especially in its account of Jesus' teaching, it expresses the 'inner truth' of his being (*Life of Jesus*, 450). The Gospel of John must be traced back to the authorial subjectivity not so much of the evangelist as of Jesus himself, whose life and person it so faithfully represents. The externalizing movement from experience to communication is to be reversed; the materiality of writing and speech is to be dissolved as the interpreter traces these secondary realities back to the primary source from which they once flowed forth. The experience that gave rise to these utterances is that of a perfect, unclouded consciousness of God. The interpreter arrives at this originating experience not by any exegetical technique but in a moment of 'divination' – an event that presupposes that 'each person contains a minimum of everyone else, so that divination is aroused by comparison with oneself' (*Hermeneutics*, 150).[14] In this case, the interpreter's own experience of God makes it possible to divine a similar, although perfect, experience of God as the true source of the utterances contained in this gospel. Interpreter and authorial source mirror one another; indeed, they can even be said to become identical, for divination 'lead[s] the interpreter to transform himself, so to speak, into the author' (96). The interpreter is in Christ, and Christ is in his interpreter; one rediscovers oneself and one's own experience in the figure of Christ. In the process of these transactions, however, the text itself has vanished. Grammatical interpretation, with its necessary but one-sided insistence on the materiality of the text, has been left far behind as interpreter and author reflect each other back to one another in an infinite regress.[15] At this point it becomes clear why, despite the necessary role of the gospel 'picture' of Jesus in ensuring that his experience of God is communicated to later generations, it is allowed to remain almost invisible as Schleiermacher develops the christology that lies at the heart of his vision of Christian faith. It is the nature of 'psychological' interpretation to dissolve the materiality of the text in retracing it to its source; and the 'grammatical-historical' interpretation in which that materiality is preserved is only a provisional moment in interpretation, useful above all in its ability to demonstrate that the particularities of the gospel narratives are secondary to the original impression created by the Redeemer and are therefore theologically indifferent. Grammatical-historical interpretation is placed at the disposal of a psychological interpretation whose goal is the dissolution of the text.[16]

From this standpoint, the reason why, unlike Calvin, Schleiermacher cannot contemplate an explicit doctrine of scripture at the outset of his work becomes clear. We have already identified the possibility of combining Enlightenment rationalist scepticism with the Romantic enthusiasm for which textuality is a barrier to immediacy that must be dissolved for the sake of the *erstaunende Anschauen des Unendlichen*; and it is now clear that this same anti-textual strategy underlies the *Glaubenslehre* at its theological heart. In opposition to the enthusiasm that separates Spirit and text, Calvin had once asserted the irreducibility of textuality, which is why his *Institutes* and his biblical commentaries can be seen as parts of a single, coherent theological project. For Schleiermacher, on the other hand, textuality as such does not belong within the sphere of theology at all. Grammatical-historical exegesis is not a strictly theological activity; theology must respect its autonomy, which is indeed a necessary condition of its own autonomy. By identifying the secondariness so characteristic of textuality, an autonomous exegesis creates space for theology's own autonomous pursuit of the original communication. Dead writing must give way to living speech.[17]

Book 2 of Calvin's *Institutes* outlines 'the knowledge of God the Redeemer in Christ, first disclosed to the fathers under the Law, and then to us in the Gospel'. In Schleiermacher's *Glaubenslehre*, this corresponds to the 'explication of the consciousness of sin' that opens part 2 and to the first, christological section of the 'explication of the consciousness of grace'. Book 3 of the *Institutes*, 'The way in which we receive the grace of Christ: what benefits come to us from it, and what effects follow', corresponds to Schleiermacher's treatment of 'the manner in which fellowship with the perfection and blessedness of the Redeemer expresses itself in the individual soul': indeed, the order here – regeneration, conversion, justification, sanctification – appears to be self-consciously Reformed. In book 4, Calvin considers 'the external means or aids by which God invites us into the society of Christ and holds us therein', and Schleiermacher again follows him in turning from the individual to the church in a section oddly entitled 'the constitution of the world in relation to redemption'. Having identified the Holy Spirit as the principle of unity in 'the new corporate life founded by Christ' (§121), Schleiermacher distinguishes 'the essential and invariable features of the church' from 'the mutable element characteristic of the church in virtue of its coexistence with the world'. Holy scripture is the first item under the former heading. Other 'essential and invariable features of the church' include the ministry of the Word of God, baptism, the Lord's Supper, the power of the keys and prayer in the name of Christ. These are arranged in pairs: scripture and preaching constitute the church's 'witness to Christ'; baptism and the Lord's Supper serve 'the formation and maintenance of living fellowship with Christ'; and the power of the keys and prayer in the name of Jesus point respectively to 'the reciprocal influence of the whole on the individual, and of individuals on the whole' (§127). It is not clear how there can be a 'witness to Christ' that does not already intend 'the formation and maintenance of living fellowship with Christ' – an anomaly arising, like many others, out of the ubiquitous drive towards systematic clarity and balance, an essentially aesthetic concern that untidy heterogeneities should be re-envisaged as parts of an ordered yet dynamic whole.[18] Otherwise, this proposal to treat holy scripture in the context of the doctrine of the church appears in itself to be reasonable and even illuminating, especially in contrast to the impression conveyed by book 1 of the *Institutes*, that God brings us to know him by means of a book. In the *Glaubenslehre*, the problem lies not in the location but in the content of the doctrine of holy scripture.

According to Schleiermacher, our Christianity, like the apostles', derives not from written texts as such but from the personal influences that proceed from Christ. This can no longer happen directly, and we are now dependent on 'the New Testament representations of Christ's personality'. If the church is the church only as the dwelling-place of the Holy Spirit, it must also be said that 'the influence of these representations of Christ will always be an indispensable precondition of the Holy Spirit's being imparted' (§127.2). Yet to speak of the 'influence' of the New Testament 'representations of Christ' is to abstract from the New Testament texts as they stand: for it is not the case that the texts as such are an 'indispensable precondition of the Holy Spirit's being imparted'. Indeed, strictly speaking, 'the fixed written letter of the New Testament' is unnecessary: 'the *actual form* [i.e. the written, textual form] in which the personality of Christ is set before us does not belong unconditionally to the *esse* but rather to the *bene esse* of the church' (§127.2). Christ's personality was originally communicated by proclamation alone, and there is no reason in principle why it should not always have been so. Scripture enables us to test our proclamation against that of the earliest witness to Christ, but its preservation of that earlier witness 'would be a mere lifeless possession if this preservation were not an ever-renewed self-activity of the Church, which reveals itself also in living witness to Christ that either goes back to Scripture or harmonizes with Scripture in meaning and spirit' (§127.2). The fixity of the scriptural preservation of the original witness to Christ is subordinate to the dynamic actualization of that witness in the church's proclamation. The church's ministry of the Word is itself 'traceable to Christ himself, for the communication of life and power' (§127.2). We have, then, two parallel divine ordinances, a fixed and therefore dead writing and a living speech. It is in fact the written text that has preserved the earliest impressions of Christ's personality, and it can therefore never be superfluous; but it is of value only in so far as its representations of Christ help to inspire the living speech through which redemption is experienced. We cannot in practice dispense with 'the fixed written letter of the New Testament', but we can at least counteract its deadening effects by postulating a ministry of the Word that is prior to, parallel to and superior to holy scripture. It seems that the phenomenon of holy scripture represents an ever-present threat of a tyranny of the letter; the doctrine of holy scripture is motivated almost exclusively by the need to contain this threat by assigning to scripture as circumscribed a role as possible.[19] Thus, faith in Christ is prior to and independent of a doctrine of scriptural inspiration (§128). The New Testament contains apocryphal as well as canonical material, and only the latter is authoritative for us (§§129.2, 130.4). Inspiration is to be ascribed to the whole activity of the apostles and not to 'the written word in its bare externality', interpretation of which must be 'guided by the rules that obtain elsewhere' (§130.2). Free, unfettered historical research is set to work on the dissolution of the canon, while dogmatic theology redefines the interests of Christian faith in the New Testament texts so as to ensure that this research will never be obstructed or inconvenienced.

The proposal to purge holy scripture 'from what does not belong to it' (§130.4) implies that we should resume the quest of the early church for the true form of holy scripture (§131.1). In fact Schleiermacher has little interest in a reconstructed New Testament canon, consisting perhaps of the Gospel of John, some parts of the synoptic gospels, and whichever of the apostolic letters prove to be genuine. The function of his critique of the New Testament canon is to further his attack on textuality as such. The next move is therefore to dispense with the Old Testament in its entirety: 'The Old Testament scriptures owe their place in our Bible partly to the appeals the New Testament scriptures make to them, partly to the historical connection with the Jewish synagogue; but the Old Testament scriptures do not on that account share the normative dignity or the inspiration of the New' (§132). This thesis is presented as a 'postscript' to the doctrine of scripture that has been developed thus far, and various reasons for it are given. The Pauline antithesis of law and Spirit means that the law cannot have been inspired (§132.2). Nowhere in the Old Testament, not even in the psalms, do we find the Christian doctrine of God stated in its pure form (§132.2). Christ and the apostles only appealed to the Old Testament because of their historical situation (§132.3). The Old Testament might in future be printed after the New, as an appendix (§132.3). In this doctrine of scripture, the concept of holy scripture has been dissolved. Neo-Marcionite enthusiasm seeks to purge the sacred texts of everything that distorts the pure moment of origin, and the purification process extends to the after-effects of the Old Testament in the New. The apostolic age as a whole cannot be regarded as normative: 'For owing to its naturally most unequal distribution of the divine Spirit, . . . it was very easily possible (since Jewish and pagan views and maxims were uneradicated and their antagonism to the Christian spirit could only be recognized gradually) that expositions of religion might be produced which, strictly speaking, were rather Judaism or paganism coloured by Christianity itself, i.e. were, if considered as Christian, in the highest degree impure' (§129.2). The proposal to separate the truly canonical from the apocryphal material in what is currently regarded as 'holy scripture' is at the same time a programme for the radical de-judaizing of Christian faith. In the form of the Old Testament and its after-effects within the New, Judaism is (for neo-Marcionism) the archetypal corrupter of Christian purity. The problem of textuality is thus in essence the problem of the Old Testament, the religion of 'the letter' in its original form, whose malign effects have distorted Christian faith from the very beginning. The model for our efforts to free ourselves from the Jewish letter in Old and New Testaments is Christ himself, whose consciousness of God derived not from the Old Testament or his Jewish contemporaries but from his own inner life alone (*Life of Jesus*, 266). In conformity with his example, we must ensure that our own awareness of God mirrors the purity of its source and is not contaminated by the 'debasing influence' of 'Jewish forms of thought and life' (*Gl.* §129.2).

The claim that pure Christianity is entirely independent of Judaism and the Old Testament has already been outlined in the section in the Introduction in which Schleiermacher offers an initial presentation of 'Christianity in its peculiar essence', claiming to derive his propositions not from Christian dogmatics but from 'apologetics' (§§11–14). Christianity is distinguished from other religions 'by the fact that in it everything is related to the redemption accomplished by Jesus of Nazareth' (§11), and the radical exclusiveness of the relation to Jesus is indicated by the claim that follows, that 'Christianity does indeed stand in a special historical connection with Judaism; but as far as concerns its historical existence and its aim, its relations to Judaism and Heathenism are the same' (§12). The 'essence of Christianity' is carefully demarcated from Judaism from the outset. Judaism – the religion of the Old Testament – has already been characterized as a deficient form of monotheism which, 'by its limitation of the love of Jehovah to the race of Abraham, betrays a lingering affinity with Fetichism' (§8.4), that is, with a religion in which one identifies oneself 'only with a small part of finite existence' (§8.2). Although its monotheism is in some sense a presupposition for the Redeemer's existence, it would be a mistake to exaggerate the significance of this historical connection. The crucial point is that 'the relations of Christianity to Judaism and Heathenism are the same, inasmuch as the transition from either of these to Christianity is a transition to another religion' (§12.2). Christian faith, like any other religious communion, 'can never be explained by the condition of the circle in which it appears and operates; for if it could, it would not be a starting-point but would itself be the product of a spiritual process' (§13.1). Like other historical phenomena, Christian faith is genuinely new. Yet, although Schleiermacher is anxious to minimize the *historical* connection between the Redeemer and the Old Testament, that does not mean that the Redeemer simply appears at random, with no preparation: the neo-Marcionite rejection of the Old Testament need not entail so radical and irrational a conclusion. There is instead an *anthropological* connection between the Redeemer and the past history of humankind; his appearance proves that 'there must reside in human nature the possibility of taking up the divine into itself', and one can therefore understand the actualization of this possibility in Christ as 'an action of human nature, grounded in its original constitution and prepared for by all its past history' (§13.1). Human nature is created for consciousness of God, and it therefore yearns for the fulfilment of its destiny that occurs in Christ.

Against this universal anthropological background, the Old Testament prophets retain a certain significance. Messianic prophecies 'disclose to us a striving of human nature towards Christianity, and at the same time give it as the confession of the best and most inspired of earlier religious communions that they are to be regarded only as preparatory and transitory institutions' (§14, *Postscript*). Thus Jeremiah, as the voice not of Judaism but of universal human nature, prophesies a new covenant which will be quite unlike the Mosaic covenant on which Judaism is based; and such passages establish the principles that 'almost everything in the Old Testament is, for our Christian usage, but the husk or wrapping of its prophecy, and that whatever is most definitely Jewish has least value' (§12.3). Since such anticipations of the Redeemer stem not from a particular historical tradition but from universal human nature, the Apologists were right to recognize that the 'striving of human nature towards Christianity' was also to be found in 'the utterances of the nobler and purer Heathenism' (§12.3). Yet the varied expression of the universal human striving towards that which was actualized in the

Redeemer is of no value for demonstrating the truth of Christianity: for the recognition of this striving is dependent on our own prior experience of it, and we therefore encounter the Redeemer as the answer to a question that arises out of *our own* nature, a question that we can only subsequently trace in its various other expressions. Although there are elements in Old Testament prophecy that express what is universally human rather than distinctively Jewish, even these are of no real significance to us. At best, the Old Testament renders 'only those of our religious emotions which are of a somewhat general nature, without anything distinctively Christian' (§12.3). The Old Testament does not 'share the normative dignity or the inspiration of the New' (§132).

Schleiermacher's *claim* is that (in general) the Old Testament remains bound by narrow nationalistic limits, whereas the New Testament (again, in general) reflects the breaking down of these limits through the universal significance of the Redeemer. Yet there is a sense in which, in his *practice*, he treats the two Testaments in parallel. In the case of the Old Testament, particularity ('whatever is most definitely Jewish') is denied all significance, and a positive role is assigned only to those prophetic utterances that express the striving of universal human nature. As we have seen, Schleiermacher's treatment of the New Testament entails an equally drastic subordination of particularity (the gospel narratives in their constituent parts) to the universality represented by the Redeemer's perfect God-consciousness. The New Testament texts themselves are said to contain 'apocryphal' material, which must be carefully distinguished from genuinely canonical elements, and the main source of this corruption is the enduring influence of the Old Testament on the early Christians. In the New Testament too, 'whatever is most definitely Jewish has least value'.[20]

Jewishness for Schleiermacher represents *textuality*, the primary obstacle to the notion of the openness of human nature to immediate experience of God which is the basic premise of his entire theology. Textuality enters the New Testament's 'picture' of the Redeemer in its repeated insistence that faith in him is dependent not on pure intuition but in the recognition that his history unfolds *kata tas graphas*. Indeed, there is no gospel 'picture' of Jesus, in the sense of a static image of a person permanently translucent to God. Instead, there are gospel *texts*, whose irreducible textuality takes the form of an equally irreducible narrativity. Like the Old Testament texts on which they draw so freely, these are material objects. They are in no sense the transparent medium for an encounter of like with like, and to hand over their particularities for historical-critical dissolution is arbitrary and high-handed. A profound intertextual relationship with the Old Testament guarantees not only the materiality of the texts but also the materiality of the Redeemer to whom, in their materiality, they bear witness: for the notion of the transparency of the texts to the Redeemer has as its correlate the transparency of the Redeemer to the all-embracing infinity which dissolves every particular into itself. The neo-Marcionite rejection of the Old Testament issues, as though inevitably, in a docetism in which Jesus' material existence is suppressed in order that the ideal image of the Redeemer might serve as a symbol corresponding to the universal human longing for absorption into the divine.

2. Harnack

The Foreword to the first edition of Harnack's *Marcion: Das Evangelium vom fremden Gott* (1921; 1924[2]) reveals an unusually intimate relationship between scholar and subject-matter.[21] In his old age, the celebrated church-historian and theologian looks back to a day that seems to belong to another world: 12 December 1870, when at the age of 19 he had been awarded a prize at the University of Dorpat for his study of 'Marcionis doctrina e Tertulliani adversus Marcionem libris eruatur et explicetur' (VI). The Faculty had requested him to revise his work with a view to publication; at the time this came to nothing, but he has always maintained an interest in the subject. Marcion 'has been my first love in church history, and this affection and veneration has, in the half-century that I have lived with him, not been diminished even by Augustine' (VI). Year after year, material has been gathered in hours snatched from more pressing duties, and there has often been doubt whether the work would ever be completed; but now, at last, first love is brought to fruition (VIII). In part, this is an affair of pure scholarship; Marcion is the key to a number of difficult problems relating to the transition between the post-apostolic and the old-catholic eras (VII). Still more significant, however, is Marcion's unique place in the general history of religion. 'He is the only thinker in Christian history to take quite seriously the conviction that the God who redeems us from the world has absolutely nothing to do with cosmology or cosmic teleology', and the result is a unique concentration on the person of Jesus Christ himself, a determination that nothing shall be allowed to undermine the purity and newness of his gospel (VII). It is, says Harnack at the end of his Introduction, 'a pleasure to occupy oneself with a deeply religious man of intellectual purity, who rejected all syncretism, allegory and sophistry' (21).

Marcion is not to be understood as a gnostic, but simply as a theologian who 'had come to know God, through the appearance of Jesus Christ, wholly and exclusively as the Father of mercy and God of all comfort, and was certain that no other assertion about him was valid, indeed that every other such assertion was the most serious error' (4). He was thus able to take to its logical conclusions 'the religion of inwardness [*die Religion der Innerlichkeit*]' (5). The religion founded by Jesus Christ was transmitted in a form corrupted by the addition of the Old Testament and all sorts of late Jewish traditions, resulting in a syncretistic 'catholicism' that differed sharply from its founder's view that 'all traditions, doctrines and forms were essentially indifferent' (7). The catholic, syncretistic Christianity which remains the foundation of official church doctrine and order is thus a christianized Judaism which has failed to comprehend the radical newness represented by its founder. Catholicism's tendency to accumulate a wealth of disparate material makes it impossible for it to function as an authentic 'personal religion [*Privatreligion*]' (10), and, so long as it endures, a reaction such as Marcion's remains a possibility. 'It is never possible to suppress the longing of the thinking religious person to appropriate *inwardly* [innerlich *anzueignen*], in its totality, what religion has brought him, or, if that is not possible, to exclude whatever is contradictory, incomprehensible and offensive' (11). We should therefore expect to encounter people in church history who 'wish to teach a Christianity that is *clear* [eindeutig]' (11), in opposition to the 'impure syncretism' of official church doctrine and order, rooted as it is in the Old Testament (13). Marcion can be seen as the discoverer of this possibility, given in the structure of catholic Christianity: for him there could be 'no syncretism, but rather the simplicity, integrity and clarity of what is authentically Christian' (18). Marcion represents the first dawning of the 'protestant' possibility of a Reformation that would clear away the rubble that chokes and conceals the pure spring from which the gospel originally issued forth. He has rightly been seen as 'the first Protestant' (198).

For Marcion, the whole church had been led astray by the false apostles and Jewish evangelists opposed by Paul, who 'had poured new wine into old wineskins and converted the gospel into the Old Testament' (198). Despite its abandonment of circumcision and other Jewish laws, 'this Christianity saw law and gospel as a unity, and thus denied the essence of the gospel' (198). Paul would have accepted much of Marcion's critique of Christian syncretism, acknowledging 'in the man who here arose as a reformer his own true pupil' (199) – although he would have been less happy about the severing of law and gospel and about the docetic christology. The figures of Jesus, Paul and Marcion represent a trajectory away from Judaism (200n). Paulinism itself was already 'a colossal revolution in the history of Jewish-Christian religion' (203), and figures such as the author to the Hebrews, Barnabas, Ignatius, Diognetus and John indicate that the general drift towards a more conservative, Jewish understanding of Christian faith was by no means universal even before Marcion (203–4): all of these occupy a position 'along the line from Paul to Marcion' (204). Yet Marcion alone offered a *historical* justification for rejecting the Old Testament (207). While his theory that Paul's letters had been corrupted by judaizing additions is historically untenable, Marcion rightly saw that the Pauline antithesis of righteousness by faith and not by works leads logically to the rejection of the Old Testament, and that the (alleged or actual) Pauline means for preserving its canonical status were inadequate (216).

All this leads to the well-known thesis asserting Marcion's significance for our own time: 'To reject the Old Testament in the second century was an error which the great church rightly rejected; to retain it in the sixteenth century was a fate which the Reformation was still unable to escape; but to preserve it during the nineteenth century and beyond as a canonical document for protestantism is the result of religious and churchly paralysis' (217). In the second century, a historical solution to the problem of the Old Testament was impossible: rejecting it meant ascribing it to another deity and the consequent loss of religiously valuable elements in the psalms and the prophets (217–18). In the sixteenth century, Luther denied the canonical status of those books that are unique to the Greek Old Testament, regarding them only as 'good and useful to read'; but the power of tradition prevented him from downgrading the rest of the Old Testament in the same way. ('What a liberation it would have been for Christianity and its teaching, had Luther taken this step!' [219].) Later, Schleiermacher, Hegel and others recognized that the distinctiveness of the Christian conception of God had to be established on the basis of Christ alone, but the evangelical churches have remained too tradition-bound to take the necessary step of placing the Old Testament among those books which are 'good and useful to read' – even though most of the popular objections to the church stem from the authority it still concedes to the Old Testament (222). While there is now no question of 'rejecting' the Old Testament, as Marcion did, 'the question of the Old Testament, first posed and decided by Marcion, remains urgent today for evangelical Christianity' (223).[22]

Marcion, or Marcion–Harnack, is therefore a reformer for our times. It is his vocation to carry the work tentatively begun by Luther to a triumphant conclusion, proclaiming a gospel purified from Old Testament and Jewish influences whose content is the God, revealed in Jesus, who is pure love and who does not condemn. Who knows what the impact of such a proclamation might be? 'Those with the deepest knowledge of the popular mind [*Volksseele*], as it exists today among the despisers of ecclesial Christianity, assure us that only the proclamation of a love that does not judge but helps us still has any prospect of being heard' (232). This moderate, reasonable neo-Marcionism concludes its case by warning against the radical neo-Marcionism which divorces God's revelation from human existence, and which tends towards a

Nietzschean 'transvaluation of values [*Umwertung der Werte*]' and a 'dissolution of culture [*Auflösung der Kultur*]' (225). Admittedly, there may be an element of truth in this position. 'Are "righteousness", morality and culture real ways to salvation for those held captive by sensual existence? Or are they mere palliatives which ultimately make evil still worse in the absence of the selfless, higher will-to-love? Do the starry heavens above me and the moral law within me really transport me to the plane of eternal truth and true eternity, which are in fact given only in love towards God and the brethren? Or are they simply powers which fail in every great test?' (231). Goethe and Kant alone cannot point the way to salvation. Yet, in opposition to contemporary 'expressionistic' theology, we can no longer be dualists as Marcion was: morality and culture must be seen 'not only' as opposed to God's revelation 'but also' as steps along the way (234). Marcion needs the moderating influence of Harnack, with his *Kultur* and his *Wissenschaft*, if he is to fulfil his vocation as a reformer for our times.[23]

To propose a figure of early church history as a reformer for our times is credible only on the basis of prior coincidences between his own thought and the relatively autonomous theological thought of the modern era. It is not the case that Harnack's Marcion wishes to proclaim previously unheard-of or forgotten truths to early twentieth-century Protestant Christianity; on the contrary, he merely repeats, in a somewhat different idiom, proposals for rethinking Christian faith that have long been familiar from the work of Schleiermacher, Ritschl and others. Unlike the second-century original, this twentieth-century Marcion has nothing new to say. His role is in fact to show that certain of the concerns of liberal Protestant theology stem from the basic structure of Christian faith as established in the first two centuries of its existence, and especially from the threat to an original Christian *Eindeutigkeit* and *Innerlichkeit* posed by the 'syncretism' of orthodox Christian faith. Liberal Protestantism can thus understand itself not only as a radicalizing of Luther's basic theological insights, but also as the present embodiment of a *permanent* Christian concern to recover *das Wesen des Christentums* from a mass of extraneous material, a concern already expressed by Marcion under quite different cultural conditions. The coincidences between Marcion and modern theology – the preconditions for his role as a reformer for our times – are thus interpreted as a confirmation that, on both its critical and its constructive sides, modern theology is rooted in problems that are as old as Christianity itself. It is not as new as it seems. The real role of Harnack's Marcion is to lend the prestige of antiquity, difference and proximity to the origin to Harnack's own reforming programme – and especially to the proposal, issued in his own name but under the patronage of his great second-century predecessor, that the contemporary church should at last abandon its obstinate, pre-critical insistence on the canonical status of the Old Testament. Harnack's 'first love' is ultimately self-love rather than love for an other in his difference. Historical difference is maintained in the detailed analyses of the origins and development of Marcionism and the reconstruction of its central texts, but this difference is intentionally dissolved by the theological framework within which this more narrowly 'scholarly' material is set. The dialectic between difference and contemporaneity is no doubt present in all historical work, and does not in itself give grounds for criticism. It does, however, raise the question whether a particular construal of contemporaneity is as natural and inevitable as it may claim to be – especially when its impact is largely dependent on its context within an impressive scholarly performance which has, in fact, no relevance at all to the case for contemporary reform. Historical scholarship serves as a *substitute* for a reasoned presentation of this case; it excuses the historian from the inconvenience of having to construct a theological *argument*. When pressed on this point, the best this historian can do is to assert the existence of a gradual and irresistible historical trend and to renew his attack on orthodox Christian faith for its refusal to share his own intuitive certainties.[24]

The illusion of a direct relationship between the historian's reconstruction of Marcionism and the theologian's opinions about the status of the Old Testament for today's church is reinforced by the methodological decision to limit the field of scholarly enquiry to a Marcionism abstracted, so far as possible, from the theologies constructed in order to oppose it. If Marcionism is deemed to be relevant for today's church, one must already have decided that the various arguments brought to bear against this theology can largely be discounted. If it was appropriate for the church in the second and third centuries to reject Marcion, it is so no longer; the failure to accept a modernized rendering of his critique of the Old Testament is *now* 'the result of religious and churchly paralysis'. The arguments that were *then* employed are dismissed at a stroke as of purely historical interest, and the texts that express these arguments are valued not for what they wish to say about the nature of Christian faith but as 'sources' for reconstructing the position they seek to refute. It is assumed that, unlike the anti-Marcionite text, this reconstruction will be theologically relevant as well as historically informative – a reversal of the older assumption that Marcion himself is of purely historical interest and that his orthodox critics were right to oppose him and thus retain their own theological relevance. One must extract the information one desires from texts biased against Marcion; and this is regarded as a problem because the historian conceives it to be a professional duty to treat the object of investigation 'fairly' and 'sympathetically', in a belated attempt to remedy the 'one-sidedness' of orthodox polemics. Historical method itself leads one to the assumption that the orthodox critique of Marcion is inherently flawed – partly because it fails to divulge information we would dearly like to possess, and partly because its dissent makes it incapable of the sympathetic understanding that is supposed to be the historian's duty. It is thus no accident that, although Harnack is at every point partially or wholly dependent on an earlier analysis of Marcionism, that of Tertullian, he goes to considerable lengths to erase traces of Tertullian's perspective from his own work. Tertullian and his arguments against Marcion cannot be admitted because they would impair the 'purity' that Harnack is determined to preserve, both as historian and as theologian. It is true that historians are always required to establish artificial limits to their subject-matter; but it is perhaps more than coincidental that these particular limits make it so easy to proceed from 'sympathetic' historical reconstruction to advocacy, as though the former constituted a sufficient argument for the latter.

Since Harnack's Marcion tells twentieth-century Protestant theology nothing that it does not already know, it should be possible to trace back the explicit neo-Marcionism of this text to tacitly neo-Marcionite aspects of Harnack's theology as a whole; that is, certain elements of this relatively autonomous modern theology should come to light when read from the perspective of his own explicit neo-Marcionism – elements that constitute the preconditions for this perspective. In order to compensate for his own one-sidedness, we shall at various points bring Tertullian's anti-Marcionite theology to bear on our reading of Harnack. This is no more an anachronism than Harnack's deployment of Marcion himself for contemporary theological ends.

(*i*) In Paul's letter to the Galatians, we read of those who 'want to pervert the gospel of Christ' (Gal. 1.7); even apostles are said to be 'not straightforward about the truth of the gospel' (Gal. 2.14). Yet the church's fourfold gospel ascribes two of the gospels to apostolic authors and another of them to a disciple of Peter – the very apostle who was the main object of Paul's accusation. In the light of the Pauline attack on the judaizing of Christian faith, in which even apostles were implicated, can apostolic gospels be regarded as reliable? Conscious of these difficulties, Marcion 'labours very hard to destroy the reputation of those gospels which are published as genuine and under the name of apostles' (Tertullian, *adversus Marcionem,* iv.3).[25] These gospels are the products of a corrupt, judaizing Christianity, and do not render the truth of the gospel of Christ in pure and trustworthy form. Even the Gospel of Luke, the work of a disciple of Paul, 'was interpolated by the defenders of Judaism, for the purpose of assimilating it to the law and the prophets so that out of it they might fashion their [Jewish] Christ' (*adv.Marc.* iv.4). Fortunately, however, the judaizing interpolations can easily be recognized, and critical scholarship is able to eradicate them and to restore the gospel's testimony to a Jesus who remains undefiled by Jewish influences.

Harnack is interested in the striking anticipations here of the position of the Tübingen school, where the conflict between Paul and Peter about the status of the Jewish law is again seen as crucial for understanding Christian origins, and where the gospels along with all other early Christian literature are said to be marked by the *Tendenz* of their respective authors in relation to that controversy (*Marcion*, 207–8). Yet the beginning of Harnack's academic career coincided with the general abandonment of many of the positions characteristic of the Tübingen school, and he himself shows no inclination to historicize the law/gospel antithesis along the lines laid down by Marcion and Baur.[26] Contrary to Marcion, the goal of a de-judaized Jesus is not to be attained by postulating a pure original impression secondarily corrupted by judaizing influences in the process of transmission; it is to be attained by acknowledging the originality of the Jewish influence on Jesus while asserting that it does not impinge upon that which lies at the heart of his teaching. There is agreement about the goal, but disagreement about the means for attaining it.

For Harnack, the essence (*Wesen*) of Christianity – that which endures amidst all the changing forms – is to be found in Jesus' gospel, summarized under the three headings of 'the kingdom of God and its coming', 'God the Father and the infinite value of the human soul', and 'the higher righteousness and the commandment of love' (*What is Christianity?* [ET 1901; German original, *Das Wesen des Christentums*, 1900], 52).[27] It is necessary to begin with Jesus' preaching of the kingdom, yet in doing so we immediately encounter a problem. Jesus' preaching of the kingdom moves, confusingly, between two poles. On the one hand, under the influence of the Old Testament, he understands the coming of the kingdom as 'a purely future event' in which 'the external rule of God' is to be established; on the other hand, the kingdom 'appears as something inward, something which is already present and making its entrance at the moment' (53). While it is no longer possible to accept the former view, the latter remains compelling. We have already been warned that to overlook the significance of Jesus' historical context leads to docetism (12–13), so there can be no question of denying the existence of the pole at which 'kingdom of God' connotes futurity, externality, derivativeness, irrelevance and Jewishness. There can equally be no question of denying the existence of the opposite pole, understanding Jesus merely as the product of the apocalyptic mentality of his time and place. Although some have taken this view, it is the historian's task to distinguish 'between what is traditional and what is peculiar, between kernel and husk, in Jesus' message of the kingdom of God' (57).[28] Parts of the gospel texts influenced by the Old Testament are to be discarded, for we can be nourished only by what is unique to Jesus. We find this edible, non-Jewish kernel especially in the parables, where we learn that the kingdom of God is 'the rule of the holy God in the hearts of individuals' (57). The kingdom is 'a purely religious blessing, the inner link with the living God' (64): corresponding to the inwardness of the kernel, preserved but concealed within its Jewish shell, is the inwardness to which this kernel bears witness. The form of the kernel is identical to its content, and the same is true also of the husk. External in form, it can speak only of externality, that is, of the external world, understood as the inferior counterpart to the infinite value of the soul in its inwardness. Only if we crack open and discard the hard Jewish shell will we truly appropriate this precious possession, which is our own innermost being.[29]

Harnack and Marcion are at one in asserting that the originality of Jesus is untouched by his Jewish context; they agree that the gospels in their churchly, canonical form are an inadequate rendering of this original essence, and that it is their duty to eliminate judaizing distortions and so to restore the original purity. Outraged by the text-critical activities that put this programme into practice, Tertullian at one point apostrophizes the instrument with which his opponent carries out his erasures: 'Let Marcion's sponge blush!' (*adv.Marc.* v.4). One way of purifying the text from Jewish defilements is to use a sponge. Harnack suggests a subtler approach, which acknowledges the reality of the Jewish 'shell' in the very act of discarding it. Rather than a sponge, he prefers to use a nutcracker. Whichever instrument is used, the gospel texts in their canonical form suffer extreme violence; for at no point do these texts imply that their complex intertextual relationship to the Old Testament is anything other than crucial to their presentation of Jesus.[30]

(*ii*) It is Marcion's view, and Harnack agrees with him, that 'the Christian concept of God must be established exclusively and without remainder from the fact of redemption through Christ' (*Marcion*, 19) – a claim primarily directed against the Christian use of the Old Testament. Harnack acknowledges the objection that Jesus recognized the authority of the Old Testament, but claims that 'Jesus himself, in his most solemn utterance, told his disciples that from now on all knowledge of God would proceed through him' (223). The reference is to a saying recorded by both Matthew and Luke: 'No one knows the Son except the Father, and no one knows the Father except the Son and anyone to whom the Son chooses to reveal him' (Matt. 11.27, cf. Luke 10.22). On Harnack's interpretation, the saying asserts the absolute originality and exclusiveness of Jesus' knowledge of God, in relation even to the Old Testament. Harnack appeals to this same saying elsewhere. In the closing paragraph of his *History of Dogma*, he tells how Luther brought the history of dogma to an end by replacing dogmatic rigidities with faith and experience: from this perspective, 'Matthew 11.27 is the basis of faith and theology' (vii.274).[31] In *Das Wesen des Christentums*, he clarifies this anti-dogmatic interpretation by explaining that, according to this text, Jesus' consciousness of sonship is 'nothing but the practical consequence of knowing God as the Father and as his Father' (131). How he arrived at the consciousness of this unique knowledge and of his mission to communicate it to others 'is his secret, and no psychology will ever fathom it' (132). This consciousness and this mission occurred 'within the framework of the Jewish nation' – but, to repeat, 'its real kernel may be readily freed from the inevitable husk of contemporary form' (133). Harnack can use the same saying to assert the autonomy of Jesus' knowledge of God in relation both to the Old Testament and to ecclesial dogma; for Old Testament and dogma are linked by their essential Jewishness.

Marcion knows Jesus' saying in its Lucan form (Luke 10.22). Tertullian acknowledges that this is an important proof-text for the Marcionite claim that 'it was an unknown God that Christ preached', adding that 'other heretics too prop themselves up with this passage, alleging in opposition to it that the Creator was known to all, both to Israel by a covenant relationship and to the Gentiles by nature' (*adv.Marc.* iv.25). His own explanation is that 'it was for this reason that he inserted the clause that the Father is known by him to whom the Son has revealed him, because it was he who was announced as set by the Father to be a light to the Gentiles, who of course needed to be enlightened about God, as well as to Israel, by imparting to it a fuller knowledge of God' (iv.25).[32] The Lucan context makes it clear that the revelation of the Father through the Son does not take place without preparation. In the transfiguration narrative (Luke 9.28–36), for example, it is true that the divine voice commands the disciples and us to hear Jesus, the Son of God, rather than Moses and Elijah. Yet how strange it is, if Jesus came not to fulfil the law and the prophets but to destroy them, that he here associates himself with their representatives! 'This is how he destroys them: he irradiates them with his own glory!' On the other hand, it is entirely fitting for the Creator, the God of the Old Testament, to manifest his Christ 'in the company of those who announced his coming, to let him be seen with those to whom he had revealed himself, to let him speak with those who had spoken of him, to share his glory with those by whom he used to be called the Lord of glory' (*adv.Marc.* iv.22).

If, unlike Marcion's, Harnack's gospel does not include the transfiguration story,[33] one might point to the saying that immediately follows the claim to an exclusive knowledge of the Father: 'Turning to the disciples he said privately, "Blessed are the eyes which see what you see! For I tell you that many prophets and kings desired to see what you see, and did not see it, and to hear what you hear, and did not hear it"' (Luke 10.23–24, cf. Matt. 13.16–17). This can only mean that the knowledge of the Father through the Son is the fulfilment of what was proclaimed in the Old Testament, and not its replacement by a reality whose links with the Old Testament are purely accidental. 'If he had not been my Christ' (the Christ who comes not to destroy but to fulfil), 'he would not have made any mention of the prophets in this passage' (*adv.Marc.* iv.25). Marcion and Harnack are too hasty in their assumption that, whatever the prophets may have expected, it bore no relation to what actually took place in Jesus Christ.

(*iii*) According to Harnack's neo-Marcionite theses, twentieth-century Protestantism must boldly do what that of the sixteenth and the nineteenth centuries failed to do: it must deny canonical status to the Old Testament. Marcion was ahead of his time when he saw in the Old Testament 'another spirit than that of the gospel', and 'refused to acknowledge that there could be two spirits in religion' (*Marcion*, 216). How are we to characterize the alien, un-Christian spirit of the Old Testament? Marcion's *Antitheses* seeks to establish that, at point after point, the God of the Old Testament is different from the God and Father of our Lord Jesus Christ: the one forbids what the other permits, and acts in ways that are incompatible with all that we know of the character of the other. That which the Old Testament ascribes to God is utterly unworthy of the God made known to us in Christ. The God of the Old Testament is angry and uncouth, lacking in refinement. Marcion and Harnack agree that he is not a fit object of our worship.

Alexandrian Judaism had developed the theory of accommodation to account for those points in the sacred texts that offended the educated Greek mind. God did not *really* walk in the garden or regret that he ever made the world: these are just simple, pictorial modes of speech which seek to convey sublime truths to people who cannot easily grasp them.[34] Tertullian offers a christological version of this theory of accommodation in refutation of Marcion's statement of the traditional objections to the Old Testament. The general principle is that 'God would have been unable to enter into communion with humankind if he had not taken upon himself human emotions and affections, tempering the strength of his majesty – which human capacity would have been unable to endure – by way of a self-abasement unworthy of himself but necessary for man – and for that very reason worthy of God, because nothing is so worthy of God as the salvation of humankind' (*adv.Marc.* ii.27). If, for the sake of human salvation, the Son of God can abase himself to the extent of incarnation and death on the cross, why should we be unable to believe that, even before the incarnation, he 'communed with patriarchs and prophets', and so prepared himself for the human existence he was one day to undergo (ii.27)? The cultured despisers of the Old Testament have failed to understand that the incarnation exemplifies and fulfils the pattern of divine communicative action towards humankind already established in the Old Testament. The imperfections that distress refined readers of the Old Testament are signs not only of human fleshliness but also – and above all – of the saving divine condescension finally disclosed in the incarnation of the Word. It therefore cannot be said that the 'spirit' of the Old Testament is fundamentally different from the 'spirit' of Christian faith.

Harnack's opposition to the canonical status of the Old Testament may perhaps be traced back to his inability to comprehend the doctrine of the incarnation. The idea that what takes place in Jesus is (exclusively, not additionally) God's own *act* of love and condescension is utterly alien to him; such a view stems, of course, from the 'ecclesial dogma' against which he so resolutely sets his face throughout his work. The overriding purpose of his *History of Dogma* is, precisely, to consign dogma to history and to replace it with something qualitatively different: faith, Christian experience, religion, inwardness, or whatever. This new reality will not need any assistance from the Old Testament as it finds its fundamental convictions reflected back to it by the figure of Jesus. The Old Testament makes sense theologically only as a witness to the particularity of divine action, and if one denies the applicability of this interpretative category to the figure of Jesus the Old Testament will have little more to say.

(*iv*) For Tertullian, the christological pattern of divine condescension is to be found not only in the Old Testament but also in the created order – in accordance with the fact that the God of whom the Old Testament speaks is the creator of heaven and earth. Unlike the Greeks, Marcion and his followers are unimpressed by the grandeur of the created order. When exhorted to recognize the divine creator in the magnitude of his works, they frivolously point to the existence of *insects* as a clear proof of his inferiority. According to Tertullian, they should learn from the extraordinary abilities of tiny creatures such as the bee, the ant, the spider and the silk-worm 'that greatness has its proofs in lowliness, just as (according to the apostle) there is power even in weakness' (*adv.Marc.* i.14). And what of our own selves? 'This production of our God [i.e. the creator] must be pleasing even to you, since your own Lord, that better God, loved it so much and for your sake went to the trouble of descending from the third heaven . . .' (i.14). It is true also of the created order that, as the apostle wrote, the wisdom of God is folly to the world: 'God is then especially great when he is small from a human point of view; especially good when not good in human judgment' (ii.2). In the creation of humankind in the image of God, 'Goodness spoke the word; Goodness formed man of the dust of the ground into so great a substance of the flesh, built up out of a single material with so many qualities; Goodness breathed into him a soul not dead but living . . . The same Goodness provided also a help meet for him, that there might be nothing in his lot that was not good' (ii.4). The divine goodness manifested in redemption is of a piece with the goodness of the creator. Contrary to Marcionite slanders against the created order, creation is the indispensable presupposition of redemption.

For Marcion, redemption occurs in the midst of a world to which it is fundamentally alien. The world as such is not its object; it is concerned only with the souls of those who believe, and reality outside this narrow compass is a hostile realm belonging to another deity. Harnack is remarkably unconcerned about the Marcionite abandonment of the doctrine of creation as the presupposition of the doctrine of redemption. When he informs us that Marcion is significant above all for his assertion that God the Redeemer 'has absolutely nothing to do with cosmology and cosmic teleology' (*Marcion*, VII), he appears to countenance the view that we acquire through Jesus a knowledge of a God who is, at best, only obscurely related to the creator of heaven and earth.[35] In *Das Wesen des Christentums*, 'God the Father' is correlated only with 'the infinite value of the human soul' (65), that is, with 'inwardness' rather than 'externality' – an antithesis not easily reconciled with a Christian doctrine of creation. Harnack has, it is true, nothing against the idea of creation: on the contrary, this is 'an element which is as important as it is in thorough keeping with the gospel', making it impossible to identify God and world and expressing faith in God's power (232). Yet it never occurs to him to assert that, since the God who redeems us in Christ is also the creator, Marcion was at this point simply *wrong*, or to give Marcion's opponents credit for pointing this out. Harnack's world-view, such as it is, is deeply marked by the question whether (as he put it in 1895) there exists 'a higher Reality, compared with which the world is as nothing' or whether 'we are altogether confined within the sphere of mechanical nature' (71).[36] Religion – the religion communicated to us by Jesus – is the guarantee that the standpoint of scientific materialism is inadequate and that we are essentially spiritual rather than material beings. As Harnack put this point four years later, 'We value that which unfolds on this higher level as the real life to which the physical life should be subordinate' (306).[37] The external world is conceded to the control of mechanistic science, and religion establishes itself in the ethereal world of *Innerlichkeit*: Luther's doctrine of the two kingdoms seems here to undergo a distinctly Marcionite radicalization.

In the absence of the Old Testament, the doctrine of creation can neither be affirmed with a clear conscience, nor denied. Inspired by Marcion's example, we are perhaps supposed to conclude that this hardly matters.

3. Bultmann

Rudolf Bultmann's theology derives much of its impetus from the decision to repudiate what he takes to be the characteristic liberal Protestant view of history.[38] History, he argues, can never be directly disclosive of God, and historical research does not allow us to transcend the relativities of history so as to behold the divine plan coming to fruition in and behind those relativities. Theologically-relevant knowledge of God's act in Christ occurs through the 'kerygma', the message of the death and resurrection of Jesus, understood as the divine word of address that discloses our creatureliness, our guilty pursuit of an illusory, self-contradictory autonomy, and our ultimate status as objects of the divine grace that frees us from the sin and death to which we have fallen victim. Through the gospel message, the possibility for which human beings were created is repeatedly actualized: that they should live before God in full awareness of their position before God. That this is the case cannot be understood by the spectator who remains detached from the life-and-death struggle for truth and meaning represented by the New Testament, but only by those who find themselves to be participants in this struggle because they have encountered the divine word that lies at its heart. Thus, theologically-relevant knowledge is not a natural consequence of a historical research which knows how to remove secondary accretions so as to make the original image of Jesus luminously clear again. This research may be able to speak impressively about the purity of Jesus' religious experience, the compelling power of his personality, his transforming effect on his contemporaries – but such matters should not be confused with God's decisive act for the salvation of humankind. History knows of various impressive and compelling personalities, but it cannot ascribe to any of them the ultimate and universal significance implied in the Christian confession of Jesus as the Christ. As a matter of fact, Jesus was a prophet of the imminent eschaton, fully comprehensible as the product of Old Testament and apocalyptic traditions. We must also recall that the gospel tradition as a whole is a primary source for our knowledge not of Jesus but of the early church. In advocating 'radical' positions such as these, critical scholarship fulfils the useful although negative role of making it clear that history as such can never become transparent to the presence of eternity. Revelation occurs only through the miracle of the kerygma.

This critique of the understanding of history implied in liberal Protestant christology is fundamental to Bultmann's mature theological position. It draws on the renewed 'Paulinism' of Barth's *Romans*, the historical scepticism of Wrede, and the apocalypticism of Weiss and Schweitzer, together with Bultmann's own historical-critical work in applying the techniques of *Formgeschichte* to the synoptic gospels. The fact that, in this context, Wrede, Weiss and Schweitzer can be named alongside Barth is an indication of a more complex relationship to the liberal Protestant tradition than Bultmann's polemical language might lead one to expect: his characteristic theological positions can often – perhaps always – be seen as transformations of elements of the liberal Protestant heritage.[39] One such element is the neo-Marcionite rejection of the canonical status of the Old Testament, which in Bultmann's rendering proceeds directly from his disjunction between general history and the specific mode of individual historicity presupposed by the kerygma. Assembling material scattered through a number of essays (Bultmann's preferred form for theological as opposed to historical or exegetical work), we discover at this point a threefold concern.[40]

(*i*) From the New Testament onwards, Christians have sought in the Old Testament prophetic anticipations of the life, death and resurrection of Jesus Christ which can be used to demonstrate the veracity of Christian claims. Bultmann argues that this procedure has been shown to be impossible on historical-critical grounds, and that, more importantly, it is theologically illegitimate. The cross of Christ is the great *skandalon* to our natural self-understanding, challenging us to acknowledge our finitude and guilt. To try to prove that we encounter God's word in the gospel of the crucified Jesus indicates simply that one has failed to hear this word; for the word is a radical question directed towards our self-understanding rather than an invitation to reflect on its own credentials. God's eschatological act of salvation does not need any extraneous support from supposed instances of miraculous foreknowledge of inner-historical happenings, for in its essence it is *not* an inner-historical happening.

(*ii*) Because God's act in Christ is eschatological in nature, there can be no question of an unbroken continuity between the events of Israel's salvation-history and the Christ-event. On the contrary, salvation-history is brought to an end in Christ; salvation is now concentrated exclusively in his person and in the word that bears witness to him. The sphere of Christ is the historicity of individual existence, and from this standpoint Israel's salvation-history cannot be differentiated from the secular sphere of history-in-general. Israel's national existence is based on the self-contradictory belief that her elect status can and should be actualized in her empirical existence among the nations, and the crucified Christ exposes this and every other identification of God's revelation and empirical, political reality as illusory. There can equally be no question of a distinctively Christian salvation-history occurring within church history; for, in its true being, the church is not an empirical, inner-historical reality but the empty space within which the event of salvation must again and again take place.

(*iii*) If the relationship between the Testaments cannot be understood on the basis of fulfilled prophecy or salvation-history and is therefore to be seen as discontinuous, this discontinuity nevertheless retains a genuine theological significance. When, in the traditional polarity of 'law' and 'gospel', the Old Testament is understood as 'law', it is rightly indicated that what comes to expression here is the essential presupposition for the proclamation of the gospel. 'Law' represents the Old Testament's understanding of human existence as standing under the demand of the divine creator, a self-understanding that tends to generate the illusion that the demand may be fulfilled autonomously and that it therefore lies within human capacity to actualize human destiny. Thus the truth that is given in and with existence is corrupted into falsehood by sinful human self-sufficiency, and knowledge of this complex, distorted reality is essential to the hearing of the gospel, in which it is overcome. The Old Testament is valuable as an *expression* – historically highly influential – of the self-understanding presupposed by the gospel, but the universality of this self-understanding means that other expressions of it are to be expected, and that no uniquely privileged position is to be accorded to the Old Testament as such. The Old Testament usefully illustrates the human situation, but it is not strictly necessary.

In each case, Bultmann's attitude towards the Old Testament can be traced back to his belief that history is theologically relevant only from the perspective of the existing individual. This excludes any appeal to the historical continuities offered by fulfilled prophecy or salvation-history; and it also means that the relationship of the Old Testament to a particular, historical people is irrelevant to the true theological significance of the Old Testament as an expression of 'law'. The criterion for theological relevance is always whether a given assertion can be said to be meaningful 'for me', as a necessary element or presupposition of the kerygma in which I encounter the God of judgment and of grace. The knowledge that the miraculous birth of Jesus was predicted seven centuries in advance, or that the people of Israel was delivered from Egypt by divine power, is of no possible significance to 'my' life-and-death encounter with the saving, judging word of God. Such knowledge would (if reliable) add some interesting and rather surprising items to my general knowledge of the world; but it would have nothing to do with the all-important question of my concrete response to the demanding, gracious divine address as encountered here and now.

The truth underlying all forms of neo-Marcionism is the insight that the christological heart of Christian faith must function as the sole criterion for determining what is and is not authentically Christian. On this basis, it is possible to identify and criticize certain kinds of appeal to the Old Testament as sub-Christian or un-Christian. Where, for example, a doctrine of God is constructed largely out of Old Testament language and overlooks the distinctively Christian grounding of the doctrine of God in the mutual knowledge of the Father and the Son in the Holy Spirit, it is important that the questionableness of this procedure should be pointed out. Neo-Marcionism knows that authentically Christian theology is radical in nature, and that this radicalism precludes a biblicism which, assuming a more or less direct correspondence between Old Testament texts and reality, sees no need to interpret them in the light of that which lies at the centre of the biblical witness. The problem is, however, that neo-Marcionite understanding of the centre is fundamentally arbitrary, since the 'Christ' whom it locates there is conceived in abstraction from much of the content of the New Testament texts themselves. Thus, the fact that these texts everywhere assume an intimate intertextual relation with an existing scripture is disregarded, along with a great deal else that is constitutive of these texts (the narrative form of the gospels, for example). The christological criterion becomes, as it were, a weapon against the texts of both Testaments. The New Testament, and to some extent the Old Testament too, is subjected to a hermeneutic which assumes an almost universal disjunction between what is said and what is meant; the surface of the texts is deemed to be systematically misleading, and attention is focused instead on the 'real intention' said to underlie this unsatisfactory form. In Bultmann's case, the programme of 'demythologizing' is the means by which the reduction of texts to their real intention is practised and legitimated. But the gulf between the texts and their real intention is often so great that in practice texts may simply be *replaced* by their supposed 'real intention', which is understood in relation to the christological heart of Christian faith as construed by the individual interpreter. In neo-Marcionism, authentic Christian radicalism degenerates into an iconoclasm or vandalism which attacks not only the Old Testament but the irreducible textual mediation of Christian faith, so as to create space for an illusory immediacy of encounter. Criticism of neo-Marcionism must therefore address the problem of the one-sided, exclusive construal of the centre that results from the reduction of textuality to immediate encounter; and it must do so by way of an inclusive, non-reductionist construal of the centre as the focal point for the reality that lies within its circumference, and not as identical with the whole. With this in mind, we turn to a more detailed analysis of the three main elements in Bultmann's rendering of the neo-Marcionite position.

(*i*) In his study of 'Prophecy and Fulfilment' (1949), Bultmann draws a comparison between New Testament interpretation of prophecy and the allegorical exegesis of Stoicism and Hellenistic Judaism. In every case, he argues, 'it is clear that what is already known is derived from the texts'. Why are texts consulted at all if they can only tell us what we already know? The answer is that 'people want to find it in the old texts so that it can count as authoritative truth' (183). Contemporary truth will only convince if it can avail itself of the prestige of antiquity, for culture's respect for tradition is such that (despite the Athenians of Acts 17.21) sheer newness is already an adequate reason for suspicion. Contemporary truth must look old if it is to make its way in the world, and it is the function of the New Testament's 'as it is written' to create a plausible simulacrum of antiquity that will ensure the credibility of contemporary truth. Critical scholarship makes it its business to expose the pseudo-antiquity of these fraudulent productions so as to separate the genuine truth they may contain from the fake.

It is therefore Bultmann's responsibility as a critic to show, by way of numerous examples, that 'the New Testament and the traditional understanding' of prophecy 'has become impossible in an age in which the Old Testament is conceived of as a historical document and interpreted according to the methods of historical science' (185). Certain proof-texts are marshalled in support of this thesis. In the use made of Isa. 7.14 in Matt. 1.23, for example, an Old Testament text is not only 'understood in a sense contrary to its original meaning' but also 'quoted quite contrary to the original wording', following the Septuagint rather than the Hebrew (185). Heb. 2.6–8 understands Ps. 8.5–7 as a prophecy of the temporary humiliation of the pre-existent Christ, although in the original text the subject is the status of humankind within the created order (186). Arbitrary exegesis of this kind is unfortunately typical of the New Testament, whose authors 'do not gain new knowledge from the Old Testament texts, but read from or into them what they already know' (187). This illegitimate procedure was indeed useful to the primitive Christian community; for, in both its anti-Jewish polemics and its mission to the Gentiles, it was thereby able 'to overcome stumbling-blocks, to answer questions, to adduce proofs, [and] to represent objectionable or astonishing facts as predestined and prophesied' (187). In our own historically-minded age, however, this way of overcoming the offensiveness of Christian truth-claims has itself become offensive. Above all, we should question its theological legitimacy: 'Can the offence of the cross of Jesus be overcome by recognizing it as long-prophesied and decided upon by God – or only by grasping its meaning and significance?' (187). The effect of the tortuous early Christian attempts to read the cross back into the Old Testament was merely to conceal 'the real stumbling-block which belief has to overcome, and so the right way to overcome it' (188). The appeal to prophecy radically falsifies the truth of the kerygma.

Before the modern era, the argument from prophecy was crucially important to all attempts to maintain the unity of the Testaments, and its rejection can therefore be virtually *identified* with the methodological decision that the two Testaments should be studied in relative isolation from each other.[41] 'In an age in which the Old Testament is conceived of as a historical document' (and the New likewise), biblical scholarship takes it for granted in its interpretative practice that there is an unbridgeable gulf between the two parts of the Christian Bible. This gulf is so familiar that one hardly notices it; it does not need any explicit defence but can simply be presupposed; and, should anyone find it a problem that the empty space between the Testaments was the very place where one had expected to encounter Jesus Christ, reliable mechanisms are in place that will automatically issue warnings about the dangers of eisegesis, anachronism and obscurantism, and extol the virtues of a scholarship that dares to restore the texts to their original historical contexts. Yet the existence of these mechanisms, ready to be operated by Bultmann or anyone else, reflects a dim awareness that the hypothesis of the gulf between the Testaments *might* still be questioned. Precisely in ruling out the counter-thesis that between the Testaments stands not an unbridgeable gulf but Jesus Christ, one tacitly acknowledges the enduring possibility of this counter-thesis.

The counter-thesis is unthinkable without the argument from prophecy, and it is important to determine exactly what this argument might be expected to achieve. If it is conceived as a strict 'proof' that brings Christian truth-claims under the jurisdiction of pure reason in order to demonstrate their veracity once and for all, the argument from prophecy has never been compelling. The Matthean appeal to Isa. 7.14 can only function as a 'proof' for one who already believes that Matthew's account of the miraculous birth is truthful, in which case it is superfluous as such. For one who is disinclined to accept the truthfulness of such stories, the citation could merely suggest that the story originates not in historical reality but in the text that is cited to support it. In purely pragmatic terms, it is not at all clear that the appeal to the fulfilment of prophecy was generally a help rather than a hindrance to early Christian mission in Gentile contexts. It is true that the appearance of antiquity thereby achieved could be an advantage; but this advantage might be offset by the fact that the antiquity in question was an alien, *Jewish* antiquity whose credentials and standing were anything but firmly established in Graeco-Roman culture as a whole. The attractiveness of Marcionite or gnostic repudiation of the Old Testament presupposes a broadly-based perception of Jewish scripture as irredeemably alien. To explain that Christ's death took place 'according to the scriptures' (1 Cor. 15.3) does not make it any less likely that the proclamation of Christ crucified will be 'foolishness to Gentiles' (1 Cor. 1.23).

The argument from prophecy is more complex than is assumed in the conventional modern polemic against 'proofs':[42]

(1) It indicates that the gospel of the incarnate, crucified and risen Jesus is not self-explanatory but requires Jewish scripture as its primary interpretative matrix. Where this textual mediation is set aside, the result will be not a purer apprehension of the gospel but the replacement of one interpretative matrix by another: for example, gnostic syncretistic mythologizing, Marcionite dualism, or the neo-Marcionite opposition between the natural or historical sphere and the sphere of inwardness or existence.

(2) It confirms that Jesus' history and its proclamation as gospel occur within the public, historical realm in which the contemporary actualization of the tradition inherited from the past is a constant dilemma. The claim that Jesus' actualization of the past is, uniquely, a *fulfilment* of that past derives from the belief that the time of Jesus' history is 'the fullness of time' (Gal. 4.4), the time during which God in Christ acts to reconcile the world to himself. The legacy of earlier times that is actualized here is therefore actualized finally and definitively; it derives its true significance from the time of fulfilment, for which it prepares the way; and, in retrospect, it can be seen that this significance is not something arbitrarily imposed upon it but an answer to the question implied in its own openness to God's future.

(3) It therefore assumes that the role of the canonical context in which we receive the scriptural texts is not to preserve artefacts from the long-dead past as though in a museum-case, but to hold them open for definitive future actualization. Even in its much-emphasized Hebrew form, it is not the role of Isa. 7.14 to satisfy scholarly curiosity about Near Eastern political realities of the eighth century BC. In its canonical context, the promise of the child who is to be Immanuel, God with us, opens up a future that far transcends its immediate historical circumstances: a future in which it becomes true that 'the people who walked in darkness have seen a great light' (Isa. 9.2; Matt. 4.16) because of the child whose name is 'Wonderful Counsellor, Mighty God, Everlasting Father, Prince of Peace' (Isa. 9.6). The Christian interpretation of Old Testament prophetic texts can read them retrospectively, in the light of their fulfilment, in the conviction that such a reading also accords with their own inherent openness to God's future.

For all the sophistication of the historical scholarship that accompanies it, the modern critique of the Christian understanding of Old Testament prophecy operates with a crude and authoritarian hermeneutic that is no less vulnerable on general hermeneutical grounds than it is theologically. Its protestations about 'the impossibility of the New Testament and the traditional understanding' of prophecy, 'in an age in which the Old Testament is conceived as a historical document', require critical scrutiny. By what sleight of hand is an institutional decision to conceive the Old Testament as a historical document, that is, to interpret it in a way that disregards its canonical role as the first part of the Christian Bible, converted into the normative demand of 'an age'? Is the proclamation of a certain 'impossibility' undermined by the inadequacy and inflexibility of the description on which it is based? Which institutional interests is this veto intended to protect? If there is to be a theological interpretation of Christian scripture, it is essential to identify and to dismantle the ideologies that divide the two Testaments from each other, allocating them to separate interpretative communities which will be sure to discover their own institutional autonomy reflected back to them by the texts. In this sense, it can be said of many biblical scholars too that they 'do not gain new knowledge from the Old Testament texts, but read from or into them what they already know'.

(*ii*) As the end of the law, Christ is the end of salvation-history: for Bultmann, the history of God's dealings with the people of Israel is of no theological importance. As the 'eschatological deed of God', Jesus 'makes an end of all ethnic history [*Volksgeschichte*] as the sphere of God's dealing with man' ('The Significance of the Old Testament for Christian Faith' [1933], 30). In contrast to the people of Israel, the church 'is not a sociological entity, an ethnic [*Volks-*] or cultural community bound together by the continuity of history, but is constituted by the proclaimed Word of God's forgiveness in Christ . . . It has no history as ethnic [*völkische*], national, and cultural communities have their history' (30–31). The Gentile church does not, as Paul mistakenly thought, find itself grafted into the richness of the Jewish olive tree (Rom. 11.17), for 'the history of Israel is a closed chapter', it is 'not our history', and 'the events which meant something for Israel . . . mean nothing more to us' (31).[43] It is true that, in a certain sense, the history of Israel has become part of 'our' western historical heritage; but the same is also true of Greek history, so that it might be said 'that the Spartans fell at Thermopylae for us and that Socrates drank the hemlock for us' (31). 'Jerusalem is not a holier city for us than Athens or Rome' (31–32).

If, on this occasion, we adopt the hermeneutic that Bultmann himself commends and interpret these statements within their original historical context (Germany in 1933), a curious ambivalence comes to light.

On the one hand, there is a repeated denial that there is anything *völkisch* about the church, together with the assertion that in its essence the church is an empty space, uncontaminated by national identity, in which God's Word is proclaimed and heard. There is no concession here to the current German Christian demand that 'the reawakened German sense of vitality' be 'respected in our Church', and that 'race, *Volk* and nation' be seen as 'orders of existence granted and entrusted to us by God'.[44] In a lecture delivered at Marburg on 2 May 1933, Bultmann argues that theological reflection on 'ordinances of creation [*Schöpfungsordnungen*]' is only legitimate where it is recognized that 'everything, possessions and family, education and law, nation and state, can become sin at man's hands': these *Ordnungen* are God's 'only in so far as they call us to service in our concrete tasks', while 'in their mere givenness they are ordinances of *sin*' (189).[45] A critical perspective is essential: 'In a day when the nation has again been generally recognized as an ordinance of creation, the Christian faith has to prove its critical power precisely by continuing to insist that the nation is ambiguous and that, just for the sake of obedience to the nation as an ordinance of creation, the question must continue to be asked what is and what is not the nation's true demand' (191). In accordance with his own demand for concreteness, Bultmann concludes his lecture by attacking the decision of the new Marburg town council to rename streets and squares in commemoration of the National Socialist revolution, and by deploring the defamation of German Jews (193–94). The widespread view that Bultmann's characteristic emphasis on freedom from the world legitimates apolitical withdrawal ignores the critical implications of this doctrine, especially within a totalitarian political context. If the only practical result is the recommendation that, as Bultmann put it in a Marburg sermon a year later, 'when our thinking and acting are taken in claim by the projects and duties of civic and political life, by the ideals of our nation and its history, we can participate in all of this only with an inner reservation' (209), one should note that, in a totalitarian context, the public call for an 'inner reservation' as a requirement of Christian faith is not as politically innocuous as it might sound elsewhere.[46]

On the other hand (to return to Bultmann's comments on the Old Testament), the *Volksgeschichte* that is a closed chapter, that is not our history and that has no meaning for us, is the history of Israel as recounted in the Old Testament. This history is secularized; for us, it is not salvation-history but simply a piece of history-in-general, significant for western Christians alongside other histories but in no way different or normative. Christian faith is thereby freed from its Jewish matrix; it is de-judaized. The Old Testament may be used, optionally, to illustrate the understanding of human existence presupposed by the kerygma, but it may equally well be replaced by other illustrative material, drawn perhaps from Greek tragedy or modern philosophy. And if 'Israel's history is not our history', the question is which concrete history it is that claims and concerns 'us' in a way that the history of Israel does not. The answer can only be the European and specifically the German history of the modern period: this alone is 'our history', in the immediate sense. Thus, although the church in its innermost essence has no *Volksgeschichte*, its members belong to the political sphere as well as the sphere of God's Word and therefore share in the *Volksgeschichte* of their own particular time and place, through which God's demand is concretely mediated. At the time and place in question, the church is the German evangelical church whose members participate (critically, with inner reservations) in the unfolding of Germany's historical destiny; and, precisely here, it is recommended that the church should abandon its commitment to the canonical status of the Old Testament, regard the history of Israel with indifference, and fix its attention exclusively on a kerygma which has left everything Jewish – including Jesus of Nazareth – decisively behind it. What is the significance, at just this historical juncture, of Bultmann's call for the de-judaizing of Christian faith? Is the attempt to free theology and church from their Jewish roots entirely unrelated to current attempts to purify other areas of society and culture from alien, Jewish influences? Or is this – in effect if not in intention – a small contribution to the solution of 'the Jewish problem in Germany', a problem whose 'complicated character' Bultmann acknowledges while courageously attacking the defamation of German Jews? A church that learned to distance itself from its Jewish roots, adapting its liturgical, homiletical and educational practices accordingly, would be recognizably a church in and for the Third Reich, whatever measures it otherwise took to ensure its essential independence.[47] Conversely, a church that emphasized its Jewish roots, asserting that the Jewish Old Testament remains integral to Christian life and practice and that to attack it is to attack Christian faith itself, would be a church that knew how to refuse accommodation to the new political realities and ideologies. It would represent a point at which the dominant identification of Jewishness with degeneracy met with significant resistance, and to that extent a point of solidarity with German Jews.

Bultmann returns to the question of the Old Testament in a study of 'Prophecy and Fulfilment' (1949), where it is argued that 'an inner contradiction pervades the self-consciousness and the hope of Israel and its prophets' (205): Israel attempts to realize the idea of the people of God within its empirical national existence, an attempt that is 'reduced to absurdity by the grotesque form of a priestly and legalistic theocracy' (206). This 'miscarriage of history' (206) can paradoxically be seen, in retrospect, as a promise fulfilled in the coming into being of the new people of God, the church, which 'does not exist as a people requiring institutional structures for its organization' (204), since it is founded on the eschatological act of God in Christ which takes us out of the world. The history of Israel illustrates the fact that 'there is nothing which can count as a promise to man other than the miscarriage of *his* way, and the recognition that it is impossible to gain direct access to God in his history within the world, and directly to identify his history within the world with God's activity' (206). The idea of the covenant and the hopes that accompany it 'are such as to seduce man into an identification of God's eschatological activity with what happens in secular history' (207). It is clear that for Bultmann Israel's error has exemplary significance, and that the attempt to identify the course of secular history with divine activity is a real temptation that can be overcome only in faith. It is therefore plausible that the 'miscarriage of history' that he has in mind is not only Israel's but also Germany's in 1933–45, and that the fundamental contradiction upon which Israel's understanding of salvation-history is supposedly based also comes to expression in the ideology of National Socialism.

This interpretation is confirmed by a wartime article on 'The Question of Natural Revelation' (1941) in which one of the claims to a 'natural revelation' that Bultmann discusses is that of people who believe 'that God confronts them in Germany – reveals himself in Germany' (92).[48] In this context, 'natural revelation' can take the form of 'revelation in history', and the question is what is meant when such a thing is asserted. Does it imply that God reveals himself in individual persons in history, in which case the figure of the 'hero' represents the point at which divine action and empirical reality coincide? But the 'hero' can at best reveal not God but heroism. 'The vision of the hero can make an appeal to my moral will, but it does not make me pure'; the real hero, preoccupied not with himself but with his cause, 'will not put up with such abuse' (104). Bultmann alludes here to the current myth of a *Heilsgeschichte* in which a single man – the Hero, the Leader – discloses and embodies the nation's sacred, divinely-ordained destiny, thereby bestowing a new purity of purpose on the devotees of his cult. This myth originates in a false understanding of history which does not realize that the meaning of national history is ambiguous. 'Where do we get our criterion for what is essentially German, if we assert the existence of such a thing? And with what right can we say that primitive German history reveals more clearly what is "German" than does the history of the German Middle Ages?' (105). Every historical phenomenon is ambiguous, and its meaning at the time of its occurrence is almost entirely obscure, whatever the enthusiasm with which it is celebrated. Seventy years later, we do not judge the victory of 1870–71 in the same way as its contemporaries did. 'Naturally every present situation requires faith for its future tasks. But such faith is not faith in God; it is rather faith in the task itself', a faith involving a risk. 'And if the person who takes the risk does what he has in mind before God's eyes, he does it not in the consciousness that he has clearly unravelled the riddle of God's plan, but in the consciousness that his work has to stand its trial before the judgement seat of God whose verdict he cannot anticipate' (105). According to the national *Heilsgeschichte*, German history consists in the gradual disclosure of a national identity already essentially present in the nation's pre-Christian origins. The present represents the full flowering of national consciousness, the acceptance of the task imposed by the nation's history in faith in the God who directs that history towards its goal. One person in particular has courageously acted upon his faith in this history, in obedience to the divine commandment mediated through this history. Bultmann's intention is to puncture this inflated mythology by pointing out that 'the message of history is obscure and there is a risk if we pay heed to it. The essential nature of the German people is not present as a clear criterion by virtue of which we may clearly judge the rightness of our action' (105). Who knows how the triumphs of 1939–40 will be judged seventy years later?

The *Heilsgeschichte* of Israel, as rendered in the Old Testament, shares with its modern German counterpart the same fatal error: it is assumed that the empirical history of the *Volk* is the sphere of divine revelation and action. Neither *Volksgeschichte* has any place in the church, where we are freed from the world and its illusions by the Word of divine forgiveness.

This analysis of Nazi ideology is, in itself, plausible and illuminating - assuming that the procedure of converting Bultmann's statements into an 'analysis' by reading between the lines, hearing in what is said what is unsaid and unsayable, is an appropriate one. The identification of Jewishness with the primordial threat to German national identity is fully compatible with a wholesale adaptation of the basic structures of Israel's national *Heilsgeschichte*. Here, as there, we have the notion of a *Volk* separated from the nations by its divine election and by the glorious destiny that this implies. This *Volk*, destined for great things, endures the catastrophe of national humiliation in the Treaty of Versailles. Through the divinely-appointed figure of the *Führer*, it is miraculously redeemed from its enslaved state and comes to a joyful consciousness of its unique identity and destiny. Its immediate task is the acquisition of *Lebensraum*, and this is to be achieved by a military conquest whose goal is the elimination or subjugation of those who inhabit what is, in fact, promised land. Bultmann's antipathy towards Israel's *Heilsgeschichte* is apparently reinforced by its contemporary reappearance in a form that is distorted, secularized, but still recognizable.[49]

Twentieth-century reappropriations of the biblical exodus-conquest pattern may also be traced in South African *Apartheid* ideology and in Zionism; these examples might seem to confirm the danger of identifying empirical history with *Heilsgeschichte*.[50] It is, however, misleading to see in these reappropriations a reason for dispensing with the Christian Old Testament. The Old Testament does not issue in a 'miscarriage of history' which may be seen as a warning of the inevitable fate of all comparable attempts to identify empirical reality with divine revelation. Its account of *Heilsgeschichte* ends with a priestly theocracy which is only 'absurd' and 'grotesque' because the priests 'have corrupted the covenant of Levi' (Mal. 2.8). But this is not a true 'ending', for there remains an openness to God's future identified here with the coming of the messenger who will prepare the way of the Lord (Mal. 3.1). The Old Testament ends where the New Testament begins, with the promise that, before the great and terrible day of the Lord, Elijah will come to turn the hearts of fathers to their children and the hearts of children to their fathers (Mal. 4.5–6; cf. Matt. 3.4; 11.7–15; 17.10–13 and parallels; Mark 1.2; Luke 1.16–17). From a Christian perspective, the function of Old Testament *Heilsgeschichte* is not to provide a pattern for nationalistic ideologies but to prepare the way of the Lord. This history could only be said to have 'miscarried' if it had failed to provide the matrix within which Jesus was nurtured and out of which he came forth to preach peace to those who were far off and those who were near, so that Gentile and Jew together should gain access in one Spirit to the Father (Eph. 2.17–18).

Bultmann's tacit identification of a modern ideology with Israel's *Heilsgeschichte* means that he cannot escape becoming entangled in the very ideology he opposes. The modern ideology does not only reproduce or parody the basic structure of the Old Testament view; it also violently attacks this view, finding in it the roots of the Jewishness that constitutes the fundamental threat to German national identity. It goes without saying that Bultmann's denial of the canonical status of the Old Testament completely lacks the crudeness and the violence of the propagandists of the Third Reich; and, still more importantly, its motivation is fundamentally different. And yet it is disquieting to find that the theologian who calls the church to a radical rethinking of its own foundations and the ideologue who stridently demands the eradication of Jewishness from German national life stand, at this point, on common ground.

(*iii*) For Bultmann, the single theological question which may properly be put to the Old Testament is the question of its understanding of human existence (*Daseinsverständnis*). 'A genuinely historical inquiry of the Old Testament is one which, prompted by one's own question concerning existence, seeks to reactualize the understanding of human existence expressed in the Old Testament, in order to gain an understanding of one's own existence. To enter into such a dialogue with the Old Testament is all the more necessary since the Christian understanding of existence, on the basis of faith, claims for itself to be the only possibility granted by God's revelation and as such can remain genuine and vital only in constant dialogue with other views' ('The Significance of the Old Testament for Christian Faith', 14). According to the Old Testament, human existence is existence under the divine demand, characterized negatively by the awareness of the possibility and actuality of sin, the failure to obey the divine demand. This self-understanding is presupposed by the gospel, and in this sense it can be said that 'the Old Testament is the presupposition of the New' (14). 'The material connection between Law and Gospel means that man must stand under the Old Testament if he wants to understand the New' (15).

On this view of the relation of the Testaments, does the Old Testament 'retain its specifically Old Testament character?' (15). The answer, for Bultmann, is that it does not. While the *Daseinsverständnis* expressed in the Old Testament remains the presupposition for understanding the gospel, the Old Testament is of no value for us in so far as it relates to the historical experiences of a particular people. The 'truly moral demands of the Old Testament' have not lost their authority, and the reason is that they are 'not specifically Old Testament demands' but are 'grounded in human relationship itself', so that 'every period finds them simply by serious reflection upon this relationship' (16). While it can still be said in traditional-sounding language that 'the New Testament presupposes the Old, the Gospel presupposes the Law' (17), it becomes clear that what is presupposed is not the Old Testament as such but the understanding of existence expressed in the Old Testament *and elsewhere*. 'The preunderstanding of the Gospel which emerges under the Old Testament can emerge just as well within other historical embodiments of the divine Law . . . Everywhere the possibility is present for man to become aware of his nothingness and to come to humility or despair; and everywhere the temptation is present for him to make the moral demand into the means of his self-justification and to suppose that through struggle and achievement, through self-discipline and the leading of a moral life, he will attain his authentic selfhood as a mature, moral personality' (17). What matters is not the Old Testament itself but the universal possibilities for true and false self-understanding represented by the concept of 'Law'. 'It can only be for *pedagogical* reasons that the Christian Church uses the Old Testament to make man conscious of standing under God's demand' (17): the Old Testament is pragmatically *useful* in this respect, but it is not *obligatory* for the church to use it. Its value lies in its *Daseinsverständnis*, and this can equally well be found elsewhere;

for the genuine knowledge of God and humankind that it contains is a purely *natural* knowledge.[51]

How do we arrive at the conclusion that the Old Testament is to be understood theologically solely as 'Law'? If we take the texts as they stand, we find that 'existence under the Law is already thought of as existence under grace . . . The people are not constituted as a people by first obeying the Law but, rather, God's grace precedes, so that obedience is always to occur through faith in God's prevenient and electing grace' (22–23). We must therefore reckon with the presence of 'gospel' in the Old Testament: 'Insofar as "gospel" means the proclamation of God's grace for the sinner, it cannot be said that the Gospel is lacking in the Old Testament' (23–24). Once again, however, a traditional-sounding statement turns out to be misleading; for if one asks what the relation is between the gospel in the Old Testament and the gospel of God's grace in Christ, the answer is simply that these are quite different. 'Jesus is God's demonstration of grace in a manner which is fundamentally different from the demonstrations of divine grace attested in the Old Testament. For in the latter case, God's forgiveness is inextricably tied up with the destiny of the people (within which the individual also has his destiny) . . .' (29). In contrast, the kerygma has no concern with past historical events significant for the life of a people. The one who is addressed by it 'is not to look to demonstrations of God's grace found in historical events of the past, deducing from them that God is gracious and accordingly may also be gracious to him; rather, God's grace confronts him directly in the proclaimed Word' (30). While from its own point of view the Old Testament is Law and Gospel, 'it is quite possible, from the Christian viewpoint, to call the Old Testament Law' (31): to understand it, in other words, purely from the point of view of its *Daseinsverständnis*, according to which human existence is existence in subjection to the divine demand. If the grace encountered in Christ is fundamentally different from the grace of which the Old Testament speaks, then it follows not only that the element of 'gospel' in the Old Testament is none of our concern but also that the Old Testament *distorts and misrepresents* the truth about God's grace, which is in fact to be found not in the past events of a particular national history but in Christ alone. Bultmann does not explicitly draw this conclusion, but it appears to follow inevitably from the distinction he draws between the Old Testament as read on its own terms and as understood from the standpoint of Christian faith. Those who make constructive use of the Old Testament view of God's grace in interpreting God's grace in Christ will inevitably be led astray: hence Bultmann's uncompromising rejection of the prophecy/fulfilment schema and of theologies of salvation-history.[52]

In this version of the neo-Marcionite position as in others, the texts of the New Testament are treated almost as ruthlessly as the texts of the Old. In both cases, the fundamental significance attributed to the texts bears little or no relation to what they actually *say*, most of which is found to be devoid of theological significance. Thus, despite the assumption of the synoptic gospels that the history of Jesus of Nazareth is from beginning to end significant for faith, Bultmann sees here only the figure of a prophet with an eschatological message whose context is that of Judaism and not Christian faith. Christian faith originates, incomprehensibly, in the moment when it is recognized that in his death this figure constitutes God's saving address to humankind, the actualization of the possibility of an authentic existence in radical dependence on divine grace. The proclaimer becomes the proclaimed, and authentic Christian faith refers us solely to the proclaimed Christ – the Christ who has become Word – and not to the historical existence of Jesus ('Christ according to the flesh').[53] Just as the Old Testament is reduced to its *Daseinsverständnis*, so the New Testament is reduced to the kerygma, understood as God's direct address to us, here and now, challenging us to abandon our sinful self-sufficiency and to live in dependence on grace. 'Man', existing under the divine demand and entangled in sinful self-assertion, finds his existence illumined by the event of the divine Word of judgment and forgiveness: that is what the scriptures of the Old and the New Testaments have to tell us, and that is, in the end, *all* they have to tell us. Despite the formidable obstacles which the texts themselves pose to a reduction of this kind, Bultmann develops a remarkable range of strategies – historical-critical and theological – for demonstrating the theological redundancy of material that resists this reduction. The perceptive insights that often result have the effect of masking the simplicity and indeed the banality of the theology of proclamation which is always the goal of Bultmann's theological investigations.

This theology claims to be the loyal servant of the New Testament texts, helpfully detaching their real meaning from their myth-ridden surface. It claims also to identify the real meaning of the Old Testament, in a way that necessitates a still higher level of abstraction from the texts themselves. The alternative possibility is that a substitution has occurred, which is then assiduously concealed behind a bewildering array of masks and veils. On that view, the final reality of this theology would be simple: the polyphonic witness of both Testaments to God's definitive self-disclosure in Jesus Christ has been *replaced* by the monotony of the kerygma, the single word that can only be repeated, over and over again. One might say that this neo-Marcionism refutes itself by interpreting the Christ-event as the radical divine challenge to human self-assertion, while practising precisely such a self-assertion in its arbitrary and high-handed treatment of the texts which provide our primary access to this event.

NOTES

1. Modern Marcionism has also been analysed by John Bright, in his *The Authority of the Old Testament*, London: SCM Press, 1967, 60–79. I have not considered two significant figures briefly discussed by Bright: E. Hirsch and F. Baumgärtel. Bright ascribes only Marcionite *tendencies* to the latter.

2. B. A. Gerrish, *Continuing the Reformation: Essays on Modern Religious Thought*, Chicago and London: University of Chicago Press, 1993, 178–95. Quotations from Calvin are from the translation of the *Institutes* edited by John T. McNeill, Philadelphia: Westminster Press, 1960; quotations from Schleiermacher's *The Christian Faith* (*Glaubenslehre*) are from the translation of the second German edition (1830), edited by H. R. Mackintosh and J. S. Stewart, Edinburgh: T. & T. Clark, 1928.

3. Compare the argument of H. Graf Reventlow's *The Authority of the Bible and the Rise of the Modern World* (ET London: SCM Press, 1984), in which the victory of 'the modern world' over the theology of Luther and Calvin is traced from the spiritualism of the 'left wing of the Reformation' through English Deism to the German *Aufklärung*. According to Reventlow, it is impossible to overestimate 'the influence exercised by Deistic thought, and by the principles of the Humanist world-view which the Deists made the criterion of their biblical criticism, on the historical-critical exegesis of the nineteenth century; the consequences extend right down to the present' (412).

4. F. D. E. Schleiermacher, *On the Glaubenslehre: Two Letters to Dr Lücke*, ET Chico, Calif.: Scholars Press, 1981.

5. The two page-references refer to the German first edition (repr. Stuttgart: Reclam, 1969) and to John Oman's translation (1893) of the third edition (*On Religion: Speeches to its Cultured Despisers*, New York: Harper & Row, 1958). Translations are my own.

6. Thus Lessing appeals as follows to Luther in the controversy following his publication of Reimarus' anonymous *Fragments* (1778): 'Thou hast freed us from the yoke of tradition. Who will free us from the still more unbearable yoke of the letter?' (cited in H. Bornkamm, *Luther im Spiegel der deutschen Geistesgeschichte*, Göttingen: Vandenhoeck & Ruprecht, 1970[2], 201). For Herder, the letter/Spirit antithesis explains the differences between the gospels, which reflect the freedom of early Christian preaching: 'This free spirit of oral discourse breathes in every line of every evangelist; the *Spirit* is not the letter' (*Vom Erlöser der Menschen* [1797]; J. G. Herder, *Against Pure Reason: Writings on Religion, Language, and History*, ed. M. Bunge, Minneapolis: Augsburg Fortress, 1993, 185). Hegel emphasizes that the Bible itself asserts that the letter kills while the Spirit gives life – thereby relativizing itself and teaching us that only the Spirit that we bring to the text brings it to life (*Lectures on the Philosophy of Religion* [1821–31], ET repr. New York: Humanities Press, 1962, 2.344).

7. F. D. E. Schleiermacher, *The Life of Jesus* (published posthumously in 1864 on the basis of lectures delivered in 1832), ET Philadelphia: Fortress Press, 1975.

8. Lessing's publication in 1778 of Reimarus' *Von dem Zwecke Jesu und seiner Jünger* brought this issue into the centre of German theological discussion (ET in C. H. Talbert [ed.], *Reimarus: Fragments*, London: SCM Press, 1971, 59–269).

9. D. F. Strauss, *The Life of Jesus Critically Examined* (1835; 2 vols.), ET George Eliot (1846), repr. ed. P. C. Hodgson, Philadelphia: Fortress Press, 1972; London: SCM Press,

1973. Strauss writes: 'In the meantime, let the calmness and *Kaltblütigkeit* with which, in the course of [this work], criticism undertakes apparently dangerous operations, be explained solely by the author's conviction that no injury is threatened to Christian faith' (lii); Eliot rendered this term as 'insensibility'. For Strauss, Schleiermacher is 'a supernaturalist in Christology but in criticism and exegesis a rationalist' (*The Christ of Faith and the Jesus of History: A Critique of Schleiermacher's Life of Jesus* [1865], ET Philadelphia: Fortress, 1977). His 'supernaturalism' is said to consist in his retaining the dogma of Jesus' sinlessness, despite the abandonment of its foundation in the doctrine of the incarnation (29). Strauss does not notice that rationalistic exegesis fulfils a positive role for Schleiermacher in enabling him to construct his christology in relative independence of the gospel texts.

10. F. D. E. Schleiermacher, *Hermeneutics: The Handwritten Manuscripts*, ed. H. Kimmerle, ET Missoula: Scholars Press, 1977.

11. Coleridge's distinction between reason and understanding exemplifies this tension. For Coleridge, reason is the human faculty that grasps the whole of existence, whereas understanding is directed towards the parts; on occasion there is said to be a dialectical relationship between them. Thus, religion is defined as 'the consideration of the Particular and Individual (in which respect it takes up and identifies with itself the excellence of the *Understanding*) but of the Individual, as it exists and has its being in the Universal (in which respect it is one with pure *Reason*)' (S. T. Coleridge, *Lay Sermons*, Collected Works 6, ed. R. J. White, Princeton: Princeton University Press, 1972, 62). Here, 'understanding' guarantees that the individual's oneness with pure reason does not simply dissolve its individuality. Elsewhere, however, understanding is seen as the source of the illusion of separateness that prevents us from grasping the absolute oneness of being. 'The groundwork . . . of all true philosophy is the full apprehension of the difference between the contemplation of reason, namely, that intuition of things which arises when we possess ourselves, as one with the whole, which is substantial knowledge, and that which presents itself when, transferring reality to the negations of reality, . . . we think of ourselves as separated beings, and place nature in antithesis to the mind, as object to subject, thing to thought, death to life. This is abstract knowledge, or the science of the mere understanding.' For reason, existence is 'the one attribute in which all others are contained, not as parts, but as manifestations'; it is 'an eternal and infinite self-rejoicing, self-loving' (*The Friend: A Series of Essays*, Collected Works 4.1, ed. Barbara E. Rooke, Princeton: Princeton University Press, 1969, 520–21). On the other hand, the particularity postulated by the understanding is in itself non-reality; the reality it has is, as it were, borrowed from the whole, and is constantly on the verge of dissolution into the whole. In the analogous case of Schleiermacher's christology, it is the narrated particularities of the gospel texts that are dissolved into the whole.

12. F. D. E. Schleiermacher, *Luke: A Critical Study*, trans. Connop Thirlwall (1825), repr. ed. Terrence N. Tice, Lewiston/Queenston/Lampeter: Edwin Mellen Press, 1993.

13. *Life of Jesus*, 257–62, 433, 450.

14. 'Every act of understanding is for Schleiermacher the inverse of an act of speech, the reconstruction of a construction' (H.-G. Gadamer, *Truth and Method*, ET London: Sheed & Ward, 1975, 166). 'Divination' requires that the interpreter possesses a 'genius' corresponding to that of the author, the possibility of which depends on the presupposition that 'all individuality is a manifestation of universal life' (166). Schleiermacher's problem is not historical distance but the mystery of the author's identity as an individual (168).

15. The claim that Schleiermacher's chief interest lies in the psychological aspect of interpretation is disputed by Heinz Kimmerle, the editor of Schleiermacher's hermeneutical manuscripts; Kimmerle argues that this view (originating with W. Dilthey) under-estimates the importance for Schleiermacher of the 'grammatical' aspect ('Introduction' to the *Hermeneutics*, 27–28). See also A. C. Thiselton, *New Horizons in Hermeneutics: The Theory and Practice of Transforming Biblical Reading*, London: Marshall Pickering, 1992, 204–36: for Schleiermacher, 'the psychological has no absolute privilege as over against the grammatical – nor the grammatical, as over against the psychological' (217–18). It is a matter simply of different interpretative strategies, 'in accordance with chosen tasks and goals' (218). Kimmerle and Thiselton rightly point to Schleiermacher's even-handedness on this issue, which stems from his quest for a 'general hermeneutics' or 'art of understanding', as opposed to the existing 'variety of specialized hermeneutics': in the face of the infinite variety of texts, a *general* advocacy of psychological interpretation over grammatical would make no sense. In the case of the gospels, however, a clear subordination of 'grammatical-historical' to 'psychological' interpretation takes place, because of the unique significance of the personal experience that here comes to expression (especially in the Gospel of John).

16. 'If the enterprise [of hermeneutics] remains fundamentally psychological, it is because it stipulates as the ultimate aim of interpretation not *what* a text says, but *who* says it. At the same time, the object of hermeneutics is constantly shifted away from the text, from its sense and its reference, towards the lived experience which is expressed therein' (P. Ricoeur, 'The task of hermeneutics' [1973], in [ed. John B. Thompson], *Hermeneutics and the Human Sciences: Essays on language, action and interpretation*, Cambridge: Cambridge University Press, 1981, 43–62, 52).

17. According to Hegel, when the ear hears speech or music, it 'listens to the result of the inner vibration of the body through which what comes before us is no longer the peaceful and material shape, but the first and more ideal breath of the soul' (*Aesthetics*, 2.890, quoted by J. Derrida, 'The Pit and the Pyramid: Introduction to Hegel's Semiology' [1968], in *Margins of Philosophy*, ET Chicago: University of Chicago Press, 1982, 69–108, 92). As Derrida notes, this 'ideal excellence of the phonic makes every spatial language . . . remain *inferior* and *exterior*', and writing is the primary example of this (94). The materiality of writing and the material side of speech mediate the life of the soul in such a way as to be 'sublated' in the process. But 'Hegel knew that this proper and animated body of the signifier was also a *tomb*. The association *soma/sema* is also at work in this semiology, which is in no way surprising. The tomb is the life of the body as the sign of death, the body as the other of the soul, the other of the animate psyche, of the living breath. But the tomb also shelters, maintains in reserve, capitalizes on life by marking that life continues elsewhere' (82). For Schleiermacher, the scriptural text (the *gramma*) is a sign of deadness which, in marking the absence of life, is a negative testimony to the fact that 'life continues else-where'.

18. Compare Barth's analysis of the title of Schleiermacher's work, *The Christian Faith Systematically Presented according to the Basic Tenets of the Evangelical Church*: 'The word "systematically" is . . . to be put in dialectical relationship to the words "according to the basic tenets"; the latter denote the breathing out, the transition from religious immediacy to reflection, the former denotes the breathing in, the return from thoughts to pure feeling, and all of them together offer a complete survey of the vital process that Schleiermacher seeks to describe in his title. Dogmatics must be a system, then, in order to restore the balance that is temporarily upset by the existence of

basic tenets of the Christian faith' (*The Theology of Schleiermacher* [lectures at Göttingen, 1923–24], ed. D. Ritschl, ET Grand Rapids: Eerdmans, 1982, 189).

19. Similar positions recur in modern Anglican writing about the Bible. Thus John Barton argues that the Christian faith 'preceded the Bible, could in principle survive without it, and is not exhausted by what is in the Bible' (*People of the Book? The Authority of the Bible in Christianity*, London: SPCK, 1988, 59). Our knowledge of God 'does not come about through the existence of a sacred text, but through the living of the life of the people of God, which continues down to the present' (57). 'We need to use our commitment to Christ as a living instrument with which to make the subordinate position of the Bible a reality' (82–83).

20. Kant's view of the relationship between Christianity and Judaism is in some respects similar to Schleiermacher's. According to Kant, Christianity completely abandoned 'the Judaism from which it sprang', being 'grounded upon a wholly new principle' (*Religion within the Limits of Reason Alone* [1793], ET New York: Harper & Row, 1960, 118). Judaism is characterized by an exclusiveness which 'showed enmity toward all other peoples and which, therefore, evoked the enmity of all' (117). In Christianity, however, we learn of 'the Teacher of the Gospel' who gave 'an example conforming to the archetype of a humanity alone pleasing to God' (119–20); his story depicts both the conflict of the good and evil principles and the victory of the former, and thus symbolizes universal human reality. In the universality of its moral claim, Christianity is the antithesis of Jewish exclusiveness. Christianity's advantage over Judaism is that it is 'represented as coming *from the mouth of the first Teacher* not as a statutory but as a moral religion . . . But the first founders of the *Christian communities* did find it necessary to entwine the history of Judaism with it', placing certain Jewish ideas 'among the fundamental articles of faith' (155). Without these Jewish corruptions of the essence of Christianity, 'nothing would be left but pure moral religion unencumbered by statutes' (154n). For Kant as for Schleiermacher and Harnack, Judaism (as the religion of the Old Testament) is identified with orthodox Christianity. Together, they constitute the archetypal opponent of pure religion.

21. Adolf von Harnack, *Marcion: Das Evangelium vom fremden Gott* (1924²), repr. Darmstadt: Wissenschaftliche Buchgesellschaft, 1960. Translations are my own.

22. Compare the view of Leslie Houlden, who argues that in its resistance to Marcionism the second-century church 'opted for a "book-centered" (rather than, for instance, philosophical) way of being religious. From then on, it was both endowed with and saddled with . . . the OT – and compelled to find ways of interpreting it . . . in the light of Christian perspectives which, as we are now vividly aware, it was never written to display' ('Christian Interpretation of the Old Testament', in R. J. Coggins and J. L. Houlden [eds.], *A Dictionary of Biblical Interpretation*, London: SCM Press, 1990, 108–12; 110). Like Harnack, Houlden argues that, 'with . . . the strengthening of the sense of the OT as belonging to days long past, the question of its Christian use, not only in theory but also in practice, must surely come once again to the fore' (111).

23. In the preface to the second edition of his *Römerbrief*, Barth acknowledges that he was 'puzzled, on reading the first reviews of Harnack's book, by the striking parallels between what Marcion had said and what I was actually writing'; he requests 'a careful examination of these agreements before I be praised or blamed hastily as a Marcionite' (XVI–XVII/13). In his open letter to Barth of March 1923, Harnack argues that, 'like Marcion', Barth is in danger of severing 'every link between faith and the human' (ET in M. Rumscheidt [ed.], *Adolf von Harnack: Liberal Theology at its Height*,

London: Collins, 92–93). The context is debate about the sixth of Harnack's 'Fifteen questions to the despisers of scientific theology': 'If God and the world . . . are complete opposites, how does education in godliness, that is in goodness, become possible? And how is education possible without historical knowledge and the highest valuation of morality?' (86).

24. P. T. Forsyth sees Harnack as illustrating a general problem: that, in many cases, 'the scholar, the historian, submerges the thinker' (*The Person and Place of Jesus Christ*, London: Independent Press Ltd, 1909, 263). Harnack is 'a great historian, and a valuable apologist; but as a theologian he is – not so great. And yet the half-taught mind concludes that eminence in the one direction makes a man an authority in the other. It really takes a great deal of theology to revolutionise theology' (264).

25. Tertullian, *Against Marcion*, in *The Ante-Nicene Fathers* (American edition), vol. III, repr. Grand Rapids: Eerdmans, 1976, 269–474. I have sometimes emended the translation.

26. See Harnack's article on 'The Present State of Research in Early Christian History' (1885), in M. Rumscheidt, *Adolf von Harnack*, 182–93, esp. 182–85, for Harnack's view of the limitations of the Tübingen school.

27. A. Harnack, *What is Christianity? Sixteen Lectures delivered in the University of Berlin during the Winter Term, 1899–1900*, ET London: Williams & Norgate; New York: Putnam's, 1904[3].

28. Harnack no doubt has in mind here the claim of Johannes Weiss that 'the Kingdom of God as Jesus thought of it is never something subjective, inward, or spiritual, but is always the objective messianic Kingdom, which is usually pictured as a territory into which one enters, or as a land in which one has a share, or as a treasure which comes down from heaven' (*Jesus' Proclamation of the Kingdom of God*, ET of German first edition [1892], London: SCM Press; Philadelphia: Fortress, 1971, 133).

29. This identification of husk and Jewishness is confirmed by a later definition of 'husk' as 'the Jewish limitations attaching to Jesus' message' (*What is Christianity?*, 183).

30. On Harnack's use of the metaphor of the kernel and the husk, see S. Sykes, *The Identity of Christianity: Theologians and the Essence of Christianity from Schleiermacher to Barth*, London: SPCK, 1984, 135–37. Sykes argues that for Harnack the metaphor does not entail 'the essential worthlessness of the husk'; the husk can be viewed 'as a means of attaining the thing itself rather than as an obstruction' (136). Yet the distinction between the thing itself and the means by which it is attained implies the disposability of the husk once its work of preserving the kernel is complete. In so far as the husk represents Jewishness and the Old Testament, failure to discard it is now 'the result of religious and churchly paralysis' (*Marcion*, 217).

31. A. Harnack, *History of Dogma*, ET London: Williams & Norgate, 1893–1900 (7 vols.). Vol. 7 was published in 1900, the German original in 1890.

32. Compare Irenaeus' treatment of this passage in book 4 of his *Against Heresies* (*The Ante-Nicene Fathers*, vol. I, repr. Grand Rapids: Eerdmans, 1975). With Marcion in mind, Irenaeus argues that in this text 'the Lord taught us that no man is capable of knowing God, unless he be taught of God; that is, that God cannot be known without God: but that this is the express will of the Father, that God should be known. For they know him to whomsoever the Son has revealed him' (iv.6.4). In the scriptural text, '"shall reveal" was not said with reference to the future alone, as if the Word began to manifest the Father only when he was born of Mary, but it applies indifferently throughout all time. For the Son, being present with his own handiwork from the beginning, reveals the Father to all; to whom he wills, and when he wills, and as the Father wills' (iv.6.7). The reference

here is not to a natural theology but to the revelations recorded in the Old Testament, the ontological basis of which is the creation of the world through the divine Word.

33. Harnack's and Marcion's subtractions from the gospel narratives sometimes coincide. Thus, in Marcionite vein although for un-Marcionite reasons, Harnack can state that 'two of the Gospels . . . contain an introductory history (the history of Jesus' birth), but we may disregard it' (*What is Christianity?*, 31).

34. Thus Philo comments that some, hearing the words of Gen. 6.7, 'suppose that the Existent feels wrath and anger, whereas he is not susceptible to any passion at all . . . The Lawgiver uses such expressions, just as far as they serve for a kind of elementary lesson, to admonish those who could not otherwise be brought to their senses . . . It is for training and admonition, not because God's nature is such, that these words are used' (*On the Unchangeableness of God*, *Philo*, vol. III, Loeb Classical Library, London: W. Heinemann; Cambridge, Mass.: Harvard University Press, 1968, 52, 54).

35. Harnack's tendency to polarize 'redemption' and 'cosmology' may also be seen in his interpretation of the controversy between Athanasius and Arius along these lines (*Outlines of the History of Dogma* [1891², ET 1893], Boston: Beacon Press, 1957, 251).

36. A. Harnack, 'Christianity and History' (1895, ET 1896), in M. Rumscheidt, *Adolf von Harnack*, 63–77.

37. A. Harnack, 'Christ as Saviour' (1899), in M. Rumscheidt, *Adolf von Harnack*, 303–12.

38. See the early article on 'Liberal Theology and the Latest Theological Movement' (1924), in *Faith and Understanding* (incomplete ET of *Glauben und Verstehen* I, 1933¹), London: SCM Press, 1969, 28–52, esp. 29–40.

39. Thus the disjunction between the absoluteness of the christological confession and the relativity beyond which historical study cannot proceed may be seen as a response to Ernst Troeltsch's critique of liberal Protestant attempts to establish the absoluteness of Christianity as 'the realization of the essence of religion' (*The Absoluteness of Christianity*, 1901, ET of third edition [1929], London: SCM Press, 1972, 59–60).

40. Bultmann's two most important articles on this subject are 'The Significance of the Old Testament for Christian Faith' (1933), first published in *Glauben und Verstehen* I, ET in B. W. Anderson (ed.), *The Old Testament and Christian Faith: Essays by Rudolf Bultmann and others*, London: SCM Press, 1964, 8–35; and 'Prophecy and Fulfilment' (1949), ET in *Essays Philosophical and Theological* (= *Glauben und Verstehen* II, 1952¹), London: SCM Press, 1955, 182–208, and in C. Westermann (ed.), *Essays on Old Testament Hermeneutics* (1960), ET Richmond: John Knox Press, 1963, 50–75. Page references to the latter article relate to the 1955 volume.

41. Hans Frei has discussed the origins of modern arguments against the fulfilment of prophecy in *The Eclipse of Biblical Narrative: A Study in Eighteenth and Nineteenth Century Hermeneutics*, New Haven and London: Yale University Press, 1974, 66–85. In his *Discourse of the Grounds and Reasons of the Christian Religion* (1724), Anthony Collins rejected the classical Christian appeal to prophecy on the grounds that it contravenes the normal assumption that a proposition has a single meaning, intended by its author, to be reconstructed on the basis of the general rules of grammar (*Eclipse*, 84). Many of his orthodox opponents shared this assumption in their insistence 'that the authors of some of the prophetic utterances personally foreknew the coming of Jesus and in that sense meant their statements to apply to him literally' (74). But it was also argued – for example, by Thomas Sherlock – that 'the claim to fulfilment represents a retrospective view from the vantage point of what had happened in the New Testament, discerning a connected,

providential scheme in the general bearing of the Old Testament texts, so that what was said and recounted there is now seen to have foreshadowed and led to the climax or fulfilment claimed by the New Testament writers' (70). For Sherlock, in opposition to Collins, 'there is . . . an interpretation which is neither literal nor meaningless' (71). 'But no matter who was right, Collins' view was the earnest of the future' (72).

42. Karl Barth concedes that 'in the early church theology was too onesidedly occupied only with explicit prophecy in the Old Testament', but criticizes 'the usual caricature' of Old Testament interpretation in the pre-modern era, according to which 'the chief occupation in this field was to hunt down in a more or less imaginative way all manner of messianic prophecies and to produce an unnaturally exact christology of the Old Testament' (*Church Dogmatics*, I/2, ET Edinburgh: T. & T. Clark, 1956, 94). Where, in more recent Old Testament theologies, this matter is not even considered, 'the result can only be a dreary emptying of the Old Testament' (94).

43. Compare Bultmann's claim that 'the history-of-salvation mystery in Rom. 11.25ff. is derived from speculative fantasy' (*Theology of the New Testament*, vol. 2, ET London: SCM Press, 1955, 132). The shape of Bultmann's presentation of 'The Theology of Paul' in part II of his *Theology* is determined by his anthropocentric interpretation of Rom. 1–8; chs. 9–11 merely present Paul's 'reflections on the history of salvation' (1.282), a topic which for Bultmann is of little theological interest.

44. Quotations from 'The Guiding Principles of the Faith Movement of the "German Christians", June 6, 1932', ET in Arthur C. Cochrane, *The Church's Confession under Hitler*, Pittsburgh: Pickwick Press, 1976[2], 222–23.

45. 'The Task of Theology in the Present Situation', in *Existence and Faith: Shorter Writings of Rudolf Bultmann*, ed. S. Ogden, London: Fontana, 1964, 186–95.

46. 'Faith in God the Creator', in *Existence and Faith*, 202–16.

47. Compare the German Christian demand, voiced at a meeting in the Berlin Sports Palace in November 1933, 'that our regional church, as a German folk church, should liberate itself from everything that is un-German in its worship and creed, especially from the Old Testament, with its Jewish "recompense" morality' (quoted by R. Rendtorff, ET *Canon and Theology: Overtures to an Old Testament Theology*, Edinburgh: T. & T. Clark; Minneapolis: Augsburg Fortress, 1993, 77). This incident and its aftermath are discussed in Klaus Scholder, *The Churches and the Third Reich*, Volume One: 1918–34, ET London: SCM Press, 1987, 551–59.

48. 'The Question of Natural Revelation', in *Essays Philosophical and Theological*, 90–118.

49. This association of *Heilsgeschichte* with Nazi ideology is confirmed by Ernst Käsemann, reflecting on what he learned from Bultmann in his 'theological youth': 'On the way to a theology of proclamation we rediscovered that Reformation doctrine of justification which had become largely incomprehensible to our fathers and grand-fathers and which had therefore ceased for them to form the centre of the New Testament message. This discovery immunized us deeply against a conception of salvation history which broke in on us in secularized and political form with the Third Reich and its ideology' (*Perspectives on Paul*, ET London: SCM Press; Philadelphia: Fortress Press, 1971, 64).

50. On South Africa, John de Gruchy writes: 'During the 1920s and 1930s, the notion of Afrikaner history as "sacred history" became the only hermeneutic filter through which Afrikaner history was to be read and interpreted by all true Afrikaners. It was during this period that the architects and ideologists of Afrikaner nationalism made capital out of the mythology of Afrikanerdom as the Chosen People. The Great Trek was the Exodus

from the bondage of British Rule at the Cape which led, in turn, to the years of struggling in the Wilderness against all odds, en route to the Promised Land of the Boer republics' (*Liberating Reformed Theology: A South African Contribution to an Ecumenical Debate*, Grand Rapids: Eerdmans, 1991, 26). Naim Stifan Ateek reports that 'since the creation of the State [of Israel], some Jewish and Christian interpreters have read the Old Testament largely as a Zionist text to such an extent that it has become almost repugnant to Palestinian Christians' (*Justice and only Justice: A Palestinian Theology of Liberation*, Maryknoll: Orbis, 1989, 77).

51. Bultmann finds exegetical support for this universalizing approach in the Pauline critique of 'works of the law'. In opposition to the view that, 'when Paul rejects works, only the works demanded by the Mosaic Law are meant', the exclusion of 'boasting' in Rom. 3.27; 4.2 suggests that 'the "works *of the Law*", on which Paul naturally concentrates in this discussion with the Jew, represent works in general, any and all works as works-of-merit' (*Theology of the New Testament*, 1.283). This is confirmed by the general contrast between 'working' and 'gift' in Rom. 4.4–5 and by 'the parallelism between Paul's polemic against "one's own righteousness based on law" and his polemic against the "Greeks"', in which the attitude of 'boasting' is again excluded (1.283–84).

52. Compare H. Conzelmann's criticism of von Rad: 'Die theologische Sachfrage ist ja nicht, ob Israel das Gebot von einem "Heilshandeln" umklammert sieht oder sogar im Gebot selbst ein Heilshandeln sieht, sondern: Ob das, worin Israel das Heil sieht, wirklich das *Heil* ist. Das Kriterium ist klar: Ob es nämlich heute als das Heil verkündet werden kann' ('Fragen an Gerhard von Rad', *EvTh* 24 [1964], 113–25; 122).

53. Bultmann's *Theology of the New Testament* opens with the claim: 'The message of Jesus is a presupposition for the theology of the New Testament rather than a part of that theology itself' (1.1; italics removed, as in the quotations that follow). 'The dominant concept of Jesus' message is the kingdom of God', and this places him 'in the historical context of Jewish expectations about the end of the world and God's new future' (1.2). On the other hand, 'Christian faith did not exist until there was a Christian kerygma, i.e. a kerygma proclaiming Jesus Christ – specifically Jesus Christ the Crucified and Risen One – to be God's eschatological act of salvation' (1.1). This reworking of the liberal Protestant disjunction between proclaimer and proclaimed continues to ignore the fact that, in the synoptic gospels, the message of Jesus is set in the context of his *history*, culminating in his crucifixion and resurrection. The disjunction is the product of the misreading of the synoptic gospels as 'the source for Jesus' message' (1.3).

PART TWO

The Old Testament
in Christological Perspective

Chapter 5

Old Testament Theology as a Christian Theological Enterprise

What is 'the Old Testament'? The answer seems self-evident: the Old Testament is that collection of writings, beginning with the five books of Moses, that forms the first part of the twofold Christian canon, and that corresponds to the sacred scriptures acknowledged within the Jewish community. Yet such an answer would be inadequate if it regarded the title 'Old Testament' merely as a convenient label for a collection of books. It is true that the anomalous use of the word 'testament' in this context might encourage the view that this title is a matter of indifference. It stems from the translation of the Hebrew *bᵉrîth* ('covenant') as *diathēkē* ('will', 'testament') in Greek and *testamentum* in Latin, and this unique usage tells us nothing about how the collection is to be understood (unless 'covenant' is substituted for 'testament'). 'Testament' in this context can be defined simply as one or other of the collections of writings that constitute Christian scripture. Yet the effect of this is to throw all the more emphasis on the polarity of 'old' and 'new'. One of these collections of writings ('testaments') is 'old', the other is 'new'. A number of important implications may be drawn from the traditional terminology.[1]

First, the old/new polarity indicates that the Christian Bible is irreducibly twofold. From a purely chronological point of view, it would be possible to argue that the Christian Bible merely adds two further parts (gospels and epistles) to a prior tripartite canon consisting of law, prophets and writings: the Christian Bible would then come into being as the result of a single, linear process. Yet such a view would radically misrepresent the subject-matter of the Christian Bible. The fact that all biblical texts fall on one or other side of the dividing-line between old and new is essential rather than accidental.

Second, there is understood to be a constitutive relationship between the two Testaments. The Old Testament is old only in relation to the newness of the New; there would be no Old Testament without a New Testament, which can therefore be said to call the Old Testament into being, that is, to constitute an existing collection of writings as Old Testament. Conversely, the New Testament is new only in relation to the oldness of the Old. Neither collection is self-sufficient; both of them are what they are only in relation to the other. The traditional terminology indicates that the twofoldness of the Christian Bible consists not in an arbitrary yoking together of two independent collections of writings but in a mutually constitutive relationship.

Third, this relationship takes the form of a preceding and a following. Jewish scripture is construed as that which comes before. It does not contain its centre in itself; it points forward to the moment that will retrospectively establish that its reality consists in whatever is implied by 'oldness'. The Old Testament does not disclose a timeless, unchanging reality behind the temporality of phenomena, for it is itself temporal through and through. The New Testament is separated from the Old by a chronological interval which is, however, not to be measured merely in years; for this interval is the time of the *kairos*, the moment that definitively establishes both newness and oldness.

It follows, fourth, that 'old' and 'new' are to be understood in a qualitative as well as a chronological sense. The relationship between old and new is not merely that of an earlier to a later, a first to a second. If that were the case, then the Old Testament would be only relatively old and the New Testament only relatively new; one would be older, the other would be more recent. In opposition to such a view, the old/new polarity ascribes an absolute, qualitative oldness and newness to the two Testaments. That which is new is always new. It cannot become superannuated, and it resists every attempt to convert its newness into oldness by supplementing it with a new form of newness, a third testament.

Fifth, in so far as the old is constituted as old by the new it is relativized. The new is assigned a certain precedence over the old. It is not the case, however, that the new simply supplants the old, for – as we have seen – new and old are in mutually constitutive relationship; newness remains dependent on the oldness of the old. In being designated 'old', the Old Testament is assigned its proper, honoured and authoritative place within the Christian canon, precisely as that which prepares the way for the moment that divides the old from the new.

This exegesis of the old/new polarity rests on the assumption that the traditional terminology is justified, and that to differentiate the two Testaments as 'old' and 'new' – rather than, say, 'first' and 'second', or

'Hebrew' and 'Greek' – is an appropriate construal of their subject-matter. In modern biblical scholarship, however, this assumption has been severely criticized. In particular, modern Old Testament scholarship can virtually be defined in terms of the rejection of this assumption and its replacement by a programme in which the Old Testament texts are to be interpreted 'in their own right' and without reference to that external point from which, according to Christian theology, their true meaning and significance retrospectively proceed.[2] It is true that, having established the autonomy of this body of texts, the question may subsequently be raised as to how the abyss that has now opened up between Old and New Testaments may be bridged. Yet it is impossible to reach an adequate solution to this problem where the relationship between old and new is understood as a secondary issue arising out of the prior reality of two relatively autonomous collections of texts, each with its own equally autonomous interpretative community. There may, indeed, be good reasons for this modern approach to the Christian Bible. If this approach involves a loss of the dialectical relationship between old and new, it may be that the texts themselves resist being read in terms of such a relationship – in which case 'Old Testament' and 'New Testament' would merely be convenient labels for two distinct bodies of writing. It may be that we should not allow ourselves to be misled by the familiar proximity to one another of Old and New Testaments, within the covers of a single volume. If the traditional terminology expresses an aspiration to read the Christian Bible as a unity within duality, it may be that, in the light of a clearer grasp of what the texts actually say, this aspiration must be regarded as illegitimate. Alternatively, and in more contemporary idiom, it might be said that the Christian Bible is open to an irreducible variety of reading-strategies, one of which – and it must never be forgotten that there are others too, equally legitimate – is to read the Old Testament in the light of the New. Why not?

These possibilities must be rejected, despite the plausible-sounding case that can be made for each of them. They fail to take into account the event that constitutes the oldness of the Old and the newness of the New. They find in the interval between Old and New an abyss which may be bridged, if at all, only with great difficulty and with many qualifications and reservations; and to find an abyss at precisely the point where Christian faith identifies the Word made flesh is simply to invalidate Christian faith. The casualness with which this point is overlooked, obscured or minimized indicates the pervasiveness of belief in the autonomy of the Old Testament, itself a projection of the autonomous interpretative community that occupies itself with these texts and strives to control their interpretation. At the root of this problem is the abstraction of these texts from the sole context in which, for Christians, they can be meaningful. This abstraction can take one of two forms. First, the texts may be understood as vestiges of particular strands of ancient Near Eastern history, essentially on a level with the 'evidence' that happens to have survived the vicissitudes of history and to have been discovered and reconstructed by archaeological means. Second, and in opposition to this, it may be explicitly and emphatically asserted that these texts are of 'more than' historical and archaeological interest – but without an adequate grasp of the precise nature of this surplus. The canonical texts are characteristically differentiated from archaeological vestiges on the basis of their continuing history of communal usage. This differentiation is, indeed, crucially important; but it is inadequate as it stands. To speak of a single history of communal usage is to assume a basic identity of function between the Old Testament in a Christian communal context and the Torah, the prophets and the writings within a Jewish one. This assumption is understandable, given that it is more or less the same texts that are operative within these two contexts; and yet it fails to reflect on the significance of the event that – for one community but not for the other – retrospectively constitutes these texts as 'Old Testament', thereby definitively shaping the way in which they are to be read. From the standpoint of Christian faith, it must be said that *the Old Testament comes to us with Jesus and from Jesus, and can never be understood in abstraction from him.* This judgment is to be understood as a theological interpretation of certain factors in early Christian history. It does not as yet imply any particular interpretative programme, except in the sense that it rejects all interpretative programmes that assume an autonomous Old Testament.

The Christian church receives the Old Testament *with Jesus.* It receives Jesus not through direct encounter but through the mediation of appointed witnesses. Prior to the birth of the church on the day of Pentecost, there exists a group of twelve chosen disciples, whom Jesus named apostles (Luke 6.13) and whose proclamation will be foundational to the community that Pentecost brings into being – along with that of others (men and women) 'who accompanied us during all the time that the Lord Jesus went in and out among us' (Acts 1.21). Yet, from the day of Pentecost onwards, Christian proclamation is never proclamation of a Jesus abstracted from Jewish scripture. On the contrary, the Holy Spirit who leads disciples and community into all truth (John 16.13), and who thereby empowers proclamation, does so by 'reminding' them of scriptural texts that can now be understood as testimony to Jesus (John 12.15–16, cf. 14.26). Peter's sermon on the day of Pentecost, as represented in Acts 2, therefore assumes both that Jesus' life, death and exaltation must be understood in the light of holy scripture and that, conversely, scripture itself is retrospectively reconstituted as its true scope and *telos* now for the first time come to light. The early church receives Jesus with – and not apart from – writings that can now in principle be understood as Old Testament: as a preparing of the way, as a body of texts whose centre and goal lie not in themselves but in that towards which they are retrospectively seen to be oriented. This is the case even with Jewish Christians, for it is precisely in the earliest Jewish-Christian communities that the radical reconstitution of scripture through the event of Jesus Christ is initially thought through. It is still more clearly the case for Gentile Christians whose first significant contact with Jewish scripture occurs through Christian proclamation. When Gentile Christians are reminded of the message of Christ crucified and risen on which their communal life is founded, they are at the same time reminded of the scriptural basis of this message: for Christ died for our sins, was buried and was raised on the third day 'in accordance with the scriptures' (1 Cor. 15.3–4).

The Christian church receives the Old Testament not only with Jesus but also *from Jesus*. Jesus, as attested in scripture, is the content of the apostolic message; but he is also its source, in the sense that to be an apostle is to be sent by Jesus. The risen Jesus sends his apostles to proclaim to all nations the history of his own life, death and resurrection in its unity as God's definitive act for the salvation of humankind. Yet that history is neither self-contained nor self-explanatory; it is to be understood in the light of those sacred writings that it retrospectively reconstitutes as Old Testament. The apostles must, as it were, bear these texts with them if they are to fulfil their commission, and they must not offer their hearers a Jesus abstracted from the texts that bear witness to him. If (conjecturally) Gentile-Christian communities derived their earliest copies of the Jewish scriptures from local Jewish communities, they did so only on the basis of the conviction that these scriptures had already come to them from Jesus, by virtue of their acceptance of the scripturally-shaped message that the risen Lord sent his apostles to proclaim.

The Christian church has not received an Old Testament that can be abstracted from Jesus. Such a collection would not be an 'Old Testament' at all. It would lack the peculiar authority – relativized authority, yet authority none the less – that it retains when the constitutive significance of its oldness is correctly understood. This abstracted 'Old Testament' is, however, clearly a possibility, for it constantly becomes real in the interpretative practice of a scholarly community whose own desire for autonomy it mirrors back. It rests upon the collective decision to exclude from consideration – or at least to minimize – the hermeneutical significance of the event of the Word made flesh. This decision is explicable historically as the product of a particular construal of the conditions that a discipline must meet in order to merit full acceptance within the wider scholarly community. Since the Word made flesh was elsewhere deemed to be a meaningless concept, this was to be the case here too; to the extent that this has been so, Old Testament scholarship accurately mirrors modern western culture's acute unease about its own Christian roots. This scholarship concerns itself with a text that cannot easily be identified as the Christian Old Testament; it is essentially uninterested in the alternative trajectory, into rabbinic Judaism; and it believes that this abstracted text is a natural and a neutral entity, failing to see that it is in fact its own creation.

The outcome of the discussion so far has been a rather sharp polarity between the Old Testament of Christian faith and the Old Testament/Hebrew Bible of modern scholarship. It seems that the latter derives, at least in part, from a systematic obscuring of factors that, for Christian faith, must be fundamental and determinative. There can, however, be no question of a theological approach to the Old Testament that dispenses with Old Testament scholarship. Despite the collective decision to operate on the basis of a relatively autonomous Old Testament, Old Testament scholarship has frequently reflected on its own significance within a Christian theological context. This ongoing reflection has made an impact on detailed exegesis (by no means always to its detriment), and it underlies the genre of 'Old Testament theology' that has played such a significant part in the discipline since the First World War. This reflection may prove to be inadequate. It may be vulnerable to counter-criticisms from within the discipline, and the pervasive influence of the theory of Old Testament autonomy may prevent it from attaining the necessary christological focus. But such critical judgments would need to be substantiated, in detail and not just in general terms. In addition, there may be a great deal to learn from attempts at constructive theology that are ultimately judged to be 'inadequate'. (What theology is not ultimately inadequate?) Those who engage in Old Testament theology from within the discipline of Old Testament scholarship will have a 'professional' knowledge on which those outside the discipline will remain in some degree dependent, however critical they may wish to be of the framework that organizes that knowledge. An attempt at Christian Old Testament interpretation that bypassed modern Old Testament scholarship would quickly reveal its own limitations and would hardly merit serious attention.

It is understandable that Old Testament scholarship should be wary of the claim that 'everywhere the Scripture is about Christ alone'.[3] Old Testament scripture is nowhere about Christ alone. It is about many things, all of which must ultimately be understood in relation to Christ, for whom they are retrospectively seen to prepare the way. In that relation to Christ, they may be said to bear witness to Christ – yet not in a single way, monotonously, but in many and various ways and as if from a certain distance. The Old Testament texts do not speak directly of Christ; they speak directly of many other things

– creation, promise, exodus, command, priesthood, kingship, prophecy – which together constitute the matrix within which Christ is to be understood, and which must themselves be understood for the sake of a fuller understanding of Christ. Christian faith requires a *christocentric* reading of Christian scripture, but this should not be confused with a *christomonism* that can find in the Old Testament nothing but thinly-veiled christological allegories or typologies. Christian faith is not christomonistic; it does not speak of 'Christ alone', eliminating both the heterogeneity of Old Testament discourse and its distance from Christ. Christian faith is, however, necessarily christocentric: for in Jesus Christ the identity of God, the creator who is also the God of Israel, is definitively disclosed in the triune name of Father, Son and Holy Spirit, for the salvation of humankind.

The studies that follow are devoted to the work of Old Testament scholars for whom Old Testament theology is integral to the project of Christian theology in general. They rightly presuppose that Old Testament theology is or should be a primary concern not just of Old Testament scholarship but of Christian theologians; for, despite the specializations imposed by the modern division of the theological curriculum, a theology unconcerned about biblical interpretation would hardly be Christian. Understood as a Christian theological enterprise, Old Testament theology rejects the view that the Old Testament can and should be interpreted in abstraction from its context within the Christian Bible. The question is whether, despite its good intentions, it is still too strongly influenced by an interpretative paradigm which radically distorts its object of study.

1. Eichrodt

The revival of the apparently defunct genre of 'Old Testament theology' after the First World War must be understood within its broad theological context.

Older works in this genre attempted a systematic presentation of 'the Old Testament view' of themes such as God, creation, sin, election, law and the messianic hope, on the assumption that this material, presented in this form, would contribute to contemporary Christian theological reflection.[4] At least from the time of Wellhausen, the apparent success of a developmental view of Israel's religion led to the replacement of the basically synchronic structure of Old Testament theology by diachronic, historical accounts of the development of Israel's religious thought within its ancient Near Eastern context. Against this background, the attempt by Walther Eichrodt and others to revive the practice of Old Testament theology presupposes major shifts of emphasis not only in Old Testament studies but in the field of Protestant theology as a whole. It presupposes a rediscovery of the significance, distinctiveness and integrity of the biblical texts; a renewed expectation that they may have something to say to us, so that the role of the interpreter is to enable us to be better listeners; and a sense of the limitations of an interpretative paradigm in which reality is accessible only to certain types of historical description. It also presupposes the emergence of new ways of speaking about God, making it once more credible that the Old Testament might have something to contribute here. Earlier optimism about the possibility and desirability of incorporating all phenomena into a single, all-embracing world-history had become problematic; and the claim of theologians such as Herrmann and Harnack that, for Christians, knowledge of God is located primarily in the religious consciousness of Jesus was challenged by a new emphasis on divine transcendence, making it possible to hear again what the Old Testament has to say about the holy majesty of the God of Israel.

Rather than outlining a general 'background' to Eichrodt's work, however, it is more important to identify a certain tension within that background which, as we shall see, prevents his *Theology of the Old Testament* from fulfilling its initial promise and achieving lasting significance as a contribution to Christian theology. In particular, it is necessary to show that the common assumption that Eichrodt's work 'was conceived entirely in the light of Barth's theology'[5] is seriously misleading. Most German-speaking theologians and biblical scholars maintained a far higher level of continuity with the liberal Protestant theology of the pre-war era than did Barth himself; and the deepest influence on Eichrodt's Old Testament theology stems not from Barth but from the liberal Protestant programme of seeking to uncover 'the essence of religion' or the 'religious *a priori*', in the light of which the biblical texts are then assessed. The Barthian critique helps to effect certain changes in language and conceptuality, but the basic structure of this programme remains clearly discernible.

(*i*) *Rethinking 'Religion'*

For liberal Protestantism, *Religion* represents not only the many empirical phenomena studied by *Religionsgeschichte* but the essence of those phenomena, religion itself, consisting not in cult or creed but in the relationship that binds the individual to God in unconditional trust. (If this is the essence of religion in general, it is above all the essence of Christianity itself, *das Wesen des Christentums*.) The history of religion is therefore, at the deepest level, the history of the development of this understanding of *Religion*, a history in which Jesus remains central, while places of honour are also awarded to certain of the Old Testament prophets and psalmists, and to Augustine and Luther.

Naturally, this history also has its darker side. The essence of religion quickly succumbs to Pauline dogma and to Greek metaphysics, just as, in the Old Testament period, it had been distorted by nationalism and legalism. It must therefore be rediscovered again and again. It is, however, important to note that the *history* of religion is not integral to its essence; for 'religion' represents the divine–human relationship in its most elemental form, and the human partner in this relationship is in a certain sense dehistoricized by it. 'He' does not belong to any particular time or place, but is simply and purely 'human' – for *Religion* is a matter of the soul, and externalities are tangential to it.

One possible modification of this basic model was to 'deepen' it by emphasizing the transcendence of the object of religion in place of a perceived overemphasis on divine immanence. The traumatic experience of the First World War was undoubtedly a factor in this shift. But inner-theological factors were also involved, not least an anti-Ritschlian trend which sought inspiration in the early theologies of Luther and of Schleiermacher. Three texts from 1917 illustrate this shift.

(1) In a sermon entitled 'Vom geheimnisvollen und offenbaren Gott', published in the journal *Die Christliche Welt*, Rudolf Bultmann reflects on the experience, occasioned by the War, of the depths of the divine hiddenness.[6] (The language and conceptuality is quite unlike that of his mature theological thought.) In our pre-war innocence, says Bultmann, we did indeed experience God – and yet we see now 'that we pictured him too small' (30). Surrounded as we are by an 'enigmatic and abysmal darkness', we find him to be 'wholly other than the picture we have made of him' (29). Yet this is no cause for alarm: it must be so, for God is infinite. 'God *must* be a hidden and mysterious God, full of contradictions and riddles. Otherwise our inner life would become static, and we would lose the power to obtain experience from life's fullness' (30). Although we might wish it were otherwise, the War has brought us an inestimable privilege: 'Never before has it been granted us to gaze like this into the depths of God' (33).

(2) When Karl Holl asks, 'Was verstand Luther unter Religion?', it is clear that he has in mind the contemporary question of *Religion,* for the term was obviously unknown to the historical Luther in its liberal Protestant sense.[7] Holl works primarily with early Luther texts such as the lectures on the Psalms (1513–15) and on the Epistle to the Romans (1516), finding in them a radical theocentricity which he contrasts with the christocentricity of modern Ritschlian theology (37, 38–40n). For Luther, *Religion* arises from the experienced tension between the absolute divine demand and the human inability to perform it. Far from being a God of love alone, God's love is

experienced only under the contradictory form of his wrath. Luther came to believe 'that man is closest to God precisely when he believes himself to be farthest separated from God. What is most terrible is not to experience God as the wrathful Judge, but, on the contrary, *not* to experience him as such' (29) – that is, to assume on the basis of one's earnest religious and moral activity that all is well, and to know nothing of the divine judgment that exposes such activity as the sinful and deceitful self-seeking that it actually is. Whereas Erasmus' 'enlightened' view of religion typifies the Renaissance's desire to integrate religion into culture, Luther's 'deeper understanding of the essence of religion [*das Wesen der Religion*]' led him to the insight that religion is not part of culture (*ein Stück der Kultur*) but unique, by virtue of its utterly unique object; and here he speaks as directly to our generation as to his own (109).

(3) According to Rudolf Otto, the phenomena of religion are mis-interpreted when they are studied with the aid of concepts that 'have a place in the general sphere of man's ideational life, and are not specifically religious' (*The Idea of the Holy*, 4).[8] The primary category of interpretation unique to religion is that of 'the holy [*das Heilige*]', which does not originally refer to a moral attribute (as Kant thought) but to that which is experienced as *mysterium tremendum*, as 'the wholly other [*das ganz Andere*]', breaking in on the every-day world as if from outside and evoking a uniquely religious feeling of dread. 'There is no religion in which it [the holy] does not live as the real innermost core, and without it no religion would be worthy of the name. It is pre-eminently a living force in the Semitic religions, and of these again in none has it such vigour as in that of the Bible' (6). At a stroke, allegedly 'primitive' elements in the Bible are restored to favour, and the wrath-less Ritschlian deity is rejected. Mosaic religion marks the beginning of a process in which 'the "numinous" is throughout rationalized and moralized, i.e. charged with ethical import, until it becomes "the holy" in the fullest sense of the word"', culminating in the prophets and the gospels (77). Yet this does not mean that the numinous has been eradicated, for it is 'at once the basis upon which and the setting within which the ethical and rational meaning is consummated' (78). The enduring presence of the numinous alongside these other elements, guaranteeing their specifically religious quality, is clear in Isaiah, Ezekiel and Job and in New Testament language about God's 'wrath'.

(*ii*) *Bible and Religion*
In Karl Barth's *Römerbrief* (1922[2]), we again encounter a God who is 'wholly other', separated from the world by an 'infinite qualitative difference', in

sharp opposition to the immanent deity of pre-war liberal Protestantism.[9] Here, however, the otherness of God has been thought through radically, in the sense that there is no human 'experience' – of the 'numinous', the War, or whatever – that may be correlated with this divine otherness. Rather than breaking the nexus between religion and culture, for the sake of a deeper understanding of religion and its object, that nexus is left intact in order to secure the otherness of God against assimilation by religion as well as by culture. Religion is 'that last and highest human possibility which . . . encounters us at the threshold and turning-point [*Wende*] of two worlds – but only on *this* side of the abyss [*diesseits des Abgrunds*] dividing sinners from those who are under grace' (222/240). 'Once the eye which can perceive this distinction has been blinded, there arises in the midst, between here and there, between us and the wholly other, the mist of religion . . . At the heart [*Kern*] of this mist is the illusion that – without miracle (vertically from above), without the annulling of everything that is given, apart from the truth that lies beyond birth and death – there exists a human capacity for relationship with God' (25/49–50).

One role of 'religion', in its later as well as its earlier liberal Protestant incarnations, was to provide criteria for separating the wheat from the chaff within the biblical texts. Where the texts failed to meet those criteria they could be subjected to a reductionist interpretation along historical-critical lines, thus preserving the essence of religion or of Christianity from defilement. The offensiveness of Barth's work was that this procedure was simply reversed. Far from the Bible being judged from the standpoint of religion, religion was now judged from the standpoint of the Bible; liberal Protestant theology became the object of the Pauline critique of Gentile idolatry and Jewish law. This substitution of Bible for religion inevitably entails a sharp critique of historical-critical scholarship, both for its failure to engage adequately with the subject-matter (*die Sache*) of the biblical texts and for its role in modern theology's assimilation of the Bible to 'religion'. This critique is made explicit in the preface to the second edition of the Romans commentary, but it is everywhere tacitly present in the very form of the work, as a commentary on a biblical text. Barth's commentary flaunts its disregard for current conventions about the appropriate practice of biblical exegesis, and it is for this reason that he – unlike other representatives of 'modern' theology such as Bultmann, Holl and Otto – could be castigated by Harnack as a 'despiser of scientific theology'. In a set of fifteen critical questions addressed primarily to Barth (1923), Harnack rightly sees that the issue of the Bible is fundamental.[10] He therefore begins by asking, 'Is the religion of the Bible . . . so completely a unity that in relation to faith, worship and life one may simply speak of "the Bible"?' (85). Barth's refusal to accept the critical dissolution of the Bible, legitimated by the quest for the essence of religion, is thus his original theological sin. The offence lies not in his understanding of God as 'wholly other', which is shared with many of his contemporaries, but in his reversal of the hierarchical relationship between *Religion* and Bible. *Religion*, and the *Wissenschaft* that helps to ensure its prestige, are denied the right to prescribe criteria which enable them to dominate the biblical texts. To their great surprise, they find themselves the objects – and no longer the subjects – of a critical interpretation, carried out this time by the Bible itself. They have become the victims of a role reversal.

Even sympathetic readers of Barth's text were embarrassed by this reversal and sought to minimize it. Unlike his Marburg New Testament colleague Adolf Jülicher, for whom Barth's *Römerbrief* tells us more about the present than about Paul himself (97), Rudolf Bultmann finds here a 'simple, Pauline radicalism' (124).[11] His appreciative review-article was seen by Barth as welcome confirmation that 'the complaint about a Diocletian persecution of historical-critical theology . . . was unnecessary' (*Römerbrief*, XIX/16). Yet Bultmann begins by characterizing the *Römerbrief* as an attempt to show 'the distinctiveness and absoluteness of religion [*die Selbständigkeit und Absolutheit der Religion*]', in the tradition of Schleiermacher's *Reden über die Religion*, Otto's *Das Heilige*, and other modern attempts to establish 'a religious *a priori*' (119). Bultmann knows that Barth himself would resist this characterization, preferring to speak of 'faith' and to assign largely negative connotations to 'religion'; but this, he thinks, is purely a decision about word-usage, not a matter of principle (120). Thus, for Bultmann, 'faith' serves as a synonym and surrogate for 'religion', seen now as a response to the *a priori* of revelation. It is one of the traditional functions of *Religion* to provide criteria for distinguishing what is permanently valid from what is merely time-conditioned in the biblical texts; and Bultmann therefore remains loyal to this tradition in criticizing Barth's own loyalty to the text. If, as Barth rightly argues, the text is to be understood from the standpoint of its subject-matter (*von der Sache aus*), it is necessary to assess 'how far the subject-matter has really received adequate expression in all the words and sentences of the text'. 'The subject-matter is greater than the interpretative word', and it is no irreverence to insist that this applies also to Paul and his Letter to the Romans (141). 'When, in the exegesis of Romans, I discover tensions and contradictions, high points and low points, when I try to show where Paul is dependent on Jewish theology or on common Christian tradition, on Hellenistic rationalism or sacramentalism, my intention is not only to practise a historical and philological criticism . . . [but also] to show where and by what means the *subject-matter* comes to expression, so that I may grasp the subject-matter itself, which is greater even than Paul' (141–42). Here, the alliance between historical-critical scholarship and the quest for the religious *a priori* remains intact as a strategy for dominating the text. Responding to Bultmann in the preface to the third edition of the *Römerbrief*, Barth argues that the interpreter who wishes to write *with* not *about* Paul must strive to show at every point how what is said bears witness to the single subject-matter (XX/17).[12]

Barth, Otto and others helped to establish the theological context within which it became possible and necessary for Old Testament scholars to raise again the question of 'Old Testament theology' and its relation to the study of the history of Israel's religion. It would be a mistake to expect exact correlations. New theological possibilities impinge upon existing scholarly disciplines from the outside, and their impact will depend upon scholars' ability and willingness to convert them into a form that makes sense *within* the ongoing life of their particular disciplines. It is clear, however, that the new emphasis on divine transcendence – whether in the name of religion or of the Bible – was heard by biblical scholars as requiring new forms of theological relevance from their disciplines.

It is this issue that Otto Eissfeldt addresses in his article of 1926, 'Israelitisch-jüdische Religionsgeschichte und alttestamentliche Theologie'.[13] According to Eissfeldt, the new theological situation raises for Old Testament scholarship the question whether the religion of the Old Testament is to be studied with the same methods as other religions of antiquity or as 'the true religion, God's revelation', that is, as 'Old Testament theology' (1). Whereas, before the War, the former option was clearly the 'modern' one, the situation is now quite different: 'Weary of the historicism, psychologism and relativism of the scientific study of religion [*die religionswissenschaftliche Methode*], people long for revelation and demand a scientific approach to the Bible which does justice to its claim to be revelation, of absolute signifi-cance, that is, a theological approach' (2). Eissfeldt acknowledges the legitimacy of this demand, but argues that the historical approach to the religion of Israel and Old Testament theology should be practised in isola-tion from one another. In this way the demands both of science and of faith will be satisfied. This separation is, however, only relative, for each side has something to offer the other. Historical science helps faith to explain away the sub-Christian aspects of the Old Testament, and faith can help historical science to see what would otherwise be overlooked: 'If current scholarship emphasizes the demonic, irrational and unpredictable dimensions of Yahweh's character, the reason for this is that this aspect of God has again become apparent in the religious experience [*religiöse Erfahrung*] of our generation' (7).

As one would expect from this unreconstructed reference to 'religious experience', Eissfeldt is critical of the tendency of Barth and Eduard Thurneysen to link revelation closely to the canon of Christian scripture, thereby breaking the primary correlation of revelation with faith (2–4n). As we have seen, a function of Barth's supposed 'biblicism' is to exclude not faith itself but faith understood undialectically as the 'experience' of revelation, a view of faith that provides criteria whereby the biblical texts may be judged. It is just this view of faith that Eissfeldt continues to assume, and this places him in the *Religion* tradition. His sketch of an 'Old Testament theology' illustrates how this tradition has also learned to speak of 'revelation':

> Because Old Testament theology is concerned with the divine revelation that, for faith, has occurred and occurs anew in the Old Testament, it cannot take the form of historical description. For faith has nothing to do with the past; it has to do with that which is present and timeless. Revelation too is exalted over the category of time. (11)

Old Testament theology must therefore adopt a systematic approach, in which the various articles of faith (*loci*) – concerning, for example, the individual attributes of Yahweh – are treated in orderly fashion without reference to the historical processes whereby Israel came to enunciate them. The theological weakness of Eissfeldt's proposal stems from his assumption of a timeless *Religion* in which divine being is divorced from divine action. He knows the view that Jesus Christ is the centre of the Bible (4–5, quoting Otto Procksch), but the framework within which he operates prevents that insight from having any real impact even on 'Old Testament theology', let alone *Religionswissenchaft*. It is excluded both by the ahistoricism of the category of 'religious experience' which continues to determine the interpretation of 'revelation' and 'faith', and by the inability to recognize that the first task of any recognizably Christian Old Testament theology would be to challenge the notion of an 'Old Testament' abstracted from christology.

It is customary to contrast Eissfeldt's methodological proposal with that of Walther Eichrodt, outlined in an article published in 1929 and entitled 'Hat die alttestamentliche Theologie noch selbständige Bedeutung innerhalb der alttestamentlichen Wissenschaft?'[14] Eichrodt argues, in opposition to Eissfeldt, that a systematic treatment of Old Testament religion would be in the interests of scientific Old Testament scholarship itself:

> It would be wrong to see in this systematic task a contrast with the historical method; it is an inadmissible restriction of the term 'historical' when one confines it to study of the process of becoming, to the genetic method, as though that were self-evident. Rather, 'historical' is to be understood only in contrast to everything normative, so that the systematic approach is to be included entirely within the historical. (86)

Old Testament scholars should not try to become amateur dogmatic theologians; theological application of their work is the responsibility of others. Yet, Eichrodt continues, the claim that Old Testament theology is a 'purely historical' discipline is misleading, as it fails to recognize that historical study is always undergirded by the subjective values and commitments of the historian and so is never 'pure' in the sense of being 'presuppositionless'. When certain historical phenomena are identified as significant and set within some overall framework of interpretation, how could this occur in the absence of subjective commitments? All 'naïve optimism about absolute objectivity' is excluded, and we must learn that the historical ideal does not consist in 'the extinction of one's individual identity' (87) but in becoming explicitly conscious of the presuppositions with which one inevitably operates. These modern insights into the nature of historical knowledge make it impossible to accept Eissfeldt's contrast between an 'Old Testament dogmatic discipline' and a 'chemically pure, objective Israelite and Jewish *Religionsgeschichte*' (88). Old Testament theology is a historical discipline which can be at the same time 'theological' in so far as it interprets its material in relation to its role of preparing the way for God's revelation in Christ, as attested by the New Testament. 'It is of course undeniable that Israelite and Jewish religion can be understood from a quite different standpoint, so long as this is preceded by methodological reflection and clarification about this standpoint too. Yet a *theological* approach is not possible on any other presupposition than the one mentioned' (88–89), that is, the christological presupposition. A more sophisticated account of the scope and nature of historical enquiry refutes the naïve positivism for which theological and historical concerns are necessarily opposed to one another.

The christological presupposition is restated at the outset of Eichrodt's *Theology of the Old Testament*, the first volume of which was published in 1933. 'To our general aim of obtaining a comprehensive picture of the realm of OT belief we must add a second and closely related purpose – *to see that this comprehensive picture does justice to the essential relationship with the NT* and does not merely ignore it' (1.27; italics original).[15] The crucial question, however, is how the relationship to the New Testament and therefore to christology is construed. Eichrodt shares with Eissfeldt the assumption that Old Testament theology must adopt a synchronic rather than purely diachronic approach. In Eissfeldt's case, as we have seen, this assumption grew out of a view of *Religion* as the elevation of the individual out of historical particularity into timeless relationship with God, an event that occurs when, through the medium of 'experience', divine revelation evokes the response of faith. The positive value of the Old Testament rests on its testimony to this relationship. Such a theology will be able to appeal to Christ as the exemplar of *Religion* in its purest form; but it will not be able to accommodate the event of the Word's becoming flesh, since its movement away from history into relationship with God is radically at odds with God's own movement into a relationship with humankind in which the historicity both of revelation and of the response it evokes is irreducible. It seems that Eichrodt's presentation of the divine–human relationship is similarly, at its deepest level, oriented not towards irreducible historicity but towards timeless presence. There is, indeed, plenty of historical particularity in evidence, but its function is to outline the uncovering, degeneration and recovery of an understanding and experience of the divine–human relationship that places it essentially beyond history.

For Eichrodt, Israel's understanding of the covenant-relation with Yahweh presupposes the divine revelation to which the traditions about Moses and Sinai bear witness. This event is, however, the historical presupposition for an essentially *present* relationship: 'With this God men know exactly where they stand; *an atmosphere of trust and security* is created, in which they find both the strength for a willing surrender to the will of God and joyful courage to grapple with the problems of life' (1.38; italics original). That is, as the section-heading puts it, 'the meaning of the covenant concept' (II.1). Unlike *Religion*, indeed, the covenant is unthinkable without institutional embodiment, and Eichrodt's basic treatment of the meaning and history of the covenant concept is therefore followed by a lengthy treatment of 'the covenant statutes', that is, 'the secular law' and 'the cultus' (III, IV).[16] But here too Eichrodt's strategy is, negatively, to insist on the qualitative difference between Israel's institutional religion and that of her Near Eastern neighbours, despite the overlap of empirical content, and, positively, to show that even on its institutional side the covenant is oriented towards personal relationship. Thus cultic atonement is firmly based on 'the free and gracious ordinance of the covenant God', requiring a response of 'trusting obedience on the part of the offerer' (1.166). 'The unique character of the Israelite conception of atonement' is to be seen in 'the personal character of Israel's relationship with God' (1.166, 167).

The 'personal' nature of the covenant God is apparent from 'the constant and emphatic connection of the divine name with cultic activity', which 'shows how vividly people were aware that in the name of the covenant God they encountered him in person and experienced his activity' (1.208). This sharply-demarcated divine personhood is defined in opposition to the unstable personification of natural forces that underlies both polytheism and pantheism (1.209). It is true that 'the more emphatically this concrete picture of God as personal guarded against any deviation which might regard him as a blind natural force acting on impulse, the greater . . . was the danger of approximating him too closely to the human' (1.210–11; italics removed). Naïve anthropomorphism was, however, a fault on the right side in the struggle against the divinizing of nature: it must be seen as 'a wise self-limitation on the part of God that he should have presented himself and caused himself to be understood primarily as personal, while leaving veiled, so to speak, the fact that he was also spiritual' (1.213). What is overlooked in this antithesis between personhood and nature, so fundamental for Eichrodt's conception of Old Testament theology, is the inseparability of personhood (divine or human) from *historicity*.[17] As presented in the Old Testament, the relationship between Yahweh and Israel is irreducibly historical; it never takes the form of a dehistoricized encounter between an abstract I and an abstract Thou. If, as Eichrodt notes, the divine personhood is guaranteed by the divine name, precisely this divine name – 'Yahweh' – indicates that a divine personhood abstracted from history is inconceivable for Israel. At the moment of its disclosure, it is apparent that this name is rooted in the past: for Moses is to announce Yahweh not as unknown but as 'the God of your fathers, the God of Abraham, the God of Isaac, the God of Jacob' (Exod. 3.15). Yet this name is also oriented towards the future: *ehyeh asher ehyeh* (v. 14). This future is partially disclosed in the promises of redemption from Egypt and of the land (vv. 7–10), but the name speaks also of a hidden future of radically free divine activity that transcends the revealed future that constitutes the horizon for Moses' own future. Although Eichrodt regards Old Testament statements about the divine attributes (power, love, righteousness, holiness and so on) as 'affirmations about the divine *activity*', this 'activity' lacks the concrete historical enactment of the Old Testament presentation and tends towards ahistorical abstraction.[18]

The historical dimension of the divine–human relationship consists, for Eichrodt, in the initial development of its properly personal form, out of and away from the unpromising soil of ancient Near Eastern religiosity in general, and in the emergence and overcoming of subsequent threats to its purity. These threats are not of a piece: to the single threat that the texts acknowledge – idolatry, the service of other gods – Eichrodt adds various other threats posed (he thinks) by the texts themselves. Thus he displays remarkable ambivalence towards his own central category, that of 'covenant': the major prophets are said to avoid this term because of the 'weakness inherent in it which makes it a potential danger to religious life', that is, 'its legal character' which encourages a contractual rather than a personal view of the divine–human relationship (1.52). Already in the seventh century BC Deuteronomy shows that this was a real danger, and the danger becomes reality in the post-exilic period as an impersonal relation to the law is increasingly substituted for a personal relation to God. Eichrodt repeatedly turns to Ps. 119 in order to illustrate this. 'Life with God is now life under the Law, and the more this conception was carried out to the letter and down to the last detail, the more did all interest centre on man's conduct, driving the personal self-communication of God into the background' (2.363–64). 'Living inner exchange with a divine Thou was forcibly supplanted by the dead authority of an impersonal entity, behind which both the infinite majesty and the love, seeking fellowship with man, of him to whom the Law should have borne witness, was all too easily hidden' (2.376). The fact that almost every verse of Ps. 119 is explicitly *addressed* to the divine Thou might have led Eichrodt to question the crude and one-sided contrast between legal and personal relationships that he here adopts. His procedure is precisely that of the *Religion* tradition: criteria for the criticism of the biblical texts are derived from a particular construal of the proper form of the divine–human relationship.

Eichrodt invests heavily in the theory of post-exilic decline from the prophetic heights, on which his christology is largely dependent. At the end of part 2 of the *Theology of the Old Testament* ('God and the World'), we visit the underworld and learn, finally, of the demons, who played a minimal role in authentic Old Testament religion but became more significant in 'later Judaism'. Eichrodt concludes his discussion (and the book, for part 2 was published separately in the original German) by stating that at this time

> it cannot be denied that there was a considerable darkening of life's horizons. In this situation only a *new* assurance of the nearness of the redeeming covenant God could lead to freedom and that religious confidence, capable of over-coming the world, which had been characteristic of the prophetic period. Hence even this line of development in the Old Testament's understanding of its faith points beyond itself to the age of the New Covenant. (2.228)

Eichrodt is here dependent on the liberal Protestant adaptation of the old schema of origin, decline and recovery. Here, the prophetic experience of God marks the high point in the Old Testament's unveiling of true *Religion*; post-exilic religion represents a degeneration; and the function of christology is therefore to restore that which has been lost and to lead it to its ultimate fulfilment. It makes little difference whether the emphasis falls on the 'newness' of God's act in Christ ('a *new* assurance of the nearness of the covenant God', 'the New Covenant') or on its restoration of what had previously been in existence ('that religious confidence . . . which had been characteristic of the prophetic period'): for the fact that God's act in Jesus Christ can be thought of as in any sense a restoration indicates that this 'newness' is only relative. Jesus is certainly a *help*, but he is not indispensable: something closely resembling the divine–human relationship in its purest form was already experienced and known centuries before his birth, and even he is in the end extraneous to that relationship, which is to do with a 'religious confidence, capable of overcoming the world'. Jesus, the prophets and no doubt many others help us to attain this religious confidence, which lies at the heart of religious experience in general and Israel's theology of the covenant in particular, but there must come a point where their help ceases. Otherwise we never acquire a religious confidence of our own, here and now; we remain dependent on others to do our trusting for us.

A christology that leads to conclusions such as these clearly operates with 'ebionite' disregard for the simple fact that in Jesus the Word has become flesh, and that this must constitute the centre and the basis of all our thinking about the divine–human relationship. Underlying Eichrodt's penetrating discussion of individual elements of Old Testament theology is a repristinated liberal Protestant theology that has learned to speak in new ways about divine personhood, holiness and revelation, but that still clings tenaciously to the dogmas of a *Religion* that has dispensed with the particularities of divine action.

2. Von Rad

Like Eichrodt, Gerhard von Rad believes that 'Old Testament theology' is distinguished from the historical study of Israel's religion by the attempt to interpret the Old Testament as Christian scripture. Unlike Eichrodt, von Rad takes this task seriously in practice and not just in principle. About a quarter of the second volume of his *Old Testament Theology* (1957–60; ET 1962–65)[19] is devoted to the relationship between the Testaments, a topic which – as von Rad notes – is at present systematically neglected. Institutional factors are to blame for the 'virtual elimination' of this issue: the 'division of labour and the development of separate departments of scholarship' have created a situation in which 'a whole category of important theological questions today lies in a kind of no-man's-land between Old Testament and New Testament theology' (2.388). The claim that the relationship between the Testaments is *typological* enables von Rad to integrate this question into his presentation of Old Testament theology as a whole, rather than permitting it to arise merely as a supplement to the primary task of understanding the Old Testament 'in its own terms'. Precisely when understood 'in its own terms', the Old Testament itself raises the question of its relation to the New. Old Testament theology is characterized by a dynamic of promise and fulfilment in which the fulfilment does not exhaust the content of the promise but, on the contrary, discloses that dimension of the promise that transcends the present and points towards the future. It is this dynamic that underlies Israel's constant reinterpretation of its own traditions, a reinterpretation that can already take typological form even within the Old Testament itself (for example, in Deutero-Isaiah's projection into the future of intensified exodus imagery). The Old Testament is a dynamic rather than a static entity, and exegesis constantly discloses an openness to the future that tacitly poses the question of the goal towards which its restless movement is directed. For the Christian, that goal is Jesus Christ, and the traditional concept of 'typology' suggests a hermeneutic in which every part of the Old Testament is read in its relation to that goal. Yet, far from imposing an extraneous criterion on Old Testament interpretation, a typological hermeneutic grows out of the Old Testament itself. It is therefore possible for von Rad both to engage in historical-critical work on, say, the origins of the Hexateuch, and to maintain that 'we receive the Old Testament from the hands of Jesus Christ, and all exegesis of the Old Testament therefore depends on whom one thinks Jesus Christ to be' (*Genesis*, 43).[20] It is true that von Rad does not normally practise the explicitly Christian typological exegesis that he advocates; but he is able to advocate it only because his own exegesis demonstrates its fundamental legitimacy and necessity on the basis of the Old Testament texts themselves.

The rationale for von Rad's understanding of Old Testament theology is most clearly set out in an article entitled 'Grundprobleme einer biblischen Theologie des Alten Testaments' (1943).[21] Von Rad begins by criticizing the recently-published Old Testament theologies of Eichrodt (1933–39), Sellin (1936) and Köhler (1936) for imposing a 'systematic' framework alien to the material itself. This procedure is justified by Köhler on the grounds that 'it is impossible to derive the lay-out and the ordering of the theological content of the Old Testament from the Old Testament itself', but for von Rad this is 'a counsel of despair [*ein verzweifeltes Kapitulieren*]' (226). Why, he asks, should we assume that the replacement of a *religionsgeschichtliche* approach to Israel's religion by a theological one necessitates a flat, static, systematic framework (226–27)? To lose Old Testament history alongside *Religionsgeschichte* is to lose the Old Testament itself: for 'the Old Testament is the book of a particular history, it wishes to recount a history of God with humankind' – the history narrated in the series of books from Genesis to 2 Kings, to which the prophets also appeal as they speak of past, present and future. 'The category of history is in the Old Testament a thoroughly theological one, and no theology of the Old Testament can evade it' (227). In accordance with this emphasis on the canonical form and coherence of the Old Testament literature, von Rad later based most of his treatment of 'the theology of Israel's historical traditions' (*Old Testament Theology*, vol. 1 part 2) on an outline derived from the canonical story, beginning with the primeval history and concluding with the Books of Kings and Chronicles. The rediscovery of the canonical form of Old Testament literature is already signalled in *The Form-critical Problem of the Hexateuch* (1938).[22] In a situation in which 'the final form of the Hexateuch has come to be regarded as a starting-point barely worthy of discussion, from which the debate should move away as rapidly as possible in order to reach the real problems underlying it' (1), von Rad's form-critical investigations have 'the merit of leading us back to the final and conclusive form of the Hexateuch' (3).[23] Systematic treatments of Old Testament theology overlook both the Old Testament's orientation towards history and the canonical form of its major literary units.

For von Rad, it would be inadequate and misleading to understand the canonical form of a text in terms of its literary coherence. His own form-critical approach reinforces the source-critical finding that the texts are *lacking* in certain kinds of literary coherence, and his attempts to rehabilitate the final form of the texts is in no sense a retreat from the basic critical claim that the texts display clear signs of incoherence and that these are to be explained on the basis of the texts' prehistory as reconstructed by modern scholarship. Thus, in the case of the Hexateuch, 'None of the stages in the age-long development of this work has been wholly superseded; something has been preserved of each phase, and its influence has persisted right down to the final form of the Hexateuch. Only a recognition of this fact can prepare one to hear the plenitude of the witness which this work encompasses' (*Hexateuch*, 78; italics removed). The 'coherence' of the Hexateuch is like that of a medieval cathedral that has been constructed and extended over a period of several centuries, incorporating a number of contrasting architectural styles. While von Rad can be criticized for his excessive confidence in the ability of historical scholarship to reconstruct the processes of a text's origin, his insistence on a *theological* understanding of the final form of the text opens up possibilities that are excluded by a purely 'literary' hermeneutic.

Theologically, the crucial categories are 'promise' and 'fulfilment'. The Old Testament recounts a history of the relationship between God and humankind, and underlying this history, in all its variety, is 'a manifold rhythm of promise and fulfilment' which is decisive for its interpretation ('Grundprobleme', 227). This history is a *Heilsgeschichte*, a history set in motion and determined by God's word. Thus, in the deuteronomic history, 'God's word, in its commandments and in the promise to David, works to create history in the twofold form of judgment and salvation' (228). The point is elaborated in a later study of 'The Deuteronomic Theology of History in I and II Kings' (1947), where von Rad draws attention to the pattern of prophecy and fulfilment that runs through the Books of Kings, to the effect of the Davidic promise in restraining God's judgment of Judah despite his rejection of the northern kingdom, and to the suggestion at the close that the favour bestowed on the exiled, captive King Jehoiachin may point to a new future for the people of God beyond the execution of the covenantal curse.[24] We are led to conclude that 'in the deuteronomic presentation of the matter Yahweh's word determines the history of Judah, and that it does so under two particular forms: first, it is a law which controls and destroys; secondly it is a "gospel", a continually self-fulfilling promise to David, which brings salvation and forgiveness' (219). As presented here, *Heilsgeschichte* is 'a course of events shaped by the word of Yahweh, continually intervening to direct and to deliver, and so steadily pressing these events towards their fulfilment in history' (221). While the theme of the covenantal curse might seem to compromise the orientation of the promise/fulfilment schema towards salvation, the ending of 2 Kings may plausibly be read in the light of Yahweh's concern that 'David my servant may always have a lamp before me in Jerusalem, the city where I have chosen to put my name' (1 Kgs. 11.36), a concern that obviously rests upon the Davidic covenant (2 Sam. 7).

The promise/fulfilment schema also underlies the entire Hexateuch, in which the outline first established by the Yahwist remains clear: 'The land of Canaan is promised to the patriarchs, although in the land of their sojourning they stand in a peculiarly broken relationship to the object of the promise. The wilderness generation finds itself in a movement towards fulfilment characterized by trouble and temptation – a fulfilment finally accomplished under Joshua' ('Grundprobleme', 228). The Hexateuch thus reaches its climax with the claim that 'Yahweh gave them rest on every side just as he had sworn to their fathers . . . Not one of all the good promises which Yahweh had made to the house of Israel had failed; all came to pass' (Josh. 21.44–45). Yet, remarkably, the promise is not exhausted in its fulfilment. Deuteronomy, 'which certainly derives from the situation after the conquest, sees Israel as still fundamentally *before* the fulfilment; all the good gifts of salvation, including that of dwelling in the promised "rest", are once again set before the community as promises' (228). Israel has entered the promised land, but has forgotten Yahweh and clung to the Baals; thus it remains true of Israel after the conquest that 'you have not as yet come to the rest and to the inheritance which Yahweh your God gives you' (Deut. 12.9). As von Rad had already argued in a study dating from 1933, in the Book of Deuteronomy 'a miracle of faith is performed before our eyes: the intervening period, wasted as it has been by sin, is expunged from the record, and Israel is carried back again to the hour of its first election' (95–96).[25] The fulfilment of the promise of rest is still open, despite the conquest and references to 'rest' in connection with David and Solomon (2 Sam. 7.1, 11; 1 Kgs. 8.56); the Epistle to the Hebrews is fundamentally right to argue, on the basis of Ps. 95, that 'there remains a rest for the people of God' (Heb. 4.9). As the author to the Hebrews argues, his own typological interpretation of this theme is already anticipated in the Old Testament itself. In this *heilsgeschichtliche* dynamic of promise and fulfilment, the fulfilment of a promise re-establishes the promise on a new level; and it is the main task of an Old Testament theology whose ordering is derived from the Old Testament itself to investigate the workings of this fundamental dynamic. How, on the other hand, could 'a synchronic [*flächenhaft*], systematic presentation grasp this ongoing salvation-historical fracturing [*Brechung*] of the Old Testament testimonies?' ('Grundprobleme', 229).

The dynamic of promise and fulfilment takes new forms in the proclamation of the classical prophets. The prophets interpret the present in the light not of a past *Heilsgeschichte* but of a future characterized in the first instance by a catastrophic divine judgment that exposes every claim to a security based on traditions of election as illusory. Yet beyond this judgment lies a definitive, eschatological act of Yahweh on behalf of his people, sometimes glimpsed as if from afar, sometimes rendered in glowing colours. Thus, 'the prophetic message differs from all previous Israelite theology, which was based on the past saving history, in that the prophets looked for the decisive factor in Israel's whole existence – her life or her death – in some future event' (*Old Testament Theology*, 2.117). The discontinuity is not, however, absolute: for 'the specific form of the new thing which they herald is not chosen at random; the new is to be effected in a way which is more or less analogous to God's former saving work. Thus Hosea foretells a new entry into the land, Isaiah a new David and a new Zion, Jeremiah a new covenant, and Deutero-Isaiah a new exodus' (2.117). The breach with the salvation-historical past is most radically expressed in Deutero-Isaiah's exhortation to 'remember not the former things nor consider the things of old – for behold, I am doing a new thing' (Isa. 43.18–19, a text that von Rad employs as a superscription to his treatment of 'the theology of Israel's prophetic traditions'). Even here, however, and with particular clarity, the new thing is analogous to the old; for the God who promises a new thing is already known as 'Yahweh, your Holy One, the Creator of Israel, your King', who 'makes a way in the sea, a path in the mighty waters, who brings forth chariot and horse, army and warrior; they lie down, they cannot rise, they are extinguished, quenched like a wick' (Isa. 43.15–17). In this typological thinking, the exodus from Egypt no longer belongs to the series of *heilsgeschichtliche* acts of God, from the election of the patriarchs to the conquest or the election of David, which together comprise a solid foundation upon which subsequent *Heilsgeschichte* can gradually unfold. This foundation and the history that flowed from it have been abruptly brought to an end by the divine judgment. Israel in exile is not to look back, in a vain attempt to re-establish continuity; she is to look forward to God's new, definitive saving act, and as she does so she will discover that the past has not been lost without trace but that it is present in the form of *promise*. Where God's future act is understood in terms derived from the past, then past and future are conceived as promise and fulfilment, type and antitype. Here and elsewhere, the promise/fulfilment schema derives from a radical reinterpretation of earlier traditions, understood now as a promise oriented towards fulfilment in the imminent future. Von Rad's detailed exegetical work on the history of traditions (*Überlieferungsgeschichte*) is thus closely related to his view of the dynamic nature of Old Testament theology in general.

Already in his 1943 article von Rad argued that this construal of Old Testament theology makes it possible to re-establish the integral relationship between the two Testaments, in opposition to the tendency to interpret Jesus in isolation from the Old Testament and the Old Testament in isolation from Jesus. In relation to the first point, von Rad claims that, without exception, the New Testament witnesses 'set the appearance of Jesus Christ in the context of Old Testament salvation-history', and that, 'theologically speaking, it is by no means open to us to abstract Jesus Christ from this context – even if this seems to make him still more problematic for us' ('Grundprobleme', 231). (One catches here an echo of the first article of the Barmen declaration of 1934, according to which 'the one Word of God which we have to hear, and which we have to trust and obey in life and in death' is 'Jesus Christ, as he is attested to us in Holy Scripture', that is, in the texts of the Old Testament as well as the New.)[26] In relation to the second point (the question whether the Old Testament can be understood, at least initially, in isolation from Jesus), von Rad rejects the objection that a typological exegesis would undermine the historical particularity of Old Testament texts and thereby show itself to be indistinguishable from allegorical interpretation. On the contrary, it is precisely a typological exegesis that could restore to the Old Testament its own peculiar value: 'If we compare it with the approach that reads the Old Testament for its "religious values" (preferably "timeless" ones), one will have to concede that typology can face the "differences" and the "sub-Christian" elements with a much clearer conscience than the other approach could' (232). It is of course true that hermeneutical caution is required in this area, at least until we see our way a little more clearly; and if the results sometimes seem forced (von Rad refers to the work of W. Vischer), it is not the method itself that is to be blamed.

Von Rad is acutely aware that to read the Old Testament in relation to Jesus Christ is a difficult project for which no clear hermeneutical guidelines are as yet available, and which is bound to evoke suspicion among those accustomed to a neo-Marcionite Old Testament abstracted from the centre of Christian faith. In a contemporary setting, this view of the goal of Old

Testament theology will evoke little sympathy where 'Old Testament theology' is understood as the quest for 'relevant' or 'liberating' aspects of the texts – an updated version of the older search for 'timeless religious values'. Von Rad, however, knows what a theology of that kind does not know, which is that 'Jesus Christ, as he is attested to us in Holy Scripture, is the one Word of God which we have to hear, and which we have to trust and obey in life and in death', whether in the Third Reich or anywhere else; and the question he raises as to how the christological orientation of the Old Testament texts is to be rendered in such a way as to preserve rather than to suppress their particularity is therefore the only serious theological question that Old Testament theology must face. All other questions are comprised within this fundamental question.

In a study of 'Typologische Auslegung des Alten Testaments' (1952), von Rad refines and extends his understanding of typology at two main points.[27]

(1) Typology is understood as a particular instance of analogical thought in general, which also comes to expression in the form of proverbs and poetry (17–18). Far from endangering the particularity of the individual phenomenon, analogical thinking is the condition for the knowability of the individual phenomenon in its particularity. This suggests that the objection to typology lies not in its use of analogy but in the particular, christological analogy that is here applied. Typological exegesis of the Old Testament claims that the Christ-event is 'the only analogy which is relevant for a theological interpretation of these texts'. It rests on the assumption that Heb. 1.1–2 is true, that 'we are concerned with a single divine speech, both to the fathers through the prophets and to us through Christ' (31). Unfortunately, this simple assumption has fallen into disrepute. During the Enlightenment, as von Rad shows, the christological analogy of traditional typological thinking was replaced by new modes of analogical thought. In his *Entwurf der typischen Gottesgelahrtheit* (1755), Michaelis sought the antitype of Old Testament types not in christology but in the general truths of religion; and in 1779 Semler wrote dismissively that 'even the greatest enthusiast for typology can hardly accord it a place among the fundamental doctrines [*Grundsätze*] of Christianity' (21). The Old Testament was still related to the *ideas* expressed in the New, especially when these happen to coincide with the interpreter's opinions about the general truths of religion or the fundamental doctrines of Christianity, but the relation to the *facts* attested in the New Testament disappears without trace.

Its place is taken by a comprehensive new form of analogical thinking, that of the historical-critical method. According to Troeltsch, 'That which makes criticism possible at all is the use of analogy', the analogy between the narrated event and 'normal, customary or at least often attested processes' of the kind that happen 'before our very eyes' ('Über historische und dogmatische Methode' [1898], as quoted by von Rad, 22). In this celebration of the 'omnipotence of analogy', it might seem that our own experience now constitutes the true antitype to the Old Testament types. Yet the type/antitype schema assumes a linear *Heilsgeschichte* oriented towards an eschatological goal, and therefore a relation of *unlikeness* as well as likeness between type and antitype; analogy is important here, but it cannot be absolutized. On the other hand, Troeltsch's omnipotence of analogy can only be established on the assumption of 'the fundamental homogeneity [*Gleichartigkeit*] of all historical occurrence', an identity underlying all difference that precludes in advance the possibility of newness and therefore of heterogeneity that is assumed in Christian faith.[28] Paradoxically, Troeltsch's historicized world is characterized in the end by an ahistorical simultaneity. When the programme of analogy and comparison is applied to the study of the Old Testament, the result is an account of 'Israel's religion' which is, for von Rad, 'to be regarded simply as a disastrous reduction of the content of the Old Testament as it actually addresses us'. What is overlooked here is the fact that 'the Old Testament is a history-book' which recounts 'a history effected by God's word, from the creation of the world to the coming of the Son of man' (23). Far from undermining the historical particularity of Old Testament texts, typological exegesis preserves their openness to a new future constituted by God's action from the departicularizing, dehistoricizing effect of the postulate of homogeneity.

(2) Von Rad wishes to integrate typological exegesis into Old Testament exegesis in general, rather than assigning it a merely supplementary role. Such a project would have to address itself to the Old Testament as a whole (and not just to the obvious instances of typology in the prophets), on the assumption that typological exegesis is appropriate to the innermost nature of the texts themselves. In prophetic texts such as Hos. 2.16–20, 'one sees that already within the Old Testament mute historical facts become prophetic and are viewed as prototypes [*Vorbilder*] to which a new and more complete divine saving action must correspond' (29). This familiar point is now extended to narrative texts, in an attempt to show that an openness to prophetic and Christian typological usage is inherent to the texts themselves. In Old Testament narrative, 'it is very common to find in the telling of the historical fact something that transcends what actually happened' (30). For example, the Book of Judges sees the judges as charismatic bearers of a comprehensive theocratic office extending to all Israel, despite their actually rather limited sphere of influence. The Book of Joshua depicts a unified

conquest of Canaan under a single leader, in contrast to the more complex and diverse process implied by Judges 1. For von Rad, it is quite inadequate to regard these and similar instances as examples of a general propensity of peoples not schooled in modern historical method to represent their own past in the heightened, intensified form characteristic of legend. Such an explanation is too superficial, failing to locate these narratives in the particular context of Israel's distinctive experience of God. What occurs here is that 'an article of faith is projected into history – that is, God's saving activity on Israel's behalf is represented in what faith sees as its unity; the event is presented in a transfigured form which goes beyond what actually occurred, because that which is believed must make itself visible as already completed in history' (30). Conversely, 'the utterances of the psalms of lament far transcend biographical experience, setting before us an image of paradigmatic suffering characterized by utter abandonment by God' (30). One way or the other, a tendency towards the radicalizing of experience becomes visible; we are compelled to speak of 'an eschatological moment in these representations, in so far as they assert that a finally-valid divine action has already become real in history' (30). Israel's utterances about both past and present are inherently open to God's future and so to typological understanding, for they are already transfigured by that future. Prophetic and Christian typological interpretation has rightly understood that Israel's traditions are characterized by a refusal to stand still and a hastening towards God's future. In these texts, through faith, God's future is anticipated. Typological exegesis cannot be clearly demarcated from 'ordinary' exegesis, for typological exegesis is precisely what *these* texts require if their true nature is to be brought to light.

Von Rad's typological hermeneutic implies an exegetical practice that goes far beyond crude and artificial correlations of Old Testament figures and institutions with Jesus Christ. What is proposed is not an anachronistic return to pre-critical exegesis but a radicalization of the modern theological and exegetical concern to identify ever more precisely those characteristics that are peculiar to the biblical texts. At the same time, it must be said that in his exegetical practice von Rad is concerned only with typological processes occurring within the Old Testament itself. By his own criteria, these are of no direct theological significance. They become significant only as the precondition for a Christian typological interpretation that sees the enfleshed Word as the goal of God's history with Israel; and von Rad's highly suggestive rationale for Christian typological interpretation does not entirely compensate for his general failure to practise it. His interpretative practice, as represented for example by all but the concluding sections of his *Old Testament Theology*, fits comfortably within the framework of an Old Testament scholarship which pursues its various historical and exegetical projects in isolation from the New Testament and Christian theology. What is distinctive about von Rad is his clear recognition of the theological problem posed by the relative institutional autonomy of Old Testament scholarship: the relation of the Old Testament to the New is for him *the* question of Old Testament theology, and yet precisely this question is obscured by the current division of labour. But even von Rad is unable to translate this insight into exegetical practice. His work as a whole may at best be seen as prolegomena to a new, typological exegesis that interprets the Old Testament texts within their total biblical context; but it is also possible – and much more usual – to understand him simply as a conventional Old Testament scholar whose interest in a distinctively Christian Old Testament interpretation remains marginal to his real achievement.[29] The reason for this ambiguity is presumably that von Rad remains inhibited by the convention that the Old Testament must be interpreted in isolation from the New, although he rejects this convention in principle. In practice, this means that he emphasizes the *forward* movement of salvation-history towards a final actualization, at the expense of the *retrospective* movement, starting from the final actualization in Jesus, that is essential to the practice of a Christian typological exegesis. Old Testament types can be identified only in the light of the antitype.

Von Rad assumes a straightforwardly linear view of time in which, as in the biblical narrative itself, we begin at the beginning (in this case, the creation of the world), and proceed through various intermediate stages (God's history with Israel) until we finally attain the goal towards which we have all along been directed (Jesus Christ). The linearity of salvation-history is fundamental to von Rad's conception of Old Testament theology, and it is clearly expressed in the basically chronological arrangement of his two volumes, where (after various preliminaries) we begin with 'the primeval history' and eventually reach our predestined conclusion with 'the New Testament fulfilment'. The assumption here is that biblical theology is bound to follow biblical chronology. Jesus is the goal of *Heilsgeschichte*, but there is much to be said about the divine saving activity in and through Israel before we speak explicitly of him. At the very end of the story of God's saving activity, we encounter the figure of Jesus, who is its goal. As such, he casts a retrospective light on earlier stages of the story, which make sense in a new way when related to him; he makes possible a typological interpretation. Yet, for von Rad, this retrospective movement is ultimately much weaker than the *forward* momentum of salvation-history, which flows onwards as inexorably as a river towards the sea. If Jesus is the goal of salvation-history, he is also its product; like any other major historical figure, he is the passive creation of the history from which he derives *before* he acts in such a way as retrospectively to impose a new meaning on the history that remains the ground for his activity.[30] The question is how, on this account, the Word that is identified with the historical existence of Jesus of Nazareth can also be the Word that was with God in the beginning; how, in other words, it can be said of Jesus that his being is ultimately grounded not in history but in God, in a sense that is true of Jesus alone and so does justice to the uniqueness of the incarnation.

If von Rad's typological exegesis were to be practised consistently, the result would be an interpretation for which the forward movement of salvation-history is complemented and indeed preceded by the retrospective movement from fulfilment back to anticipation. The 'Old Testament', as Christian scripture, only comes into existence in the moment of absolute newness represented by Jesus, and should be interpreted on the basis of its moment of origin; only the antitype makes the types visible as such. Von Rad himself recognizes that 'we receive the Old Testament from the hands of Jesus Christ, and all exegesis of the Old Testament therefore depends on whom one thinks Jesus Christ to be' (*Genesis*, 43). Only from the standpoint of the salvation fulfilled in Jesus does it become clear that the fundamental meaning of the Old Testament lies in its testimony to salvation-history, and von Rad's interpretation of Old Testament theology therefore *proceeds in principle from a Christian starting-point*. It is, in other words, precisely an interpretation of the 'Old Testament', the first part of the two-part Christian canon. The object of this interpretation is not a religiously-neutral collection of texts abstracted from its former context, and interpretation therefore cannot occur in a religiously-neutral manner, extended in the direction of fulfilment in Jesus only in a secondary, subsequent movement that remains tentative and optional. The goal of the Christian Old Testament must be the starting-point for interpretation: without this starting-point, it is by no means clear that the narrated movement into God's future should be regarded as the fundamental substance of this body of writings. Von Rad's conception of Old Testament theology is therefore based on a Christian foundation. Unfortunately, this is obscured by the constraints imposed by disciplinary structures within which a Christian foundation is declared to be redundant and illegitimate. Yet von Rad's advocacy of a typological exegesis and his conception of Old Testament theology indicate an awareness that Jesus is Alpha as well as Omega, theologically and therefore methodologically as well.[31]

In the concluding paragraph of an article entitled 'Offene Fragen im Umkreis einer Theologie des Alten Testaments' (1963), von Rad asserts again that Old Testament theology can be a genuinely theological undertaking only when it 'relates [the Old Testament] to the witness of the evangelists and the apostles with complete openness [*in aller Öffentlichkeit*], and makes credible their interdependence [*Zusammengehörigkeit*]'.[32] The credibility of this relationship is dependent on showing how the process of tradition leads Old Testament theology 'from one actualization to another, so that the question of the ultimate fulfilment arises in the end out of its own content'. If, on the other hand, Old Testament theology 'analyses the Old Testament in isolation [*für sich*] – no matter how devotedly this is done – the designation "history of Old Testament religion" would be more appropriate' (416/428– 29). Old Testament theology has a future only as an explicitly Christian enterprise, on the basis of the Christian Bible in which Jesus marks the point where the two Testaments divide and meet. Without this presupposition, to discuss the future of Old Testament theology – its 'problems and prospects', how it is to be 'reconstructed' – is in fact to talk about something quite different. Old Testament theology is incompatible with an interpretation of the Old Testament *für sich*. In both Testaments, although in different ways, Jesus is the beginning and the end.[33]

An attempt to put this theological hermeneutic into practice would face three major objections. First, it might be said that the logic of the movement from one actualization to another does not require an inner-historical moment of fulfilment. Second, one might challenge the assumption that what is to count as 'theology' must be determined on an exclusively christological basis. Third, this hermeneutic might be criticized as a retreat into confessionalism and an abandonment of the ecumenical ethos of historical-critical scholarship.

(1) The inner-historical moment of fulfilment is to be understood not only as the end but also as the beginning of Old Testament theology; it cannot be deduced from the texts if they are abstracted from the actuality of this fulfilment. In abstraction, the texts might be said to initiate an entirely open-ended process of reinterpreting tradition that has continued into our own times and for which we are now responsible. The result would be a pluralistic and relativistic hermeneutic in which traditions and texts are placed at the disposal of each new generation of readers, to be understood in the light of their varied situations.[34] Such a hermeneutic is incompatible with the existence of the Christian Bible, according to which the confession that Jesus is the Christ presupposes an inner-historical moment of fulfilment that retains its ultimate significance in the relativities of each new situation. Yet the foundational significance of this christological starting-point does not mean that von Rad's quest for an interpretation of the Old Testament that proceeds 'out of its own content [*von ihrem Stoff selbst*]' has to be abandoned. The prophetic application of Israel's salvation-historical traditions to the eschatological future clearly 'poses the question of a final fulfilment' rather than legitimating an entirely open-ended process of reinterpretation. If, on the Christian view, the moment of fulfilment is different from anything that

could have been known in advance, it should be possible to show that it is still recognizably an answer to the question implied in the Old Testament texts themselves.

(2) To claim, with von Rad, that Old Testament theology must begin and end with the confession of Jesus as the Christ is not to reduce theology to christology. It is to claim, first, that Christian faith has a *centre*, and that it is not a set of unconnected assertions about God, humankind and the world. And it is to claim, second, that this centre is the self-disclosure in Jesus of the triune God, and that every assertion of Christian theology must be able to demonstrate a relationship to this centre. It might be said that Old Testament theology can and should reflect theologically on themes such as creation or suffering without reference to any christological centre. Yet such a theology could only operate by interpreting certain texts in isolation from their context within the Christian Bible, the centre of which is marked by the figure of Jesus. Since it is only within the Christian Bible that there is an Old Testament at all, the Old Testament itself would be dissolved by a theological reflection basing itself exclusively on Old Testament texts.

(3) Historical-critical scholarship understands itself as a terrain upon which Jews, Protestants and Catholics can meet, contrasting its own generous ecumenicity with the exclusiveness it believes it detects in every 'confessional' approach to biblical interpretation.[35] Yet, in adopting this self-understanding, this scholarship reveals its own exclusiveness. Jews, Protestants and Catholics can meet on this terrain only in so far as they have submitted to the demand to exclude their religious identities from the work of biblical interpretation; the religious commitments that initially motivate biblical interpretation are deemed to be a purely private matter, unsuitable for public discourse. Whether this drastic disjunction between biblical interpretation and religious identity is or can be acceptable to Jews is not for a Christian to say. What can be said is that it is a sign not of ecumenicity but of a rigid, doctrinaire exclusiveness when Christians are denied the right to practise a biblical interpretation on the basis of the confession that Jesus is the Christ. The separation of the two Testaments, which on von Rad's view Old Testament theology must strive to overcome, is one of a number of expressions of this illiberal and intolerant ethos.

3. Childs

At least in English-speaking contexts, the Christian theological dimension which is so central to von Rad's conception of Old Testament theology has rarely been taken seriously. The publication and translation of von Rad's major work coincided with mounting criticism of the 'biblical theology movement', which had sought (at least in one of its variants) to maintain the unity of the Testaments by way of a salvation-historical theology of the 'mighty acts of God';[36] and one of the casualties of this criticism was the possibility of sustained and constructive reflection on the relationship between the Testaments.[37]

In his *Biblical Theology in Crisis* (1970), Brevard Childs analysed the American 'biblical theology movement' and argued that its downfall created space for new approaches.[38] According to Childs, biblical theology originated in a post-war rediscovery of the theological dimension of the biblical texts, in sharp reaction against the 'liberal' scholarship of the 1930s (23). Although the phenomenon of the canon was not explicitly discussed, there was a general desire to overcome the separation of the two Testaments, as scholars began to work in both fields (36). A central tenet was the belief that God reveals himself in history, in opposition to every claim that the truths with which religion concerns itself are somehow 'eternal' (39). Also characteristic was a belief in a distinctive biblical mentality: we were supposed 'to put ourselves within the world of the Bible', understanding it 'in its own categories', and above all noting the sharp difference between Hebraic and Greek world-views (45). The Bible was held to be utterly distinctive within its ancient Near Eastern and Graeco-Roman environments (47). This approach to biblical interpretation aligned itself with the 'neo-orthodox' theology especially of Emil Brunner, who taught at Princeton from 1938 onwards, and could make little of other contemporary theologians such as Tillich and Bultmann (56); and, with the waning of neo-orthodoxy's influence in the late 1950s and early 1960s, biblical theology's characteristic positions came increasingly under attack. For various reasons, it no longer seemed compelling or persuasive to talk of divine acts in history, the unity of the Bible or the distinctive biblical mentality (62–72): too many significant questions had been suppressed. According to newly-fashionable theologians such as Harvey Cox and Paul van Buren, 'God had abandoned the sanctuary and gone out into the streets' (85), and a new theological generation who thought along these lines would obviously 'find the emphases of the Biblical Theology Movement increasingly foreign' (83).

Yet, Childs continues, biblical theology should not be abandoned; instead, it should rethink its own foundations (92). It should recognize that 'the canon of the Christian church is the most appropriate context from which to do Biblical Theology' – for the canon delineates the area in which the church hears the Word of God, and interpretation must reflect the function of the canon within the community of faith (99). The older biblical theology 'accepted uncritically the liberal hermeneutical presupposition that one came to the Biblical text from a vantage point outside the text' (102); over against this, it must be recognized that 'Scripture does not exist as a book of truth in itself' (103) and that the false dichotomy between book and community must be removed (102–3). Biblical theology's traditional ambivalence towards conventional historical-critical scholarship is maintained here. In this scholarship, useful material is amassed but 'the scale of priorities' is all wrong (142); older exegesis – including that of the New Testament itself – is arrogantly dismissed as 'pre-critical' (139); the diachronic emphasis means that the final stage of the text is ignored (146).

Although in his Exodus commentary of 1974 Childs sought to rehabilitate 'pre-critical' modes of interpretation, subsequent work – especially the *Introduction to the Old Testament as Scripture* (1979) and *The New Testament as Canon: An Introduction* (1984) – has shown that his rediscovery of the hermeneutical significance of the canon is his most important contribution to a renewed 'biblical theology'.[39]

One might argue that the value of Brevard Childs' characteristic emphasis on the canonical form of the biblical texts lies in its contribution to *textual criticism*. Textual criticism as traditionally understood is the modest but indispensable endeavour to re-establish a text freed, so far as possible, from the alterations introduced by generations of over-zealous or incompetent scribes, on the assumption that it is this purified text that is the appropriate object of interpretative activity. Childs has rightly seen that the over-zealousness or incompetence of modern scribes too poses a threat to the integrity of the biblical texts. Obsessed with reconstructing the circumstances of the texts' genesis, critics prise them out of their received canonical context and subject them to the mutilations characteristic of source, form and redaction criticism. Childs' achievement is to have re-established the reality of the texts in their canonical form, challenging the assumption that the modern scribal activity is indispensable for their interpretation. In order to understand something, does one first have to destroy it? But that is what happens when, for example, the four gospels are no longer understood canonically as the fourfold narrative rendering of the one gospel but as separate, sharply differentiated texts which cannot be understood without a reconstruction of their interrelations and of the other circumstances that brought them into being.

The work of the textual critic is an indispensable preliminary to interpretation, establishing what it is that is to be interpreted. Childs, however, wishes to be an interpreter as well as a textual critic; that is, he wishes to reflect theologically on the texts whose canonical form he has succeeded in re-establishing. There is no reason why he should not do this, and indeed every reason why he should; but it must be emphasized that textual criticism and interpretation are different operations and that significant achievement in one field does not guarantee success in the other. Although Childs insists on the unity of his hermeneutical proposal and his work of theological interpretation, there are unfortunately major theological shortcomings in his two more recent works in this area: the relatively modest *Old Testament Theology in Canonical Context* (1985), and the more substantial *Biblical Theology of the Old and New Testaments* (1992).[40] The main problem lies in the assumption that the decision to include the Jewish scriptures in the Christian canon without alteration gives the Old Testament a relatively autonomous status in relation to the New.

In the earlier of the two works, Childs reverts to a pre-von Rad systematic or thematic approach. Here, Old Testament theology begins with treatment of 'The Old Testament as Revelation', 'How God is Known' and 'God's Purpose in Revelation', and proceeds to discuss the Mosaic Law and the roles of judges, kings, priests and prophets. A certain bias towards theological anthropology may be detected in the concluding chapters, which include treatment of 'Male and Female as a Theological Problem', 'The Theological Dimension of Being Human' and 'The Shape of the Obedient Life'. Methodologically, this work is significant for its reliance on the canonical form of the texts and its consequent independence from the historical-critical work that continues to shape other 'systematic' treatments of Old Testament theology. The diachronic dimension is virtually eliminated, and Old Testament theology is presented in a much more consistently systematic, synchronic form than anything envisaged by von Rad's predecessors. The various texts are present to one another in the form of a pure simultaneity, with the result that intertextual relationships can be established without recourse to historical question about priority, influence, authorial intention and so on. Thus Childs can draw on a wide range of Old Testament material to illustrate and clarify each of the commandments of the Decalogue, claiming that 'the effect of the canonical collection is to provide a new intertextuality which relates these various witnesses within a literary corpus' (64). The concern with chastity in the Book of Proverbs makes it a suitable source for reflection on the seventh commandment despite its lack of explicit reference to Sinai and the law: for 'a theological understanding of Sinai is at work in the canonical process which is different in kind from a modern reconstruction of the historical origins of Israel's laws' (55). But the new understanding of intertextuality will be successfully established only if the canonical texts are rescued from the ravages of critical hubris. Thus, 'the challenge of Old Testament exegesis is not to rest content with refocusing the biblical text in order to reconstruct its prehistory. Rather, its theological responsibility lies in following the direction which is given by the shaping of the biblical text itself' (153). We should note, for example, that 'within the canonical context of II Kings the Josianic reform has been assigned a much more modest role than that afforded it by critical scholarship' (151–52). The hypotheses about Israel's early religion that Wellhausen and Gottwald derive from the Book of Judges are in clear breach of the canonical representation of a period of apostasy from the norms of Mosaic religion (151, 179). All this represents a sophisticated, post-critical quest for a 'second naïvety'. After the great disturbance wrought by criticism, everything is to be restored to its proper place – although, if the moment of restoration is itself to be preserved, it will also be necessary to preserve the memory of the disturbance that made it necessary.

All this relates to the 'text-critical' side of Childs' work; its translation into theological assertions is quite another matter. For the present, however, we turn to the more recent and more ambitious attempt at a biblical theology of both Testaments. Here, remarkably, there is a definite retreat from the canonical project. The early chapter on creation opens with an account of 'The Growth of the Tradition in Oral and Literary Stages' in which the Priestly and the Yahwistic narratives are treated separately, and in which the hegemony of German critical scholarship is effectively re-established. This chapter opens Childs' treatment of 'The Discrete Witness of the Old Testament', which proceeds 'from Eden to Babel', to the patriarchal traditions, and so on, following biblical chronology up to the exile and restoration. The layout recalls von Rad's first volume, but otherwise the canon does not fulfil the major hermeneutical role that one might have expected. In the discussion of 'The Discrete Witness of the New Testament', the subject-matter is in fact not the New Testament and its witness but the history of the development of early Christian tradition, theology and literature – precisely the type of illegitimate substitution to which Childs was once so sensitive. The third and final major constructive section purports to offer 'Theological Reflection on the Christian Bible', but in fact merely discusses a series of well-worn topics ('God the Creator', 'Covenant, Election, People of God', 'Law and Gospel') in a thoroughly conventional way that consistently maintains the distinction between 'the Old Testament witness' and 'the New Testament witness'. Childs tacitly acknowledges his shift towards a hermeneutically more conservative position by distancing himself from the assumption which underlies his *Introduction to the Old Testament as Scripture,* that 'the major antagonist to serious theological reflection on the Bible' stems from 'the diachronic legacy of nineteenth-century historical criticism' (722). More recently, he tells us, he has become disenchanted with the synchronic approaches that he once helped to make fashionable, on the grounds that they can be used to 'propagate a fully secular, non-theological reading of the Bible' (723). It was (one may speculate) the shock of this unsurprising discovery that led Childs to conclude that there is, after all, much to be said for the diachronic legacy.

Whatever their methodological differences, Childs' *Old Testament Theology* and his *Biblical Theology* are at one in their insistence that the Old Testament requires a theological interpretation that maintains its relatively independent status. Childs begins by observing that 'the Christian church recognized the integrity of the Old Testament for its own faith within its canon of authoritative scripture' (*Old Testament Theology*, 7). Yet, Childs continues, the term 'Old Testament' already indicates that the canonical collection has been set in a new, Christian framework, and this framework continues to shape the discipline of 'Old Testament theology', even if only in a secularized and attenuated form. The crucial question is *how* this framework should affect the discipline. Clearly, 'to suggest that the Christian should read the Old Testament as if he were living before the coming of Christ is an historical anachronism which also fails to take seriously the literature's present function within the Christian Bible for a practising community of faith' (8–9). Yet, on the other hand, 'the Old Testament functions within Christian scripture as a witness to Jesus Christ precisely in its pre-Christian form. The task of Old Testament theology is, therefore, not to Christianize the Old Testament by identifying it with the New Testament witness, but to hear its own theological testimony to the God of Israel whom the church confesses also to worship' (9). It is theologically significant that 'the Christian canon treasures a portion of the scripture in which the name of Jesus is not mentioned': for 'the continuing, authoritative function of the Old Testament for the church' indicates that 'the perception of God through the witness of the old covenant remains a constitutive stance for Christian theology' (30). In other words, the church worships a God who is known in the New Testament through Jesus but who is known in the Old Testament through his self-disclosures to Israel. Old and New Testaments offer distinct although complementary ways to the knowledge of the one God, and the Old Testament serves to *limit* the extent to which it can be said that God is known in and through Jesus. Underlying this theological judgment are, first, the existence of Old Testament scholarship as a relatively autonomous institution, and, second, the assumption that the canon establishes a synchronicity and simultaneity that extends even to the relationship between the two Testaments. Scriptural 'authority' is, as it were, spread evenly across this flat surface, and the church is no less obliged to confess God as Yahweh, the God of our fathers who delivered us from slavery in Egypt, than it is to confess him as the God and Father of our Lord Jesus Christ. The Old

Testament confession of God retains its place *alongside* the New Testament one, for the Old Testament itself coexists with the New in a state of pure, dehistoricized textuality.

If followed through consistently, this view of scriptural authority would lead to a radical judaizing of Christianity characterized, for example, by the expansion of the creeds to include the great events of Old Testament *Heilsgeschichte* and by the incorporation of the Jewish feasts within the Christian liturgical calendar. Male circumcision would have to be reintroduced: for, according to the scripture that the church acknowledges as authoritative, the God of Abraham, Isaac and Jacob is the God who has established circumcision as the unsubstitutable sign of his everlasting covenant. There can be no appeal to the New Testament treatment of these matters; on the contrary, we must resist 'the Christian temptation to identify Biblical Theology with the New Testament's interpretation of the Old, as if the Old Testament's witness were limited to how it was once heard and appropriated by the early church' (*Biblical Theology*, 77). Indeed, the dangerous adjectives 'Old' and 'New', suggestive both of diachronicity and displacement, would presumably have to be replaced by a more neutral terminology that does not compromise the enduring, 'vertical' authority of the so-called 'Old' Testament. In other contexts Childs knows that both Testaments in their different ways 'bear witness to Jesus Christ' (*Biblical Theology*, 78); and he also knows that 'it is incumbent on the interpreter, especially of the Old Testament, not to confuse the biblical witness with the reality itself' (379). Yet his language often betrays an uncontrolled drift towards a biblicism that assumes a uniformly direct relationship between text and reality. The most notable theological consequence of this is the remarkable relativizing of the Christian acknowledgment of the triune God definitively disclosed in Jesus, accomplished by the simple expedient of setting the Old Testament alongside the New in a relationship of pure simultaneity.

The most charitable explanation for this state of affairs is that it derives from an understandable although misguided over-reaction against arbitrary and forced christological readings of Old Testament texts. For Childs, the New Testament itself sets a dangerous precedent here, and we must recognize that 'the hermeneutical practice of the New Testament does not in itself provide a theological warrant for the church's imitation of this approach' (381). The apostles were granted the authority to interpret scripture in a manner controlled by the Christ-event rather than by the literal sense; but we are not apostles, and this rules out 'any direct imitation of the New Testament's hermeneutical practice' (381).[41] It seems that the Old Testament is endangered by too close a proximity to the New Testament in general and to Jesus in particular. If it is not kept at a certain distance, its distinctive voice will be overwhelmed. Childs is of course right to claim that 'the recognition of the one scope of scripture, which is Jesus Christ, does not function to restrict the full range of the biblical voices', or to 'replace a coat of many colours with a seamless garment of grey' (725). But his treatment of 'the discrete witness of the Old Testament' is in practice characterized by the absence of a single, christological centre as the object of this discrete witness.

To claim that Childs' position is inadequate is not to deny that the problems he identifies are real ones. What is needed by way of a response is an alternative theological hermeneutic for Christian Old Testament interpretation, outlined in the brief remarks that follow.

(1) It is superficial and misleading to point to the more imaginative or eccentric examples of New Testament scriptural exegesis (e.g. Matt. 2.23; 21.5–7; 1 Cor. 9.9; 2 Cor. 3.7–18; Gal. 3.16; 4.21–31), and to conclude that, since these cannot possibly be imitated, Old Testament exegesis must maintain its independence. The New Testament's use of the Old is a product of the early Christian understanding of Jesus as God's definitive self-disclosure, the consequent displacement of Jewish scripture in so far as it appears to speak of a definitive divine self-disclosure other than that which has now taken place in Jesus, and the reinterpretation of that scripture as attesting and enacting the preparing of the way for Jesus. Recognition of these basic presuppositions of Christian faith and theology makes it possible to accept the theological rationale for New Testament exegesis of the Old without obliging us either to imitate it in detail or to rule this out on principle.[42] On this view, it would also be impossible to understand the New Testament's use of the Old merely as a particular instance of the general hermeneutical phenomenon of the openness of all texts to radical rereading within new and unforeseen contexts.

(2) It is not the case that the early church incorporated Jewish scripture unchanged into its authoritative canon. On the contrary, this incorporation only occurred on the basis of a reinterpretation of scripture in the light of the Christ-event. In its canonical form, the Christian Old Testament is a quite different entity to a scripture understood in abstraction from what Christian faith takes to be its *telos*, for the Christian Old Testament can only be understood as attesting and enacting the preparing of the way for Jesus. Old Testament exegesis can only be Christian in so far as it recognizes that this alone is the canonical role of the texts and learns to interpret them in the light of this role. It must recall that we receive the Old Testament only from Jesus and with Jesus.

(3) There can, however, be no unbridgeable gulf between what the Old Testament texts 'originally' or 'actually' meant and what they come to mean in the context of Christian faith. Such a view would legitimate the existence of two separate exegetical methods, confirming the widespread impression that to understand these texts as the Christian Old Testament is to impose an arbitrary construal that goes against the grain of the texts themselves. This impression derives from the practice of contrasting a traditional Christian interpretation of an Old Testament text with its 'original meaning', while overlooking the traditio-historical continuum that unites them. The Old Testament itself does not simply preserve 'original' meanings, as though in a museum-case, but subjects the traditions it preserves to continual re-interpretation and recontextualization. It is, indeed, the concern with so-called 'original' meanings that must often proceed against the grain of the texts, arresting the forward momentum of the process of tradition in order to arrive at hypothetical reconstructions of an 'original' meaning by way of various complex archaeological procedures. Christian Old Testament interpretation need not deny that the texts might be interpreted differently if read within an interpretative framework other than that of Christian faith; but it must at the same time maintain that a Christian theological hermeneutic uncovers the true theological dynamic of the texts themselves.[43]

(4) To assert that Christian Old Testament exegesis must always be related to that which lies at the centre of Christian faith is not to claim any absolute superiority for the New Testament over the Old. The New Testament is not a hermeneutical filter through which the Old Testament must pass in order that what is theologically significant in it should be identified; the value of the Old Testament does not lie only in its capacity to reinforce or duplicate the assertions of the New. The obvious and fundamental differences in both form and content are indispensable to their respectives roles, and it would be misguided to try to flatten them out for the sake of some ahistorical homogeneity.

(5) Christian confession of Jesus as the Christ ascribes to him a universal and ultimate significance. It should therefore not be assumed that a christologically-oriented Old Testament interpretation will inevitably reduce the polyphony of the Old Testament texts to monotony. If the scope of the Christ-event is the whole of reality, then there is no danger that any of the breadth and depth of the experience reflected in the Old Testament will be lost. And if the universal scope of the Christ-event preserves particularity rather than eliminating it, then Old Testament particularities too will be seen in their full significance. A christological interpretation that

impoverished the Old Testament could only stem from an impoverished christology.

(6) According to the doctrine of Jesus' virginal conception, understood by the early church as the divinely-ordained sign of his incarnation, Jesus' being is uniquely grounded in God before it is shaped by the life, traditions and scriptures of the people of Israel. Yet his human existence is determined by this particular context, which may therefore be said to prepare the way of the Lord in the sense that it establishes the categories within which Jesus' person and work become intelligible. Christian Old Testament interpretation should therefore be attentive to the ways in which fundamental Old Testament conceptuality establishes the preconditions for the intelligibility of Jesus' person and work, without assuming that he can be adequately 'explained' on this basis.

(7) Modern exegesis of the Old Testament often betrays the influence of Christian presuppositions even when it believes itself to be engaged in a purely 'neutral' and 'historical' enterprise. Those who wish to detach Old Testament scholarship from Christian theology make this a ground for reproach, rejecting interpretations influenced by Christian presuppositions and advocating interpretations as far removed as possible from what are taken to be the concerns of Christian faith.[44] Granted that there can and should be a Christian Old Testament interpretation, however, and that without it an 'Old Testament' cannot even exist, Christian presuppositions are not in themselves a cause of reproach. They must be made explicit, and they must constantly be tested to see if they are appropriate both to Christian faith and to the text that is being interpreted. Yet there is still much to be gained from engagement with the tradition of modern Old Testament exegesis, even if it may also be necessary for an explicitly Christian exegesis to go its own way at many points. To imagine that a radical breach with this tradition is needed, as though Christian Old Testament exegesis had to begin all over again, would be sheer *hubris*.

It is the great merit of Brevard Childs' work that he has pursued the question of authentically Christian Old Testament interpretation with a single-mindedness and tenacity unprecedented in modern Old Testament scholarship, where this issue is often regarded as marginal or as already taken care of in normal exegetical practice. Unlike most of his critics, Childs has recognized that there is a problem here, that this problem is fundamental, and that at least part of the answer lies in our understanding the phenomenon of the Christian canon. He is – again, unlike most of his critics – sensitive to the concerns of Christian theology, and the theological problems I have identified represent not so much a final position as a one-sided, unbalanced development of certain genuine insights at the expense of others.

Eichrodt, von Rad and Childs are clear that Old Testament theology can only be practised within a Christian theological framework; and this means that Old Testament theology – the theological understanding of the Old Testament – is a concern not only of Old Testament scholarship but of Christian theology in general. The fact that Old Testament scholarship as a whole offers only half-hearted support to this view may account in part for the theological flaws and limitations that have come to light here, especially in the area of christology. Yet permanently valuable insights remain, requiring only the will to exploit them properly.

NOTES

1. Compare the discussion of the terminological issue in Walter Moberly, *The Old Testament of the Old Testament: Patriarchal Narratives and Mosaic Yahwism*, Minneapolis: Fortress Press, 1992, 155–66.

2. The present terminological debate derives from the traditional structure of the discipline of 'Old Testament studies', and not just from contemporary political sensitivities. If 'the Old Testament' is in interpretative practice accorded an autonomous status in relation to Christian theology, then there can be no objection to replacing the traditional title with a neutral expression such as 'Hebrew Bible' or 'First Testament'. Where, on the other hand, it is the Christian Bible that is the object of interpretation, to surrender the traditional terminology would be to risk losing the Bible's basic theological structure. John Goldingay's claim that 'the expressions "Old Testament" and "New Testament" tend to downgrade the Hebrew scriptures in a way that would have been repugnant to the early Christians', and that they should therefore be abandoned even by Christians, is therefore theologically disastrous as well as factually erroneous (*Models for Scripture*, Grand Rapids: Eerdmans; Carlisle: Paternoster, 1994, 2n).

3. Luther's claim, cited as the title of an article by W. Vischer, in B. W. Anderson (ed.), *The Old Testament and Christian Faith: Essays by Rudolf Bultmann and others*, London: SCM Press, 1964, 90–101.

4. See the discussion of Old Testament theology in the nineteenth century in J. H. Hayes and F. C. Prussner, *Old Testament Theology: Its History and Development*, Atlanta: John Knox Press, 1985, 73–142.

5. R. Rendtorff, *Canon and Theology: Overtures to an Old Testament Theology*, Minneapolis: Augsburg Fortress; Edinburgh: T. & T. Clark, 1993, 95.

6. R. Bultmann, 'The Hidden and the Revealed God', ET in *Existence and Faith* (ed. S. Ogden), London: Collins, 1964, 25–38.

7. K. Holl, 'Was verstand Luther unter Religion?', in *Gesammelte Aufsätze zur Kirchengeschichte*, I, Tübingen: J. C. B. Mohr, 1948, 1–110.

8. R. Otto, *The Idea of the Holy: An Inquiry into the Non-Rational Factor in the Idea of the Divine and its Relation to the Rational*, ET Oxford: Oxford University Press, 1931.

9. K. Barth, *Der Römerbrief,* Munich: Chr. Kaiser, 1922[2], repr. Zürich: Theologischer Verlag, 1978; ET *The Epistle to the Romans*, Oxford: Oxford University Press, 1933. Translations are my own. Page references are to the German original and to E. C. Hoskyns' English translation.

10. ET in M. Rumscheidt (ed.), *Adolf von Harnack: Liberal Theology at its Height*, London: Collins, 1989, 85–87. The exchange between Harnack and Barth was first published in the journal *Die Christliche Welt*, Jan.–May 1923.

11. These and other early reviews are reprinted in J. Moltmann (ed.), *Anfänge der dialektischen Theologie, Teil I*, Munich: Chr. Kaiser, 1974: A. Jülicher, 'Ein moderner Paulus-Ausleger', 87–98 (a review of the first edition of 1919), R. Bultmann, 'Karl Barths "Römerbrief" in zweiter Auflage', 119–42. Bultmann had earlier been more critical of the first edition.

12. Bultmann's response to this is contained in a letter dated 31 December 1922, in which he continues discussion of the hermeneutical issue and argues that the Schleiermacher of the *Reden* should be regarded as an ally and not as an enemy (B. Jaspert, *Karl Barth, Rudolf Bultmann: Letters 1922–66*, trans. and ed. G. Bromiley, Grand Rapids: Eerdmans; Edinburgh: T. & T. Clark, 1982, 4–6).

13. O. Eissfeldt, 'Israelitisch-jüdische Religionsgeschichte und alttestamentliche Theologie', *ZAW* 44 (1926), 1–12.

14. W. Eichrodt, 'Hat die alttestamentliche Theologie noch selbständige Bedeutung innerhalb der alttestamentlichen Wissenschaft?', *ZAW* 47 (1929), 83–91.

15. W. Eichrodt, *Theology of the Old Testament*, ET (two vols.) of fifth edition, London: SCM Press, 1961–67.

16. D. G. Spriggs points out that 'covenant' only serves as the controlling concept for part 1 of Eichrodt's *Theology of the Old Testament;* Eichrodt attempts to resolve this structural problem by a system of cross-references and, in part 3 ('God and Man'), by emphasizing the relationship between God and Israelite man (*Two Old Testament Theologies: A Comparative Evaluation of the Contributions of Eichrodt and von Rad to our Understanding of the Nature of an Old Testament Theology*, SBT 2nd series, 30, London: SCM Press, 1974, 5).

17. Underlying this dehistoricizing of personal relationship is the philosophical assumption that the first of what Martin Buber calls the basic words or word-pairs, *Ich–Du*, can be sharply distinguished from the second, *Ich–Es* (*I and Thou*, ET of third edition, New York: Scribners, 1970, 53). On this issue, see Hans W. Frei, *Theology and Narrative: Selected Essays*, ed. G. Hunsinger and W. C. Placher, New York and Oxford: Oxford University Press, 1993, 58–73: 'A person's identity is known to us in the inseparability of who he was and what he did' (73). Personalistic theologies and philosophies tend to divorce identity from agency.

18. Eichrodt cites Exod. 3.14 primarily for its association of *yhwh* with the verb *hwh* or *hyh;* the divine name emphasizes existence and presence (*Theology*, 1.189). 'I am that I am' means 'I am really and truly present, ready to help and act, as I have always been' (1.190). The suggestion in Exod. 3 of *particular* divine actions, and their significance for divine identity and thus the divine name, is overlooked.

19. G. von Rad, *Old Testament Theology*, two vols., ET Edinburgh and London: Oliver & Boyd; New York: Harper & Row, 1962–65.

20. G. von Rad, *Genesis: A Commentary* (1949), ET of ninth German edition, London: SCM Press, 1972.

21. G. von Rad, 'Grundprobleme einer biblischen Theologie des Alten Testaments', *TLZ* 68 (1943), 225–34.

22. G. von Rad, *The Problem of the Hexateuch and Other Essays*, ET London and Edinburgh: Oliver & Boyd, 1966, 1–78.

23. Compare the statements in the introduction to von Rad's Genesis commentary: 'It is particularly important today that we should turn once again to exegesis of the texts in their present form, that is, that we should take up the question of the meaning that was gradually attached to them . . . The exegete must take into account the fact that the sources are no longer separate from each other, but have been combined together' (42). This aspect of von Rad's exegesis is emphasized by H. W. Wolff: 'Am vollen Verstehen des gegenwärtigen Textes lag ihm alles . . . Überlieferungsgeschichtliche Hypothesen sind wandelbar; die konstante Aufgabe bleibt der zu erklärende Text' ('Gerhard von Rad als Exeget', in H. W. Wolff, R. Rendtorff, W. Pannenberg, *Gerhard von Rad: Seine Bedeutung für die Theologie*, Munich: Chr. Kaiser, 1973, 9–20; 17).

24. G. von Rad, 'The Deuteronomic Theology of History in I and II Kings', in *The Problem of the Hexateuch*, 205–21.

25. G. von Rad, 'There remains still a Rest for the People of God: An Investigation of a Biblical Conception', in *The Problem of the Hexateuch*, 94–102.

26. English translations in A. E. Cochrane, *The Church's Confession under Hitler*, Pittsburgh: Pickwick Press, 1976[2], 237–47; E. Jüngel, *Christ, Justice and Peace: Towards a Theology of the State in Dialogue with the Barmen Declaration*, ET Edinburgh: T. & T. Clark, 1992, xxi–xxix.

27. G. von Rad, 'Typologische Auslegung des Alten Testaments', *EvTh* 12 (1952), 17–33. Translations are my own. There is an English translation in C. Westermann (ed.), *Essays on Old Testament Hermeneutics*, ET Richmond: John Knox Press, 1963 (= *Essays in Old Testament Interpretation*, London: SCM Press, 1963), 17–39. For a bibliographical account of the discussion stimulated by this article, see H. Graf Reventlow, *Problems of Biblical Theology in the Twentieth Century*, ET London: SCM Press, 1986, 24–31.

28. W. Pannenberg rightly points to the danger of levelling 'the particularity of phenomena, on which genuine historical interests must be focused', on the basis of 'a one-sided orientation toward the typical' (*Basic Questions in Theology*, vol. 1, ET London: SCM Press, 46). God's activity gives rise to what is new, and theology is thus (like history) 'interested primarily in the individual, particular, and contingent' (48). Troeltsch's principle of analogy may reflect the earlier phase of *religionsgeschichtliche* research, in which 'the particularity of the biblical witnesses seemed to disappear behind the parallels from the history of religion' (48).

29. See, for example, James L. Crenshaw, *Gerhard von Rad*, Waco: Word Books, 1978.

30. According to Pannenberg, von Rad's *Old Testament Theology* shows (in opposition to kerygmatic theology) that 'Jesus himself and also primitive Christianity must now be understood in connection with the history of the transmission of the tradition of Israel' (*Basic Questions in Theology*, 1.88). Von Rad makes possible a 'biblical theology' that would treat intertestamental and early Christian history of tradition as he did the traditions of Israel (1.92–93). Where this emphasis on the onward flow of salvation-history is not balanced by the presupposition of an inner-historical fulfilment characteristic of typology, the result is that revelation is postponed until the end of history and is only 'anticipated' in the life, death and resurrection of Jesus ('Dogmatic Theses on the Doctrine of Revelation', in W. Pannenberg [ed.], *Revelation as History*, ET New York and London: Macmillan, 1968, 123–58; 131–35).

31. On the basis of von Rad's 1935 review of the first volume of W. Vischer's *Das Christuszeugnis des Alten Testaments*, R. Rendtorff feels able to present him as a critic of 'christological interpretation as a way of "salvaging" the Old Testament' (*Canon and*

Theology, 76–91). In 1943, however, von Rad writes as follows about Vischer: 'Sofern er die typologische Methode handhabt, dürfte u. E. das Gespräch nicht zu einer Infragestellung der Typologie überhaupt führen, sondern sie hätte sie abzugrenzen gegenüber äusserlichen oder willkürlichen Sachassoziationen. Sie muss sich dem Kerygma der jeweiligen Texte unterwerfen' ('Grundprobleme', 232). Rendtorff fails to acknowledge that von Rad too advocated a form of 'christological interpretation' – one that respects the integrity of the individual texts.

32. G. von Rad, 'Offene Fragen im Umkreis einer Theologie des Alten Testaments', *TLZ* 88 (1963), 401–16. Translations are my own. The article is included in the English translation of von Rad's *Old Testament Theology*, 2.410–29. Page references are to the German and to the English.

33. Recent work on Old Testament theology has distanced itself from von Rad's concern about the relationship of this discipline to Christian faith and theology: see, for example, Leo G. Perdue, *The Collapse of History: Reconstructing Old Testament Theology*, Minneapolis: Augsburg Fortress, 1994; Jesper Høgenhaven, *Problems and Prospects of Old Testament Theology*, Sheffield: JSOT Press, 1988; R. Rendtorff, *Canon and Theology*. (1) For Perdue, 'the primary question that stimulates all Old Testament theology is that of revelation and . . . the knowledge of God' (*Collapse of History*, 301). His own answer to that question relates Old Testament texts to topics such as 'liberation, creation, canon, feminism, story, and imagination' (302, summarizing the main concerns of the book). Despite his recognition that biblical theologians must 'become more theologically literate' (305), Perdue consistently moves between the Old Testament and 'contemporary issues' (304) without any reference to Jesus or the New Testament – and therefore without any reference to Christian faith. (2) Høgenhaven understands biblical theology as a purely historical discipline whose task is 'to establish the main lines within each book, and to explain how the concepts and ideas of the various parts of the Bible are interrelated' (*Problems and Prospects*, 93). Yet this does not extend to the relation between the Testaments. The separation of Old Testament and New Testament theology rightly recognizes the 'historical and literary differences' between these collections; the question of the unity of the Bible 'is a matter for systematic theology to consider' (95), beyond the competence of exegetes and biblical theologians. (3) Rendtorff is aware that the Old Testament is part of the Christian Bible and is thus related in some way to the New Testament, but he qualifies this by posing the question: 'Does the interpreter consider the pre-Christian (i.e., Jewish) meaning of the text to be theologically relevant or not?' (*Canon and Theology*, 14). Rendtorff is looking for 'a common Jewish-Christian reading of the Hebrew Bible' (31), a 'common biblical theology' (34) which minimizes 'Christianity's claim to absoluteness' and acknowledges that 'both Judaism *and* Christianity are successor religions of biblical Israel' (36).

34. Compare James A. Sanders' understanding of the canon in terms of its 'adaptability': just as the biblical tradents constantly reinterpreted community traditions within ever-changing contexts, so it has been ever since, up to and including contemporary believing communities (*From Sacred Story to Sacred Text*, Philadelphia: Fortress Press, 1987, 172). For von Rad, on the other hand, the 'openness to the future' characteristic of the Old Testament texts means 'the conviction of a future event from which alone the narrated event receives its decisive illumination' ('Offene Fragen', 412/422).

35. This view of biblical scholarship is attacked by Jon Levenson, in *The Hebrew Bible, the Old Testament, and Historical Criticism: Jews and Christians in Biblical Studies*, Louisville: Westminster/John Knox Press, 1993, 82–105 and *passim*. 'In what way and to what degree

are the Jews who meet Christians in biblical studies Jewish? . . . What is Christian about the premise that the Hebrew Scripture "speaks from its own complete integrity" over against the New Testament?' (83, 84). If the ground on which Jews and Christians meet is merely that of historical relativism, 'then the designation of those who so meet as "Jews" or as "Christians" is really only vestigial' (98). 'Unless historical criticism can learn to interact with other senses of scripture – senses peculiar to the individual traditions and not shared between them – it will either fade or prove to be not a meeting ground of Jews and Christians, but the burial ground of Judaism and Christianity, as each tradition vanishes into the past in which neither had as yet emerged' (105).

36. The reference is to G. Ernest Wright, *God who Acts: Biblical Theology as Recital,* London: SCM Press, 1952. Critics of the 'biblical theology movement' have tended to identify it with the positions characteristic of this book (so, for example, James Barr, *Explorations in Theology* 7, London: SCM Press, 1980, 1, 10).

37. James Barr's *Old and New in Interpretation: A Study of the Two Testaments* (London: SCM Press, 1966) exemplifies this loss. Although the 'central theme' of this book is ostensibly 'the relation between the Old and New Testaments' (171), the claim that the Old Testament scholar's theological task is the 'critical testing . . . of the way in which the special place and function of the Old Testament is represented within various general currents of theology' (169) illustrates its generally negative tenor.

38. Brevard Childs, *Biblical Theology in Crisis,* Philadelphia: Westminster Press, 1970.

39. Brevard Childs, *Exodus,* Old Testament Library, London: SCM Press, 1974; *Introduction to the Old Testament as Scripture,* London: SCM Press, 1979; *The New Testament as Canon: An Introduction,* London: SCM Press, 1984. There is an extensive secondary literature on Childs; see especially Mark Brett, *Biblical Criticism in Crisis? The Impact of the Canonical Approach on Old Testament Studies,* Cambridge: Cambridge University Press, 1991. I have discussed Childs' work in ch. 2 of my *Text, Church and World: Biblical Interpretation in Theological Perspective,* Edinburgh: T. & T. Clark; Grand Rapids: Eerdmans, 1994.

40. Brevard Childs, *Old Testament Theology in a Canonical Context,* London: SCM Press, 1985; *Biblical Theology of the Old and New Testaments,* London: SCM Press, 1992.

41. Elsewhere Childs argues that to allow Old Testament interpretation to follow New Testament models is 'hermeneutically in error in assuming that every time-conditioned feature of the New Testament can be used as a warrant for its continued use without properly understanding the theological relation of its authority to its function as kerygmatic witness' (*Biblical Theology,* 84–85). What is notable in this rather opaque sentence is the standard critical appeal to the 'time-conditioned' character of this or that feature of the New Testament texts as a way of excluding it from serious theological and hermeneutical consideration.

42. Recent literary theory can also contribute to reflection in this area; see Richard B. Hays' creative use of the concept of 'intertextuality' in his *Echoes of Scripture in the Letters of Paul,* London and New Haven: Yale University Press, 1989, 14–24 and *passim.* Childs' assumption that 'theological' and 'literary' approaches to biblical texts are mutually exclusive should be resisted.

43. 'A unity of the Bible is not to be established artificially . . . A unity exists already because of tradition history. The supposed gulf between the Old and New Testaments does not exist traditio-historically at all, and no dubious bridges are needed to span it' (H. Gese, 'Tradition and Biblical Theology', in D. A. Knight [ed.], *Tradition and Theology in the Old Testament,* Philadelphia: Fortress Press, 1977, 301–25; 322). 'Biblical theology must . . . see that the biblical Isaiah is not the historical Isaiah but the dynamic force, the

Isaiah tradition, which stems from Isaiah and achieves its effect traditio-historically, stretching from the first redaction all the way to the New Testament view of "fulfillment"' (325).

44. Philip Davies' claim that broad acceptance of the Old Testament picture of 'ancient Israel' is theologically-motivated and thus illegitimate is a typical recent statement of this widely-held view. Davies appeals to 'the practitioners of traditional biblical criticism' to abandon 'a theologically-dictated form of historical criticism', promising both theological and historical benefits from this divorce (*In Search of 'Ancient Israel'*, Sheffield: Sheffield Academic Press, 1992, 155). In debate with Childs, Davies accepts that a theological reading might be 'a legitimate option *among others*', but only if this were to be based on the communal function of the biblical text and not on 'a claim about the objective character of its contents' (19n). The idiosyncratic and arbitrary restriction imposed here can only stem from one of the 'religious commitments' whose tendency to 'parade as scholarly methods' Davies claims to deplore (19n).

Chapter 6

Creation in the Beginning

'In the beginning God created the heavens and the earth': in the Bible's own beginning, the act of creation is identified as the beginning. This need not have been the case. The act of creation might have been preceded by all kinds of esoteric histories purporting to explain its possibility; gnostic mythologies rewrite the Genesis narrative along these lines. Alternatively, the act of creation might have been conceived as an eternal event incapable of the narrative rendering announced by the opening reference to 'the beginning'. Or the creation of heaven and earth might have been identified with the single, constantly-unfolding world-process, the work of a God who never ceases to create, who does not rest on the first sabbath and whose creative activity therefore cannot be confined to 'the beginning'. The content of the familiar opening verse of the Bible is in fact anything but obvious. It represents a choice of one particular rendering at the expense of all other possibilities, whether exotic and far-fetched or plausible and reasonable. The chosen rendering rests upon the presupposition that God's activity, in creation and beyond, is appropriately depicted in narrative form.

As Aristotle noted in the *Poetics*, a properly integrated narrative has a beginning, a middle and an end. 'A beginning is that which does not necessarily come after something else, although something else exists or comes about after it.'[1] Most occurrences are incapable of providing the beginning of a narrative, since they are too closely bound to preceding occurrences and lack the capacity to serve as the foundation for the middle and the end that a true beginning must possess. According to the biblical narrative, however, the creation of the world does possess that capacity. It is, indeed, an absolute beginning that precedes and grounds all the relative beginnings that we experience and narrate. Yet a beginning – even this absolute beginning – is. *only* a beginning; something else takes place after it. Corresponding to the beginning is the end, 'that which naturally follows something else either as a necessary or as a usual consequence, and is not itself followed by anything'. The biblical narrative concludes with an imaginative rendering of the event in which the heavens and the earth established in the beginning pass away and are no more, superseded by new heavens and a new earth; an absolute end to all worldly occurrence which transcends all the relative endings that we experience and narrate, corresponding in the comprehensiveness of its scope to the absolute beginning. The divine–human history conforms to Aristotle's rule that 'well-constructed plots must neither begin nor end in a haphazard way'. But an end does not immediately succeed a beginning; the plot must also contain a middle. 'A middle is that which follows something else [i.e. a beginning], and is itself followed by something [i.e. an end].' The middle bears the main weight of the narrative as it moves between its two limits. Put crudely, more happens in the middle than at the beginning or the end. In this case, it is striking that the way from the universality of the beginning to the universality of the end takes place in the narrowest particularity: biblical narrative recounts not world-history in general but the call of Abram, the history of Israel, and the story of Jesus' birth, life, death and resurrection.

Aristotle's simple analysis of plot obviously cannot do justice to the complex theological structuring of biblical narrative, but it does suggest that the proper interpretative context for the first verse of the Bible is not simply the 'Priestly creation-narrative' in isolation, or even the Book of Genesis or the Pentateuch, but the Christian Bible as a whole. The beginning that it announces is open to indefinite future development which it must serve to make explicable. While it would be possible to develop this point along literary-critical lines, it is more important to ask about the theological significance of the biblical rendering of the creation of heaven and earth as 'the beginning' of the comprehensive history of the divine–human relationship; and this will involve attempting to understand the text in its relation to the extratextual reality it intends. To abstract this text from its truth-claim is radically to misunderstand it. Yet it is not immediately clear how and on what basis it can be held that God created heaven and earth 'in the beginning'. The theological significance of this claim will have to be developed by way of a dialogue with two alternative approaches to a Christian doctrine of creation.

First, it may be argued that the notion of creation in the beginning does not do justice to the total biblical presentation of creation as an ongoing, dynamic divine activity oriented not towards origins but towards an eschatological goal. 'Creation' would then refer to the totality of God's activity towards the world, and it would be inappropriate to assign it specifically and primarily to 'the beginning'. Against this extension of the doctrine of creation, a theological rationale will be developed for retaining the association of creation with the beginning. Creation is *only* the beginning; that which follows – the middle and the end – is not creation but something else.

Second, it may be argued that the integration of the narrative of creation into the total biblical narrative is a contingent factor that cannot determine how the concept of creation is to be understood. On this view, the world may be understood as divine creation on general rational grounds and not simply on the basis of authoritative texts. The scriptural texts themselves may be held to affirm this possibility of an independent knowledge of the world as God's creation, in which case the narrative connection between creation and the history of salvation is as it were relativized from within. Against this claim that the scriptural texts affirm an autonomous knowledge of God as creator, it must be shown that creation is *truly* the beginning of God's history with the world: it is not a self-sufficient, self-contained idea but can only be understood in the light of that which succeeds it, for which it lays the foundations.

The notion of creation 'in the beginning' is an indispensable element in a Christian doctrine of creation and in a biblical theology of creation. It is not the task of biblical theology in this area merely to assemble the relevant biblical material, pointing to common and divergent strands, assessing various scholarly positions, and perhaps expressing the hope that the biblical presentation might offer some 'positive resources' for responding to current ecological problems. Biblical theology must interpret the biblical material in the light of the question of its truth and significance, and this will make it necessary to co-ordinate the truth and significance that are found here with the other truths and significances that the biblical texts assert and imply. The biblical presentation of creation must be understood not in isolation but in its context, and it is the purpose of this study to show how and why its relation to that context is to serve as the beginning and foundation of all that follows.

1. Creation as Foundation

In his *God in Creation* (1985), Jürgen Moltmann advocates an interpretation of creation in the light of its eschatological goal.[2] According to Moltmann, 'creation' does not refer only to the past divine activity that brought into being the relatively stable world that we know. That static view must be replaced by a dynamic approach in which God's creative activity lies not only in the past but in the present and above all in the future, in such a way that the future goal of creation – the transfiguring of the world in the immanent divine glory, the perfection of the community of creation – draws past and present creative activity towards itself as its innermost *telos*. Hope lies at the heart of Christian faith, which does not live in a fulfilled present but out of a future for the world and for humankind that is yet to be disclosed.[3] This hope is articulated by humans, but it is not a purely human hope: traditional theological anthropocentrism must give way to a theocentrism which locates human beings within the wider community of creation and which sees the revelation of the immanent divine glory in the world as the goal of creation as a whole. God's covenant-partner is not simply the human being but every creature, and his covenant-faithfulness protects creation and its future from every threat. It is true that, as Paul puts it, 'the whole creation groans in travail together until now', and that it is 'subjected to futility'; but creation's groaning at its subjection is merely the negative side of its hope for liberation from futility. There is no special human hope distinct from the hope of creation as a whole. Humans are, however, able to articulate the hope of the rest of creation, not by virtue of any natural knowledge but through God's self-disclosure in the history of Israel and above all in Jesus the Messiah, whose death and resurrection mark the dawning of the messianic age in which hope for the future is assured by anticipatory experiences through the Spirit in the present. The God whose ongoing creative activity is the source and object of this hope is not the God of an abstract monotheism, who in his legitimation of human domination is in part responsible for the current ecological crisis, but the trinitarian God of Christian faith; the rediscovery of trinitarian theology is therefore a Christian contribution to resolving that crisis. Creation is the work of a God who is not only transcendent but also the immanent Spirit in whom it comes into being, who seeks in it a dwelling-place in which the fullness of the divine glory can ultimately be disclosed.[4] The term 'creation' is thus applied to the entire process or history of God's covenant-relationship with the world, and old dogmatic and credal distinctions between creation, redemption and eschatology are dissolved in the dynamic flux of the single unceasing divine activity.

Moltmann is anxious not to concede too great a significance to the creation accounts of Gen. 1–2, which clearly locate creation in the past. In the Christian theological tradition, he argues, 'it was not sufficiently noted that the stories about creation in the Priestly Writing and in the Yahwist's account do not as yet present a *Christian* doctrine of creation, for the messianic orientation is here not yet overtly present' (*God in Creation*, 55). To reduce belief in creation to a theory about origins would fundamentally impair it; for 'creation' represents 'the quintessence of the whole divine creative activity', and the doctrine of creation must therefore 'embrace creation in the beginning, creation in history, and the creation of the end-time' (55). This messianic doctrine of creation must appeal to the whole biblical teaching and not just to individual passages isolated from their broader context; and it must identify the centre around which biblical teaching as a whole must be organized. That centre is to be found in the New Testament, whose testimony about creation occurs 'in the resurrection kerygma and in the experience of the Holy Spirit, who is the energy of the new creation' (65). 'Because eschatological creation proceeds from the process of the resurrection and the creation of life, in the New Testament the Creator God is given the new messianic name of *ho egeiras Iēsoun*, the Father of Jesus Christ, the God who raises the dead, the God of hope (Rom. 15.13). Faith in the resurrection is therefore the Christian form of belief in creation' (66). And, for the New Testament, the power of the resurrection is the Holy Spirit, whose gifts already anticipate and actualize the energies of the new heavens and the new earth for which the whole creation yearns (cf. Rom. 8.18–27). 'The messianic era does not merely bring an *outpouring* of the gifts of the Spirit on men and women. It also *awakens* the Spirit itself in the whole enslaved creation' (69).[5]

This messianic doctrine of creation can appeal especially to Pauline material. But the equation of 'Christian' with 'messianic' relativizes the distinction between Christian faith and Judaism, and makes it possible to relate Christian hope not only to the life and destiny of Jesus but also to Old Testament prophecy. In the Old Testament, 'the world does not disclose itself as God's creation just by itself', for 'Israel learnt to understand the world as God's good creation in the light of the saving events of the exodus, the covenant and the settlement in the Promised Land . . . The *special* experience of God which emerged from "God the Lord's" revelation of himself moulded and interpreted Israel's *general* experience of the world' (54). But this means that, as Israel's experience and understanding of God's saving activity changes, her experience and understanding of creation will change correspondingly. Hence the exhortation in Isa. 43.18f.: 'Remember not the former things, nor consider the things of old. For behold, I will create a new thing . . .' The prophets experience the rupture of salvation-history, and must therefore look to the future and not to the past for God's decisive saving activity. 'It is true that the prophets describe God's new creation with the images of times belonging to the faraway past, which cannot be brought back again. But they paint this new creation in incandescent colours' (121): there will be new heavens and a new earth (Isa. 65.17).[6] There is therefore a continuity between the messianic, future-oriented New Testament doctrine of creation and the turn towards the future of the Old Testament prophets. Apostles and prophets agree that God's creative activity is to be understood in relation to the future and not merely to the past. The static view implied by Gen. 1–2, read in isolation, is relativized and set in motion.

The fact remains that according to the biblical narrative creation marks *the beginning* of God's dealings with the world and with humankind – *only* the beginning, and not the middle and the end as well.[7] It is not a foregone conclusion that this simple literary and exegetical observation is theologically significant; there may often be good reasons for putting a certain distance between the literal sense of a particular biblical text and a contemporary theological assertion. On the other hand, it is theologically important to remain open to what particular texts actually *say*. I shall argue that the biblical notion of creation in the beginning is still a theological necessity.

(*i*) Laying the foundation

The creation-narratives in Gen. 1–2 represent God's activity in creation as belonging, in some sense, to the past. Gen. 1.1–2.4a locates the divine acts of creation within the framework of the first seven days, 'the beginning' (1.1) of the temporal continuum presupposed by the entire biblical narrative as it gradually unfolds, a continuum in which the reader is also located. God rested on the seventh day because 'the heavens and the earth were finished [*way‘kullû*] and all the host of them' (2.1), and the first sabbath therefore marks the boundary between the time of God's primary creative activity and the ongoing divine activity that the biblical narrative will subsequently describe.[8] Rest presupposes completion. The first account ends with the words, 'These are the generations of the heavens and the earth when they were created' (2.4a), and the strange use of the genealogical formula '*ēlleh tōl‘dōth* (cf. 5.1; 6.9; 10.1, etc.) integrates the creation-narrative into the temporal continuum represented by the genealogical material in Genesis.[9] The second narrative (Gen. 2.4b–25) opens with a reference to 'the day when Yahweh Elohim made the earth and the heavens' (2.4b), and the setting of the first man and woman in a place from which they and their descendants were subsequently barred underlines again the pastness of the time of creation. In both narratives, a limit is placed on the time of creation: the sabbath in one, the expulsion from Eden in the other.

Yet this is a quite different past to the near-oblivion into which, for example, the descendants of Adam have fallen (cf. Gen. 5), for the effects of this past are immediately and directly perceptible in the present. The creative works of the first six days are oriented towards the world of our present experience: God brings into being day and night, the blue sky, the sea and the dry land, to serve as permanent structures for the foreseeable future; and he bestows on plant, animal and human life the creative power to secure its own future by reproducing itself. The first plants and trees contained seed, each according to its kind (1.12); sea creatures, birds, humans and (presumably) other animals were blessed, and commanded to 'be fruitful and multiply' (1.22, 28). The reference is obviously to the familiar environment of ordinary human experience. Having this environment directly before him, and having acquired a systematic knowledge of its basic structure, the narrator imagines and describes the orderly divine activity necessarily presupposed in its present existence. The second narrative too is about the realities of present experience: the human affinity with the dust of the ground, the animals in their likeness and unlikeness to humans, the longing that causes a man to leave his father and his mother and to cleave to his wife, the hard labour of childbirth and agriculture, the symbolism of nakedness and clothing. These narratives locate the time of creation in the past, 'in the beginning', precisely in order to understand the basic structures of present experience. And this present is not just the present of the writer or the reader but the entire time during which human life is lived within an environment of the kind here described; a present that encompasses every imaginable human time and place.

What is valued in this all-encompassing present is its *stability*. The writer perceives that this stability is contingent upon the original creative decision of God and his subsequent decision not to deluge the world a second time, despite human evil. 'I establish my covenant with you that never again shall all flesh be cut off by the waters of a flood . . . When I bring clouds over the earth and the bow is seen in the clouds, I will remember my covenant which is between me and you and every living creature of all flesh' (Gen. 9.11, 14–15). 'While the earth remains, seedtime and harvest, cold and heat, summer and winter, day and night, shall not cease' (8.22).[10] The language here already indicates the close link between creation and Israel's distinctive experience of covenant, yet this is not a one-way movement in which creation is interpreted in the light of covenant, but not the reverse. The relation between creation and covenant is one of interdependence and circularity: God's covenant-faithfulness casts a retrospective light on his faithfulness in creation, but the faithfulness of the creator to his creation is a necessary presupposition of Israel's experience of the covenant. The limiting of the time of creation to the beginning serves a representation of the created order as stable and dependable, a permanent manifestation of God's covenant-faithfulness to all living creatures, even if only some of them have eyes to see it as such.[11]

In Moltmann's theology, on the other hand, the 'static' view of creation offered by Gen. 1–2 is subordinated to the more 'dynamic' view that is supposed to emerge when the link between creation and covenant is properly understood. In Israel's thinking, it is said, God is first the God of the covenant, the God of exodus, Sinai and conquest, and only as such and secondarily is he the God of creation. 'In the biblical traditions of the Old and New Testaments, experience of the world as creation is determined by belief in the revelation of the creative God in Israel's history' (54). This is to restate the widespread view that Yahweh is known to Israel first as redeemer and only secondarily as creator, except that Yahweh's redemptive activity is now redescribed as an ongoing *creative* process.[12] Yet, in the biblical texts, the relationship between creation and covenant is in fact one of interdependence. Creation has a certain priority in the sense that it refers us to 'the beginning'. But the beginning is no more significant than the middle or the end; indeed, the question of relative importance does not arise. Some exegetical examples will help to clarify this point.

(1) Creation occurs 'in the beginning', whereas covenant belongs to the middle – 'covenant' denoting the entire complex history that begins with the call of Abraham and that culminates in the story of the life, death and resurrection of Jesus. The middle arises out of the beginning; and, at least in retrospect, the beginning of the story is seen to prepare the way for the middle. The world whose origin is described in Gen. 1 is the stage upon which Abraham, Sarah and their descendants act out their parts in the unfolding historical drama. When the Lord commands Abram to leave Haran and to migrate to the land that will eventually belong to his descendants (Gen. 12.1), his authority to do this stems from the fact that he is the creator who separated land from sea and to whom the land – any land – belongs. The promise of descendants as numerous as the stars in the sky (15.5) presupposes the creator's power to bless humankind, male and female, by commanding and enabling them to be fruitful and to multiply (1.28). The creation of humankind in God's image and likeness suggests a unique affinity between the creator and this particular creature, and this is confirmed by the possibility of divine–human dialogue actualized for the first time when the Lord God confronts the first human couple with their act of disobedience. This possibility of divine–human dialogue and interaction is fundamental to the concept of the covenant, in which God's speech or action evokes responsive human speech or action. Moving forward into Exodus, the plagues and the parting of the sea presuppose that the God who liberates his people is the creator who exercises power and authority over his non-human creatures. At every point in the biblical narrative, the God who acts and speaks in it is no other than the creator of heaven and earth. Gen. 1–2 is therefore a true beginning, the foundation and presupposition of everything that occurs subsequently.[13]

(2) The interdependence of covenant and creation is also evident on a smaller scale in a number of passages in which the divine name 'Yahweh' is associated with creation as well as redemption.

In the version of the Decalogue given in Exod. 20, the speaker of these commandments introduces himself as 'Yahweh your God, who brought you out of the land of Egypt, out of the house of bondage' (20.2). Does this mean that the name 'Yahweh' is associated exclusively with the exodus, as Moses' encounter with him at the burning bush might suggest (Exod. 3)? Even there, however, the divine response to Moses' sense of his deficiencies as a speaker is grounded in creation: 'Who has made man's mouth? Who makes him dumb, or deaf, or seeing, or blind? Is it not I, the Lord?' (Exod. 4.11). That Yahweh is creator as well as redeemer, the redeemer as the one who is already the creator, is confirmed in the fourth commandment: the sabbath is to be observed because 'in six days Yahweh made heaven and earth, the sea and all that is in them, and rested on the seventh day; therefore Yahweh blessed the sabbath day and hallowed it' (20.11). It is striking that, despite the obvious link with the seven-day creation tradition represented by Gen. 1, 'Yahweh' is here substituted for 'Elohim'; and this confirms that it is as the creator that Yahweh is also the God of the exodus. Yahweh's role as creator is also presupposed in the second commandment, the prohibition of idolatry. Israel is not to make 'a graven image or any likeness of anything that is in heaven above, or that is in the earth beneath or that is in the water under the earth' (20.4). Why? As we have seen, in the fourth commandment Yahweh is identified as the creator of heaven, earth and sea, and to worship the creature as divine would be to deny the truly divine creator. It is as the creator that Yahweh is the redeemer. Yet, on the other hand, to know Yahweh only as the creator and not as the redeemer from Egypt would be arbitrarily to isolate the beginning of the story from the middle. No character in a narrative can be adequately known from his or her first appearance, however significant or fundamental this may be.

Similarly, Amos initially defines Yahweh in terms of the exodus: 'Hear this word that Yahweh has spoken against you, O people of Israel, against the whole family which I brought up out of the land of Egypt' (Amos 3.1). Yet in a series of possibly liturgical fragments (4.13; 5.8–9; 9.5–6), the name Yahweh is associated not with exodus but with creation: 'For lo, he who forms the mountains and creates the wind, and declares to man what is his thought; who makes the morning darkness, and treads on the heights of the earth – Yahweh the God of hosts is his name!' (Amos 4.13). Once again, the name 'Yahweh' implies both creation and redemption.[14] The interdependence of the two roles is also clear in a similar passage in Jer. 31.35–36: 'Thus says Yahweh, who gives the sun for light by day and the fixed order of the moon and the stars for light by night, who stirs up the sea so that its waves roar – Yahweh of hosts is his name: "If this fixed order departs from before me, says Yahweh, then shall the descendants of Israel cease from being a nation before me for ever".' The creator is also the God of the covenant, and the divine faithfulness disclosed in the stability of the created order illustrates and guarantees the faithful maintaining of the covenant. This passage immediately follows the depiction of the new covenant, which will be 'not like the covenant which I made with their fathers when I took them by the hand to bring them out of the land of Egypt, my covenant which they broke' (31.31–32). Interpreting the two passages in the light of each other, it seems that the unlikeness of the new and the old covenants is ultimately intended to ensure the stability of the single covenant in which God promises to be the God of Israel; a covenant which, despite human sin, is as firmly fixed as those earlier divine works, the sun, moon and stars in the heavens. While the history of Israel is moving through disaster towards the goal of salvation, creation here functions as a stable backdrop to this dramatic history.

To summarize these exegetical discussions in a single sentence: *Because God is creator as well as redeemer (the creator as the future redeemer and the redeemer as the creator), creation constitutes the stable foundation for the history of the covenant, from beginning to end.* But this statement is the product of Old Testament exegesis, and its credentials as a claim of Christian theology remain unclear. Surely the overwhelmingly eschatological orientation of the New Testament will compel us to replace this static view of creation with a more dynamic one? In the light of the New Testament and of modern science, can it still be maintained that the doctrine of creation refers us only to 'the beginning'? Before we turn to the New Testament, however, there are two preliminary considerations that suggest caution at this point.

(1) We should ask why is it that the terms 'static' and 'dynamic' have respectively attracted negative and positive connotations in modern usage. An answer may be found in the use of this polarity in the ideology and practice of modern capitalism. Capitalist ideology applauds dynamism, the restless dissatisfaction with the way things are and the quest for the new. It approves inventiveness, adaptability, expansion, mobility and (of course) 'freedom' – to such an extent that that which endures and does not change becomes a troubling enigma that must either be passed over in silence or denounced as inflexible, outdated and dogmatic.[15] Theology should be more wary of the subtle but pervasive pressure of contemporary ideologies on its own thought-processes and language.

The representation in the Genesis texts of a divinely-given, stable created order obviously stems from an agricultural society in which the rhythm of the seasons, seedtime and harvest, rainfall and the soil are basic categories of experience. These texts do not encourage romantic nostalgia for the simplicity of rural life; they acknowledge that the ground brings forth thorns and thistles, and that it condemns those who till it to unending hard labour. But they also shed light on an anomaly of our own situation: that, on the one hand, even industrialized urban cultures are still ultimately dependent on agriculture and the fecundity of the created order; and that, on the other hand, this situation of dependence is concealed by an ideology that can see in the human situation nothing more than the need for free, dynamic, inventive human activity. In opposition to this ultimately atheistic myth of human self-creation, the Genesis texts draw our attention to the stable structures which still constitute our own basic environment, on which we remain dependent and which speak (to those with ears to hear) of our further dependence on God, the creator of heaven and earth. Without such a critical consciousness, the prayer 'Give us this day our daily bread' is meaningless.

(2) The modern scientific tendency to perceive the natural order in dynamic rather than static terms obviously cannot be interpreted merely as a product of the capitalist ideology of dynamism, although the two are probably not unrelated. Yet science knows not only of dynamic change and adaptation within the natural order but also of the regularities that are so much more obvious and important to ordinary, non-scientific perception. Science too knows of the regular alternation of seedtime and harvest, cold and heat, summer and winter, day and night, and in so far as it does so it remains closer to human experience of the natural order than a science that converts nature into history.[16] Yet, although science itself is an exclusively human project, the 'anthropocentrism' of the Christian world-view is regarded as problematic; and Gen. 1 is seen as a classic expression of that now-superseded anthropocentrism. For science, the emergence of so-called 'intelligent life' capable among other things of scientific research is a strange, ungraspable anomaly: by a remarkable irony, the random play of natural powers manages not only to *mimic* purposive creative action, through devices such as 'natural selection', but also to bring into existence creatures capable of *genuine* purposive creative action. For the biblical texts, on the other hand, the grounding of human existence in divine creative action results in a basically non-paradoxical, non-ironic interpretation of human existence. While the scientific story of the continuing evolution of the world-process is not without theological significance, it should not be permitted to supplant the biblical creation accounts or to influence the basic shape of Christian theology. Christian faith cannot abstract the natural world either from human existence or from the divine creative intention that gives rise to both for the sake of covenant-partnership with the human creature; and for that reason the biblical creation story in its wider biblical context remains the definitive account of our place in the world.[17]

(ii) The creaturehood of Jesus

In the New Testament, the language of creation (e.g. *ktizein, ktisis*) normally refers us back to 'the beginning' (e.g. *ho ktisas ap' archēs* [Matt. 19.4]; cf. Mark 10.6; 13.19; 2 Pet. 3.4) which remains the foundation of present historical existence (cf. 1 Tim. 4.3). Creation-language can also be used metaphorically to depict the radical newness experienced by Gentile Christian communities under the impact of the gospel of Christ (2 Cor. 5.17; Gal. 6.15: *kainē ktisis*; cf. Rom. 4.17; Eph. 2.10, 15). However, rather than engaging in a close study of vocabulary, it seems preferable to confront directly the question whether and to what extent our summary statement about the Old Testament material also applies to the New. Creation, we said, constitutes the stable foundation for the history of the covenant, from beginning to end; it is not consistently historicized.

Moltmann's eschatological doctrine of creation is dependent on the premise that Christianity itself is wholly eschatological, in the sense that all of its component parts ultimately point in the same direction: the future of God's promise.[18] It is held that, as a matter of historical fact, the original proclamation of Jesus and the early church was entirely eschatological, and that this historical finding can be and should be exploited theologically. The hermeneutical privileging of texts that imply an eschatological understanding of creation is inevitable on these presuppositions. Yet there are major difficulties with this theological hermeneutic. The canonical collection as a whole does not in itself imply that early Christian faith was entirely eschatological. The collection opens not with four apocalypses but with four gospels, which appear to direct our attention towards the past more than the future. Eschatological expectation is of course emphatically present – in the synoptic apocalypse, some of the Pauline letters, and the Book of Revelation – but always in conjunction with a variety of other issues which bind the Christian community as firmly to the past and the present as to the future. The claim that early Christianity was wholly eschatological in fact derives not from the New Testament texts as they stand but from a reconstruction of the history that preceded them. This reconstruction gathers together eschatological texts from the synoptic gospels and the earlier Pauline letters, and announces that here alone is to be found the key to Christian faith at its moment of origin.[19] But, if the earliest Christians had their eyes turned so resolutely towards the imminent future, it is hard to see why they were evidently so concerned with the careful preservation and development of traditions relating to Jesus' past existence. And if, on the evidence of the Pauline letters, the Thessalonian community lived for a time in an atmosphere of intense eschatological expectation, can this also be said of the Galatians or the Philippians?[20]

If in the New Testament past and present retain their reality, the life, death and resurrection of Jesus may be understood as the inner-historical culmination of God's covenant with Israel. A human being, a son of man, lives in total obedience to the covenantal requirement that he should love the Lord his God with all his heart, soul and strength, and his neighbour as himself; and his love of God and neighbour is lived out in conditions of total solidarity and identification with his neighbour, so that his own obedience encloses and perfects the imperfect obedience of those who are drawn to him by his call. The universal implications of this particular life are to be worked out through the church's mission to all nations, and it is therefore this universal mission that is central to the gospel resurrection narratives, rather than eschatology (Matt. 28.18–20; [Mark 16.15–18]; Luke 24.45–49; John 20.21–23; 21.15–17; cf. Acts 1.6–8).

What role does the created order play in this history of the culmination of the covenant? As in the Old Testament, it serves as foundation: ever present, always necessary, often almost unnoticed because of the pressure of historical developments, rarely an object of exclusive attention for its own sake, yet constantly and unobtrusively insinuating itself into the historical narrative. This point can be illustrated by observing correlations between the creation-narrative of Gen. 1 and the gospels.

On the first day of creation, God separated the light from the darkness, thus setting in motion the regular alternation of day and night; and so 'there was evening and there was morning, the first day'. Like all humans, Jesus is subject to this same alternation. At the beginning of his ministry, the Marcan narrator tells how in the evening, at sundown, the sick were brought to Jesus, and how in the morning, before dawn, he rose from sleep and went to a lonely place to pray (Mark 1.32, 35). At the end of the story, Joseph of Arimathea arranges for Jesus' burial 'when evening had come', and Jesus arises from death early on the first day of the week, before the sun had risen (Mark 15.42–16.2). The interval between the beginning and the end is also measured out in days: 'after some days' (2.1), 'in those days' (8.1), 'after six days' (9.2), 'on the following day' (11.12), 'on the first day of unleavened bread' (14.12). The time of creation establishes the necessary foundation also for the life of Jesus.

On the second day, God created a firmament which he named 'heaven' or 'sky', separating the waters above from the waters below and thus establishing the space in which the world as we know it might come into being. Jesus' life occurs within this space beneath the sky – the single space within which all humans must live and move and have their being, from the beginning of human history to its end. It is noticeable how much of his ministry takes place in locations that are open to the sky: the lake and its shores, the road, the mountains. Although he is sometimes to be found within the enclosure of house or synagogue, he has no fixed dwelling-place but is often compelled to sleep under the sky. Unlike the foxes and the birds, the Son of man has nowhere to lay his head (Matt. 8.20).

On the third day, God separated the sea from the dry land. The sea is present in the gospels in the form of the Sea of Galilee (Mark 1.16), also known as the Sea of Tiberias (John 6.1) or the Lake of Gennesaret (Luke 5.1). We hear of the shore that marks the division of sea and land: there, Jesus is hemmed in by a large crowd so that he has to preach from a boat (Mark 4.1). As fishermen, Jesus' first disciples belong to both land and sea (Mark 1.16–20), and this may account for the frequent journeys from place to place by way of the sea. But the main sphere of Jesus' activity is of course the land, its various locations differentiated by place-names or by natural features such as mountains. On the third day, God also created plants and trees, which (as it later emerges) are to provide food for humans and animals. In his parables, Jesus speaks of sowing and harvest (Matt. 13.1–30); and he knows that it is through the mediation of these and other human activities (cf. Luke 13.21) that the prayer 'Give us this day our daily bread' is answered. He also knows of fruit-bearing trees – fig-trees and vines, for example – and of less valuable vegetation such as thorns, thistles and tares. But for Jesus this part of the created order can be valued for its beauty as well as for its usefulness: 'Consider the lilies of the field, how they grow; they neither toil nor spin, yet I tell you even Solomon in all his glory was not arrayed like one of these' (Matt. 6.28–29).

On the fourth day, God created the sun, moon and stars. Jesus speaks of a time when the sun will be darkened, the moon will not give its light, and the stars will fall from heaven (Mark 13.24–25). But that time is not yet: for the present, the sun still rules the day and the moon the night. God makes his sun to shine on the evil and on the good, on all people indiscriminately (Matt. 5.45). Nothing is hidden from its heat, which scorches the seed sown in rocky ground so that it withers (Mark 4.6) and which increases the burden of labourers who must endure its fierceness in the middle of the day (Matt. 20.12).

On the fifth day, God created the living creatures of sea and air, fish and birds. Jesus knows that if a son asks his father for a fish, he will be sure to give him one – and not a snake (Luke 11.11). He calls his first disciples away from their fishing; but he also twice secures for them a miraculous catch (Luke 5.1–11; John 21.1–8); he divides two fish between more than five thousand people (Mark 6.41); after his resurrection, he himself both eats fish (Luke 24.42–43) and cooks fish for his disciples (John 21.9–13). As regards the birds of the air, we are told to observe how, though 'they neither sow nor reap nor gather into barns', they are nevertheless fed by our heavenly Father (Matt. 6.26). Although they are of little value in the market-place, 'not a single sparrow falls to the ground without your Father's will' (Matt. 10.29). The Father's care for them is also apparent in the fact that 'birds of the air have nests' (Matt. 8.20), possibly among the branches of the mustard-tree, 'the greatest of shrubs' (Matt. 13.32).

On the sixth day, God created land animals; and he created humankind, men and women, in his own image, to exercise dominion over all creatures of sea, sky and land. Jesus knows of this relationship in various forms: fishermen and fish (Mark 1.16–20), shepherd and sheep (Luke 15.3–7), and his own riding a colt into Jerusalem (Mark 11.1–7). He knows that, even on the sabbath, people untie their ox or ass from the manger and lead it away to water it (Luke 13.15); and if, on the same day, a sheep should fall into a pit, they will be sure to rescue it (Matt. 12.11–12). He knows that foxes have holes (Matt. 8.20) but that camels are unable to step through the eye of a needle (Matt. 19.24); and he speaks of the violence of dogs and pigs (Matt. 7.6). Animals can pose a threat to humans, and they can be threatened by one another, as in the case of sheep among wolves (Matt. 10.16). Jesus also knows that the human creature, made uniquely in the image of God, is of more value than all other creatures. Two sparrows are sold for a penny, but 'you are of more value than many sparrows' (Matt. 10.31). The practice of rescuing a sheep from a pit on the sabbath vindicates the practice of healing on the sabbath because a human is infinitely more valuable than a sheep (Matt. 12.12).

On the seventh day, God rested from his labours. The inhabitants of Galilee mark the sabbath by attending the synagogue, and Jesus does likewise. But what is the meaning of the sabbath? 'The sabbath was made for man, not man for the sabbath' (Mark 2.27). Men and women must pass their time within the created order in hard labour: on the sea, in the fields, among the mountains, in the home. For one day in seven, however, they must share in the creator's rest and hear the law and the prophets read to them; and they will find themselves reminded, week by week, of the ultimate source, norm and goal of their labours in the midst of the creation.

These correlations between the creation-narrative and the gospels indicate that creation remains the foundation of the covenant-history in the inner-historical culmination of the covenant in the life of Jesus. Christologically, we may say that these correlations *help to make visible Jesus' creatureliness*.[21] He is, as we have seen, God's covenant-partner, the one in whom the history of the covenant attains its inner-historical culmination and perfection. The history of the covenant is no longer a history only of disobedience and failure, of hopes at best only partially and ambiguously realized. But God's human covenant-partner is also a creature; he has a history, but he is also fully integrated into the foundational, non-historical realm of creation, as a creature among other creatures. The prominence of the created order within his own particular life-history reminds those who are drawn into the new covenant he initiates that they too are creatures among other creatures. The structure of the created order is the same in first-century Galilee as in the world of our own experience, and the creation-narrative that describes this stable, ahistorical or pre-historical structure therefore overarches these and all other times and places in which there is human existence.

To be aware of creatureliness is to be aware of dependence upon God. But to be God's covenant-partner is also to be dependent upon God, for God is the sole initiator and guarantor of covenant and creation alike. The dependent being of the covenant-partner is grounded in the prior dependent being of the creature; and, conversely, the dependence of the creature becomes fully conscious and explicit in the dependence of the covenant-partner. The realm of creation does not fall outside the realm of the covenant. We cannot love God and neighbour on the one hand while on the other hand acting slightingly and high-handedly towards the created order, regarding it as mere raw material for our own autonomous purposes and activity. Covenant is, as it were, superimposed upon creation, its foundation, in such a way as to incorporate creation wholly within itself.

The relationship between creation, covenant and christology can be brought into sharper focus by noting that Jesus' covenantal practice of the love of God and neighbour requires him to offer true worship to God on behalf of his neighbour. (Thus Jesus appropriates and applies to himself the saying from Deuteronomy, 'You shall worship the Lord your God, and him only shall you serve' [Deut. 6.13; Matt. 4.10].) In the context of the covenant, it is the Book of Psalms that best represents the full range of human worship of God. Thus, the sinless Jesus identifies himself with the penitents of the psalter who confess their sins (for example, in Ps. 51) when he himself submits to John's baptism of repentance (Matt. 3.13–15, cf. vv. 1–6, 11). Jesus also worships God in the words of righteous sufferers who express their faith and hope in the form of a complaint: 'My soul is very sorrowful, even to death' (Matt. 26.38, cf. Pss. 42.5, 11; 43.5); 'My God, my God, why hast thou forsaken me?' (Matt. 27.46; Ps. 22.1). Such complaints cannot be the last word, however, for the psalmists also express a joyful confidence in resurrection and vindication, and these texts too can be seen as the means by which Jesus worships the Lord his God as he moves towards his own suffering and resurrection: 'The very stone which the builders rejected has become the head of the corner; this was the Lord's doing, and it is marvellous in our eyes' (Matt. 21.42; Ps. 118.22–23); 'The Lord said to my Lord, "Sit at my right hand, till I put thy enemies under thy feet"' (Matt. 22.44; Ps. 110.1). These examples suggest that Jesus' vicarious, representative worship of the Lord his God entails the whole gamut of expression that the psalter makes available. This worship lies at the heart of his high-priestly ministry.

The psalter also includes texts that address God primarily as creator. These include an expression of rapt amazement at the beauty of the night sky and the near-divine privileges bestowed on humankind (Ps. 8, cf. also Ps. 19); a lovingly detailed enumeration of God's earthly works of creation (Ps. 104); and the ecstatic songs at the end of the psalter, in which the worshippers call upon all created things to join in their songs of praise (Pss. 148, 150). These poems evoke and celebrate the glory and the mystery of the created order with a power that rivals the nature-poetry of Romanticism. But this comparison provokes an anxiety. Do these songs of praise have a place within the Christian worship of God? Or are they too close for comfort to the paganism which exults in the glories of nature because it knows nothing of God's history with humankind, of which the created order is only the foundation? The danger of a dichotomy between creation and covenant is overcome, however, if it can be shown that this praise of the creator for his works belongs within the covenant. And if Jesus, the Son of man, is God's true covenant-partner, then these psalms too must be credible as part of the high-priestly worship that he offers on our behalf to the Lord his God.[22] The many and various allusions to the created order that we discovered in the gospels suggest, at least at certain points, a mind that has learnt to *notice* the good gifts of creation and to reflect on their significance: '*Look at* [*emblepsate eis*] the birds of the air . . .'; '*Consider* [*katamathete*] the lilies of the field . . .' (Matt. 6.26, 28).[23] It is precisely this act of 'looking at' or 'considering' the created order that the psalter converts into psalms of praise; and, whether or not Jesus learned it from them, these psalms may credibly be seen as an element in his vicarious, high-priestly worship of the Lord his God. Praise of God the creator therefore has an indispensable role within Christian worship.

Creation is the foundation of the covenant. In terms of the biblical narrative, creation is only the beginning, whereas the covenant occupies the middle of the narrative in which most of the action occurs. But creation and covenant are interdependent, bound to one another by many connections and analogies, and it is theologically disastrous to separate them or to exalt one at the expense of the other. The theological significance of creation only emerges, however, when the doctrine of creation is kept within its proper limits. Creation is the beginning and the foundation of everything that follows; it is not the whole story.

2. Creation in the Beginning and 'Natural Theology'

Creation, the beginning of the story of God's dealings with the world and with humankind, establishes the framework within which the history of the divine–human covenant can unfold, the foundation upon which all subsequent occurrence takes place. An eschatologically-oriented doctrine of creation will tend to overlook this limitation, subsuming the history of the covenant into the history of creation: an act, one might judge, of theological *hubris* that lays claim to a knowledge of the future of God's creation as a whole for which (despite Rom. 8.18–23) we have insufficient warrant.

Yet there is another way in which the biblical understanding of creation can be misstated. God's creation of the world can be removed from its proper context as the beginning of the divine–human history attested by the biblical narrative, and re-established as an independent idea isolated and abstracted from the history of the covenant. Thus, in response to public concern over environmental issues and to movements such as 'creation spirituality', and in reaction against an earlier tendency to minimize the significance of creation within biblical theology, one might declare that the biblical texts relating to creation have a particular contemporary significance.[24] Reread in a contemporary light, they are said to offer invaluable resources in our struggle to shape appropriate responses to our various ecological and spiritual crises. Exegesis of selected texts (especially from Genesis, the Psalms, Job and Deutero-Isaiah) will then be motivated by the apologetic concern to demonstrate not the integrity and truth of Christian faith but the relevance of the Bible.[25] The assertion of biblical 'relevance' refers us to the interpreter's confidence in his or her ability to relocate the biblical texts within the constraints of the current discourses that circulate around certain publicly-accredited 'problems' or 'issues'; and since these problems or issues are constructed in a post-Christian culture on which the Bible has already left a deep impression, it is not difficult to show that the Bible is 'still relevant' to them. For this post-Christian culture, however, 'creation' is synonymous with 'the natural world'. The natural world is foundational to our human existence, but our human existence within the natural world is no longer seen as deriving from and oriented towards the triune God of Christian faith. Contemporary culture has constituted itself as post-Christian precisely by its declaration of autonomy over against this God, and the project of demonstrating the Bible's relevance to one or other of its accredited problems or issues has to accommodate itself to the constraints of this situation. The tendency will therefore be to abstract biblical texts relating to the created world from their total biblical context, and the apparent naturalness of this procedure is reinforced by biblical scholarship's long-standing concern to assert and defend the autonomy of the individual text over against the whole.

Theologically, this means that creation is no longer understood as the beginning and foundation of the history of God's covenantal relationship with humankind. It has become an independent theme; it is no longer an element in a narrative. This procedure can be defended theologically by appealing to the possibility of a 'natural theology', according to which not only the existence of God but also his relationship to the world as its creator, and therefore the status of the world as creation, may be considered without recourse to any criteria internal to Christian faith. Natural theology promises a knowledge of God, the world and humankind which is immediately accessible by virtue of human rational faculties. Establishing the possibility and scope of natural theology in relation to the history of divine self-disclosure attested in the Bible has long been a contentious matter, but the existence of this theological possibility seems to lend credibility to the procedure of isolating the biblical creation material from its narrative context. Indeed, it is arguable that the narrative context of the biblical presentation of creation is a contingent matter, and that the biblical texts themselves affirm the possibility of a natural knowledge of God and of the world as his creation that can be detached from whatever else they may wish to say about God. On that view, biblical faith itself would *require* natural theology.

That is in fact the argument of James Barr in his 1991 Gifford lectures, published under the title *Biblical Faith and Natural Theology* (1993).[26] Unlike most other contemporary writers on biblical creation material, Barr has no interest in asserting the relevance of the biblical texts to our environmental crises. Nor is he interested in natural theology as such; he shows no particular desire to commend this approach to theology, let alone to practise it. He is concerned to establish the single point that the biblical texts themselves commend and practise various forms of natural theology, and that the Barthian critique of natural theology in the name of the biblical revelation is therefore self-contradictory. One cannot oppose natural theology on the basis of the biblical texts if the biblical texts themselves promote natural theology. If Barr is right, then one could no longer insist on understanding the biblical presentation of creation solely on the basis of its function within the total biblical narrative. It would have an independent significance; knowledge of the world as God's creation would derive from an independent source.

In Barr's view, 'natural theology' asserts not only that 'natural' knowledge of God is possible but that it is foundational to all other knowledge of God: 'The "natural" knowledge of God, however dim, is an awareness of the true God, and provides a point of contact without which the special revelation would never be able to penetrate to people' (1). Biblical warrant for this view has conventionally been found in passages such as Acts 17.16–34 (Paul's speech to the Areopagus) and Rom. 1.18–23, and Barr devotes his second and third lectures to detailed discussion of these texts.

Characteristic of Acts 17 is 'the complete absence of support adduced from the history, the law, and the experience of Israel; the strong universalism, with God seen as determining alike the bounds and times for *all* human peoples; the clear prospect that any of these might feel after him and find him; the conjunction of the high transcendence of the deity and his close presence and immanence; especially the idea that we live and move and have our being within him, the nearest approach, no doubt, to pantheism in the Bible, coupled with the idea that we, i.e. all humans, are his offspring . . .' (25). This passage, we are told, 'cannot be fully expounded without opening the gate towards some sort of natural theology' (26). Recognizing this is simply a matter of *honesty*. If one rejects natural theology on principle, one would have to conclude 'that Paul, as represented by Luke in this chapter of Acts, was *wrong*, and wrong in one of the most essential elements dominating the structure of Christian faith' (26) – to the detriment of 'the total authority of scripture' (27). It is true that there is an argument to the effect that 'the approach described in Acts 17 was indeed carried out by St Paul but was a momentary lapse or mistake on his part' (29); his attempt to argue on the basis of natural theology miscarried, and it was this experience that led to his decision to 'know nothing among you except Jesus Christ and him crucified' (1 Cor. 2.2) when he moved on from Athens to Corinth. Yet there is nothing in Acts which indicates that, for the narrator, Paul had failed in any way: 'He makes Paul deliver a magnificent oration, and several people believed and attached themselves to Paul, including Dionysius the Areopagite, who, even if he was not the great theologian he was later reputed to have become, was at least an important person . . . Along with him there was a woman called Damaris, and some "others". Even in numbers this was no "failure". If it was only "some" who believed, it was only "some" again who "mocked", and "others", perhaps about the same proportion, who wanted to hear more' (30). In his proclamation of a natural theology, Luke's Paul remains a reliable spokesman for what Luke takes to be the truth of the matter.

According to Rom. 1.18–23, God's anger is revealed against human impiety and unrighteousness. Those who stand accused cannot claim to have been ignorant of God, for God's nature and power have from creation onwards been disclosed through created entities. God made himself known, and humans turned their backs on this self-disclosure, devoting themselves instead to the manufacture and worship of idols. They knew the truth but preferred falsehood, and they are therefore without excuse; that is why

God is angry with them. Barr cites the view of C. K. Barrett that 'it is not Paul's intention in this and the following verses to establish a natural theology', and of C. E. B. Cranfield that 'the result of God's self-manifestation in his creation is not a natural knowledge of God on men's part independent of God's self-manifestation in his Word . . . , but simply the excuselessness of men in their ignorance' (41). For Barr, such an exegesis is 'no more than a reiteration of certain dogmatic traditions' (42). If, as the passage states, there is a self-disclosure of God in creation, and if this is 'accessible and available to *everybody*, indeed in some degree attained or possessed by everybody, Jew or Gentile, it seems to come to the same thing as natural theology in effect. They all know it, or know some trace of it. If they all know this trace of it, why can one not build some theology upon this fact?' (41).[27] The passage from Rom. 1 may amount to 'something like a revealed natural theology', which suggests 'that the traditional boundaries between revealed and natural theology cannot be sustained' (42). To reject the possibility of a knowledge of God attained independently of the will and activity of God is beside the point, for natural theology has never supposed any such thing. 'The kind of exegesis which will refuse any openness to natural theology in Romans 1–2 is the kind of negative exegesis which will also deny a doctrine of incarnation in John or a doctrine of the Trinity in Paul' (50).

Barr's discussion of Old Testament material is more broadly based; here, a single example will suffice, that of Ps. 104. It may be argued that this text 'is not concerned to perform the function that most normally and directly forms natural theology, namely to suggest that the nature of God can be known through contemplation of the universe and its workings' (82). Yet it is a mistake to distinguish too sharply between a theology of nature and a natural theology. The psalm ascribes various realities in the world to God, and there is no indication here of any special knowledge deriving from revelation: 'Everyone knew that the springs give water to the wild asses, that the lions roar at night, that men go to work in the morning and come home to rest in the evening. And that all this came from God, this was no new idea either: everyone in that ancient culture took it as obvious' (83). This is confirmed by the very close parallels between this text and 'the hymn to the Aten or sun-disk associated with the religious reform movement of Akhenaten' (84). The psalm is typical of 'Hebrew natural theology' in 'focusing on the existing cosmos as evidence and manifestation of the divine beneficence' (84). It confirms the hypothesis that 'Hebrew and Jewish ideas were a highly formative source which did much to form the background of natural theology' – in opposition to the tendency to see Hebrew and Greek thought as polar opposites, and to find in the latter 'the seeds of natural theology and of more or less all theological errors' (56).

Woven into Barr's exploration of the natural theology of the Bible is an outspoken and sustained polemic against the theology of Karl Barth (or of 'Barthianism', 'Barthian theologians', 'the Barthian tradition'). Barth's claim that Reformation theology implies a rejection of natural theology is said to be 'simply preposterous' (9). In attacking modern Protestantism for its reliance on natural theology, Barth misunderstood it (9). Indeed, his antipathy towards natural theology was actually *derived* from the liberal Protestantism of Ritschl, Herrmann and Harnack, rather than from the Bible (106). 'His theology was at bottom a dogmatic-philosophical system, in which the biblical exegetical foundation, however many pages it occupied, was logically incidental' (131). 'The long-term effect of Barthianism has been to create a wider gap between theology and the Bible than there was before' (202). It is Barth's rejection of conventional biblical scholarship that is to blame for 'the countless pages of wearisome, inept, and futile exegesis in the *Church Dogmatics*, especially in the later volumes . . . Some of the most truly ridiculous and useless pieces of biblical interpretation in this century came from the Barthian tradition, and it was precisely the false intellectual assurance that that theology offered that was the cause of their ludicrousness' (203). Despite Barth's opposition to Nazi ideology, his theology betrays the influence of the context in which it was formed: 'Features of aggressiveness and totalitarianism are manifest in the Barthian tradition, and its own rejection of natural theology, which carried with it an inability to use open-minded and reasoned forms of discussion, easily led on to a dependence on rhetorical and propagandist means of persuasion' (116). 'Barthianism managed to combine the dreariest conservative traditionalism with the same unseemly boastfulness about its conformity with recent trends that it had castigated in the liberals' (117). It might be said of 'the Barthian movement' that, in Pauline language, 'Professing themselves to be wise, they became fools . . . [they are] whisperers, backbiters' (125). Intense personal experience is from time to time obscurely intimated: 'The great ultimate disappointment about Barthianism is that, when it claimed to be able to tell us, richly and fully, about God, as a matter of Christian faith, we found that we learned nothing about God from it, but only a mass of historical assertions, or sometimes plain myths, which were intended to convince us that Barthianism as an intellectual system was right' (132). We asked for bread, and they gave us a stone.[28]

Barth's theology of creation is important for the present argument because of his insistence that there is no knowledge of God as creator independent of knowledge of God as reconciler (and vice versa): the God who created heaven and earth is no other than the triune God disclosed in Jesus as Father, Son and Holy Spirit. Creation for Barth too is, in the first instance, creation in the beginning: 'The distinctive element in creation consists in the fact that it comes first among God's works. The Bible begins with it and so does the creed' (*Church Dogmatics*, III/1, 42–43). Yet, 'as God's first work, again according to the witness of Scripture and the confession, creation stands in a series, in an indissolubly real connection, with God's further works' (43). God has decreed that the final goal of creation is the covenant of grace, and this 'requires a stage corresponding to it, the existence of man and his whole world'; thus, 'creation must not be separated from this context' (44). It must be shown that 'the whole circumference of the content of Scripture, including the truth and reality of the creation of the world by God, can be understood only from this centre' (24). This point must be maintained in opposition to the biblicism that absolutizes and fetishizes the individual text – a biblicism that may well take the form of a historical-critical hermeneutic in which any personal concern with the truth-claims of the texts is absent. In all of its forms, 'conservative' and 'radical', biblicism misrepresents the Christian Bible in its twofold, canonical form by regarding Jesus 'merely as one object of its witness among others. It regards the Bible as a repository of all sorts and degrees of pious knowledge. It knows nothing of the triunity of the God whose revelation and work are attested. It may also confess a belief in the triunity of God in isolated connections, but it does not take it seriously. It thinks it can talk about God the Father and Creator on the basis of Scripture, i.e. in the light of this or that passage of Scripture, without allowing itself to be taught by Scripture, i.e. the whole of Scripture, to know the Father through the Son, the Creator through the Redeemer' (24). Barth's hermeneutic simply follows the old hermeneutical rule that the individual text must be understood within – and not against – its context, the part in the light of the whole. It differs from the historical-critical hermeneutic in assuming that the Christian Bible in its canonical form does actually *exist* as a structured whole – an assumption integral to the concept of 'canon', which (*pace* Barr) entails far more than a mere list of books.[29]

Like all other exegetes, Barth is not always convincing in exegetical practice, and it is no harder to find examples of inconsistent, unclear or implausible exegesis in the *Church Dogmatics* than it is anywhere else. Nor do the many volumes of this *magnum opus* maintain a consistently high level of theological discussion. As in all other theologies, there are high points and low points, and some of the latter may possibly occur in the discussions of 'natural theology'. But this merely means that – again like all other exegetes and theologians – Barth's work must be used with discrimination. It does not require the rigid, fanatical adherence to a single party line characteristic of the nightmarish 'Barthianism' evoked by Barr. Barr's polemic seeks to enforce an either/or decision for or against Barth and 'Barthianism', and it is therefore in danger of replicating precisely the totalitarianism that it wants to unmask and denounce in its opponent. Such tactics effectively rule out every attempt critically to assimilate whatever is to be learned from Barth as theologian and exegete. Instead, there is only the stark choice between two uninteresting and unimaginative responses to Barth's rich and many-sided theology, one declaring itself to be *for* it, the other *against* it. If there existed, in Scotland in the years following the War, a 'Barthianism' which came to seem oppressive and intellectually bankrupt to at least one of those influenced by it, there seems little to be gained by returning to this scene of earlier disappointment in order to denounce the oppressor and to vindicate the act of self-liberation that occurred at that time.

Disregarding Barr's polemics, however, it is still an open and a proper question whether the Bible itself assumes or teaches that a knowledge of God as creator may be obtained from the created order, without reference to God's self-disclosure in Israel and in Jesus; whether it relativizes the distinctive thing it wishes to say by postulating as its own foundation a universal knowledge of God as creator, which it merely confirms, before proceeding to say that God is more than just the creator; whether there can be a true and appropriate understanding of the world as God's creation where creation is abstracted from its biblical context as the beginning of the history of God's covenant. It is not a question of hunting for individual texts that will 'open the gate' to 'some kind of natural theology'. There are, perhaps, a number of texts which, as they stand, could permit one to develop a 'natural theology' whose definition is left so conveniently vague. But it is only a biblicistic and legalistic thinking that operates along these lines. The real question is whether or not it is granted that the Christian canon exists, that it has a centre, that this centre is the self-disclosure in Jesus of the triune God who is creator, reconciler and redeemer, and that an exegesis of a particular text cannot be regarded as *theologically* normative if it conflicts with what must be said at this centre.

Yet the Bible also consists of individual texts, and there can be no evasion of exegesis. I shall therefore return to the three passages already discussed, to look more closely at their treatment of the theme of the knowledge of God as creator.

(i) Paul in Athens (Acts 17)

When Paul preaches to the Athenians in the middle of the Areopagus, it is evident that there exists between Paul and his audience an *Anknüpfungspunkt* ('point of contact', a crucial concept in the Barth–Brunner debate about natural theology), in the form of the Greek language. This language offers him a vocabulary that is 'religious' as well as 'secular'. Even if what he has to say is genuinely 'new' (vv. 19, 21), this newness cannot be absolute; for his message would then be unintelligible and incommunicable, an instance of *glossolalia*. Initially, prior to his appearance in the Areopagus, this had indeed appeared to be a danger. Epicurean and Stoic philosophers meet him, and decide that he is a *spermologos* (v. 18) – one who 'picks up seeds', like a bird, a 'gossip, chatterer, babbler, one who makes his living picking up scraps', in this case scraps of alien religions: 'he seems to be a proclaimer of foreign divinities [*xenōn daimoniōn kataggeleus*]', divinities oddly named *Iēsous* and *Anastasis* (v. 18).[30] Yet communication can occur, even about foreign gods, and the Athenians are confident of their ability to grasp what is at present 'new' (v. 19) and 'strange' (v. 20) if it is adequately explained to them. Language (here, the Greek language) promises, in principle, universal intelligibility; there is nothing so new and strange that it cannot be made at least partially comprehensible through dialogue. Paul, commissioned to preach the gospel to Jews and Gentiles, cannot but share this confidence in language as a medium of communicating even the newness and strangeness of his gospel. As he addresses the Areopagus, he must therefore provide his hearers with enough of the familiar linguistic landmarks to enable them to orient themselves in relation to the unfamiliar things he does with them. Thus, this stranger with his strange message begins his speech by speaking not of foreign divinities but of the religion of the Athenians themselves. His audience is invited to see itself through the eyes of this foreigner, and the resulting picture is not unflattering. The speaker has concluded that they are *deisidaimonesteroi*, remarkably zealous in their reverence for the gods (v. 22), thereby indicating that their own religious practices and traditions have some bearing on the topic of his discourse. This conclusion is based on the observation that, among their various *sebasmata*, there was to be found an altar to an unknown god (*agnōstō theō*, v. 23). What zeal for the gods, what reverence, to have ensured that even unknown, unnamed divinities receive their measure of human tribute along with the familiar, known members of the pantheon! In this altar, with its dedication and the rites presumably performed there, the speaker discovers the 'point of contact' he needs in order to inaugurate his discourse: the unknown god is to be made known. An existing, linguistically-organized knowledge of divinity is to be subjected to drastic revision; and yet the revision could not take place without the existing knowledge. The Greek language already conveys the knowledge that there is said to exist an unseen reality, that of *theos* or *to theion* (v. 29), that this reality is partially *gnōstos* and partially *agnōstos*, that this difference is reflected in different and perhaps conflicting human religious traditions, and that this reality requires not only speculation but also action in the form of rites connected with particular places and objects and motivated by a sense of reverence and piety. If the speaker to the Areopagus is to make intelligible the strange and new things he has to say

(vv. 19–20), then he must speak not in a foreign tongue but in the language of his audience, operating within and in relation to the *epistēmē* of divinity that this language makes available.

The availability of a certain vocabulary organized around terms such as *theos* and *to theion* means that, even where strange things (*xenizonta tina*, v. 20) are asserted about this reality, there will exist a formal analogy between what is now said and what has previously been said: for the topic of conversation is the same. It may be 'strange' to hear the proposition *not-p* asserted of *to theion* where the received view is *p*, but the common concern with *to theion* presupposes a formal analogy between the two propositions that is precisely the condition of their difference. Yet the analogy constituted by the use of a common vocabulary can take a variety of forms. A new assertion about *to theion* may simply repeat a position already acknowledged within the existing *epistēmē* – in the form, for example, of the various well-known assertions about *to theion* associated with Epicurean Stoic philosophers (v. 18). Having taken up a familiar position within the existing *epistēmē*, one might then propose to supplement this with something new; for an *epistēmē* – a linguistically-organized field of knowledge – is a fluid, shifting entity whose internal organization is always a matter of negotiation and renegotiation.[31] Alternatively, the new discourse on *to theion* might adopt a confrontational approach, denying what is generally asserted and asserting what is generally denied, on the basis perhaps of an 'alien' discourse on *to theion*; and that is what is to be expected in this case, for the speaker to the Areopagus appears to be *xenōn daimoniōn kataggeleus* (v. 18). This antithetical relationship to an existing *epistēmē* is compatible with an eclectic use of propositions drawn from it. It is a simple extension of the necessary use of individual terms such as *theos* or *to theion* to redeploy an assertion derived from the existing *epistēmē* such as *tou gar kai genos esmen* (v. 28).

The universal claim of the Christian gospel presupposes its universal intelligibility, that is, its translatability into any existing human language. Paul's discourse to the Areopagus rests on the presupposition expressed in the Pentecost story, that the mighty works of God may be announced in the tongues of Parthians, Medes, Elamites, residents of Mesopotamia, and therefore also in the tongue of the Greeks. How could the apostles be Jesus' witnesses 'to the end of the earth' (Acts 1.8) except on this presupposition? The gospel message is never a linguistic *creatio ex nihilo* but must always avail itself of existing linguistic resources and therefore of an existing knowledge. There must always be an 'analogy of language' between the 'new teaching' (Acts 17.19) and the old teaching, between the 'strange things' (v. 20) and the familiar things. Yet it makes a considerable difference whether this relationship to existing language and knowledge is understood in terms of *repetition and supplementation* on the one hand or *antithesis and eclecticism* on the other. In the first case, an existing knowledge is given retrospective sanction by the gospel, which presents itself as the completion of that which already exists. Existing knowledge is deficient only in its incompleteness. In the second case, existing knowledge is declared to consist largely in distortion and falsehood. Certain fragments can be rescued from the overthrow of the old *epistēmē* and redeployed in the service of the new one, but this does not alter the fundamental fact that the old *epistēmē* has suffered an invasion that has penetrated to its very heart, subverting it from within, seizing control of its constituent elements and either discarding them or placing them at the disposal of 'alien divinities'. On this view, the formalized politeness of the speaker to the Areopagus would be that of the would-be invader, representing a new and potent threat from the east.

If Acts 17 is to provide scriptural support for the project of a natural theology that would provide a basis and a hermeneutic for the Christian gospel, then Paul's address would have to consist of a *repetition* of what is already known, supplemented by distinctively Christian ideas which presuppose and complete this existing knowledge. On this view, 'the specifically Christian content of the speech is presented only in the last two verses' (M. Dibelius), where we learn of the man whom God raised from the dead in order that he might be our judge, and of the consequent need for repentance.[32] Parallels to everything else that is said here can be found in Graeco-Roman authors. When Paul speaks of a God who is Lord of heaven and earth, who does not live in shrines, who is not far from each one of us, and who cannot be depicted through human artistry, he is repeating what is already known. The age of enlightenment has long since dawned in Athens, bringing with it a fundamental rift between the popular religiosity that naïvely perpetuates the traditional stories and rites and the philosophical knowledge that these things are at best only a parable pointing to the One who truly is, immortal, immutable and impassible, the unmoved mover who is the ground of being. Only in the sudden reference to judgment and Jesus' resurrection do Dionysius, Damaris and the others hear the new thing that supplements and completes their existing knowledge, drawing them into a Christian faith that incorporates former knowledge rather than discarding it.[33]

This interpretation of Acts 17 can avail itself of an impressive range of material, assembled by accredited scholarly procedures so as to create the impression of an almost unanswerable case.[34] If scholarship discovers that something very similar to what is said here was independently enunciated by Aelius Aristides or Zeno of Cytium, how can one avoid the conclusion that its role within Paul's discourse is simply to repeat what is already known, reassuring the audience that what is 'new' and 'strange' is only a slight extension of what is already old and familiar? The scholarship capable of deploying this material does not expect to encounter dissent. Yet, preoccupied with its highly successful quest for parallels, it neglects to *read* the text it is supposedly illuminating. In this text, we read nothing of a Hellenistic enlightenment that has already anticipated the gospel's critique of popular religion. Although Stoic and Epicurean philosophers are mentioned (v. 18), the *andres Athenaioi* (v. 22) of the Areopagus are addressed as a single group corporately responsible for the many-sided religious practice of their city. The altar to an unknown god is a sign not of an individual act of piety but of the remarkable piety of the city as a whole. Paul's true feelings about Athenian religiosity are disclosed in the narrator's disclosure that 'his spirit was provoked within him as he saw that the city was full of idols [*kateidōlon ousan tēn polin*]' (v. 16); but there is no indication that, when he encountered Epicurean and Stoic philosophers in the *agora* (vv. 17–18), he and they hailed one another as allies in a common crusade against the errors of popular religion. The narrator presents the religious life of Athens as a seamless web, capable of assimilating the immanent critique of Epicureans or Stoics without a fundamental crisis of practice or belief.

The altar 'to an unknown god' serves as a point of contact between Paul and his audience, but not in such a way as to establish a common ground on which both parties can agree. On the contrary, this small fragment of Athenian religious life is identified as the weak point which makes it possible to destroy the entire edifice. Athenian *deisidaimonia* has constructed a remarkable range of *eidōla* and *sebasmata*, devoted to the service of gods whose names and identities are known. And it has gone further still, acknowledging that the sphere of *to theion* is only partially known and that in its shadowy hinterland there may be deities which, though unknown, are still deserving of human reverence and worship. But what if the secret of the whole system were contained in the tiny portion of Athens, easily overlooked, that is dedicated to the worship of an unknown god? What if the unknown god turned out not to be merely a distant relative of the gods of Olympus, but a god who is greater than and other than these deities, separated from them by an infinite qualitative difference? The altar to an unknown god speaks of the potentially radical crisis that might befall both the known gods and the human service that is devoted to them. What would become of the *eidōla* and the *sebasmata* if that possibility became real? An obscure altar is the point at which the deconstruction of the Athenian sacred canopy can begin; and that is the only sense in which it constitutes a 'point of contact' between Paul and his audience.[35]

A purely immanent deconstruction would identify only an obscure possibility. Paul, however, proclaims a reality. The god who is unknown to the Athenians is known to him; and this god is identified without apology or qualification as 'the God who made the world and everything in it', who is 'Lord of heaven and earth' (v. 24). There is nothing to indicate that the audience is already familiar with this god. On the contrary, the identification serves only to prepare for a critique of assumptions that are fundamental to Athenian piety: that deity somehow 'dwells in temples made by human hands [*en cheiropoiētois naois*]' and that within these temples it is the object of human service and devotion (vv. 24–25). In this radical doctrine of creation, 'making' is the prerogative of the creator God alone, who 'made [*epoiēsen*]' all things (v. 24) in a sense that precludes any reciprocal 'making' accomplished by 'human hands' (*ouk en cheiropoiētois naois, oude hupo cheirōn anthrōpōn*). None of the gods served in the temples is the creator of heaven and earth. They are finite beings, bounded (as humans are) by their relationships to one another and to the world, and the religious practice which assumes a reciprocity between finite divinities and finite human action is therefore internally consistent. Yet a radical understanding of the nature of *to theion* would have to reject this practice in its entirety, on the grounds that God is the one upon whom all things are dependent for their existence and persistence; he is the 'Lord of heaven and earth' who 'gives to all people life and breath and everything' (v. 25). If that is what the word 'God' means, then the human service of finite deities will have to cease; the very idea of 'a finite deity' would become impossible. Within the realm of *to theion*, there is no room for the multiplication of lesser deities and their cults. There can only be one God, for the knowledge of God the creator does not permit a knowledge of any other gods.

This is not the voice of a philosophically enlightened Hellenism, whose postulate of an ultimate unity poses no radical threat to the practices of reciprocity between humans and finite deities, however much it may claim to see into or beyond these traditional practices. The only cult of a radically exclusive deity is Judaism, and it is the Jewish doctrine that the creation of heaven and earth is integral to the meaning of 'God' that comes to expression at the beginning of Paul's address. 'Heaven and earth' alludes to Gen. 1.1 and 2.4, and the reference to God as source of *zōē kai pnoē kai ta panta* (Acts 17.25) recalls Gen. 2.7, where God formed (*eplasen*) a man from the dust of the ground and bestowed on him the breath of life (*pnoēn zōēs*), so that he became a living being (*psuchēn zōsan*). As for the doctrine that the divine–human relationship is radically non-reciprocal, that too is Jewish: 'If I were hungry, I would not tell you; for the world and all that is in it is mine. Do I eat the flesh of bulls, or drink the blood of goats?' (Ps. 50.12–13).[36] And yet even Judaism proves unable to escape the notion of divine–human reciprocity that determines the religious practice of the Athenians. Opposition to the idea of a divine dwelling in temples made with human hands (*cheiropoiētoi*) may therefore be directed not only against pagan temples (Acts 17.24–25) but also against the temple of the one true God in Jerusalem: Solomon built it despite the fact that 'the Most High does not dwell in places made with hands [*ouch ho hupsistos en cheiropoiētois katoikei*]' (Acts 7.48), and this relativizing even of the one true temple is confirmed by a quotation from Isa. 66.1–2 (Acts 7.49–50). Over against all theories of divine–human reciprocity, and all institutions that embody those theories, Paul's address to the Areopagus opens with a distinctively Christian assertion of the sole divinity of the creator whose relation to the world is to be understood in terms of sheer giving (*autos didous pasi . . . ta panta*, Acts 17.25). It is assumed throughout that this God is 'unknown' to the audience.

The roots of this radical theology of creation in Jewish scripture are confirmed by the claim that God 'made from one every nation of men to live on all the face of the earth [*epi pantos prosōpou tēs gēs*]' (v. 26), a summary of Gen. 1–11. Following the story of the origins of the human race from Adam to the sons of Noah, Gen. 10.32 refers for the first time to 'the nations' which 'spread abroad on the earth after the flood'. In the Babel story, it is said that 'the Lord scattered them abroad from there over the face of all the earth [*epi prosōpon pasēs tēs gēs*]' (Gen. 11.8), in language that apparently underlies Acts 17.26. As regards the allocating of the temporal and spatial limits of the various nations (*horisas prostetagmenous kairous kai tas horothesias tēs katoikias autōn*, v. 26), Deut. 32.8 similarly tells how, 'when the Most High separated the nations and scattered the sons of Adam [*huious Adam*], he established the boundaries of the nations [*horia ethnōn*] . . .' (In this passage, LXX – like Acts 17.26 – traces the nations back to Adam, taking the Hebrew *'ādām* as a proper name.) In the following verse, however, Paul goes beyond the Old Testament in claiming that this providential arrangement was motivated by concern for ultimate human well-being: it took place 'that they should seek God, so as perhaps to touch and find him [*ei ara ge psēlaphēseian auton kai heuroien*] – though indeed he is not far from each one of us, for in him we live and move and exist' (v. 27). Despite the emphasis on the beneficent divine intention and the divine nearness, touching and finding cannot be taken for granted. The language is tentative because a seeking and finding of God among the nations is not something for which there can be unproblematic evidence; instead, it is an extrapolation derived from the universality of God's will for human salvation as disclosed in Christ. Thus, when Peter is commanded to disregard the laws of cleanness and uncleanness and to preach the gospel to the Gentiles, he concludes from this that 'in every nation any one who fears him and does what is right is acceptable to him' (Acts 10.35): the notion of a prevenient divine grace operating among the Gentiles and preceding the dawning of the Christian gospel is not a general truth but a conclusion drawn from the gospel itself.[37]

In Acts 17.27 this conclusion is expressed only tentatively because, after all, there is little sign that any seeking and finding has occurred in Athens; the city is full of idols (v. 16), and even its acknowledgment of unknown divinity is of only limited significance. On the other hand, certain of the Greek poets have uttered sentiments about God that may be accepted as truthful, especially if they are set within a Christian context. One such is quoted in v. 28: 'For we are his offspring.' Is this modest statement a sign that seeking and finding has truly occurred? Perhaps it is; why should it not be? Yet it is drawn into its present context not in order to set the Christian gospel on the foundation of a prior natural theology, but in order to identify an internal inconsistency within Greek religious belief and practice. The quotation therefore leads directly into a critique of images: 'Being then God's offspring, we ought not to think that the Deity [*to theion*] is like gold, or silver, or stone, a representation by human art and imagination' (v. 29). The poets and philosophers may on occasion make statements which are *useful* to the preacher of the gospel, who is at liberty to draw upon them in an eclectic manner in the interests of communicating his strange and new message to his hearers, drawing them towards an understanding of the 'strange things' (*xenizonta tina*, v. 20) by way of what is familiar. If a theological rationale is required for this rhetorical strategy, it may be tentatively asserted, as an extrapolation from the gospel and therefore as a statement of faith, that through God's prevenient grace a seeking and a finding has occurred among the Gentiles, and that certain symptoms of this may perhaps be discerned. But nothing much may be built on this tentative discernment. It is not a foundation for the gospel, which must everywhere reckon not with a pure universal knowledge of God, given in and with human existence, but with idolatry, distortion and ignorance. On the contrary, the gospel is the foundation of the tentative hypothesis of a prevenient divine grace operating in spite of the universality of idolatry. The hypothesis does not merit independent treatment, in the form for example of a grand theory about the universal operation of a *logos spermatikos*.

To lay a foundation for the gospel in natural theology might mean to show the continuities between the age-long, universal human quest for God, with its occasional though partial moments of finding, and the moment of fulfilment through Christ, in which the restless longing of the human heart is finally stilled and perfect peace descends. But Paul does not offer his audience a sublimated eroticism of this kind. If God established the nations in order that, like Israel, they too might seek and perhaps find him, it remains the case that – in the light of a history of idolatry (v. 29) – the past, including the Greek past, must be characterized as 'times of ignorance' (*chronous tēs agnoias*, v. 30), which God mercifully 'overlooks'. The divine purpose that the nations should seek and find him is fulfilled 'now', in the divine call for universal repentance that issues from his act of raising Jesus from the dead to be our saviour and judge (vv. 30–31). The God who is not far from us, in whom we live and move and have our being, whose offspring we are, is the God who raised Jesus from the dead. In this act God 'gives proof to all' (*pistin paraschōn pasin*, v. 31) that humankind is oriented towards God as its goal, just as it derives its being from the creative act of God. The resurrection of Jesus is thus the universal revelation of the universal human relationship to a God who is the beginning and the end, the origin and the goal, of all existence. There can be no question of setting aside this universal revelation, even for a moment, in order to search for traces of another universal revelation in, for example, the Greek poets and philosophers. To do so would be a simple evasion of the divine command to repent that issues from the raising of Jesus.

As even the Epicurean and the Stoic philosophers of Athens were dimly aware, the content of the Christian gospel is nothing other than 'Jesus and the resurrection' (v. 18): there is disclosed here the end of God's ways with humankind, and therefore also the true significance of the beginning. That God created heaven and earth in the beginning cannot be adequately understood in isolation. To understand a beginning one must understood what it is that is begun, and such an understanding will remain open-ended and ambiguous without a knowledge of the end. If the raising of Jesus is the divine disclosure of the end, it must therefore also disclose the beginning; not in the sense that an understanding of the world as God's creation was impossible before Jesus (a possibility belied by the existence of Gen. 1), but in the sense that the full meaning of the concept of 'creation' includes a knowledge of the final goal for which creation was brought into being. In spanning the beginning and the end of God's history with humankind, Paul's Areopagus speech therefore cannot be seen as an exercise in natural theology with a concluding unscientific postscript derived from Christian faith. It is, simply, a proclamation of the Christian gospel – at Athens.

(ii) Paul to the Romans (Rom. 1)
In Acts 17.30, despite the preceding quotation from one of the poets (v. 28), the pre-Christian past is characterized in terms of an 'ignorance' (*agnoia*) that God is prepared to 'overlook'. In Rom. 1.19–20, on the other hand, we are told that all humans have been granted a knowledge of God's power and

deity through the created order, and that their rebellion against him is therefore inexcusable. Far from 'overlooking' their conduct, God responds to it by disclosing his 'wrath'. Do we have here one of those well-known 'contradictions' between the Paul of Acts and the Paul of the authentic letters?[38] To speak of a 'contradiction' is to postulate the impossibility of dialogue between texts. They simply confront one another, for all time, as hard, impermeable objects, one asserting one thing and the other asserting the contrary. The interpreter who establishes the contradiction may perhaps display some of this same hardness: for in establishing a 'contradiction' between canonical texts one is at the same time 'contradicting' the principle of non-contradiction that is implied in their canonicity. The contradiction between text and text is enclosed within the contradiction between interpreter and canon. While the presence of different texts within a canonical collection does not entail a freedom from tensions, it does imply that the canonical texts must at least remain on speaking terms and should not turn their backs on one another. We might suggest, therefore, that Paul's reference to 'times of ignorance' was motivated by the need to assert the radical newness of the present moment ('but now', Acts 17.30), the moment when, through Paul's preaching, the god worshipped as unknown during the times of ignorance became the known God, the creator who raised Jesus from the dead. Rom. 1.18–23, on the other hand, indicates that the 'natural' human relation to God is more than a simple, straightforward *agnoia*. Does this mean that God's universal disclosure of the goal of creation in the raising of Christ is preceded by and grounded in a prior universal self-disclosure given in creation? Paradoxically, the Acts text which speaks of 'ignorance' prior to Christ also hints at something like a true knowledge of God, occurring through God's prevenient grace, whereas the Romans text which speaks of a universal self-disclosure of God in creation knows only of the violent distortion of the knowledge of God that takes the form of idolatry.

In Rom. 1, the question of the knowledge of God the creator arises in the context of a reference to the wrath of God: 'The wrath of God is revealed from heaven against all the ungodliness and wickedness of those who by their wickedness suppress the truth [*tōn tēn alētheian en adikia katechontōn*]' (v. 18). The following verses elaborate the claim that humans possess yet suppress the truth by describing the universal divine self-disclosure in the created order (vv. 19–20) and its equally universal distortion into idolatry (vv. 21–23). The universal human contempt for the truth of the incomparable divinity of the creator renders humankind 'without excuse' (v. 20) and thus subject to 'the wrath of God' (v. 18). That humans disobey God knowingly is, it seems, a necessary presupposition of the concept of the wrath of God. At the judgment every mouth will be stopped (3.19), for no one can plead ignorance. If it is true of Jews and Greeks alike that 'no one understands, no one seeks for God', and that 'there is no fear of God before their eyes' (3.11, 18), the behaviour of those who sin 'without the law' is no more excusable than the behaviour of those who sin 'under the law' (2.12). All knew the truth, yet all have suppressed it. When it is said that 'what can be known of God is manifest to them' and that they 'know God' (1.19, 21), it is therefore a very strange knowing that is spoken of. So deeply is this knowledge of God suppressed that there can be no question of regaining it by a simple act of recollection; for a darkness has fallen upon the senseless human heart, and true wisdom has been distorted into a folly masquerading as wisdom (1.21–22). In order for the human heart to find its own way out of the labyrinth into which it has wandered, some small part of it would have to have been preserved intact from the illusory perceptions reflected back to it from the distorting mirrors with which it has surrounded itself. It would have to have been capable of recognizing its perceptions of self and world as illusions and distortions and of breaking free from them in order to undertake the arduous journey out into the fresh air and sunlight. Yet, in its own terms, the wisdom built upon the folly of suppressing the truth of the creator makes excellent sense, and the senseless human heart is well content with it. This wisdom, founded upon folly, is expressed in the project of human religion, the creation of images of the unknown through an arbitrary human artistry that takes as its pattern the reality of the creatures: they 'exchanged the glory of the immortal God for images resembling mortal men or birds or animals or reptiles' (v. 23). In this situation, a 'natural theology' would merely be a natural extension of the wisdom that is founded upon folly, a sophisticated divinizing of creaturely realities.[39]

It is not yet clear how it happens that the truth of the human situation can be grasped in such a way that illusions and distortions are clearly seen as such. Obviously this does happen, for otherwise this text could not have been written. It is also not clear how and why it is that the empirical reality of 'idolatry' is interpreted as a symptom of the suppression and distortion of a universal knowledge of God as creator. Although the divine–human relationship is empirically observable only in its distorted form, it is evidently possible to speak of this relationship abstractly, in a pure form as yet undistorted by human folly. Thus, we learn in Rom. 1.19–20 that to be human is to be the recipient of God's self-disclosure of his invisible, eternal and omnipotent divinity. This self-disclosure occurs not in an unmediated moment of vision but through the mediation of created beings. Yet the indirectness of this self-disclosure does not prevent the divine–human relationship from being fully personal in character. The notion of an alien deity, inaccessible in his inscrutable power, is not to be read into this passage, for such a notion stems from the false wisdom of those who suppress the truth. In fact, the authentic human response to this divine self-disclosure through created beings is not to flee from an inscrutable power but to honour God as God and to give thanks to him (v. 21). Since God's self-disclosure is not a mere general fact about the world but aims at personal relationship with humankind, thankful acknowledgment of the good gifts of 'life and breath and everything' (Acts 17.25) is the human response it necessarily seeks to evoke. To be human is to be that creature which – unlike stones, birds or reptiles – knows its own being and the being of its world as the gifts of the divine creator. Furthermore, it is to be that creature which not only knows the divine ground of being but is conscious of this knowledge itself as a gift of God. The primary gift of being has been bestowed on all creatures, but the secondary gift of a true knowledge of being has been granted to the human creature alone; or rather, the single gift of the being of this particular creature includes within itself this unique dimension of a true knowledge of being that is at the same time a truthful relationship to the divine source of being, expressed in worship and thankfulness. A true 'natural theology' would be a reflection on the prior reality of this 'natural' relationship between the divine creator and the human creature.

The problem for such a 'natural theology' is that the human creature whose relationship to God is given in and with creation simply does not exist in this pure and abstract form. If there had been any question of partial realizations of this ideal, of positive counter-examples to offset the general negativity, this abstract portrayal of the divine–human relationship would not occur in an exposition of the universal character of the wrath of God. Instead, it would take the form of an exhortation, a proclamation of the gospel that the good life corresponding to the original structures of human existence is still accessible, despite the prevalence of human wickedness and folly, if we will only come to our senses and grasp it. Yet such a gospel would merely be another production of the folly that masquerades as wisdom, and it is not Paul's intention that any such abstract gospel should be preached. That does not mean that this 'ideal' picture of the divine–human relationship hovers uncertainly between reality and unreality: precisely in analysing the human condition as he does, Paul demonstrates that he himself speaks from a position of relative freedom from the entanglements of the wisdom that is founded upon folly. But it is not yet clear what this position is, or how it relates to the abstract position of the unfallen human creature who naturally knows the divine creator. Paul is aware that the critic's posture of superiority over those who are criticized is undermined by his or her deep complicity in that which is criticized (2.1), and his own analysis of the human situation cannot mean that he has adopted the general role of the critic, proud of his or her ability to see through human illusions to the realities concealed behind them. Paul also knows of a distinctively Jewish claim to have acquired through the Law of Moses that true knowledge of the human situation which makes it possible to expose falsehood (2.17–20); but, although Paul is himself a Jew (just as he is also a critic), it is not his Jewishness *per se* that enables him truthfully to assert the truth about the universal human suppression of the truth. The relative difference between Jews and Gentiles can no more be absolutized than the relative difference between the critic and the criticized: hidden connections and complicities undermine the claim to difference and bind the two sides together in a single web.

In fact, Paul has already explained, carefully and in some detail, how it is that he is able to write the truth about the universal human suppression of the truth. He is 'a slave of Jesus Christ, called to be an apostle, set apart for the gospel of God' (1.1). As such, he is 'under obligation both to Greeks and to barbarians, both to the wise and to the foolish' (1.14). And he is 'not ashamed of the gospel', since it is 'the power of God for salvation to everyone who has faith, to the Jew first and also to the Greek' (1.16). Paul is able to speak the truth about the universal human suppression of the truth not because he is in himself exempt from this indictment but because it is more fundamental to his being even than his participation in human fallenness that he is called by God in Jesus Christ, and that his own calling is a single moment in the comprehensive divine plan to extend salvation in Jesus Christ to Jews, Greeks and barbarians alike. He writes to those who have experienced the divine calling to 'belong to Jesus Christ' (1.6) as he has, and he can therefore write on the assumption that they will grasp and accept what he has to tell them. It is therefore on the basis of the existence of the Christian community, called to belong to Jesus Christ, that truth about human falsehood can be truly uttered and truly understood, not from the superior standpoint of the critic who is exempt from the indictment he or she pronounces but from the standpoint of those whose human fallenness has been overtaken by the grace of God in Jesus.[40]

For that reason, unlike those who suppress the truth, Paul is thankful to God. His thankfulness is not, however, the pure and abstract thankfulness of the unfallen human creature to the divine creator. 'I thank my God through Jesus Christ for all of you, because your faith is proclaimed in all the world' (1.8): if in the abstract unfallen world there can be thankfulness for the sheer fact of existence, in the concrete world of human fallenness it is cause for thankfulness that at particular locations – Rome, for example – there is clear evidence of the reality of 'the power of God for salvation', actualized through the human preaching of the gospel. Thankfulness can also relate to one's own self: 'Wretched man that I am! Who will deliver me from this body of death? Thanks be to God through Jesus Christ our Lord!' (7.24–25a). Here, the human existence that has become utterly problematic, deeply entangled in the labyrinth, is brought to recognize and to confess its own fallenness and to be thankful for the concrete divine act that has liberated it. Yet it is not the case that this concrete thankfulness to God 'through Jesus Christ' has *replaced* the abstract ideal of the thankfulness of the human creature to the divine creator. On the contrary, it is precisely here that what is otherwise abstract becomes concrete. The fallen human creature who gives thanks to God for reconciliation through Jesus Christ is still the creature of the divine creator; fallenness may entail a *subjective suppression* of the fact of createdness, but there cannot be any *objective loss* of createdness. In giving thanks to God through Jesus Christ, one is thankful for createdness in and with thankfulness for reconciliation; for to experience 'peace with God through our Lord Jesus Christ' (5.1) is to have attained, by a circuitous route, the relationship with God which is the ultimate goal of human createdness. Our createdness might have ended in the nightmare of final alienation between creator and creature. That it did not do so makes it possible and necessary to be thankful for the createdness that has issued in reconciliation in and with our thankfulness for reconciliation itself. In this way, the thankfulness which is the human creature's proper response to the divine creator is actualized – not in isolation but in the context of grateful acknowledgment of the full scope of God's action on behalf of humankind as creator, reconciler and redeemer.

According to Paul, the intended thankfulness of the human creature to the divine creator is actualized only in and through Jesus Christ; otherwise it can only be said that 'although they knew God they did not honour him as God or give thanks to him' (1.21). If, apart from Jesus, the thankfulness of the human creature to the divine creator is abstract and unreal, it seems that the same cannot be said of the universal divine self-disclosure that is uniquely bestowed on human creatures, unlike other creatures, together with being itself. That general revelation must be a reality: for it is said quite definitely, without qualification or evasiveness, that 'what can be known about God is plain to them, because God has shown it to them' (1.19), indicating that the general revelation must – in some sense – have been subjectively perceived. Yet no attempt is made to recover this primal revelation through recollection, and there is therefore not the slightest indication that it could ever constitute an alternative or a rival to the universal revelation of 'the righteousness of God through faith in Jesus Christ to all who believe' (3.22). The effect of the primal revelation was, simply and solely, its own distortion into idolatry. It can be said of this revelation as of the divine commandment that, through sin, that which 'promised life proved to be death to me' (7.10). In abstraction, both the primal revelation and the law of God might seem to have failed;

concretely, the true knowledge and life that they intend are fulfilled in Christ through the Spirit. Retrospectively, the primal revelation that underlies and is distorted by the phenomena of human religion can be understood as pointing towards the universal scope of God's concern for human salvation presupposed in the preaching of the gospel of Jesus Christ.[41]

This does not open the gates to a natural theology that *begins* from the phenomena of human religion, for the negative verdict on these phenomena is a conclusion drawn from the content of the gospel itself. Natural theology can happily avail itself of the Pauline description of the primal revelation, but it will be baffled by its Pauline context within an analysis of the wrath of God. Unlike Paul, it will be interested in uncovering the particles of truth it thinks it can find even in idolatry; traces that prove that, contrary to Paul, a knowledge of God's eternal power and deity has never been wholly lost and can even now be brought back to life, without reference to Jesus. Such a project can find in Rom. 1 only a pretext.

(iii) The praise of the creator (Ps. 104)
In Ps. 104, Yahweh is praised not as the God of salvation but solely as the creator. In vivid mythological language, he is addressed as 'thou . . . who coverest thyself with light as with a garment, who hast stretched out the heavens like a tent, who hast laid the beams of thy chambers on the waters, who makest the clouds thy chariot, who ridest on the wings of the wind . . .' (vv. 2–3). The context suggests that the 'waters' in question are those of Gen. 1.6–7, the heavenly waters above the firmament (cf. Rev. 4.6; 15.2), in which case what is described here is the creation of the upper world, 'heaven', God's own dwelling-place. Having established a place for himself, God turns his attention to the lower world. The earth is set firmly on its foundations, and it is then inundated with water, which – as in the days of Noah – covers even the mountains (vv. 5–6). But this is only temporary, for 'at thy rebuke they fled, at the sound of thy thunder they took to flight', and 'the mountains rose, the valleys sank down to the place which thou didst appoint for them' (vv. 7–8), secure from the threat of any further inundation (v. 9). Having described the primeval divine acts that established the foundations for life on earth, the rest of the psalm meditates on the continuing divine creative activity in the present. This may be described directly, in language addressed to God ('Thou makest springs to gush forth in the valleys' [v. 10]), or indirectly, in language that describes the being of things without explicit reference to their divine source ('By them the birds of the air have their habitation, they sing among the branches' [v. 12]). Human life enters the scene unobtrusively, in parallelism with the cattle: 'Thou dost cause the grass to grow for the cattle, and plants for man to cultivate, that he may bring forth food from the earth'

(v. 14). Although the good gifts of wine, oil and bread are noted, there is here no particular sense that human being is the pinnacle of creation. It is not said that humans are little less than God, that God crowns them with glory and honour, or that he has given them dominion over all other living creatures, as it is in Ps. 8.5–8. In Ps. 104, human existence is described – or describes itself – with becoming modesty. It is not of such absorbing interest that, having introduced this topic, the psalmist finds himself unable to move on to other topics. On the contrary, the focus immediately shifts to the varied divine provision for birds and animals: the stork, the wild goats, the badgers, the young lions (vv. 16–22). The creatures of the sea are briefly but admiringly mentioned (v. 25), and the taming of this potentially hostile sphere is implied by the reference to 'ships' which appear to pass over it in safety, quite unmolested by 'Leviathan' (v. 26). From this point on, general statements about the dependence of all living things upon God replace the more specific earlier statements (vv. 27–30), and the psalm closes with a series of invocations in which the psalmist gives voice to the joy that has suffused the entire psalm (vv. 31–35).

Can this text be regarded as an early testimony to the possibility of a 'natural theology' within the faith of Israel, even in pre-Hellenistic days? In other words, does this psalm enunciate a knowledge of God that arises solely out of his works in creation, without reference to his covenantal relationship with Israel? In fact, the question of a 'natural theology' became acute only in the encounter with Hellenism, and it would be anachronistic to apply this terminology to Ps. 104 without qualification. Yet it might be possible to argue that texts such as this provide some kind of scriptural legitimation for later, more conscious experimentation with natural theology. The question is therefore how we are to understand the absence from this text of reference to the distinctive relationship between Yahweh and Israel.

The name 'Yahweh' is in fact used ten times in this text (vv. 1, 16, 24, 31, 33–35), and it is 'Yahweh my God' (v. 1) who is addressed throughout as 'thou'. The more general term 'God' (*'elōhîm*), which might seem more appropriate to divine activity not specifically oriented towards Israel, occurs on its own only in v. 21, where it is said that the young lions seek their food 'from God'. Yahweh is the object of the exhortation to bless that the psalmist addresses to his own soul at the outset of the psalm (v. 1). He is addressed as 'my God' and his greatness is celebrated (v. 2). Among his innumerable works (v. 24) the 'trees of Yahweh' are singled out. In the final verses of the psalm, reference is made to his own glory and joy (v. 31) and to the praise and joy he evokes in his worshippers (vv. 33–35). There is little sign here that the proper name 'Yahweh' is used in a way fundamentally distinct from the use of this name elsewhere; on the contrary, the language associated here with this name is entirely characteristic of the psalter. And if the name 'Yahweh' here refers to the God whose praises are sung throughout the psalter, then the attempt to isolate this psalm from its context within the psalter becomes problematic; it becomes implausible to suppose that the name 'Yahweh' refers here to a God whose activity is confined to creation and who is generally known beyond the confines of Israel. How could the orderliness and the beauty of the created world reveal that the name of its creator is Yahweh? This name also distinguishes the contents of this psalm from the closer or more distant parallels that may be found in the literatures of other peoples. Even if the literature of, say, Egypt contained a text identical to this psalm except for the substitution of another divine name for 'Yahweh', it could not be said that this psalm articulated a general knowledge of God derived from the created order; for everything in it stands or falls with the identification of the 'thou' whose creatures are celebrated in it with Yahweh, the creator who is also the God of Israel, the object of the praises of Israel alone. It is characteristic of the semantics of biblical language that the particularity of this unsubstitutable divine name is emphatically maintained.[42]

If in Ps. 104 the exclusive focus on creation has nothing to do with 'natural theology', a literary explanation might be more helpful. It is characteristic of a number of the psalms of praise that they demarcate a particular sphere of Yahweh's manifold, universal activity for their reflection, not because the psalmist believes that this sphere alone is theologically significant but in order to ensure the literary unity of their poems. This is the case in each of Pss. 103 to 107. Ps. 103 celebrates the mercies of the God of steadfast love and forgiveness. Ps. 105 praises God for preserving and guiding his people from the time of the patriarchs until the entry into Canaan. In less optimistic vein, Ps. 106 gives thanks that God has maintained his covenant with his people despite their long history of rebellion against him. Ps. 107 reflects on various experiences of Yahweh as redeemer. The fact that Ps. 104 focuses exclusively on creation has more to do with aesthetics than with its author's idiosyncratic theology. It would be utterly lacking in literary sensitivity to claim that the more optimistic account of God's history with Israel in Ps. 105 'conflicts with' the more pessimistic account in Ps. 106, and that the respective authors represent 'fundamentally opposing views' of the national history. Similarly, it is unnecessary and implausible to argue that the author of Ps. 104 is 'uninterested' in Yahweh's covenant-relationship with Israel and that his theology is fundamentally different from that of his colleagues. The author is 'uninterested' in Yahweh's covenant-relationship with Israel only within the confines of this particular act of literary production. In other contexts, he might have been as interested in this topic as anyone; indeed, there is no reason why he should not also have been the author of any or all of Pss. 103 and 105–107.

The literary relationship between Pss. 104 and 103 is especially close, considering the difference of subject-matter. Both begin and end with an identical self-exhortation, 'Bless the Lord, O my soul' (*bārªkî naphshî 'eth-yhwh*, 103.1, 2, 22; 104.1, 35), which does not occur anywhere else in the psalter. Both reflect on the fact of transience. In language that recalls Isa. 40.6–8, Ps. 103.15–16 tells how man's days 'are like grass; he flourishes like a flower of the field; for the wind passes over it and it is gone, and its place knows it no more'. Ps. 104.29, which compasses all animal life, tells how 'when thou takest away their breath, they die and return to their dust'. Ps. 103.19 states that 'Yahweh has established his throne in the heavens', and the construction of his heavenly dwelling-place is presented as the first of the divine acts of creation in Ps. 104.2–4. Ps. 103.20–21 exhorts God's 'angels' (*malākāyw*) and 'ministers' (*mªshārthāyw*) to 'bless the Lord', and the same terms are used when Ps. 104.4 speaks of the winds as Yahweh's 'messengers' and fire and flame as his 'ministers'. Both psalms refer to Yahweh's 'works' of creation (Pss. 103.22; 104.24, 31). Ps. 103 focuses on Yahweh's attribute of 'steadfast love' (*ḥesed*, vv. 4, 8, 11, 17), whereas in Ps. 104 it is the greatness of the creator and his works that is celebrated: 'O Yahweh my God, thou art very great!' (v. 1). But these respective divine attributes are obviously complementary. Ps. 103.19–22 knows of the greatness of the creator, who has established his throne in the heavens and whose kingdom rules over all, whereas in Ps. 104 the steadfast love of the redeemer (*haggō'ēl*, Ps. 103.4) is presupposed in the knowledge of the goodness of the creation which leads both the psalmist and Yahweh himself to rejoice (Ps. 104.31–34). The 'soul' exhorted in Ps. 104.1, 35 to 'bless Yahweh' should not be distinguished from the 'soul' exhorted in the same terms in Ps. 103.1–2, 22, which has experienced a range of divine benefits that include forgiveness, healing, redemption from death, steadfast love, mercy and renewal (Ps. 103.2–5). The links between the two psalms are a further indication that it is wrong to read into Ps. 104 a theology of creation independent of Israel's historical experience of Yahweh.[43]

As we have seen, Pss. 103 to 107 each confine their meditations to a particular aspect of Yahweh's many-sided activity. They may be contrasted with texts such as Pss. 136 and 147, in which – again in the context of praise – very different divine works are considered within the scope of a single text. In Ps. 136, Yahweh is initially praised as the creator who made the heavens, the earth, and the sun, moon and stars, in language that obviously reflects Gen. 1 (Ps. 136.4–9). The enumeration of divine works of creation is cut short at this point, however, and there is a sudden change of scene to Egypt, where Yahweh smote the first-born and led his people out through the Red

Sea into the wilderness (vv. 10–15). It is as if material from Pss. 104 and 105 had been tacked together – although a concern for literary and theological unity is expressed in the repeated refrain, 'for his steadfast love endures for ever', which indicates that a consistent divine *ḥesed* is manifested in very different divine works. In Ps. 147.5, God's 'greatness' is praised, as in Ps. 104.1, and, in both cases, this greatness is manifest in works of creation. According to Ps. 147.8–9, 'He covers the heavens with clouds, he prepares rain for the earth, he makes grass grow on the hills, he gives to the beasts their food, and to the young ravens which cry' – language which, apart from its third person form, would be entirely in place in Ps. 104 (cf. Ps. 104.13–14, 21, 27). Other works of creation mentioned here include the stars (147.4) and snow, frost and ice (vv. 16–17). Yet, unlike Ps. 104, Ps. 147 does not confine itself to the praise of the creator; juxtaposed with this there is also a highly particular concern with Yahweh's activity on behalf of Israel and Jerusalem. 'Yahweh builds up Jerusalem and gathers the outcasts of Israel' (v. 2). He binds up their wounds – and he determines the number of the stars (vv. 3–4). He strengthens the gates of Zion, blesses her sons, bestows peace within her boundaries – and sends snow, frost and ice (vv. 12–17). His word brings winter cold to an end, and his word declares his will to Israel, uniquely among the nations (vv. 18–20).

The striking juxtaposition in Pss. 136 and 147 of very different divine works emphasizes that the God of Israel is indeed the creator of heaven and earth, and that the creator of heaven and earth is indeed the God of Israel; a single, consistent purpose of *ḥesed* runs through all God's works. Yet, granted that this is the case, there is no reason why psalmists should not on occasion demarcate a particular aspect of God's activity for their meditations. Ps. 104 can only be read as articulating an autonomous theology of creation (on the way to a 'natural theology') if it is torn from the intertextual matrix that is, as it were, its native habitat. As the stork has her home in the fir-trees and the wild goat in the high mountains (Ps. 104.17–18), so the psalm has its home in the scriptural record of the praises of Israel. To remove it from this context is an act of violence against the ecology of the psalter.

The tendency to interpret scriptural texts relating to creation in isolation from their canonical contexts arises out of a variety of mutually-reinforcing factors. Natural theology makes it seem 'natural' to reflect on the being and nature of the creator without any regard for subsequent divine works which – unlike stars, rocks and reptiles – may be dismissed as inadequately attested or as accidental truths of history. Interpretation of the biblical creation material in the light of contemporary ecological concerns is sure to be *popular*. In post-Christian societies, on the other hand, the idea that the appropriate context for the concept of creation is the framework of orthodox Christian belief is quite clearly *not* popular, to the extent that it is deemed unworthy even of the dignity of an explicit rejection. Biblical scholars who isolate texts relating to creation from their canonical context are in fact reflecting and reinforcing assumptions and prejudices characteristic of their own particular time and place. They are also displaying a tendency, deeply ingrained in modern biblical studies, to emphasize and to exaggerate the boundaries that demarcate one text from another. Within a canonical context, one can afford to be fairly relaxed about textual boundaries, since the significant boundary is that which divides canonical from non-canonical writings. In its long-standing conflict with the concept of the canon, however, modern scholarship strives to reinforce textual boundaries within the canonical writings. The parts are no longer seen as taking up various functions within the whole, for each part is itself construed as a whole, a self-contained theological position that can be played off against other such positions. The proposal to isolate Ps. 104 from its context within Israel's praise of the God of covenant and creation is a typical example of this entrenched resistance to the possibility that the canon remains hermeneutically normative.

For biblical theology, creation represents the beginning of the history of God's covenant-relationship with humankind. It is *only* the beginning of that history, and not the totality; it establishes the foundation or stage upon which the rest of that history can unfold. And it is *truly* the beginning of that history, and not an independent topic that can be considered in abstraction from its narrative context. Theology and exegesis alike must attend more closely to the simple fact that, like any well-formed story, the true story that is constitutive of Christian communal identity has a beginning, a middle and an end.

NOTES

1. Aristotle, *Poetics*, ET in *Classical Literary Criticism*, Harmondsworth: Penguin Books, 1965. The quotations here are all from ch. 7.

2. J. Moltmann, *God in Creation: An Ecological Doctrine of Creation*, ET London: SCM Press, 1985.

3. Thus, early in his book, Moltmann announces his intention of presenting 'a deliberately and emphatically Christian doctrine of creation', understanding 'the word "Christian" in its original sense as "messianic"; but messianic as the word has been moulded by Jesus' proclamation and his history . . . This messianic doctrine of creation therefore sees creation together with its future – the future for which it was made and in which it will be perfected' (4–5). Moltmann links this dynamic, eschatologically-oriented account of creation with the claim of modern physics that 'there is no such thing as a stationary universe; the universe as a whole, and all the bodies in it, are involved in a unique movement, and in an *irreversible "history"'* (198).

4. For Moltmann, 'The trinitarian concept of creation integrates the elements of truth in monotheism and pantheism', the result being a trinitarian panentheism in which 'God, having created the world, also dwells in it' (98). God's immanence in the world is associated especially with the Spirit: 'Through his cosmic Spirit, God the Creator of heaven and earth is present *in* each of his creatures' (14). But to postulate a God who is both transcendent and immanent might suggest a duality in God rather than a triunity, a God who is both the transcendent Father and the immanent Spirit. This may explain why christology plays so small a part in Moltmann's doctrine of creation.

5. The striking image of the 'awakening' of the Spirit immanent in creation stems from Moltmann's conception of spirit as the dynamic principle of order, interaction and development whose activity can be discerned in all strata of creation. In particular, 'Spirit is the quintessence of the human being's self-organisation and his self-transcendence' (18), gradually attaining to ever-fuller consciousness. The awakening of the Spirit in the messianic era must therefore relate to the opening up of the human consciousness of creation's messianic future in the light of Jesus' resurrection. It is not clear how far this somewhat Hegelian interpretation of *Geist* is compatible with the notion of the transcendence of the divine Spirit implied in the New Testament metaphor of 'outpouring'.

6. Moltmann's emphasis here on the prophetic material's orientation towards the future (119–21) recalls his discussion of 'promise in the eschatology of the prophets' in his *Theology of Hope* (ET London: SCM Press, 1967, 124–33). In both cases, the major influence is vol. 2 of G. von Rad's *Old Testament Theology* (ET London: SCM Press, 1965). The more recent book makes it clear that what is hoped for embraces not only all people but the whole of creation.

7. According to Moltmann, evolutionary theories compel theology to develop a doctrine of *creatio continua* to complement the *creatio ex nihilo* that occurs 'in the beginning' (*God in Creation*, 208). This would emphasize not only the divine preservation of the world (the traditional view) but also the preparation of its completion and perfecting (209). If, however, creation in the beginning is *creatio ex nihilo*, it is not clear that the various aspects of God's continuing involvement with creation are still to be regarded as *creatio*. 'Creation' *is* creation out of nothing, and therefore creation in the beginning. In Kantian terminology, the relation of the phrase *ex nihilo* to *creatio* is analytic rather than synthetic. Barth argues that to understand preservation as continual creation 'would not merely presuppose an imperfection in the original creation but it would also involve in some measure its continual dissolution and complete renewal, so that its continuing existence would consist in a permanent fluctuation between life and death and life, between being and non-being and being' (*Church Dogmatics* III/3, 68). A terminological distinction must be maintained between 'creation' and 'preservation'.

8. 'The seventh day implies a break between the work of creation and all the divine work which follows – a break which we must not forget when we consider the relationship between Creator and creature' (K. Barth, *Church Dogmatics* III/3, 7).

9. B. W. Anderson argues that Gen. 2.4a is a superscription to what follows, rather than a summary of what has preceded (*From Creation to New Creation: Old Testament Perspectives*, Minneapolis: Augsburg Fortress, 1994, 54). But the second creation story has little to say about the creation of heavens and earth, and the use of *bara* also suggests a link with Gen. 1. Gen. 2.4a is to be understood as an *inclusio*, referring us back to 1.1.

10. The significance of the Noachic covenant for the Old Testament's theology of creation is rightly emphasized by R. Rendtorff, *Canon and Theology: Overtures to an Old Testament Theology*, ET Minneapolis: Augsburg Fortress; Edinburgh: T. & T. Clark, 1993, 109–13.

11. Thus in Ps. 136 the same divine *ḥesed* is manifested both in the works of creation and in the events of the exodus.

12. In his influential article on 'The Theological Problem of the Old Testament Doctrine of Creation' (1936), G. von Rad argued that 'in genuinely Yahwistic belief the doctrine of creation never attained to the stature of a relevant, independent doctrine', that it is 'invariably related, and indeed subordinated, to soteriological considerations' (*The Problem of the Hexateuch and other essays*, ET London and Edinburgh: Oliver & Boyd, 1966, 131–43; 142). Much hangs on how one understands the terms 'independent' and 'subordinated'. Old Testament 'soteriology' (von Rad apologizes for the necessary use of theological terminology of this kind [133]) is itself not 'independent', if 'independence' implies that the Old Testament presentation of redemption could in principle dispense with the idea of creation altogether. If there is a 'subordination' of creation to redemption, this is a subordination within a relationship of interdependence.

13. Although Brevard Childs knows that 'according to Israel's sacred history the formation of the heavens and the earth constituted the beginning of God's creative activity', he loses sight of this canonical perspective when (following von Rad) he argues that 'Israel's faith developed historically from its initial encounter with God as redeemer from Egypt, and only secondarily from this centre was a theology of creation incorporated into its faith' (*Biblical Theology of the Old and New Testaments*, London: SCM Press, 1992, 107, 110). Theologically, this implies that there could be a knowledge of God as redeemer which is not at the same time a knowledge of God as creator, a view otherwise associated with Marcion.

14. Although these passages are normally taken to be the insertions of later editors (so James L. Mays, *Amos*, Old Testament Library, London: SCM Press, 1969, 83–84), that does not mean that they are to be left out of account in discussing the theology of this text (compare M. D. Carroll R., *Contexts for Amos: Prophetic Poetics in Latin American Perspective*, Sheffield: Sheffield Academic Press, 1992, 216–18).

15. 'Constant revolutionizing of production, uninterrupted disturbance of all social relations, everlasting uncertainty and agitation distinguish the bourgeois epoch from all earlier ones. All fixed, fast-frozen relations, with their train of ancient and venerable prejudices and opinions, are swept away, all new-formed ones become antiquated before they can ossify. All that is solid melts into air, all that is holy is profaned . . .' (Marx and Engels, *The Communist Manifesto* [1848], in D. McLellan, *Karl Marx: Selected Writings*, Oxford: Oxford University Press, 1977, 221–47; 224).

16. Moltmann argues that 'the knowledge of the history of nature relativizes natural laws, because it nullifies the impression of the regularity of happening, which is the real basis on which natural laws rest' (*God in Creation*, 199). It is not clear what it would mean to 'relativize' the regularities of seedtime and harvest, cold and heat, summer and winter, day and night, on which all human beings – including scientists and theologians – remain entirely dependent. If there is any 'relativizing' in this area, it is surely the regularities of the natural world as humanly experienced that relativize the significance of the histories of nature proposed by physicists or biologists.

17. At the close of his interesting and informative critique of earlier attempts to harmonize Gen. 1 with the findings of geology, C. W. Goodwin argued that this text had now been definitively superseded ('The Mosaic Cosmogony', in *Essays and Reviews*, London: John W. Parker & Son, 1860, 207–53). 'For ages, this simple view of creation satisfied the wants of man, and formed a sufficient basis of theological teaching, and if modern research now shows it to be physically untenable, our respect for the narrative which has played so important a part in the culture of our race need be in nowise

diminished' (253). The verbs associated here with the Genesis view of creation are all in the past tense ('satisfied', 'formed', 'played'), suggesting that – whatever respect may still be due to it – it has had its day. In its assertion of the unity of the world it 'anticipated the highest revelation of modern enquiry' (253), as type to antitype. This view is rooted in Anglican traditions of natural theology which seek to evade the textual mediation of divine self-disclosure.

18. 'From first to last, and not merely in the epilogue, Christianity is eschatology, is hope, forward looking and forward moving, and therefore also revolutionizing and transforming the present. The eschatological is not one element *of* Christianity, but it is the medium of Christian faith as such, the key in which everything in it is set . . .' (J. Moltmann, *Theology of Hope*, 16). Why this strange ambition to set 'everything' in a single 'key', to be maintained 'from first to last'? The fact that this would be musically intolerable should be a warning to systematic theology.

19. Albert Schweitzer's work as a New Testament scholar is a particularly ruthless example of this procedure. For Schweitzer, 'the thought of Jesus must have been either eschatological or non-eschatological; it could not have been both' (*The Quest of the Historical Jesus*, ET London: A. & C. Black, 1954³, viii). Similarly, 'Instead of the untenable notion that Paul had combined eschatological and Hellenistic ways of thinking we must now consider either a purely eschatological or a purely Hellenistic explanation of his teaching.' If with Schweitzer we take the former alternative, the result is 'the complete agreement of the teaching of Paul with that of Jesus' (*The Mysticism of Paul the Apostle*, ET London: A. & C. Black, 1931, viii). The result is also the complete reduction and subjugation of the New Testament to the will of the interpreter, with his single, arbitrarily-selected master-concept.

20. John Barclay has rightly emphasized the significance for Pauline interpretation of social and ideological differences between Pauline congregations ('Thessalonica and Corinth: Social Contrasts in Pauline Christianity', *JSNT* 47 [1992], 49–74).

21. Compare Colin Gunton's claim that the gospels depict the creatureliness of Jesus in their rendering of 'the network of relationships he had with particular groups of people and with the material world' (*Christ and Creation*, Carlisle: Paternoster, 1992, 43); for 'to be a creature is to be constituted, to be made what one is, by and in a network of relationships' (36). Tracing the elements of the Genesis narrative in the gospels is one way of bringing to light the relation of Jesus as a human creature to the non-human world.

22. Of course, not everything in the psalter can credibly be understood as part of Jesus' worship. The prayer, 'Father, forgive them, for they know not what they do' (Luke 23.34) could be understood as a *refusal* to employ some of the psalter's more vindictive language (e.g. Ps. 109).

23. In such passages, 'an imaginative apprehension of the wonder and beauty of nature, and of the unity of nature and man under the care of the Maker of both, has brought forth the appropriate literary form for its expression . . . Clearly we are in touch with a mind of poetic and imaginative cast' (C. H. Dodd, *The Founder of Christianity*, London: Collins, 1971; Fontana edn. [1973], 50).

24. Christoph Schwöbel rightly warns of the danger of repeating 'die Fehler der negativen Isolierung des Schöpfungsthemas durch Nichtbeachtung in der positiven Isolierung durch Nicht-Integration' ('Theologie der Schöpfung im Dialog zwischen Naturwissenschaft und Dogmatik', in *Unsere Welt – Gottes Schöpfung*, FS for E. Wölfel, Marburg: N. G. Elwert Verlag, 1992, 199–221; 202).

25. 'Concern over the environmental crisis' has 'triggered [a] new focus on the role of the natural world in the religion and culture of Israel', in the hope of identifying 'the role

that the Bible might play in the discussion of the current crisis' and of translating certain aspects of the 'biblical worldview' into 'an environmentally relevant theology' (Ronald A. Simkins, *Creator and Creation: Nature in the Worldview of Ancient Israel*, Peabody, Mass.: Hendrickson, 1994, 257, 262).

26. J. Barr, *Biblical Faith and Natural Theology*, Oxford: Clarendon Press, 1993.

27. And yet Barr refuses to avail himself of this permission to join the biblical authors in their vigorous natural theologizing. 'To me', he confesses, 'the arguments of natural theology are not a congenial field' (*Biblical Faith and Natural Theology*, 102) – any more than the arguments of theologies of revelation. 'What really interests me is the effect that the whole question has upon biblical studies and upon the place of the Bible in theology' (103). To be more specific, Barr's primary interest is in arguing that, 'if it is true . . . that natural theology in some way underlies the Bible . . . , the effect upon Barth's total theological position must be devastating' (103).

28. It is no pleasure to quote some of these statements. The one that it is worth taking a little trouble to refute is the claim that Barth was wrong to see modern Protestantism as compromised by natural theology, since from Schleiermacher onwards natural theology had repeatedly been repudiated by liberal Protestant theologians. Barr is under the mistaken impression that the pages of the *Church Dogmatics* are peppered with ill-tempered polemics against 'natural theology'; but that is not the case, even in the earlier volumes. On Barth's reading of post-Reformation Protestant theological history, certain Reformation insights are already subverted by the increasing prominence of *theologia naturalis* in seventeenth-century Protestant orthodoxy (*Church Dogmatics*, I/1, 192), which prepared the way for a 'devastating inrush of natural theology' in the eighteenth century (I/2, 123). Barth is of course aware that, in the wake of Kant's *Critique of Pure Reason*, Schleiermacher and his successors no longer practise a traditional natural theology, which is now understood as an exercise in an illegitimate metaphysics, and for that reason he does not generally use the expression 'natural theology' when speaking of them. It is therefore said of Schleiermacher not that he practised natural theology but that he laid a foundation for theology in an anthropological account of a general human capacity for religion that could be known apart from Christian faith (see, for example, *Church Dogmatics*, I/1, 192–93, among countless similar passages). For Barth, this obvious distinction between old-fashioned natural theology and modern interest in a universal human 'religious *a priori*' is less significant than what the two projects have in common: the attempt to establish a foundation for Christian faith that is prior to and independent of Christian faith. The broader use of 'natural theology' assumed by Barr appears to stem from the 1934 debate between Brunner and Barth, in which Brunner self-consciously applies the archaic expression *theologia naturalis* to his own programme of theological apologetics: it is, he claims, 'the task of our theological generation to find the way back to a true *theologia naturalis*' ('Nature and Grace: A Contribution to the Discussion with Karl Barth', ET in E. Brunner and K. Barth, *Natural Theology*, London: Geoffrey Bles, 1946, 59). Barth here accepts this new usage because he agrees with Brunner that modern anthropological starting-points for theology are in continuity with pre-Kantian natural theology. Thus he can write: 'By "natural theology" I mean every (positive *or* negative) *formulation of a system* which claims to be theological, *i.e.* to interpret divine revelation, whose *subject*, however, differs fundamentally from the revelation in Jesus Christ and whose *method* therefore differs equally from the exposition of Holy Scripture' ('No! Answer to Emil Brunner', *Natural Theology*, 74–75).

29. Barr defends his assertion that 'canon' means no more than 'list' by claiming that this is 'the normal meaning of the word in English when applied to scripture' (*Holy*

Scripture: Canon, Authority, Criticism, Oxford: Clarendon Press, 1983, 49n). In its normal meaning, the English word 'list' refers to a series of items – names, dates, titles – assembled in random order or in accordance with a simple system (alphabetical or chronological, perhaps), but without reference to the structured relationships that may exist between members of the series. Structured relationships are, however, integral to the concept of the canon: someone who has merely memorized a list of titles, from Genesis to Revelation, without (for example) understanding the rationale of the division into two parts or the relative weight assigned to some books in comparison to others, has a very imperfect understanding of the canon.

30. Suggested translations of *spermologos* are taken from the Bauer–Arndt–Gingrich lexicon, which in turn refers to E. J. Goodspeed.

31. This usage of *epistēmē* is borrowed from M. Foucault, and may be compared to Thomas Kuhn's concept of the *paradigm*, the set of tacit conventions that determines the structure of what counts as 'knowledge' or 'truth' within a given community at a particular time. Foucault attempts to bring to light 'the *episteme* in which knowledge, envisaged apart from all criteria having reference to its rational value or to its objective forms, grounds its positivity and thereby manifests a history which is not that of its growing perfection, but rather that of its conditions of possibility' (*The Order of Things: An Archaeology of the Human Sciences*, ET London and New York: Tavistock/Routledge 1970, xxii).

32. M. Dibelius, 'Paul on the Areopagus' (1939), in *Studies in the Acts of the Apostles*, ET London: SCM Press, 1956, 26–77; 27. 'The Areopagus speech is a hellenistic speech with a Christian ending' (58).

33. Following Dibelius, this interpretation of the Areopagus speech is also accepted by P. Vielhauer in his influential article 'On the "Paulinism" of Acts', ET in L. E. Keck and J. L. Martyn (eds.), *Studies in Luke–Acts*, London: SPCK, 1968, 33–50; 33–37.

34. Even if the parallels were as significant and far-reaching as they are said to be, one would still have to recall that the encounter between early Christianity and Hellenism involved not only a 'hellenisation of Christianity' but also a 'Christianisation of hellenism' (for this point see C. Schwöbel, 'Theologie der Schöpfung', 207). As W. Pannenberg states, 'A "hellenization" in the sense of being overcome by foreign interests, e.g., by the philosophical idea of God, does not necessarily appear already where theology undertakes to come to grips with it, but only where theology fails in the midst of this struggle by losing its assimilative, transforming power' ('The Appropriation of the Philosophical Concept of God as a Dogmatic Problem of Early Christian Theology', in *Basic Questions in Theology*, II, ET London: SCM Press, 1971, 119–83; 140).

35. According to Dibelius, the altar to an unknown god is employed in the speech as a sign of 'man's "feeling after" and honouring the God he believes must exist' ('Paul on the Areopagus', 60), that is, as a positive 'point of contact'. Barth's interpretation is more plausible: 'If they had really known this unknown God, they would not have erected a special altar to him in distinction to their relationship to other deities whom they also worship. He is indeed – they do not know this, and Paul tells it to them – the Lord who has formed the heavens and the earth and all that is therein, who as the Lord of the heavens and the earth dwells not in temples made with hands . . . It is on this ignorance of theirs in regard to God, which betrays itself even in their best possibilities but of which they are quite insensible, that Paul addresses these Athenians' (*Church Dogmatics*, II/1, 122–23).

36. Dibelius' interpretation of the Areopagus speech as almost exclusively Hellenistic in content causes him to deny its obvious Old Testament roots. ('The emphasis of

Old Testament piety is quite different from this' – 'The Old Testament cannot even be considered as the place of origin of this motif', etc. ['Paul on the Areopagus', 44, 52].)

37. Thus Barth argues that 'the order of reconciliation . . . is also the confirmation and restoration of the order of creation', that 'in the life of Jesus Christ there takes place, with the establishment of the new order, the reconstitution of the old'. The general description in Acts 17.27–28 of the nearness of God to all humans is 'grounded – firmly grounded, so that no other ground need be sought – in the particular . . . , namely, that the life of Jesus Christ is the life of grace, the life of the Saviour' (*Church Dogmatics*, IV/3, 43).

38. Such contradictions are said to establish an infinite qualitative difference between the Paul of Acts and 'the real Paul', in this case the Paul of the Letter to the Romans (M. Dibelius, 'Paul on the Areopagus', 62). It can be said of 'the Areopagus speaker' that 'his distance from Paul is just as clear as his nearness to the apologists' (P. Vielhauer, 'On the "Paulinism" of Acts', 37). The two are not just different but '*utterly* different' (36, my italics), for their difference is the difference between Protestant and Roman Catholic theologies: in contrast to Rom. 1, Acts 17 is said to confirm the dictum that 'grace does not destroy nature but presupposes and completes it' (36). It is one of the merits of Brevard Childs' canonical perspective that it eliminates hyper-Protestant exegesis of this kind (see, for example, *The New Testament as Canon: An Introduction*, London: SCM Press, 1984, 228–40).

39. It is because of the radical, total nature of the human distortion of the original revelation of God that Paul can build nothing on this original revelation apart from human inexcusability and divine wrath. According to C. E. B. Cranfield, 'The result of God's self-manifestation in his creation is not a natural knowledge of God on men's part independent of God's self-revelation in his Word, a valid though limited knowledge, but simply the excuselessness of men in their ignorance. A real self-disclosure of God has indeed taken place and is always occurring, and men ought to have recognized, but in fact have not recognized, him' (*The Epistle to the Romans*, I, International Critical Commentary, Edinburgh: T. & T. Clark, 1975, 116). This does not quite do justice to Paul's claim that the disclosure is not only objectively given but also subjectively received (cf. *phaneron estin en autois* [v. 19], *nooumena kathoratai* [v. 20], *gnontes ton theon* [v. 21]), although only in such a way as to lead to the fundamental distortion of the disclosure in the form of idolatry. Yet there is no call for Barr's high-handed judgment that Cranfield is here offering 'confessional assertions rather than exegetically backed interpretations', 'expressions of loyalty to a basically Barthian viewpoint' (*Biblical Faith and Natural Theology*, 43). Cranfield's interpretation remains closer to Paul than that of earlier commentators such as Sanday and Headlam, who – no less influenced by confessional assertions, in this case Anglican ones – simply find in Rom. 1 an ordinary instance of 'the argument from the nature of the created world to the character of its Author', well-known to both Greeks and Jews (W. Sanday and A. C. Headlam, *The Epistle to the Romans*, International Critical Commentary, Edinburgh: T. & T. Clark, 1895, 43).

40. Paul criticizes Gentile idolatry not merely as a critic (2.1) or a Jew (2.17–20), but as an apostle of Jesus Christ – the difference being that this entails his own solidarity with those who are criticized (for 'all have sinned' [3.23], including Christians and apostles), ruling out any claim to a secure standpoint outside that which is criticized. A very different interpretation is offered by Graham Shaw, for whom 'Paul uses the message of God's judgment to express his own antagonism and repudiation of the Gentile world. At the same time he elevates himself by proclaiming a condemnation from which he is exempt.

Amid the fury of the invective one scarcely notices that the speaker emerges unscathed'
(*The Cost of Authority: Manipulation and Freedom in the New Testament*, London: SCM
Press, 1983, 143–44). On this view, Paul can simply be identified with the critic whose
self-aggrandizing behaviour he claims to unmask in Rom. 2.1. That would in fact only be
possible if one knew in advance that the message of a God who did not 'repudiate the
Gentile world' but in Christ reconciled it to himself was untrue, a mere front for a human
will-to-power that can easily be unmasked with the assistance of a few elementary strategies
derived from an all-purpose 'hermeneutic of suspicion'.

41. The Pauline notion of the distorted primal revelation is therefore an interpretation
of the phenomena of 'Gentile' (non-Jewish, non-Christian) religion. To take this interpretation seriously, rather than regarding it as an embarrassing expression of Jewish and
Christian 'exclusiveness', would involve considerations such as the following: (1) It would
not be adequate to leave the phenomena of religion theologically uninterpreted. For
example, to say that 'a religion can be viewed as a kind of cultural and/or linguistic
framework or medium that shapes the entirety of life and thought' (G. A. Lindbeck, *The
Nature of Doctrine: Religion and Theology in a Postliberal Age*, London: SPCK, 1984, 33)
is to renounce theological interpretation by assimilating religion to the sheer givenness of
a culture or language. (2) Religion is a human response to the primal divine revelation
given in and with human existence. In it, the truth is *suppressed* (Rom. 1.18), but it is
nevertheless the *truth* that is suppressed, the truth that all worldly existence is dependent
on the power of the eternal divine creator, and that for humans, made for relationship
with this creator, this is cause for thankfulness. (3) This human response is distorted from
the very beginning, and consists in an arbitrary divinizing of the creature, of which the
production of idols – physical artefacts representing divinity – is only the most tangible
symptom (Rom. 1.21–23). The Christian gospel implies an unmasking and a demystifying
of idols, undertaken not in a destructive spirit but in the name of the triune God disclosed
in Jesus. (4) However 'negative' this interpretation may seem, the phenomena of religion
are at least taken seriously. Religion is not patronized as a picturesque vestige of humankind's naïve past; it is regarded as a distorted, unconscious witness to the truth of God
that encompasses the world and human existence and is revealed in the Christian gospel.

42. This emphasis on 'Yahweh' as proper name suggests that the question of the
'meaning' of this name is of only limited significance. While in certain passages a meaning
is associated with names such as 'Yahweh', 'Abraham', 'Esau', 'Jacob' and 'Jesus' (Exod.
3.14–15; Gen. 17.5; 25.25–26; Matt. 1.21), it is characteristic of proper names that such
meanings are incidental to their primary function of addressing or referring to an unsubstitutable individual. W. Eichrodt rightly notes that 'in Israel there was less interest in
the etymological significance of the divine name than in the concrete content which it
conveyed', expressed in the historical actions of the owner of that name; yet he still persists
with the question as to the 'meaning' that 'originally [*sic*] lay behind the name Yahweh'
(*Theology of the Old Testament*, I, ET London: SCM Press, 1961[5], 187). It is notable that,
in the account of divine self-naming in Exod. 6.3, no meaning is assigned to the new
name, 'Yahweh'.

43. According to A. Weiser, 'The psalmist is a man who combines the capacity for
profound religious thought with the gift of reflecting on nature with an affectionate
intimacy . . . The way in which he sees beauty and purpose in the world extolling the
glory and wisdom of its Creator, however, also shows his independence of tradition . . .
[T]he psalmist has made use of the most varied features of the contemporary world-view,
to which we can find numerous parallels in Babylonian, Egyptian, Greek and Nordic
mythology' (*The Psalms*, Old Testament Library, ET London: SCM Press, 1962, 666). It

is remarkable that Weiser can allude to parallels even in Nordic mythology without mentioning the most obvious 'parallels' of all, which arise from the pervasive intertextuality of the psalter and which relativize the boundaries of individual psalms. The entirely false impression is given that the author has expressed an intense individuality by writing a text that is not really 'Israelite' at all.

Chapter 7

---- ᛝ◆ᛝ -·-

In the Image of God

In Gen. 1.27, it is said that, unlike other creatures, humans were created 'in the image of God'. They are like all other creatures and unlike God in being created by God. They are like the living creatures of sea, air and land in their need for nourishment and in their capacity to be fruitful and to multiply, and here too they are unlike God. Yet, despite the many similarities that bind humans to other creatures and that differentiate them from God, at some point they may still be said to be like God and, for that very reason, unlike all other creatures.

If humans are unlike other creatures in being in some sense like God, then it might be possible to identify this point of God-likeness by determining empirically what it is that differentiates humans from all other creatures and makes them distinctively human. It would then be possible to solve the exegetical problem posed by the notion of 'the image of God' simply and directly, without recourse to complex exegetical, hermeneutical and theological procedures. The truth about human being is surely something we can know directly, not something we must laboriously extract from sacred texts? At any rate, that has been the assumption of a long tradition of exegesis. An ancient and a modern example will suffice to show the essential continuity that has existed at this point.

In his treatise *De opificio mundi,* Philo informs his readers that 'the word "image" is used with reference to the mind that is the ruler of the soul [*kata ton tēs psuchēs hēgemona noun*]' (69).[1] Humans are like God not in their bodily form but in their possession of a mind: 'for after the pattern of a single mind, even the mind of the universe as an archetype, the mind in each of those who successively came into being was moulded' (69). The human mind is related to the body as the divine mind to the world, invisible and incomprehensible and yet seeing and comprehending all things. This likeness creates in the human mind a longing to return to the divine mind that is its pattern and origin:

And so, carrying its gaze beyond the confines of all substance discernible by sense, it comes to a point at which it reaches out after the intelligible world, and on descrying in that world sights of surpassing loveliness, even the patterns and originals of the things of sense which it saw here, . . . it seems to be on its way to the Great King himself; but, amid its longing to see him, pure and untempered rays of concentrated light stream forth like a torrent, so that by its gleams the eye of the understanding is dazzled. (71)

It is here regarded as self-evident that Moses' doctrine of the image refers us to the Platonic eroticism in which mind is both attracted and repulsed by its divine archetype. Where else might the image of God be found than in the human mind? Philosophical anthropology makes further exegetical reflection superfluous.

In the first volume of his *The Nature and Destiny of Man* (1941), Reinhold Niebuhr traces back to Augustine an authentically Christian doctrine of the *imago Dei* that interprets human nature 'in terms which include [man's] rational faculties but which suggest something beyond them' (1.173).[2] According to the Christian doctrine of the image of God,

Implicit in the human situation of freedom and in man's capacity to transcend himself and his world is his inability to construct a world of meaning without finding a source and key to the structure of meaning which transcends the world beyond his own capacity to transcend it . . . [A] mind which transcends itself cannot legitimately make itself the ultimate principle of interpretation by which it explains the relation of mind to the world. The fact of self-transcendence leads inevitably to the search for a God who transcends the world. (1.176, 177)

The context of these remarks is a treatment of the 'biblical basis of the doctrines', that is, of 'man as image of God and as creature'. Man is image of God in that human self- and world-transcendence mirrors divine transcendence. As in Philo, biblical language here flows, easily and straightforwardly, into the language of philosophical anthropology – in this case, the language of a theistic existentialism whose roots in a Platonism mediated by Philo, Augustine and many others are transparent. Exegesis of the biblical *imago Dei* passages is unnecessary where it is assumed that 'the Christian doctrine of man' is statable in broad and general terms such as these. As it pursues its basically antiquarian interests, exegesis may by chance uncover previously-overlooked elements which can be pressed into the service of this doctrine; but these will be inessential ornaments, for the doctrine has been established directly and without textual mediation.

If there is to be a theological anthropology, it will have to take account of the existence of other anthropological possibilities, not all of which it will wish simply to reject. At numerous points, there will surely be analogies and convergences between theological and non-theological reflection on the phenomena of the human. Yet a theological anthropology sensitive to the textual mediation of Christian faith will not assume too readily that the particularities of holy scripture can be effortlessly assimilated to supposedly 'broader' conceptions. It will not assume that, whatever may be the case with its doctrine of God, its doctrine of the human will necessarily occupy much the same ground as other conceptions. There is no reason to suppose that the Christian doctrine of the human is any less distinctive and idiosyncratic than the Christian doctrine of God. Indeed, there is every reason to suppose that the distinctiveness of the one will be reflected in the other. If the Christian view of God articulates not a general conception of deity but a highly distinctive conception of a triune God uniquely disclosed in Jesus, then this will leave its mark on theological anthropology too. And if this definitive divine self-disclosure is textually mediated, the same will be true of the anthropology that corresponds to it. If that is the case, there can be no easy route from biblical *imago Dei* language to a general philosophical conceptuality. Far from being an antiquarian exercise, exegesis would then be integral to theological construction.

1. Anthropology in Christological Perspective

In Gen. 1.26–28, we read:

> And God said, 'Let us make man ['*ādām*] in our image, according to our likeness [*b'ṣalmēnû kid'mûthēnû; kat' eikona hēmeteran kai kath' homoiōsin*]; and let them have dominion over the fish of the sea, and over the birds of the air, and over the cattle, and over all the earth, and over every moving thing that moves upon the earth'. So God created man in his image, in the image of God he created him; male and female he created them. And God blessed them, and God said to them, 'Be fruitful and multiply, and fill the earth and subdue it; and have dominion over the fish of the sea and over the birds of the air and over every living thing that moves upon the earth'.

(The translation of '*ādām* as 'man' rather than 'humankind' [NRSV] is necessary for the sake of the contrast between 'he created him' and 'he created them'.) The link between the likeness of God and creation as male and female recurs in Gen. 5.1–3:

> This is the book of the generations of Adam ['*ādām; anthrōpon*]: when God created man ['*ādām; ton Adam*], he made him in the likeness of God [*bid'mûth '*lōhîm; kat' eikona theou*]. Male and female he created them and named them man ['*ādām; Adam*] when they were created. When Adam had lived a hundred and thirty years, he became the father of a son in his own likeness, after his image [*bid'mûthô k'ṣalmô; kata tēn idean autou kai kata tēn eikona autou*], and named him Seth.

Whereas in Gen. 1.26–27 'likeness' is subordinated to 'image' (which occurs three times), in Gen. 5.1–3 this is reversed: 'image' is subordinated to 'likeness'. The two terms are clearly synonymous in both passages, and the difference in the prepositions is of no importance. 'Image' returns, however, in Gen. 9.6, where the implication of Gen. 1.26–27, that the image of God is that which differentiates humans from every other creature, receives a particular application. Although animals may now be killed (v. 3), humans may not be: 'for in [the] image of God [*beṣelem ʾelōhîm, en eikoni theou*] he made man'.

At this point the doctrine of the *imago Dei* simply disappears from the Old Testament, thereby showing itself to be specific to the biblical history of origins that precedes the history of the covenant. It is rediscovered in the Judaism of the Hellenistic period, which finds in it the welcome possibility of a fundamental anthropological reflection rooted in distinctively Jewish traditions. For ben Sira, human existence is marked by a dual origin out of the dust of the ground (cf. Gen. 2.7; 3.19) and in the image of God:

> The Lord created man out of earth, and turned him back to it again. He gave them few days, a limited time, but granted them authority over the things upon it [*sc.* the earth]. He endowed them with strength proper to them [*kath' heauton*] and made them in his own image [*kai kat' eikona autou epoiēsen autous*]. He placed the fear of him [*sc.* humans] upon all flesh, and gave dominion over animals and birds. He gave them counsel and tongue and eyes, ears and a mind [*kardia*] for thinking. He filled them with knowledge and understanding, and revealed to them good and evil. He set his eye upon their hearts to show them the majesty of his works [*ta megaleia tōn ergōn autou*]. And they will praise his holy name, to proclaim the majesty of his works. (Sir. 17.1–8)

Here, God's 'image' is linked initially to the promise of dominion over animals and birds, along the lines of Gen. 1.26, 28; and, following Gen. 9.2, the 'fear' of humans evident in the animal realm is seen as an empirically-observable sign of this dominion. Yet this raises the further question of the nature of the human superiority to and difference from the animal realm. This is not a matter of physical strength, which is bestowed on humans in a form 'proper to them' but which does not especially distinguish them. It is a matter not of a quantitative but of a qualitative divine bestowal: the gifts of knowledge and understanding, given to enable not an autonomous human existence but the recognition of the greatness of the creator in his works and the life of praise that flows from this recognition. The image of God is that point where recognition of the creator arises from within the created order. Humans are unique because they alone recognize the creator in his works and offer him the praise that is his due. This interpretation of the divine image already excludes the *hybris* that, in another context, the concept of human God-likeness might evoke, and a further check is provided in the sober recognition that humans are unlike God in that they originate in and return to the dust of the ground. The life of praise occupies only the short span that God grants; praise is silenced in death.[3]

In its own way, this might seem an exemplary interpretation of the concept of the image of God. The link with dominion over the animal realm indicates an intention to interpret the image-of-God concept within its textual context in Gen. 1. Yet the author rightly poses the further question as to the basis of the distinction and difference that is here implied, and finds this not in the Platonizing understanding of mind which proved so irresistible to Philo but in the capacity to recognize and to praise the creator – a capacity that is actualized in the existence of Israel, God's covenant people, among whom there takes place the true worship of the only true God, the creator of heaven and earth. In Israel's praise of God the universal human vocation comes to expression: for praise is the *telos* of the divine image in humankind. The isolated *theologoumenon* of the image of God, confined to a small number of texts in Gen. 1–9, is thus given an interpretation consonant with the entire scriptural record of God's dealings with Israel. The author acknowledges both the textual particularity of this concept and the universal claim about human existence that he rightly finds here.

Might this scripturally-based, non-Platonizing interpretation of the image of God serve as a model for a Christian interpretation? This possibility is excluded by the New Testament, which radically reinterprets the image of God by identifying it with Christ.

Unbelievers fail to see what believers see, which is 'the light of the gospel of the glory of Christ, who is the image of God [*hos estin eikōn tou theou*]' (2 Cor. 4.4). It is Jesus Christ, God's Son, 'who is the image of the invisible God [*hos estin eikōn tou theou tou aoratou*], the first-born of every creature' (Col. 1.15). It might be argued that this language is not intended as an interpretation of the anthropological image-of-God concept in Genesis, and that the linguistic convergence is mere coincidence.[4] (When the author to the Hebrews describes Christ as *apaugasma tēs doxēs . . . autou* [Heb. 1.3], the meaning is presumably similar to the Pauline 'image-of-God' christology, but in apparent independence of Genesis.) Yet in Col. 3.9–11 Paul clearly alludes to Genesis:

> And do not lie to one another, having put off the old nature [*ton palaion anthrōpon*] with its practices and having put on the new which is being renewed in knowledge according to the image of its creator [*kat' eikona tou ktisantos auton*], where there is neither Greek nor Jew, circumcision or uncircumcision, barbarian, Scythian, slave, free, but Christ is all and in all.

Here, *kat' eikona* clearly recalls *kat' eikona theou* in Gen. 1.27 and 5.1; and *tou ktisantos auton* recalls the use of *ktizein* in Old Testament creation traditions (e.g. Gen. 14.19, 22; Deut. 4.32; Pss. 32[33].9; 88[89].47; Eccl. 12.1), although the reference here is to the new creation rather than to the old. Since the *neos anthrōpos* is closely correlated with Christ, in whom hostility and inequality are abolished (3.11), the allusion to Gen. 1 in Col. 3.10 confirms that in 1.15 the christological title *eikōn tou theou* is drawn from Gen. 1 and has not been independently formulated. The original creation provides conceptuality for describing the new creation.[5]

In the case of 2 Cor. 4.4, the identification of Christ as image of God again occurs in the context of other creation-language.[6] The God who has given us the light of the knowledge of his glory in the face of Jesus Christ is the God who said, 'Let light shine out of darkness' (2 Cor. 4.6) – an obvious allusion to Gen. 1.3. As there was an original creation, heralded by the dawning of life, so there is now a new creation: 'If anyone is in Christ, there is a new creation – the old has passed away, behold, the new has come' (2 Cor. 5.17). In the context of this creation-language, the reference to Christ as the *eikōn tou theou* must again allude to Gen. 1. As in Col. 3.10, Christ as the image of God is the pattern according to which believers are being recreated – as, beholding in Christ the mirror image of the glory of the Lord, they are changed into the same image (*tēn autēn eikona*), from glory to glory, through the transforming activity of the Lord who is the Spirit (2 Cor. 3.18).[7]

If Jesus Christ is the image of God, and if this expression occupies as it were the same semantic space as its counterpart in Genesis, then a Christian interpretation of the anthropological concept of the image of God will have to take account not only of the Genesis texts but also of their christological transformation. *The Genesis texts in themselves do not provide the basis for a theological anthropology*, even if, like ben Sira, one resists seduction by philosophy and remains scrupulously within the parameters of Old Testament representations of humankind in relation to God. It is impossible to explain how humankind is created in the image of God without explaining how the image of God is Christ. Admittedly, it is initially unclear how the anthropological concept and the christological title are to be related to one another. It does not seem possible simply to adopt a christological reading of Gen. 1.26–27, as though the image of God in which humans are created could straightforwardly be identified with Christ. Nor should one adopt the Marcionite view that the original creation in the image of God belongs to 'the old' which has passed away with the dawning of 'the new' (2 Cor. 5.17). The anthropological and christological facets of the *imago Dei* must be combined in a way that respects the integrity of the Old Testament text, neither imposing upon it a later, alien christological content nor replacing it with that content. With this proviso, however, the crucial point is to avoid the usual practice of reflecting on the anthropology implied in the Genesis texts in abstraction from christology. This practice often stems from a biblicism concerned only that the 'voice' of the individual text be heard, without attempting to relate it to the *centre* of Christian scripture that lies in the space between the two Testaments and is enclosed by them, the event of the becoming flesh of the Word through whom all things were made. Like the rest of Christian scripture, the Genesis texts that speak of the creation of humankind in the image of God must be interpreted both in their particularity and in their relation to this centre.

Before returning to the Old Testament texts in the light of all this, however, some potential objections to the way so far taken must be answered. In the interpretation of image-of-God texts in both Testaments that I am here developing, the exegesis is intended to establish the thesis that *we learn from Jesus what it is to be human.*[8] Can this Pauline thesis still be seriously and responsibly maintained by a contemporary theology? Identifying and weighing various possible objections to it is a necessary discipline that will also enable us to define more closely what the thesis actually entails.

(1) Paul's image-of-God christology is accompanied by light-imagery which may seem alienating to us. God has enabled us 'to see the light of the knowledge of the glory of Christ, who is the image of God', he 'has shone in our hearts to give the light of the knowledge of the glory of God in the face of Jesus Christ', he enables us to 'behold the glory of the Lord', and to be 'changed into his likeness from glory to glory' (2 Cor. 4.4, 6; 3.18). The Christ who is the image of God, is, it seems, a being of light: one recalls Paul's own conversion, when he was encompassed by 'a light from heaven, brighter than the sun, shining round me' (Acts 26.13), and the revelation to John of Patmos of a Christ whose head and hair were 'white as white wool, white as snow', whose eyes were 'like a flame of fire', and whose face was 'like the sun shining in full strength' (Rev. 1.14, 16). Unlike the early Christians, we do not, I think, find ourselves impressed or attracted by light-imagery of this kind. A general background acceptance of light as a symbol or manifestation of an awesome, other-worldly purity, essential for the effectiveness of New Testament light-imagery, has largely disappeared. We might ask how, why and when this event – which one might describe as a loss of symbolic resonance – occurred. The question is, of course, unanswerable; but as good an answer as any might be to point to the coincidence on 6 August 1945 of the Feast of the Transfiguration with the dropping of the atomic bomb on Hiroshima. By re-enacting and indeed surpassing the transfiguration after its own fashion, modern science has burdened the image of the light

shining brighter than the sun with sinister, inhuman and demonic connotations. We cannot and must not dispense with Christian light-imagery;
but it has undoubtedly been contaminated for us by the pseudo-miracles of
light which John of Patmos, with his usual sober realism, would correctly
have identified as an epiphany of the beast that ascends from the bottomless
abyss.

Yet the light-imagery which, in the New Testament, surrounds the figure
of the exalted Lord is not intended to identify him as some half-mythological
light-being. The one who appears to Paul on the Damascus road is not an
angel, for he identifies himself as 'Jesus of Nazareth' (Acts 22.8), a name
denoting a human origin and therefore implying a normal human way through
birth, childhood, adulthood, activity, passivity and relatedness to others –
concluding in death and the grave. Saul the persecutor discovers on the
Damascus road that this Jesus of Nazareth has indeed been raised from the
dead, but his resurrection does not transform him into some phantasmal
light-being who has discarded his human past, as a snake sloughs off its skin.
The exalted Lord is no other than Jesus of Nazareth: that is why the New
Testament discourages speculation about the Lord's present mode of existence
(cf. Acts 1.11a) and – especially in the form of the fourfold gospel testimony
– insistently points us back to an earthly life. Jesus as the image of God is no
inhuman image characterized by mere brightness.

(2) If Jesus is the image of God, then it is in him that we learn who we
are, what it is to be human. But this seems an impossible claim. We already
know who we are and what it is to be human. Jesus as the image of God is
perhaps necessary to tell us about *God*, whom we do not know; but that he
should tell us about something as well known as *ourselves* is impossible to
accept. The laborious disciplines and educational processes in which we
participate from childhood onwards tell us who we are. To a lesser or greater
extent, we gradually acquire critical faculties that enable us to discriminate
between the truthful and the false and meretricious self-images that are
constantly dangled before our eyes by the arts and the sciences, by the media
and the advertising industry, by local conventions relating to class, race or
gender. We are familiar with the partial, specialized answers to the question
of our identity supplied by medicine, philosophy and history. Jesus, along
with many others, might have a contribution to make to our self-image. But
we do not learn from him that we are embodied beings, that we are linguistic
agents, that we have been born and that we are destined to die. We know
who we are.

In fact we do not know who we are, for in Jesus, the image of God, we are
told who we are; and we would not have been told if we had not needed to

know. The people who walked in darkness have seen a great light, and those who dwelled in a land of deep shadow, on them has light shined – enabling them to see themselves, their way and their neighbour for the first time. Without this illumination, our self-knowledge is a mess. It includes a 'natural' self-knowledge, essential although limited. Human being entails participation in the constraints and capacities of bodiliness, it commits one to certain necessary relationships with other humans and with the non-human environment – and, as the characteristically human phenomenon of speech indicates, it also entails a knowledge that all this is the case. Yet this natural self-knowledge is available to us not in pure form but in indissoluble connection with another self-knowledge – the wisdom of the serpent, the fruit of the ever-renewed human attempt to establish an autonomous knowledge of human existence without reference to the true God. We might understand the ever-expanding class of *-ism* words as a symptom of this. Rationalism, nationalism, capitalism, socialism, historicism, Darwinism, Fascism, existentialism, feminism, postmodernism: *-ism* denotes the solidification of a constellation of ideas into a theory about human existence which aims at comprehensiveness and which competes for power and influence in the market-place or battleground of the ideological realm. An *-ism* may not be *only* a theory about human existence. It may also be a practice or set of practices, it may also theorize about non-human entities, but it will always display the unmistakable marks of its fabricators' self-image. The *-ism* is a device that enables us to tell ourselves who we are. Perhaps some if not all of them do indeed give us true if partial insights into human being. But their partial insights can only be distinguished from the chaos of their various illusions and falsehoods by means of an appropriate criterion. Jesus as the image of God is the criterion that makes this discrimination possible.

(3) It is in Jesus, the image of God, that God tells us who we are. But Jesus was a man, not a woman. Can he really embody the image of God in its wholeness? Can a woman learn from Jesus what it is to be a woman? Does she not need to look elsewhere, to other women and not to this one man? But if women do not learn from Jesus what it is to be women, neither do men learn from him what it is to be men. It is not his purpose to give us authoritative guidance about gender roles. Men may learn from him to see through certain characteristically male illusions (about power and status, for example), but they learn this from Jesus and not from Jesus' maleness. Jesus was a male and not a female, but the either/or of gender does not preclude the fullness of humanity. We must of course learn to be either men or women, but, if Jesus is the image of God and therefore the disclosure of humanity

rather than of maleness, it is more fundamental to us that we learn what it is to be human.

That the question of our common humanity is more fundamental to us than the question of our gender roles is not something that we can simply assume, perhaps in reaction against some feminist claims about the qualitative difference between female and male experience and perception of the world. An issue of that kind cannot be eliminated by availing oneself of the commonsense maxim that, after all, we are all human. We do not know whether and how far we are entitled to speak of our common humanity as underlying and preceding gender differences. Feminism is critical of any discourse that treats humanity in abstraction from gender differences, just as Marxism is critical of every abstraction from class differences, on the grounds that the universality claimed by such discourses is false, a mere cover for male or class interests. It is critiques of this kind that have generated the widespread contemporary unease with the concept of a universal 'human nature'. Are they simply wrong?

In so far as they treat of a certain range of phenomena of the human, the critiques may be judged to be more or less helpful, necessary and illuminating. In so far as they imply claims about the ontology of the human, however, they are to be resisted.[9] If in Jesus we learn what it is to be human, then part of what we learn is that to be human is not in the first instance a matter of gender, race or class. Jesus was male, a Jew and an artisan, but to describe him as the image of God is to assert that his humanity transcends his maleness, his Jewishness and his artisan-status: 'For there is no distinction between Jew and Greek; the same Lord is Lord of all and bestows his riches upon all who call upon him' (Rom. 10.12). To rethink the significance of Jesus on the assumption of an irreducible difference between Jew and Gentile, male and female, would be to part company with Christian faith: for we learn from Jesus that to be human precedes and transcends differences of ethnic origin and gender.

(4) We learn from Jesus, the image of God, what it is to be human. This statement is more precise and accurate than another statement that might be ventured, that we learn from *scripture* what it is to be human. We do not learn what we need to know merely by assembling and analysing various converging and conflicting scriptural statements, concluding perhaps with the opinion that a *single* doctrine of the human is not to be found in scripture, and that such a doctrine would be the result of imposing alien systematic concerns on the essentially heterogeneous scriptural material. Scripture contains optimistic (Ps. 8) and pessimistic (Job 14) accounts of the human condition; its emphasis on divine–human likeness (Gen. 1.26, 28) is counter-

balanced by an emphasis on divine–human unlikeness (Isa. 40.18, 25; Eccl. 5.2); it contains an indictment accusing the entire human race of apostasy from the divine will (Rom. 1.18–3.20), but it also knows of the purely natural goodness of the Samaritan (Luke 10.29–37); it teaches both the bondage of the human will (Rom. 9.14–29) and its freedom (Luke 15.11–20). The two hermeneutical options (which are also theological options) are to allow this diversity to stand or to insist on the methodological priority of the *centre* of scripture (the event of the Word become flesh), which both relativizes the individual statement and establishes it in its true significance.

The hermeneutical-theological thesis of the centre of Christian scripture will not readily be accepted by exegetes. If we subordinate the individual text to the centre, we will in practice be subordinating one text to others; but on what basis do we conclude that some texts are more fundamental than others? How, on this approach, can the particularity of the non-fundamental texts be preserved from dogmatic encroachments proceeding from the (perhaps arbitrarily-defined) centre? Why, in any case, should scripture *need* a 'centre'? The metaphor of the 'centre' stems – it might be argued – from old-fashioned convictions about scriptural unity that have long since ceased to convince. Might there not be good *theological* reasons for abandoning this metaphor and for welcoming the fact of scriptural heterogeneity? The idea that any one person – even Jesus – can single-handedly teach us 'what it is to be human' is, after all, rather far-fetched. Would we not do better to welcome scriptural diversity on the grounds that no single doctrine of the human has a monopoly of the truth, and that a collage of different insights and experiences gives us a much richer account of ourselves than we are likely to acquire from the vain pursuit of an authoritative or authoritarian dogma?

This popular and specious argument makes a virtue out of its supposed concern for the 'integrity' of the individual text. What it conceals is the extent to which this concern is bound up with a concern to subvert the integrity of holy scripture as a whole. Concern for the integrity of the individual text legitimates an understanding of scripture as consisting in nothing more than an arbitrary accumulation and juxtaposition of heterogeneous material. It is in fact a very simple and obvious observation about the Christian canon that it is structured around a clearly-defined centre which represents the point of division between 'old' and 'new'; and it should not be entirely unexpected that Christian theology might want to operate on that basis. And yet most modern biblical interpretation completely disregards the question of the hermeneutical significance of this canonical structuring.[10] Modern biblical interpretation generally operates on the assumption that the texts must be understood in abstraction from their canonical location and status, and this assumption is so widely accepted that it is hard even to make an alternative proposal comprehensible. The thesis that Jesus stands at the centre of Christian scripture will not preclude particularity, diversity or richness; it will preclude only the incoherence and the arbitrary preferences which are otherwise inevitable.

2. Image and Dominion

In Jesus as the image of God we learn what it is to be human. But that is purely an epistemological statement, and tells us nothing of the *content* of the knowledge we acquire from Jesus. Because the full content of this disclosure is infinitely diverse and rich, we need a particular standpoint from which to approach this matter; and we may find this in the Genesis image-of-God statements. To claim, with Paul, that Jesus is the image of God is by no means to forget Genesis. The Genesis texts have already influenced the discussion so far by suggesting that the christological image-of-God concept should be understood anthropologically, and it is time to draw on them further.

The Genesis texts do not explain why they speak of humankind as in the image and likeness of God. Nevertheless, two aspects of this language stand out particularly clearly.

(1) The terms 'image' (*ṣelem*) and 'likeness' (*dᵉmûth*) refer in the first instance to visual representations. The Israelites are commanded to 'drive out all the inhabitants of the land from before you, and destroy all their figured stones, and destroy all their molten images [*kol-ṣalmê massēkōthām*], and demolish all their high places' (Num. 33.52), and the images in question are clearly visual representations of other deities. Later, the Philistines enquire of their priests and diviners how to escape the disasters that their own capture of the ark of the covenant has brought upon them, and are told: 'You must make images [*ṣalmê*] of your tumours and images [*ṣalmê*] of your mice that ravage the land . . .' (1 Sam. 6.5). Image (*ṣelem*) denotes similarity of appearance. The same is true of likeness (*dᵉmûth*). When King Ahaz travelled to Damascus to meet King Tiglath-Pilezer of Assyria, he was impressed by an altar there and decided to commission a copy of it; he therefore sent the high priest Uriah a likeness or model (*dᵉmûth*) of the altar, 'exact in all its details' (2 Kgs. 16.10).

This is in essential agreement with the usage of Gen. 5.3, which tells how, 'when Adam had lived a hundred and thirty years, he became the father of a son in his own likeness, after his image [*bidᵉmûthô kᵉṣalmô*], and named him Seth'. Seth was in Adam's likeness and after his image in the sense that, broadly speaking and *mutatis mutandis*, he looked like his father. The reference, two verses previously, to God's creation of *'ādām* (male and female) in his own likeness (Gen. 5.1) indicates that here too the relationship is one of physical resemblance. Broadly speaking and *mutatis mutandis*, humans look like God. The people of Israel is not to make for itself 'a graven image or any likeness [*pesel w⁽kol-t⁽mûnah*] of anything that is in heaven above, or that is in the earth beneath, or that is in the water under the earth' (Exod. 20.4; Deut. 5.8); for the person who contemplates making a surrogate image of the divine in the shape of one of the creatures of air, land and sea is himself or herself already the only authorized divine image. Humans are not to create an image of God because they are already that image, created by God.[11]

If humans look like God, it seems to follow that God himself bears a form similar to the human one. Having observed for a while the bewildering movement of the four living creatures and the wheels associated with each of them, the prophet Ezekiel notices

> the likeness [*d⁽mûth*] of a firmament, shining like crystal, spread out above their heads . . . and above the firmament over their heads there was the likeness [*d⁽mûth*] of a throne, in appearance like sapphire; and upon the likeness of a throne was a likeness as it were of a human appearance [*d⁽mûth k⁽marʾēh ādām*]. And upward from what had the appearance of his loins I saw as it were the appearance of fire enclosed round about; and downward from what had the appearance of his loins I saw as it were an appearance of fire, and there was brightness round about him. Like the appearance of the bow that is in the cloud on the day of rain, so was the appearance of the brightness round about. Such was the appearance of the likeness of the glory of Yahweh [*hû marʾēh d⁽mûth k⁽bōd-yhwh*] . . . (Ezek. 1.22, 26–28)

Unlike humans, Yahweh is manifest in fire and brightness; and yet, his form is recognizably a human one. Ezekiel's teaching corresponds to that of Genesis: if humans are made in the likeness of God, then God will resemble the human form if and when he makes himself visible (cf. Exod. 33.18–23; Isa. 6.1; Dan. 7.9).[12]

This disconcerting teaching is no doubt the reason why Ezek. 1 was not read in the synagogue. As the Mishnah notes, 'the chapter about the Chariot may not be used as a reading from the prophets' – although it duly records the dissenting opinion of R. Judah, who 'permits this' (*Megilloth* 4.10). It is equally disconcerting to realize that the familiar Genesis image-of-God concept is most straightforwardly interpreted along similar lines as an assertion of likeness of appearance. The claim that the Genesis narrator has 'spiritualized' the originally visual connotations of *ṣelem* and *d⁽mûth* cannot account for the recurrence of precisely this vocabulary in the case of the relationship of Adam to Seth (Gen. 5.3). It is perhaps because such language was understood to be dangerous that it evokes so few echoes in the rest of the Old Testament. The divinity of God is not to be compromised by dangerous speculation about the humanity of God. 'To whom then will you compare me [*t°damm°yûnî*, from the same root as *d°mûth*] that I should be like him? says the Holy One' (Isa. 40.25).

Rather than simply rejecting the postulate of a divine–human likeness, understood in primarily visual terms, an alternative would be a christological interpretation. In his *Adversus omnes haereses*, iv.20, Irenaeus argues against the heretical view that 'he who was seen by the prophets was a different God, the Father of all being invisible'.[13] The saying 'No one shall see God and live' (Exod. 33.20) was said 'in respect to his greatness and his wonderful glory', and does not contradict the truth that 'when [God] pleases he is seen by men, by whom he wills and when he wills and as he wills' (iv.20.5):

> Inasmuch, then as the Spirit of God pointed out by the prophets things to come, forming and adapting us beforehand for the purpose of our being made subject to God, but it was still a future thing that man, through the good pleasure of the Holy Spirit, should see God, it necessarily behoved those through whose instrumentality future things were attested, to see God, whom they intimated as to be seen by men . . . (iv.20.8)

It is especially clear in the case of Ezekiel

> that the prophets saw the dispensations of God in part, but not actually God himself. For when this man had seen the vision of God, and the cherubim and their wheels, and when he had recounted the mystery of the whole of that progression, and had beheld the likeness of a throne above them, and upon the throne a likeness as of the figure of a man . . . , and when he had set forth all the rest of the vision of the thrones, lest anyone might happen to think that in all this he had actually seen God, he added: 'This was the appearance of the likeness of the glory of God.' If, then, neither Moses, nor Elias, nor Ezekiel, who had all many celestial visions, did see God; but if what they did see were similitudes of the splendour of the Lord, and prophecies of things to come, it is clear that the Father is indeed invisible, of whom also the Lord said, 'No-one has seen God at any time'. But his Word, as he himself willed it, and for the benefit of those who beheld, did show the Father's brightness and explained his purposes . . . (iv.20.10–11)

The prophet sees God in human likeness not because God is human in form – for God is the Holy One, spirit not flesh – but because, without abandoning his holiness and his spirituality, God purposes to become human, in the incarnation of his Word, and to be seen as such. If Jewish scripture is the primary semantic matrix for the early Christian understanding of Jesus, then the scriptural passages that appear to compromise the divine incomparability to everything created take on a new significance (compare the interpretation of Isa. 6 in John 12.41). Their claim is that, when God reveals himself in visions to his prophets, he does so in a quasi-human form; and, in retrospect, they must be understood to play a part in the work of the whole Christian Old Testament, which is to prepare the way of the Lord and to make straight his paths.

Transferring all this to the Genesis image-of-God concept, we must first exclude the possibility that Gen. 1.26–28 could ever warrant any talk of God as *inherently* human in form. To that extent, the refusal of the rest of the Old Testament to take up this concept is understandable and appropriate. Yet the notion of a visual likeness between God and humans, implied here as in the Ezekiel parallel, is not simply to be rejected. It is to be understood as a prophetic anticipation of the incarnation. The incarnate, human Jesus is the image of God; his action for human salvation is at the same time God's action, his speech is at the same time God's speech, and to see him and hear him is to see and hear God. 'He who has seen me has seen the Father' (John 14.9). But the person, the action and the speech that discloses the Father is still a human person, action and speech. It is the person, action and speech of the human Jesus that makes him like God in the sense that he discloses God. 'Truly, truly I say to you, the Son can do nothing of his own accord but only what he sees the Father doing; for whatever he does, that the Son does likewise [*homoiōs*]' (John 5.19). Accompanying and preceding the visible action of the Son is the invisible action of the Father that becomes indirectly visible in the action of the Son. The Son's person and action are therefore the one true *homoiōma* of the Father's person and action; this particular human person is the image and likeness of God in the strictest possible sense.

Yet Gen. 1.26–28 is speaking not directly of Jesus but of all humans. All humans may be said to be like God in the sense that they are like Jesus. He shares their human existence, the path they must traverse from birth to death; and they share his human existence. If Jesus is like God, then, in so far as they are like Jesus, all humans are like God. Without this christological reference, the concept of the image and likeness of God should be handed over as quickly as possible to the Platonizers and the spiritualizers, who insist that the image is to be found in the human mind but is absent from the human body. Yet, in Genesis, it is not the mind but the whole human person who is made in the image and likeness of God; and that is the case with Jesus, who mirrors God not only in his mind but also in his bodily action. If he is indeed the paradigmatic case of the human likeness to God, then the notion of an original universal creation of humankind in the image of God must be understood to be retrospectively constituted. Thus, when murder is prohibited on the grounds that 'God made humankind in his own image' (Gen. 9.6), we may understand this to mean that acts of violence against the human person are incompatible with the honouring of the human person that occurs when God in Christ establishes a likeness and identity between the human person's being and activity and his own. The human person is prophetic of Jesus, the Son of man. Wherever the human person is honoured rather than dishonoured, it may therefore be said that 'as you did it to one of the least of these my brethren, you did it to me' (Matt. 25.40).

In Jesus we learn who we are; and 'we' here encompasses not Christians alone but all humans, since it is all humans who are created in the image and likeness of God. We are like God in the sense that we are like the human Jesus, whose person and actions are identified with the person and actions of God. God has created a human counterpart who stands not on the far side of an ontological abyss but within God's own being; and this fact is the hermeneutical key not only to the divine identity but also to our human identity. We are that creature which, in the person of the one man Jesus, has been singled out for an utterly unprecedented role as counterpart to God within God.

The point of this singling out of the one man Jesus is not to identify a transaction that occurs within God but without us. Jesus is the image of God not for his own benefit but for ours. If God has enabled us to 'see the light of the gospel of the glory of Christ, who is the image of God' (2 Cor. 4.4), the purpose is not that we should simply gaze and remain untransformed but that, through the action of the Holy Spirit within the Christian community, we should be 'changed into the same image, from glory to glory' (2 Cor. 3.18).[14] God has determined us to be 'conformed to the image of his Son [*summorphous tēs eikonos tou huiou autou*], in order that he might be the first-born among many brothers and sisters' (Rom. 8.29), and this 'conformation' is not a magical process but, negatively, a refusal to be 'conformed to this world [*mē sunschēmatizesthe tō aiōni toutō*]', and, positively, a being 'trans-formed by the renewal of the mind [*metamorphousthe tē anakainōsei tou noos*] so that you may discern what is the will of God, what is good and acceptable and perfect' (Rom. 12.2). In this way, a being and an action occur within the world in which the perfect likeness of Jesus' being and action to God's being and action is partially and fragmentarily reproduced. As this occurs, we are conformed to the image of God's Son and participate directly in the image of God that is uniquely his.[15]

We should therefore distinguish a universal human likeness to God, deriving from the universal human likeness to Jesus, from the direct par-ticipation in Jesus' God-likeness that occurs within the Christian community and through the Holy Spirit. Conformation to the image of God's Son is the goal of human creation in the image of God, and human creation in the image of God is the ontological presupposition for conformation to the image of God's Son.

(2) In Gen. 1.26, the divine decision to create humankind in the image and likeness of God is immediately followed by the decision that they are to 'rule over [*rdh*] the fish of the sea, and over the birds of the air, and over the cattle, and over all the earth, and over every moving thing that moves upon the earth'. The transition from creation in the image of God to human rule over the creatures is repeated in the following verses. Having created humankind in his own image, the creator communicates his intention for them: 'Be fruitful and multiply, and fill the earth and subdue it; and rule over the fish of the sea and over the birds of the air and over every living thing that moves upon the earth' (v. 28). The image of God does not *consist in* rule over the creatures, for it can be asserted without reference to this (Gen. 5.1; 9.6); but rule over the creatures appears at least to be an immediate *consequence* of creation in the image of God.

What is meant by this rule over the creatures? Gen. 1.26 and 28 both begin their accounts of the objects of this rule by referring to 'the fish of the sea' and 'the birds of the air'. In what sense do humans rule over all fish and birds? The use of these creatures for food is not yet envisaged, as the diet of humans and animals alike is originally vegetarian (1.29–30). Another Old Testament author finds the idea of a human dominion over the birds highly implausible:

> Is it by your wisdom that the hawk soars, and spreads his wings toward the south? Is it at your command that the eagle mounts up and makes his nest on high? On the rock he dwells and makes his home in the fastness of the rocky crag. Thence he spies out his prey; his eyes behold it afar off. His young ones suck up blood; and where the slain are, there is he. (Job 39.26–30)

A similar independence of human concerns could no doubt be attributed to the fish. As for the 'cattle' (the third item in the list in Gen. 1.26), the word *bᵉhēmah* denotes domesticated animals as opposed to the wild 'beasts of the earth' (*hayyath hā'āreṣ*); these categories of animal are carefully differentiated in Gen. 1.24, 25; 2.20; 3.14. Human 'rule' over domesticated animals is the most readily comprehensible aspect of the promise of dominion. Gen. 1.26 proceeds, however, to extend this rule to 'all the earth', and to 'every moving thing that moves [*rmś*] upon the earth' (cf. v. 28: 'every living thing that moves [*rmś*] upon the earth') – probably a comprehensive reference to all land-creatures. What kind of rule do humans exercise over the animal kingdom as a whole?

The problem lies not in the connotations of violence that accompany the verb *rādāh*. The verb can mean 'tread down' (cf. Joel 3.13 [4.13 MT], with reference to the wine-press), but Israel's sacred writers know quite well how to differentiate a just from an unjust rule. The verb can be used for both. In Ezek. 34.4 Israel's shepherds are condemned for their treatment of the sheep: 'With force and harshness you have ruled them [*rᵉdîthem 'ōthām*].' Yet in Ps. 72.8 the wish that the king may 'rule [*wᵉyērᵉd*] from sea to sea' follows the wish in v. 7 for the flourishing of justice and peace. There is no reason to imagine that the human rule over the animals referred to in Gen. 1.26, 28 is to be a rule of force and harshness rather than of justice and peace. It is true, however, that at a later point in the narrative it is said that 'the fear of you and the dread of you shall be upon every beast of the earth and upon every bird of the air, upon everything that moves on the ground and all the fish of the sea . . . Every moving thing that lives shall be food for you; and as I gave you the green plants, I give you everything' (Gen. 9.2–3). Human rule over the creatures is now expressed in the new form of using them for nourishment.

Yet even this does not seem fully to explain the notion of human rule over the creatures. Humans do not eat all creatures: cross-cultural parallels to the distinctions in Lev. 11 between clean creatures that may be eaten and unclean ones that may not would not be hard to find. The notion of a universal human rule over all creatures appears to express not so much an active relationship as a general conviction of human superiority to the creatures. Humans are involved in active relationship with some creatures – domesticated animals, creatures of land, sea and air used for food, wild animals that pose a threat to life or property – but by no means with all. The promise of dominion does not confine itself to these particular relationships but is universal in scope. It is a promise that humans transcend the world of the creatures in significance and value – as in Jesus' assurance that 'you are of more value than many sparrows' (Matt. 10.31, cf. 12.12). The world contains many species of living creature, but humans rule over them all because they transcend them all.[16]

A very similar view is expressed in Ps. 8.3–8:

> When I look at thy heavens, the work of thy fingers, the moon and the stars which thou hast established; what is man, that thou art mindful of him, and the son of man that thou dost care for him? Yet thou hast made him little less than God [*mᵉᶜat mē'ᵉlōhîm*; LXX *braxu ti par' aggelous*] and dost crown him with glory and honour. Thou hast given him dominion [*tamshîlēhû*] over the works of thy hands; thou hast put all things under his feet, all sheep and oxen, and also the beasts of the field, the birds of the air, and the fish of the sea, whatever passes along the paths of the sea.

The creation of humans as 'little less than God' resembles the Genesis concept of the image of God: LXX's decision to treat *'ᵉlōhîm* as a plural is a possible reading (cf. Ps. 82.1, where *'ᵉlōhîm* is clearly plural), but probably reflects embarrassment at the assertion of a human proximity to God.[17] In parallel with Genesis, the assertion of human God-likeness leads to the idea of human rule over all the creatures – not only domesticated ones ('sheep and oxen') but also wild animals, birds and fish. The image of kingship is more prominent here than in Genesis, occurring not only in the reference to 'rule' (*mšl*, v. 7 [EVV v. 6]; cf. *rdh*) but also in the coronation-language of the preceding verse: 'Thou dost crown him with glory and honour' – *kābōd wᵉhādār* are particular prerogatives of the king in Ps. 21.6 (EVV v. 5). As in Genesis, it is difficult to see what this *universal* dominion amounts to; and the most plausible solution is again that a general human transcendence over the world of the creatures is asserted, but without any clear reflection on the concrete *relationships* between humans and the creatures. The result is that the psalm's answer to its own question, 'What is man . . .?' (v. 4), is curiously abstract and undefined. Humans are said to be incomparably greater than all other creatures, but it is not clear that this statement makes a difference to anything. Humans often believe in their own superiority to the other creatures, but what matters is not the bare fact of this superiority but its nature and implications. In what sense are humans that creature uniquely crowned by God with glory and honour? Neither the psalm nor Genesis help us much here.[18]

Theologically, the reason why the notion of human transcendence of the creatures is left abstract and incomplete in the Old Testament is that it can only be filled out and made concrete by Jesus. The Epistle to the Hebrews therefore interprets Ps. 8 (and, by implication, Gen. 1.26, 28) as follows:

> For it was not to angels that God subjected the world to come, of which we are speaking. It has been testified somewhere, 'What is man that thou art mindful of him, or the son of man that thou carest for him? Thou didst make him for a little while lower than the angels, thou hast crowned him with glory and honour, thou hast subjected everything under his feet.' In 'subjecting everything' to him, he left nothing outside his control. At present, we do not yet see everything in subjection to him. But we see the one who 'for a little while was made lower than the angels', Jesus, by way of the suffering of death 'crowned with glory and honour', so that by the grace of God he might taste death for everyone. (Heb. 2.5–9)

Despite the possible christological connotations of *huios anthrōpou*, the psalmist's opening question is probably understood here in general anthropological terms. The reference to *huios anthrōpou* is subordinated to the first half of the question (*ti estin anthrōpos hoti mimnēskē autou*), where nothing suggests a christological reference for *anthrōpos*. In any case, the christological expression occurs not as *huios anthrōpou* but as *ho huios tou anthrōpou*.[19] If this is correct, the author to the Hebrews understands the psalm as returning a christological answer to the anthropological question why humankind is the concern of God.[20] The answer unfolds in three successive stages. First, God made him (Jesus) 'for a little while lower than the angels'. Like MT's *m^e'at*, the LXX's *brachu ti* can have a temporal sense (cf. Isa. 57.17: *di' hamartian brachu ti elupēsa auton* . . ., in contrast to 2 Sam.16.1: *kai David parēlthen brachu ti apo tēs Roos* [=summit]); and that is how the author to the Hebrews takes it. It is important for him that this relative lowliness is only temporary, for the superiority of the Son to the angels has been the theme of the whole of his first chapter. Second, God 'crowned him with glory and honour': the reference is to Jesus' exaltation to the right hand of the Father, following his death. Other psalm texts (notably Pss. 45.6–7 and 110.1) have already been applied in Heb. 1 to Jesus' exaltation. Third, the author omits the line 'and thou hast set him over the works of thy hands' (Ps. 8.7a LXX) and applies the next line, 'thou hast subjected everything under his feet', to the eschatological future when Jesus triumphs over all his enemies. This chronological, three-stage christological reading of the psalm text is clearly implied in the author's commentary in vv. 8–9. The text, he argues, speaks of a subjection of *everything* to Jesus, and this we do not yet see; the reference is therefore to the future (v. 8). What we do see is a Jesus once 'made a little lower than the angels' and now 'crowned with glory and honour' (v. 9). The answer to the anthropological question why humankind is the object of God's concern is given in a three-stage christology of humiliation, exaltation and final victory. The psalm's description of human transcendence over the creatures is given a concrete application to Jesus, and the universality implied in the notion of the subjection of everything (*panta*) is emphasized: there is therefore no need to specify sheep and oxen, birds and fish.[21]

It might seem that this early Christian exegesis of Ps. 8 has virtually nothing in common with responsible literal exegesis as now understood, and that an attempt to defend it would necessarily be an extreme case of special pleading. The author, we might argue, has been led astray at two points: first in his interpretation of *brachu ti*, which introduces an element of temporal progression into the text that is not present in the original; and second in the LXX's substitution of 'angels' for 'God'. The result is that an anthropological statement about the near-divine glory of humankind ('Thou hast made him little less than God') is replaced by a christological statement about the temporary humiliation of Christ ('Thou didst make him for a little while lower than the angels'). The result is a contrast with the next clause ('Thou hast crowned him with glory and honour') rather than the smooth continuity of the original; and a further temporal distinction is found between this clause and the following one ('Thou hast put everything in subjection under his feet'), on the grounds that this must refer to an eschatological reality. The fact that in the original 'everything' refers to sheep and oxen, birds and fish is suppressed. As so often with New Testament interpretation of the Old (we might conclude), we can see exactly why it takes the form it does, and yet find ourselves quite unable to affirm it.

Let us suppose, however, that the author to the Hebrews is here engaging not in literal exegesis but in *critical* exegesis of the psalm text in the light of its subject-matter. The criticism of the text begins with the LXX translator, who, rightly seeing that nothing in the human relationship to sheep, oxen, birds and fish justifies the claim that humans are 'little less than God', took *ᵉlōhîm* as a plural (as in Ps. 82.1) and rendered it 'angels'. To the criterion of divine transcendence the author to the Hebrews added a christological criterion. In the light of Jesus, it simply cannot be true that God's intention for humankind is fulfilled in a general, abstract human superiority to the world of the creatures. Jesus died for us and was exalted to the right hand of the Father; and at the end of all things his cause will triumph. Since he is a being of flesh and blood like ourselves (cf. Heb. 2.14), his is a human death, exaltation and triumph; and these events chart our own destiny, for Jesus is 'the pioneer of our salvation' whose role it is not to achieve something for his own benefit but to bring 'many sons to glory' (v. 10). If the psalm is to answer truthfully its own question about why humankind is God's concern, it must enunciate not a general anthropology but an anthropology shaped and determined by christology. Can it be read in this way? Retrospectively, in the light of the Christ-event, it can be and must be. There is no human apart from Jesus who is truly 'crowned with glory and honour' (Heb. 2.7), and if the psalm is to speak truly it must therefore be taken to refer to him. There is no subjection of all things to humankind apart from the one that is taking place in Jesus; and so, by insisting on a strict interpretation of *panta*, the author can find a reference to Jesus here too. Jesus' present glory and honour and his future victory are rooted in a human life that culminated in humiliation and death, and if the psalm in its Septuagintal form can be read as referring to a temporary residence in the human, sub-angelic sphere, then that is again to the advantage of its ability to enunciate the truth. The psalm is read in the critical light of God's own answer, in Jesus, to the question 'what is man, that thou art mindful of him?' The text is reoriented towards the divine answer that has occurred in the life, death and exaltation of Jesus, in such a way that it too can share in the enunciation of that divine answer.

In Jesus as the image of God, we learn what it is to be human; and we learn in him what is the true nature of the rule over the created order that was promised in the beginning. The notion of a general superiority to the creatures is only a beginning. Far more significant is the overcoming in Jesus of perhaps the most terrible of creaturely realities, death: because he has 'tasted death for everyone' (Heb. 2.9), Jesus is able to 'deliver all those who through fear of death were subject to lifelong slavery' (v. 15). Paul too understands the promise of Ps. 8.6 that 'he has put everything in subjection under his feet' to include a reference to the defeat of 'the last enemy', death (1 Cor. 15.25–27). To be human is therefore to share with Jesus a way which has its final goal in the overcoming of death. The promise of human transcendence of the creaturely sphere finally amounts to nothing less than that. The Old Testament must in the end remain agnostic about the scope of this human transcendence: for, after all, 'who knows whether the human spirit goes upward and the spirit of the beast goes down to the earth?' (Eccl. 3.21). In his resurrection, however, Jesus is the guarantee of a transcendent human destiny. That does not diminish the significance of human existence (including human relations with the creatures) on the near side of death: the significance of the way is greater, not less, if it is a way towards a goal rather than petering out in the middle of nowhere. Jesus himself represents not only the goal but also the way. In order to be 'perfected' he too had to tread this way, sharing the joys, sorrows and temptations common to flesh and blood in our sub-angelic, human sphere, 'learning obedience through what he suffered' (Heb. 5.8), in faith enduring the cross and despising the shame (12.2). Discipleship requires us to embrace the way too, and not only the goal.

The danger of a Christian obsession with the far side of death is in any case much less than the danger of an utter neglect of this topic. Where the 'glory' that is the final human destiny is neglected, then it can no longer be said that 'we see Jesus . . . crowned with glory and honour' (Heb. 2.9); and, failing to see the exalted Lord, we will no longer see his earthly way, since it will have lost its goal. He will have become largely superfluous to us, and we may even be attracted by the thought that 'man . . . is like the beasts that perish' (Ps. 49.12, 20), and conclude that the notion of a human transcendence of the creatures is an illusion.

In the Genesis texts, as we have seen, humans are created in the image of God in the sense that they physically resemble God: God himself bears the 'likeness as it were of a human form' (Ezek. 1.26). There is also a close connection between the image of God and rule over the creatures, although the latter should not be identified with the former but is presented in Gen. 1.26, 28 as its immediate corollary. One further idea associated with the image of God must be mentioned: the creation of humankind as male and female. According to Gen. 1.27, 'God created man in his own image, in the image of God he created him; male and female he created them.' Similarly, in Gen. 5.1–2 it is said that 'when God created man, he made him in the likeness of God. Male and female he created them and named them Man when they were created'. It is not clear, however, exactly what the relationship is between creation in the image of God and as male and female. Are these ideas essentially independent? Or is creation as male and female a key, perhaps *the* key, for understanding the image-of-God concept?

Although the latter view is currently popular,[22] it seems preferable to regard the two ideas as independent, for the following reasons:

(1) Creation in the image of God *differentiates* humankind from all other creatures, and for this reason its consequence is human rule over the creatures. Yet human creation as male and female emphasizes the *connection* with other creatures: for to be male and female is characteristic of 'all flesh' (Gen. 6.19; 7.16), that is, of all the living creatures, human and non-human, who entered the ark (cf. also 7.2–3, 8).[23] Of course, men and women are male and female in a distinctively human way, whereas birds and beasts are male and female in non-human ways, but the Genesis text does not reflect on this difference.

(2) The language of Genesis implies that the individual person is made in the image of God: 'In the image of God he created *him*' (Gen. 1.27, cf. 5.1). In Gen. 9.6, the prohibition of murder is based on human creation in the image of God, which must therefore be predicated of the individual. The individual created in the image of God is of course not considered in abstraction from social relationship, yet it would go beyond the text to claim that it is *only* in human interrelatedness that the image of God is manifested.

(3) The reference in Gen. 1.27 to creation as male and female therefore does not imply 'that the image of God came through the distinction of sex, but that the image of God belongs to both sexes', as Aquinas rightly notes (*ST*, Ia.93.7).[24] Men and women are created in the image of God, but the image of God is not to be found specifically in their interrelatedness.[25]

(4) The traditional trinitarian reading of the plural 'Let us make . . .' in Gen. 1.26 may be correlated with the human plurality of male and female; God and humans are then alike in being communal or relational beings. The parallel is not exact, however: for the text stresses precisely that aspect of human relatedness (existence as male and female) which, on the trinitarian hypothesis, is absent from the divine being. Theologically, this interpretation tends to assert a parallel between human society and the immanent trinity that can be established without reference to christology.[26] At the root of this interpretation is perhaps another philosophical anthropology (in which the

human person is a person-in-relation), which the Genesis texts and the doctrine of the immanent trinity then appear to confirm.

In contrast to this exegetically and theologically flawed approach, I have tried here to be attentive both to the Old Testament texts, read on their own terms, and to the radical nature of the christological transformation of all theological concepts. Having established the methodological significance of the identification of Jesus as the image of God, it would have been possible to develop this theme from texts other than Genesis – most obviously, the gospels. The decision to retain the traditional approach by way of Genesis has resulted in certain limitations: even in christological transformation, the Genesis image-of-God concept and the corollary of human rule over the creatures have, as it were, a finite theological content beyond which they should not be pressed. Humans are like God in the sense that they look like God; their appearance is similar to his. This was interpreted with reference to Jesus, God's counterpart whose entire being exists only within the being of God: the human Jesus is paradigmatically like God, and all other humans are therefore like God in that, as humans, they are like Jesus. This external likeness has as its goal an internal likeness, as, through the Holy Spirit operative within the Christian community, there occurs a human being and action corresponding to Jesus' and therefore participating directly in the image of God. The corollary of human creation in the image of God, human rule over the creatures, also required a radical christological interpretation, following the critical rather than literal exegesis practised by the author to the Hebrews. A consequence of the human God-likeness disclosed in the being and action of Jesus is that the human destiny actualized in him involves the overcoming and transcending of death itself. Jesus therefore discloses what it is to be human, and the Genesis texts are to be understood as prophetic of that event.

NOTES

1. *Philo*, vol. I, Loeb Classical Library, trans. F. H. Colson and G. H. Whittaker, London: Heinemann; Cambridge, Mass.: Harvard University Press, 1929.

2. R. Niebuhr, *The Nature and Destiny of Man, I: Human Nature*, London: Nisbet, 1941.

3. Contrast the view of the Wisdom of Solomon, where to be created in the image of God is to participate in his eternity: 'God created man for incorruption, and made him in the image of his own eternity [*eikona tēs idias aidiotētos epoiēsen auton*], but through the devil's envy death entered the world, and those who belong to his party experience it' (Wis. 2.23–24).

4. The view of James Barr, *Biblical Faith and Natural Theology*, Oxford: Clarendon Press, 1993, 164.

5. According to Lohse, commenting on Col. 1.15, 'Even though the term "image" . . . suggests Gen. 1:27, it is out of the question to interpret it as a direct reference to the biblical account of creation. When the word *eikōn* is defined as the "image" of the invisible God, the Hellenistic understanding of the term is to be assumed' (E. Lohse, *Colossians and Philemon*, Hermeneia, ET Philadelphia: Fortress, 1971, 46). In the background here is an understanding of the cosmos as God's image (attested in Plato and the Corpus Hermeticum), which was transferred by Hellenistic Judaism to Wisdom (cf. Wis. 7.26, where Wisdom is an 'image of [God's] goodness [*eikōn tēs agathotētos*])' (47). Lohse acknowledges that in Col. 3.10 'God's eschatological new creation is described . . . with reference to Gen. 1:26f' (142), but does not see the relevance of this to the interpretation of the christological title in 1.15. He also fails to see that, if Christ is the image of the invisible God, his own visibility and thus his humanity must be implied.

6. There is even less need for theories of a 'background in [the] Wisdom speculation of Hellenistic Judaism' here than in the case of Col. 1.15 (against V. P. Furnish, *II Corinthians*, Anchor Bible, Garden City, NY: Doubleday, 1984, 222). 'The glory of Christ, who is the image of God' is, according to 2 Cor. 4.4, the content of 'the gospel', and what is proclaimed in the gospel is not a metaphysical speculation but 'Jesus Christ as Lord' (v. 5). Furnish's claim that 'this christological use of the concept [of *eikōn tou theou*] has close affinities with Philo's application of it to the Logos' (222) overlooks the fact that there really are significant differences between the Philonic Logos and the Pauline Jesus.

7. In 2 Cor. 3.18 *katoptrizomenoi* probably means 'beholding as in a mirror' (*katoptron* = 'mirror'); *tēn autēn eikona* would then be a reference to that which is beheld in the mirror, 'the glory of the Lord' – that is, 'the glory of God in the face of Jesus Christ' (4.6). He is the image of God and mirrors the glory of God to us, and we are transformed into 'the same image'. This seems a more plausible interpretation than the view that 'the "mirror" in which Christians see reflected the glory of the Lord is not . . . the gospel itself, or even Jesus Christ. It is one another' (N. T. Wright, *The Climax of the Covenant: Christ and the Law in Pauline Theology*, Edinburgh: T. & T. Clark, 1991, 185; italics removed). 2 Cor. 3.16–18 applies to Christians Moses' practice of removing the veil when he went in to speak with the Lord (Exod. 34.34a, quoted freely in 2 Cor. 3.16) and to be transfigured by his glory (Exod. 34.34b–35); a 'direct' encounter with Christ through the Spirit is therefore relevant here. The view that *tēn autēn eikona* should be understood in the light of the reference to Christ as *eikōn tou theou* (4.4) is preferable to the claim that 'Christians are changed into the same image as each other' (188).

8. I follow here Barth's plea for 'the founding of anthropology on Christology' (*Church Dogmatics*, III/2, 44). 'As the man Jesus is himself the revealing Word of God, he is the source of our knowledge of the nature of man as created by God' (3).

9. This distinction between the phenomena and the ontology of the human is derived from K. Barth, *Church Dogmatics*, III/2, 71–132.

10. Even Brevard Childs' valuable attempt to recover the hermeneutical significance of the canon fails to reflect adequately on the interrelatedness of the two Testaments, tending to see them merely as juxtaposed. Childs argues one-sidedly that 'the Old Testament bears its true witness as the Old which remains distinct from the New', and that we should resist 'the Christian temptation to identify Biblical Theology with the New Testament's interpretation of the Old, as if the Old Testament's witness were limited to how it was once heard and appropriated by the early church' (*Biblical Theology of the Old and New Testaments: Theological Reflection on the Christian Bible*, London: SCM Press, 1992, 77).

11. Rejecting this interpretation of the image of God, John Sawyer advocates an approach that dispenses with the usual source-critical distinction between the so-called 'P' and 'JE' narratives and reads Gen. 1–3 as a whole ('The Image of God, the Wisdom of Serpents and the Knowledge of Good and Evil', in P. Morris and D. Sawyer [eds.], *A Walk in the Garden: Biblical, Iconographical and Literary Images of Eden*, Sheffield: Sheffield Academic Press, 1992, 64–73). Gen. 1 and 2–3 are to be read in parallel: Gen. 2–3 tells how the image or likeness of God mentioned in 1.26–27 was actually acquired – by the decision of the first human pair, inspired by the serpent, to eat the forbidden fruit, thus acquiring the knowledge of good and evil and becoming 'like one of us' (3.22). But 1.26–27 indicates that God *intended* human creation in his own image and likeness, whereas in chs. 2–3 the likeness to God that consists in the knowledge of good and evil was actually *forbidden*. On Sawyer's view, chs. 2–3 effectively subvert ch. 1.

12. According to G. von Rad, it is 'without question' that 'in the broader background of this Priestly statement about God's image in man there is the notion of Yahweh's human form' (*Genesis*, ET London: SCM Press, 1972⁹, 59; compare von Rad's *Old Testament Theology*, vol. 1, ET London: SCM Press, 1962, 145–46). In both contexts von Rad emphasizes the significance of Ezek. 1.26. W. Eichrodt agrees that the word *ṣelem* 'denotes a statue, that is, a plastic representation', and that it is therefore 'certain that the original idea was of Man's outward form as a copy of God's' (*Theology of the Old Testament*, vol. 2, ET London: SCM Press, 1964⁵, 122); Eichrodt argues that the term is qualified by the addition of the more abstract *dᵉmûth*, which marks a shift 'from physical similarity to spiritual correspondence' (124). In Gen. 5.1, 3; 9.6, however, *ṣelem* and *dᵉmûth* appear to be synonymous and interchangeable. Westermann is critical of the thesis that 'the image and likeness of God is seen in the external form' (also advocated by H. Gunkel, P. Humbert, L. Köhler and W. Zimmerli), finding 'a very telling objection' in the fact that 'the Old Testament knows nothing at all of a separation of a person's spiritual and corporeal components; it sees the person as a whole' (*Genesis 1–11*, ET Minneapolis: Augsburg, 1984, 149–50). It is not clear how this broad generalization about OT anthropology is relevant to the point at issue.

13. Translations are taken from *The Ante-Nicene Fathers*, vol. 1, repr. Grand Rapids: Eerdmans, 1975.

14. I assume here that *hēmeis pantes* (the most probable reading) refers to the Christian community. Although in 2 Cor. 1–7 the first person plural characteristically refers to Paul and his co-workers, the addition of *pantes* suggests a more comprehensive reference here (against L. Belleville, *Reflection of Glory: Paul's Polemical Use of the Moses-Doxa Tradition in 2 Corinthians 3.1–18*, JSNT Supplement Series, Sheffield: Sheffield Academic Press, 1991, 275–76). 2 Cor. 3.16–17 is compatible with the broader reference.

15. 'The form of Jesus Christ takes form in man. Man does not take on an independent form of his own, but what gives him form and what maintains him in the new form is always solely the form of Jesus Christ himself. It is therefore not a vain imitation or repetition of Christ's form but Christ's form itself which takes form in man. And again, man is not transformed into a form which is alien to him, the form of God, but into his own form, the form which is essentially proper to him. Man becomes man because God became man' (D. Bonhoeffer, *Ethics*, ET London: SCM Press 1978, 63).

16. Moltmann argues that 'human lordship on earth is the lordship exercised by a tenant on God's behalf. It means stewardship over the earth, for God' (*God in Creation: An Ecological Doctrine of Creation*, London, SCM Press, 1985, 224). (For Moltmann, in line with Gen. 1.29 but not Gen. 9.3, this stewardship is best practised by vegetarians.)

Do all animals, birds and fish need to be 'stewarded', and is any such universal stewardship actually exercised?

17. H.-J. Krauss argues that, in a psalm addressed to Yahweh (v. 1), *'elōhîm* must refer to heavenly, divine beings (*Psalms 1–59*, ET Minneapolis: Fortress, 1993, 183) – in which case the LXX translator was correct. Is this view compatible with Krauss's thesis of a close dependence on Gen. 1.26–28 (180)?

18. Krauss writes: 'The shepherding and the slaughtering of animals, the hunting and catching of wild game and fish is a sovereign right emanating from God by which the superiority of the human being over all created things – even more, their *'elōhîm*-status – is revealed' (*Psalms 1–59*, 183). Yet the psalm does not mention these activities, confining itself to the *fact* of human superiority.

19. The only exception is John 5.27. On this point see W. L. Lane, *Hebrews 1–8*, Word Biblical Commentary, Waco: Word, 1991, 47.

20. On this interpretation, the 'man' or 'son of man' in v. 6 is not simply to be identified with Jesus (against H. W. Attridge, *Hebrews*, Hermeneia, Philadelphia: Fortress, 1989, 73): the anthropological question receives a christological answer in vv. 7–8a. Thus to say that for the author to the Hebrews the psalm is 'not . . . a meditation on the lofty status of humankind in the created order, but an oracle that describes the humiliation and exaltation of Jesus' (72) is to make a false distinction. The author surely believes (*i*) that Jesus was human, and (*ii*) that his death and exaltation have direct implications for human destiny.

21. I assume here that, after the anthropological question of Heb. 2.6, the rest of the quotation from Ps. 8 is understood christologically: the anthropological question receives a christological answer. It is possible to interpret Heb. 2.7–8 in purely anthropological terms and only to find an explicit christological reference in v. 9, where Jesus is named. The argument would then run: 'Ps. 8 speaks of man's complete authority over the universe. But we see no sign of this at present. What we do see is Jesus, abased for a time, but now exalted in glory' (P. Ellingworth, *Commentary on Hebrews*, New International Greek Testament Commentary, Grand Rapids: Eerdmans; Carlisle: Paternoster, 1993, 150; Ellingworth discusses this question in some detail [150–52]). But the contrast in vv. 8–9 is not between 'man' and 'Jesus': it is between the non-fulfilment (as yet) of the promise of universal subjection (v. 8a) and the fulfilment in Jesus of the psalmist's language about humiliation in this sub-angelic world followed by exaltation.

22. See, for example, A. E. McFadyen, *The Call to Personhood: A Christian Theory of the Individual in Social Relationships*, Cambridge: Cambridge University Press, 1990, 31–39. McFadyen's discussion is, however, based largely on Gen. 2 rather than Gen. 1, and it is not clear that he needs the concept of the image of God in order to derive a relational view of the person from Gen. 2.

23. Compare J. Barr, *Biblical Faith and Natural Theology*, 171. I agree with Barr that Barth's doctrine of the image of God (worked out primarily in *Church Dogmatics* III/1, 181–206) is untenable, but I would dissociate myself from his crude and exaggerated claim that this is 'a particularly ill-judged and irresponsible piece of exegesis' (160).

24. Translation from the 1911 Dominican translation of the *Summa theologica*, repr. Westminster: Christian Classics, 1981. Aquinas bases his statement on the traditional view that the image of God is in the mind, 'in which there is no sexual distinction'; Col. 3.10 and Gal. 3.28 are conflated in order to confirm this point (*ST* Ia.93.7).

25. Phyllis Trible argues that 'in Genesis 1:27 the formal parallelism between the phrases "in the image of God" and "male and female" indicates a semantic correspondence between a lesser known element and a better known element' (*God and the Rhetoric of Sexuality*,

Philadelphia: Fortress, 1978, 17). Trible finds here the basis for the Old Testament's God-language, usually masculine (father, husband, king, warrior), sometimes feminine (mother, midwife, mistress). 'In contrast to the dominant language of scripture . . . , this equal stress upon the image of God male *and* female provides a hermeneutical impetus to investigate female metaphors for God' (22). Yet nothing in Gen. 1.27 requires the hypothesis of a 'semantic correspondence'. After the emphatic chiastic repetition in v. 27ab, v. 27c gives the impression of providing a new piece of information.

26. Compare Moltmann's view: 'In human likeness to God, the analogy is to be found in the differentiation in relationship, and the wealth of relationship in the differentiation. It is this which, in the triune God, constitutes the eternal life of the Father, the Son and the Spirit, and among human beings determines the temporal life of women and men, parents and children. This socially open companionship between people is the form of life which corresponds to God' (*God in Creation*, 223). Although I accepted this view in *Text, Church and World: Biblical Interpretation in Theological Perspective* (Edinburgh: T. & T. Clark; Grand Rapids: Eerdmans, 1994, 107–8, 149–51), I am no longer convinced of either its exegetical basis or its theological value.

Chapter 8

——— ⋈ ———

Scripture in Dialogue:
A Study in Early Christian
Old Testament Interpretation

The Enlightenment's radicalizing of the Reformers' disjunction of text and tradition has led to a fundamental rejection of the entire history of classical Christian interpretation of Christian canonical texts. Although it is conceded that pre-critical exegesis may occasionally have had interesting and sensible things to say (especially where it appears to anticipate modern insights), this tradition as a whole is placed under a cloud of suspicion.[1] However charitable towards it one might wish to be, one is constantly offended by the arbitrariness of interpretations which defy the plain, literal-historical sense of the text in their zeal for the defence and maintenance of orthodox Christian belief. One might choose to blame the notion of a uniform scriptural inspiration, the fatal seductiveness of allegorical approaches, or the rigidities of christological orthodoxy for this state of affairs; but, wherever the problem stems from, it is widely agreed that this tradition must simply be abandoned and that a new start must be made. Henceforth biblical scholars will not assume that they can be assisted by the biblical interpretation of Irenaeus or Augustine, Luther or Calvin. On the contrary, they will assume – in principle and above all in practice – that nothing is to be gained from engagement with the long history of misinterpretation represented by these figures. Various elements of the displaced interpretative tradition still survive within the Christian community, and this situation typically occasions reflection on the unfortunate gulf between modern scholarship and the irrationalities of popular piety. A future is imagined in which it will be possible to proclaim even the more 'radical' results of historical-critical research from the pulpit. In the meantime, the task is to preserve the freedom of this research from those who would subvert it in the name of one or other of the various ecclesiastical orthodoxies.

Current hermeneutical thinking is gradually disclosing the extent to which this modern interpretative tradition is itself riddled with implausibilities and arbitrarinesses. It is, for example, a mistake and an illusion to imagine that the meaning and significance of texts are determined by their relation to their immediate circumstances of origin. This does not mean that all interpretations are to be accorded an equal validity, for reception of earlier interpretation has always been – to a greater or lesser extent – a *critical* activity in which one may have to take issue with one's predecessors as well as building on their achievements. To criticize significant aspects of the exegetical tradition does not place one outside that tradition; on the contrary, critical appropriation – rather than naïve repetition – is the most fruitful way of indwelling that tradition. This critical appropriation will have the positive goal of identifying those aspects of the interpretative and hermeneutical tradition that can assist the renewal of theologically-oriented biblical interpretation and hermeneutics in our own time.

What is required is not simply greater scholarly attention to the history of exegesis. In itself, this would certainly be a good thing, and commentaries sensitive to the history of the text's reception – Childs on Exodus, Luz on Matthew – are a valuable corrective to the usual scholarly insensitivity towards classical Christian exegesis.[2] Yet presentations of the history of a text's interpretation encounter a number of problems. First, the vast mass of available material makes it hard to avoid offering a selective and superficial account, lacking in analytical rigour. Second, to present the history of a text's interpretation is not in itself to indwell the Christian interpretative tradition. That would require one to participate in the tradition's quest for discernment of God's truth as mediated through the biblical text, drawing on the history of interpretation with that goal in mind. Third, the Bible has traditionally been understood as more like a single book than a collection of separate individual books, and this makes it difficult to isolate a reception-history of individual texts and passages from the broader contexts in which they are discussed. It is true that some individual passages acquire prominence in doctrinal debate, and in such cases a relatively self-contained interpretative tradition may develop. Yet such texts are a minority, and in most cases a focus on individual texts will distort the process of reception, projecting onto it the exaggerated modern concern with the distinctiveness and integrity of the individual text over against the whole.

It would seem that surveys of the history of a text's interpretation will have only a limited value. It may prove more valuable to practise a hermeneutically- and theologically-sensitive reading of individual interpretative texts, motivated not by purely historical interests or a misplaced desire for comprehensiveness but by the expectation that these 'secondary' texts will assist us in our endeavours to hear the witness of the primary texts with which they and we are concerned.

The foundations of classical Christian Old Testament interpretation were laid in the attempts of second- and third-century theologians to establish a *via media* between non-Christian Judaism on the one hand and the rejection of the Old Testament by Marcionites and gnostics on the other. Most of the interpretative strategies characteristic of patristic exegesis are already exemplified in Justin Martyr's *Dialogue with Trypho*, a text which represents the coming to maturity of a Christian Old Testament exegesis that is only fragmentarily and unsystematically present in the New Testament itself, and that takes an erratic and one-sided form in the work of Barnabas and Clement. There are, it is true, a number of reasons why a positive assessment of Justin's work might seem fundamentally implausible and even potentially dangerous. A basically *negative* assessment of early Christian Old Testament interpretation might wish to argue a case such as the following:

(1) The distinctive Christian approach to the Old Testament is largely the work of Gentile Christians insufficiently sensitive to the Jewish cultural milieu both of Jewish scripture and of earliest Christianity. For example, the determination to trace un-Jewish doctrines such as the incarnation and the Trinity back into the Jewish scriptures led to serious distortions.

(2) Early Christian history is marked by a growing rift between the church and the Jewish community which leaves an indelible mark on Christian Old Testament interpretation: Jewish scripture is employed for the purposes of anti-Jewish polemic. While this situation is perhaps understandable historically, a responsible contemporary interpretation will play down difference and emphasize possibilities of consensus.

(3) Christian Old Testament exegesis is dominated by an appeal to proof-texts detached from their contexts and interpreted prophetically and christologically. This procedure presupposes an understanding of prophecy as divinely-inspired foretelling that is no longer tenable.

In the discussion that follows, I shall try to show that such claims are at best one-sided and at worst seriously misleading. Early Christian hermeneutics is – at least potentially – more sophisticated and more nuanced than is recognized by its detractors.

The *Dialogue with Trypho* dates from the mid-second century, between about AD 155 and 165, although the dramatic date of the action is *c*.135–

140 since Trypho identifies himself as a refugee who escaped from the Bar Cochba revolt and who now lives mainly in Corinth (*dial.* 1).[3] Trypho and his companions are initially drawn to Justin by the prospect of philosophical conversation, the availability of which is signified by Justin's retention of the philosopher's distinctive dress. Trypho is no stranger to such conversations, having learned from a certain Corinthus the Socratic the value of philosophical discourse. For Trypho, philosophy is compatible with the practice of Judaism because the philosophers seek to investigate the existence and nature of the divine being no less than do Moses and the prophets. This Jew knows that he can receive instruction about God from Gentiles as well as from fellow-Jews; and his Gentile conversation-partner must now account for the fact that, despite his philosopher's clothing, the instruction he proposes to give is in the right interpretation of the law and the prophets. The Jew consults the Gentile about God, but what this particular Gentile knows about God has been derived from Jews – and yet is a quite different knowledge from that which the Jew Trypho already possesses. This complex situation requires the complex literary device of a dialogue within a dialogue: after an account of a philosophical quest for God which eventually led him to Platonism (*dial.* 2), Justin tells of the collapse of his Platonic beliefs and the dawning of Christian faith by recounting a dialogue with an old man, met by chance near the seashore, who plays the role of the Socratic midwife (3–7). Justin encounters the full force of sceptical arguments against the Platonic doctrine of the soul's natural immortality and kinship to God, and is saved from scepticism and disillusion by a reference to the prophets who, long predating the philosophers, announced the future occurrence of certain events that have only recently taken place (8).

Trypho's friends merely laugh at the evangelistic appeal to receive Christ which concludes the autobiographical section (8), but Trypho himself criticizes Justin for having abandoned Plato without having properly understood the Judaism which, as a Christian, he also rejects. If Justin is to be saved, he must be circumcised and observe the sabbaths, the feasts, and the law in its entirety – and he should forget the so-called Christ (8). Justin promises a full justification of his position, if his hearers are willing to listen (9), and, after further preliminaries, embarks on a long explanation of the Christian attitude towards the Mosaic law in response to the charge that Christians wilfully neglect some of its central requirements (11–30). This explanation makes extensive use of prophetic reinterpretations of sacrifice, sabbaths, fasting and circumcision: one point at which the Christian Old Testament differs from the law and the prophets of the Jewish community is in the hermeneutical privileging of the prophets over the law. The prophets point forward to a new order (a new covenant) which will include the Gentiles and in which certain purely Jewish observances will cease; and, more specifically, the prophets point forward not to a single eschatological event but to a twofold advent of the Christ, who will come first in humility and suffering and second in power and glory (31). The effect of this, as Trypho points out, is to install the disgraced, crucified Christ at the heart of the existing Jewish schema of promise and (still future) fulfilment – a thoroughly implausible move, as he thinks (32).

Justin wishes to show that the Christ who comes in this manner is rightly acknowledged as God (36); for scripture teaches that, despite the divine unity, there is a twofoldness in God. Thus, addressing the same person, it is said both that 'thy throne, O God, is for ever and ever' and that 'thy God hath anointed thee with the oil of gladness above thy fellows' (Ps. 45.6, 7; *dial.* 38). That 'Christ existed as God before the ages' (48) is also demonstrated by the theophany of Gen. 18, in which the Lord who appears to Abraham is distinguished from the Lord who remains in the heavens (56–57); by the figure of wisdom in Prov. 8 (61); and by the remarkable plural ('Let *us* make man . . .') in Gen. 1.26 (62). But how, Trypho enquires, are we to know that this God and this Lord, one with and yet distinct from the one Lord and the one God, is to be identified with Jesus (63)? Much hangs on the promise that the child Immanuel, God with us, is to be born of a virgin (Isa. 7.14; *dial.* 66–78). Does this text prefigure the miraculous sign that attests the incarnation, or does it merely speak of the birth of the future King Hezekiah to a young woman? That the Christ should die as well as being born is indicated both by veiled types, such as Moses' lifting up of the serpent (91), and by the clearest prophetic assertions, as in the first-person description of crucifixion in Ps. 22, in which David obviously speaks in the person of another (97–106). Christians are the true high-priestly race; it is they who, from the rising of the sun to its setting, offer to God the pure offering of which the prophet Malachi speaks (Mal. 1.11; *dial.* 116–17); it is they who are the nation promised to Abraham, the father of many nations and the prototype of the Gentile believer (119).

Is this text a true dialogue at all? Justin does most of the talking, whereas Trypho's interventions are comparatively brief. Yet Trypho is a real character and not just a cipher: generally courteous although sometimes indignant, well-informed about Jewish alternatives to Christian readings of key proof-texts, a loyal Jew who is nevertheless independent enough to distance himself from official opinion at various points, not least in being willing to converse with a Christian at all. No agreement is reached at the end of the dialogue, and yet the dialogue-partners take leave of one another in the most affectionate terms. Trypho is also, of course, a literary device enabling Justin to present a mass of complex exegetical argument in as attractive a manner as possible.

But behind this literary dialogue there stands, no doubt, the experience of real dialogues between Christians and Jews; dialogues where there could apparently be room for courtesy even in the midst of serious and fundamental disagreement.[4] This is confirmed by Origen's reference to a lost work similar to the *Dialogue with Trypho* and perhaps roughly contemporary with it: the *Controversy between Jason and Papiscus regarding Christ*, in which, we are told, 'a Christian is described as conversing with a Jew on the subject of the Jewish scriptures, and proving that the predictions regarding Christ fitly apply to Jesus; although the other disputant maintains the discussion in no ignoble style, and in a manner not unbecoming the character of a Jew' (*c. Cel.* iv.52).[5] Evidently Jews could take part in debates with Christians without acrimony, and Christian authors and readers were capable of acknowledging this. The assumption that pre-modern Jewish–Christian dialogue was invariably acrimonious betrays only our own inability or unwillingness to engage in genuine dialogue with the past.

The claim that this text can be understood as a resource for Christian theological interpretation of the Old Testament will obviously need to be qualified at numerous points. Even after every allowance has been made for different hermeneutical conventions, the quality of Justin's exegesis is – to say the least – variable. To assess this text positively will require us to read it in a certain light, frequently distinguishing what is said from what is meant, moderating its naïve confidence in the rightness of its own arguments, and allowing much that seems central to Justin to be relegated to the periphery. On the other hand, it will also mean learning to appreciate the extraordinary theological and hermeneutical achievement that underlies it: the transformation of Jewish scripture into the Christian Old Testament, not by converting these texts into a mere quarry for an *ad hoc* polemic or apologetic, but by reimagining the whole in the light of the Christ-event and its enduring aftermath.

1. From Athens to Jerusalem

The Christian dialogue-partner acknowledges his incalculable debt to the prophets of Israel and therefore to the Jewish matrix from which his own faith springs. Without the prophets, Justin would be a Platonist or a sceptic. It is possible, he acknowledges, to find 'some who are called Christians' who 'dare to blaspheme the God of Abraham and the God of Isaac and the God of Jacob' (*dial.* 80).[6] But such people are not real Christians at all. Opposition to the anti-Judaism characteristic of second-century Christian heterodoxy is rarely made explicit in this text; yet it was written in the heyday of Marcion and Valentinus, quite probably in precisely the place (Rome) where their systematic denigration of the God of the Jews and of Jewish scripture was first articulated, and it is therefore in part an act of resistance to the new Christian anti-Judaisms.[7] The real 'parting of the ways' occurs not between Justin and Trypho but between Trypho and Marcion. Justin rejects the programme of a radical de-judaizing of Christianity, and it is precisely because he and Trypho have not gone their separate ways but still appeal to the same texts that the disagreement can be so fundamental. If Justin's text falls into the hands of readers tempted by radical Christian de-judaizing, it will be perceived as an appeal to recognize the reality and the richness of the Jewish matrix of Christian faith. This matrix consists not only of the writings of the prophets but also of the tradition that has preserved them in the Hebrew language and, in recent times, presented them to the world in the priceless gift of the Greek translation produced by the seventy elders (*1 apol.* 31, *dial.* 71). Gentile Christians, 'having learned the true worship of God from the law and the word which went forth from Jerusalem by means of the apostles of Jesus, have fled for safety to the God of Jacob and God of Israel' (*dial.* 110). Gentile Christians have undertaken the pilgrimage to Mount Zion of which the prophet Micah wrote when he foresaw how the nations would say, 'Come, let us go up to the mountain of the Lord, and to the house of the God of Jacob' (Mic. 4.2; *dial.* 109).

In Justin's case, the pilgrimage to Jerusalem begins from Athens, and it occurs in his conversion from Plato to the prophets as described in the early chapters of the dialogue; a conversion from a Greek understanding of the divine–human relationship to a Jewish one. Justin's initial attraction to Platonism – after unsuccessful experimenting with other philosophies – is motivated by his quest for God. When he discovered Platonism, he recalls, 'The perception of immaterial things quite overwhelmed me, and the contemplation of ideas gave wings to my mind, so that I quickly supposed myself to have become wise; and such was my folly, I expected immediately to look upon God – for this is the goal of Plato's philosophy' (*dial.* 2). Philosophy, this Platonist tells the old man encountered by chance near the sea-shore, 'is the knowledge of that which is [*epistēmē tou ontos*] and the understanding of the truth'; it is the knowledge of God, who may be defined as 'that which always remains the same and is the cause of existence to all else' (3). Knowledge of God is possible because of the natural affinity between God and the mind. Plato says 'that the mind's eye [*to tou nou omma*] is of such a nature, and has been given for this end, that, when the mind is itself pure, we may see that very Being who is the cause of everything perceptible to the mind [*tōn noētōn hapantōn*] . . . , beyond all essence, unutterable and inexplicable, but alone beautiful and good' (4). This is eloquently said, no doubt, but Justin's conversation-partner rightly presses the epistemological question. 'Does our mind, then, possess such and so great a power? Or does it perceive reality only through the senses? Can the human mind ever see God if it is not assisted by the Holy Spirit? . . . What affinity [*suggeneia*] is there between us and God?' (4). In reply, Justin the Platonist argues that the mind's ability to know God is grounded in its likeness to God, and its likeness to God consists in the fact that it too is immortal and uncreated. That which now hinders it from perfect union with its divine counterpart is the body; but when the soul is separated from the body, it will soar upwards and be united with that which it loves; however, returning to corporeality in the cycle of rebirth, it will forget what it has seen in the world above.

The power of the Platonic vision is such that it can draw even Judaism into its orbit. The familiar stories can be read as allegories of Platonism, as they are by Philo of Alexandria. Alternatively, Judaism can resist seduction by Plato; and this can be done not only by strengthening the barriers demarcating the chosen people from the Gentiles but also at a philosophical level. The old man, a Gentile Christian rooted in a Jewish understanding of God, gently probes the foundations of Justin's Platonism. If the re-embodied soul forgets the vision it enjoyed in its disembodied state, how are we to know that it ever experienced such a vision? If the world's existence is contingent rather than necessary, may this not be the case with the soul also? If that is so, and if the soul is reintegrated into the created order, does it possess a natural immortality, or is its future existence like its present existence entirely dependent on the will of God? God and the soul are unlike; they are related to one another asymmetrically as creator to creature; and if God does not continue to hold the creature in being, it ceases to be. This philosophically-articulate Judaism confronts Platonism with a radical doctrine of creation and a critique of the myth of the uncreated and godlike soul.

If the soul no less than the body is radically dependent on God for its being, then it can no longer understand the knowledge of God as the quest of an active subject for a passive object. God can be known only if God gives himself to be known. In principle, this situation might lead to philosophical scepticism. But to become a sceptic would be to overlook the fact that God has already given himself to be known, in a manner that, like creation itself, is contingent rather than necessary. 'Long ago, before the time of those regarded as philosophers, there lived certain men, blessed and righteous and beloved by God, who spoke by the divine Spirit' (*dial.* 7). It is here made explicit for the first time that the source of the old man's critique of Platonism is the Jewish understanding of God as creator and revealer; and in what follows it also becomes explicit that this understanding of God is subject to a distinctive Christian modification. Those who spoke by the divine Spirit 'foretold future events [*ta mellonta*], which are now taking place. They are called prophets . . . Their writings are still extant, and whoever reads them and believes them is greatly helped in the knowledge of the beginning and end of things [*peri archōn kai peri telous*], and of whatever else the philosopher ought to know' (7). Immediately, Justin recounts, 'a flame was kindled in my soul, and a love of the prophets and of those who are friends of Christ possessed me; and as I reflected on his words I found this philosophy alone to be well-founded [*asphalē*] and profitable. Thus, and for this reason, I am a philosopher' (8). The philosopher has learnt that the knowledge of God is historical rather than natural, *a posteriori* rather than *a priori*, communal rather than merely individual.

Justin's account of his intellectual pilgrimage from Athens to Jerusalem serves to establish his credentials as a philosopher who offers instruction in the Jewish prophets and as a dialogue-partner for the Jew Trypho. This Jewish–Christian dialogue takes place on the premise of the Jewishness of Christianity. The Jewishness of Christianity is integral to orthodox Christian belief from the outset; it is not a modern discovery that requires Christian belief to subject itself to extensive reformulation. Among the foundations of the Christian faith represented by Justin are a Jewish view of God as the creator and revealer, and the Jewish prophets who point forward to the day when the divine Word himself will be manifested in the form of a Jewish humanity, born of a Jewish mother. To deny the Jewishness of Christianity is only possible on the premise of a docetism such as Marcion's. The dispute between Justin and Trypho is indicative not of the insensitivity of the Gentile outsider to a supposed essence of Judaism but to a profound rupture within Judaism or Jewishness itself.[8]

2. Torah as Divine Accommodation

Justin's dialogue with Trypho is occupied almost exclusively with the interpretation of the law and the prophets – a further sign that dialogue occurs on the ground of a Jewish tradition fundamentally divided against itself. Neither side is interested in leaving this ground, and both sides are concerned not only with individual texts but with overarching hermeneutical frameworks within which individual texts can be located.

On learning that Justin is a Christian, Trypho's initial complaint is

that you, who claim to be religious [*eusebeis*] and suppose yourselves better than others, are in no way separated from them, and do not practise a way of life any different from that of the Gentiles; for you observe no festivals or sabbaths, nor do you practise circumcision . . . Have you not read that that soul shall be cut off from his people who is not circumcised on the eighth day? And this precept applies also to foreigners and to slaves. But you, rashly despising this covenant, reject the duties that follow from it and try to persuade us that you know God, while failing to practise those things that God-fearing people [*hoi phoboumenoi ton theon*] would do. (*dial.* 10)

The situation would be simpler if Christians worshipped a different God. Yet, Justin replies, 'we do not think that there is one God for us and another for you, but that he alone is God who led your fathers out from Egypt with a strong hand and uplifted arm' (11). A new covenant has come into effect: 'For the law promulgated on Horeb is now old, and belongs to yourselves alone', and 'an eternal and final law – Christ himself – has been given to us', which is 'for all without exception' (11). Justin must show that the divine commandments to which Trypho appeals represent a *temporary* stage in the history of God's dealings with humankind, and that this stage has now been brought to an end. And he must be able to offer a *coherent* account of that history as a whole, in response to Trypho's accusation of arbitrariness. Is it really possible for largely Gentile communities to read the scriptural texts as their own story? Or would they do better to leave Judaism to the Jews and to understand Jesus Christ as the revealer of a previously unknown God?

One possible strategy in interpreting the Torah is to exploit the hermeneutical possibilities implied in Matt. 19.8 ('For your hardness of heart Moses allowed you to divorce your wives, but from the beginning it was not so'). The beginning may be held to possess greater authority than that which later supplements it, especially if the supplement can plausibly be understood as a divine accommodation to human weakness. The principle of the secondariness of the supplement is applied by Paul to the issue of circumcision, crucial for Justin and Trypho as well: Abraham was declared to be righteous on the grounds of his faith *before* he was circumcised (Rom. 4.9–12). Circumcision therefore cannot be a necessary element in the divine–human relationship. As Justin says, extending the Pauline argument backwards, if circumcision were necessary

God would not have made Adam uncircumcised, would not have looked with favour on the sacrifice of the uncircumcised Abel, and would not have been pleased with the uncircumcised Enoch, who was not found because God had translated him . . . Melchisedek, the priest of the Most High, was uncircumcised; yet Abraham, the first who received circumcision after the flesh, gave tithes to him and was blessed by him; after whose order God declared by the mouth of David that he would establish the everlasting priest. (19)

The uncircumcision of Gentile Christians under the new covenant represents the restoration of the divine–human relationship in its original form. In this original form, the relationship is not gender-specific – 'for God has given to women too the ability to observe everything that is righteous and virtuous', and women's inability to receive circumcision therefore indicates that circumcision is irrelevant to righteousness (23).[9]

If a present reality is justified by appeal to the beginning, an explanation of the supplement must also be offered. Human obduracy, weakness, ignorance and forgetfulness require divine accommodation rather than merely abstract ideals, if these deficiencies are eventually to be overcome, and the incident of the golden calf (Exod. 32) is an occasion for divine pragmatism of this kind. In response to this incident, God, 'adapting [*harmosamenos*] to that people, commanded them to offer sacrifices to his name, so that you might not serve idols ... Moreover, he commanded you to abstain from certain kinds of food, so that while you eat and drink you might keep God before your eyes, being liable to depart from the knowledge of him, as Moses also says: "The people ate and drank, and rose up to play"' (19, 20). Like circumcision, neither sacrifices nor the food laws are an original element in the divine–human relationship, and it is possible to please God without them; the theory of accommodation explains the addition of the non-original supplement in such a way as to deny its permanent validity.[10] Supporting evidence is found in the prophetic critique of sacrifice (22), in the fact that Trypho too must practise a Judaism without sacrifice in the absence of the temple (40), and in the prophetic promise of a universal worship of the one God. Speaking through the prophet Malachi, God says: 'I will not accept your sacrifices at your hands; for from the rising of the sun to its setting my name is glorified among the Gentiles, and in every place a sacrifice is offered unto my name, even a pure sacrifice; for my name is honoured among the Gentiles, saith the Lord' (Mal. 1.11; *dial.* 28) – a reference to the Christian Eucharist, 'offered by Christians in all places throughout the world' (*dial.* 117, cf. 41). This universal vision is, Justin thinks, preferable to the contemporary rabbinic preoccupation with learned exegetical investigations into 'why so many measures of fine flour and so many measures of oil are used in the offerings' (112), and suchlike matters.

The new covenant is thus not only new but represents a return to a beginning that is still older than the old covenant, the supplement. The now-restored beginning is characterized negatively by the absence of some though not all of the boundary-markers characteristic of the Jewish community, and positively by the restoration of the universal horizons established by the early chapters of Genesis, from creation to the covenant with Noah. The God who is now worshipped from the rising of the sun to its setting is the God who, from the beginning, has been the God not of the Jews only but also of the Gentiles.[11] The accusation of arbitrary disregard for the law is answered not by appealing to individual texts in isolation but by locating them within a comprehensive hermeneutical schema. This schema has the effect of relativizing the normative status of the law, and the intention is not only to show why Gentile Christians do not observe it but also to create space for the new, extratextual reality of Christ and the communities that acknowledge him. It is this comprehensive new reality or new covenant that generates the hermeneutic that declares the Mosaic covenant to be 'old'.

This distinctive Christian interpretation of central themes in the Jewish scriptures clearly represents a *possible* reading of these texts. Yet it insists that it is – in broad terms, if not in exegetical detail – the *only* possible reading of these texts, and that the reading favoured by Trypho and his rabbinic mentors is illegitimate. Might the exclusiveness of the two opposing standpoints be overcome by a more pluralistic hermeneutic capable of accommodating them both?[12] Trypho himself suggests this at one point, in relation to the interpretation of the prophets; the basic argument could easily be extended to the law. Let Jesus 'be recognized as Lord and Christ and God, as the scriptures indicate, by you Gentiles, who have from his name all been called Christians; but we, who are servants of the God who made him, do not need to confess or worship him' (*dial.* 64). In other words, there might be a peaceful coexistence between Jews and Gentile Christians, each reading the scriptures differently but neither encroaching on the beliefs and practices of the other. Justin here accuses Trypho of a frivolous disregard for the constraints of truth; but the modern pluralistic paradigm will be interested in developing and exploiting Trypho's tentative suggestion in opposition to Christian exclusiveness. If this paradigm were to be accepted, both Christian and Jew would have to abandon a particular identification of God's definitive and unsurpassable self-disclosure, committing themselves instead to the new truth-claim that Moses and Jesus represent alternative and equally valid ways of relating to God. There would then be two parallel covenants rather than an old covenant and a new; two views of the divine–human relationship, each of which is appropriate and adequate only in so far as it allows itself to be relativized not so much by the other as by the pluralistic paradigm itself.[13] The relativizing movement would be unlikely to stop at this point, however. As we have seen, there is a third dialogue-partner in this text: a Platonist (Justin himself in a previous identity), in dialogue with a Christian. The Platonist's way to the divine will also have to be accorded a relative justification, along with the alternative philosophical ways that he tries out and rejects during the philosophical stage of his religious quest (*dial.* 2). Each way (it will be said) has its own relative justification; no way is entirely bereft of the truth, and no way can claim a monopoly of the truth – for monopolies deny customers the freedom to choose that is their birthright. The proposal of a pluralistic hermeneutic intends not to resolve the differences between Justin and Trypho but to persuade them to abandon the model of difference that the dialogue normally presupposes. Pluralism seeks to annex difference, converting it into an aestheticized diversity in the name of an underlying identity.[14]

If we do not wish to take sides, it is perhaps best to allow Justin and Trypho their difference and thereby to respect their otherness. But it is not clear that Christian faith and theology can avoid the problems that Justin struggles with as he seeks to show that the Jewish scriptures should be read as the Christian Old Testament. And if the questions are unavoidable, then there may also be something to be learnt from Justin's answers.

3. Prophecy and Proof

Justin must demonstrate the ability of the Christian paradigm to produce a coherent reading of the law and the prophets, if he is adequately to answer Trypho's accusation that Christians are arbitrary in their treatment of the sacred texts. The foundational status of the law is opposed, by appeal to criteria internal to the scriptural texts themselves: far from being foundational, its proper role is to prepare the way for the new, universal covenant that is to succeed it. The prophetic texts must also bear the weight of the argument about the nature and identity of the Christ, and much of the dialogue is preoccupied with this single point: whether the Christian claim that the Christ is Jesus, the Word made flesh, born of a virgin, crucified and exalted, coheres with the normative scriptural texts.

It is true that Justin tends to assume that his scriptural argument demonstrates not only the *coherence* of the Christian claim but also its *truth*: that Jesus is the Christ is supposedly *proved* by exegesis of texts such as Isa. 53 or Ps. 22. There are, however, grounds for thinking that the argument from fulfilment of prophecy should be interpreted differently.

(1) In the argument from prophecy, the basic Christian truth-claim is elaborated 'by means of the contents of those Scriptures you accept as holy and prophetic [*tōn par' humin hagiōn kai prophētikōn graphōn*]' (*dial.* 32). In other words, the argument must presuppose the dialogue-partner's acceptance that scripture is inspired; the possibility of a criticism of scripture itself is thus excluded. On the other hand, where there is no inhibition against criticizing scripture, the argument from prophecy is vulnerable. Celsus makes this point forcefully: 'If the prophets foretold that the great God . . . would become a slave, or become sick, or die, would it therefore be necessary for

God actually to die or suffer sickness or become a slave, merely because such things had been foretold?' (Origen, c. Cel. vii.14). More succinctly expressed: 'If these things were predicted of the most high God, are we to believe them of God merely because they were predicted?' (vii.15). In fact, 'we need not inquire whether a thing has been predicted or not but whether the thing is honourable in itself and worthy of God' (vii.14). To take a hypothetical case: it is foretold that God will become human and suffer sickness, and on the basis of this it is claimed that a particular sick person represents the fulfilment of this prophecy. This is a valid although not a compelling argument if the authority of the original prophecy is granted; but if this is not granted, then the prophecy itself and the argument derived from its supposed fulfilment are vulnerable to the *a priori* claim that the concept 'God', properly understood, is incompatible with suffering sickness. Celsus' argument would not be so effective where the fulfilment of prophecy is said to take the form of a miracle, as in the case of the virgin birth or resurrection; for the actual occurrence of such events might imply that the *a priori* concept of God is incorrect. But debate will here be concentrated not on prophecy but on historicity, since Celsus believes that purely natural and indeed discreditable accounts of the birth and post-mortem appearances of Jesus are more plausible than the Christian claims. In such a debate, the role of the argument from prophecy would be to suggest that the Christian claims are not invented and arbitrary, but that they make possible a coherent account of the history of the divine–human relationship. In this form the argument would retain a certain force, not only in refuting the charge of arbitrariness but also in countering the *a priori* conception of God with an *a posteriori* narrative account of divine being and action, on the basis of which certain limitations in the *a priori* conception might be exposed.

(2) Even where Justin is arguing intrasystematically, on the basis of a shared belief in the authentic prophetic status of scripture, his argument does not compel assent. If Trypho is to be persuaded, it will be on the basis not of formal proofs but of a cumulative argument whose impact depends on its ability to re-imagine the meaning of scripture as a whole.

According to Justin, the prophets foretold events that have now taken place. To fore-tell (cf. *prophētēs*; *pro-phēmi*, pre-dict) is to tell of an event, but to do so in advance rather than after the event. Foretelling is nevertheless a mode of telling rather than, say, the expression of a strong probability, because telling presupposes not the probability but the actuality of the event to be communicated; and foretelling likewise presupposes actuality rather than probability or possibility. To tell is also to communicate, and to foretell is therefore to communicate in the first instance with those who hear the original prophetic utterance. If foretelling occurs, it must enable its hearers to imagine certain definite events that are to be actualized in the future, and believing it would entail a confident expectation of this actualization. At this point, however, the identification of prophecy with foretelling becomes problematic; for the very fact that Justin is attemping to persuade a Jew of the truth of Christian claims is already an indication that no such confident expectation existed in the community which preserved and believed the prophetic writings. If foretelling occurred, why did its hearers act as if they had been told nothing at all? Why is the proclamation of a Christ who was born of a virgin and crucified as strange to Jews as it is to Gentiles?

A possible answer is that the Jews misunderstood their own prophets; scriptural language suggesting hardness of heart, blindness and deafness lies ready to hand. But the failure of the community to understand what it was supposedly told has the effect of diminishing the plausibility of the alleged foretelling, and evokes the question what it is about prophecy itself which makes it possible for it to be misunderstood on such a massive scale. At certain points Justin effectively concedes that the model of prophecy as foretelling cannot be sustained. In exegetical practice, he discovers that prophecy is often obscure. 'What the prophets said and did . . . they disclosed in parables and types [*parabolais kai tupois*], so that, because they concealed the truth in this way, it was not easy for most of what they said to be understood by the multitude, that only those who take the trouble to seek might find and learn' (*dial.* 90). But if prophetic discourse is characterized by concealment, then it lacks the straightforwardness of telling. It operates by way of hints and suggestions, enigmatic allusions to the possibility that the horizons of the present may be open to a qualitatively different and ungraspable future. The degree of concealment is such that prophecy is comprehensible only after the event. 'If through the prophets it was obscurely [*parakekalummenōs*] declared that the Christ would suffer and afterwards become Lord of all, this could be understood by no-one until he himself persuaded the apostles that such statements were expressly declared in the scriptures' (76). In a Pauline image, it is only in Christ that the veil that conceals the face of scripture is removed. But in that case what is to be demonstrated out of scripture – that Christ must suffer and be raised – must first be known in the light of its actualization if the demonstration is to take place. Without Christ, scripture remains obscure, and where the text is shrouded in obscurity multiple interpretations simply cancel each other out. Prior to Christ, the claim that the Christ must suffer and be raised would simply have been one opinion among many, entirely unable to authenticate itself in the face of competing claims.

It follows that, despite their shared acceptance of the prophetic character of scripture, the positions of Justin and Trypho are to some extent incommensurable. A dialogue conducted solely on the basis of the texts would not vindicate the view that the Christ must suffer and be raised. Justin seeks to evoke in Trypho the willingness to attempt a reading of holy scripture based on the premise that the Christ is Jesus, the incarnate Word who is God himself, born of a virgin, crucified and exalted; a premise derived not from foretelling in isolation but from an actuality which from the first both interprets and is interpreted by the prophetic writings. According to Justin, the gulf between himself and Trypho can ultimately be overcome not by dialogue alone but by the grace of God, and the appropriate response to this situation is prayer. At the time of his conversion, Justin was exhorted to 'pray that, above all else, the gates of light may be opened to you; for these things [i.e. the prophetic writings] cannot be perceived or understood by all, but only by the person to whom God and his Christ grant understanding' (*dial.* 7). The gulf between Justin and Trypho persists until the end of the dialogue, which therefore concludes in prayer. The argument from the fulfilment of prophecy should not be understood as requiring the unanswerable cogency of the ideal mathematical or legal proof. The coherence that it may succeed in demonstrating is the coherence of a faith whose ultimate grounds are mysterious but which must nevertheless give a partial account of itself in the face of rival truth-claims.

4. The Old Testament and Christological Construction

Justin presents a remarkable variety of christological interpretations of scriptural texts. For him, the whole of scripture is prophetic. Even Moses is first of all a prophet and only secondarily the lawgiver of the Jewish people, and testimonies to Christ may therefore be found at every point. If much of the exegesis seems unconvincing to typical modern readers, the reason may lie – at least in part – in the enduring influence of a historically-oriented hermeneutic that lacks the analytical tools to grasp the phenomenon of a *Wirkungsgeschichte* that propels canonical texts far beyond their immediate circumstances of origin. A typology that sees a foreshadowing of the crucified Christ in the outstretched hands of Moses, interceding for Israel in the battle against Amalek, may have nothing to do with the origins of the story; but it is at least aware of the pervasive intertextuality that makes the hypothesis of scriptural unity defensible on literary as well as on theological grounds.[15] But the notion of intertextuality does not adequately account for the basic shape of Justin's christological hermeneutic, which is dictated by theological commitments. If the detailed exegesis is defensible at all, it is so only within the context of a theological framework which is often more implicit than explicit.

A crucial element in this theological hermeneutic is Justin's theory of the two advents of Christ, first introduced at an early stage of the dialogue, following extensive quotations from Isa. 52–55 (*dial.* 13–14), in order to elucidate the antithesis in these chapters between the suffering of the servant of the Lord and the glorious outcome of God's saving activity:

> 'Of these and suchlike words written by the prophets, O Trypho', said I, 'some refer to the first advent of Christ [*eis tēn prōtēn parousian tou Christou*], in which he is proclaimed as having appeared in disgrace, obscurity and mortality; but others refer to his second advent, when he shall appear in glory and above the clouds . . .' (*dial.* 14)

The effect of this view is that the symbol 'Christ' can serve to unify a range of biblical material that might otherwise have seemed disparate and unimportant. When, after the discussion of the law (*dial.* 11–30), the theme of the two advents returns (*dial.* 32), Justin's strategy is to supplement the basic text in Isa. 53 with texts from the psalms that can be used to bridge the gap between the two sides of the antithesis. At his first advent, Jesus endured death on the cross; and yet, in his resurrection and ascension, he was himself addressed as 'Lord' and exalted to the Lord's right hand, in accordance with the prophecy of Ps. 110 (*dial.* 32, 33). The ministry that he has obtained through his human history is a priestly one, again in accordance with the words of the psalm: 'Thou art a priest for ever after the order of Melchizedek' (Ps. 110.4; *dial.* 33). The promise in Ps. 72 of the world-dominion of the Davidic king is fulfilled in him (*dial.* 34), as is the language of Ps. 24 about the entry of the king of glory into the holy place (*dial.* 36). Many other texts are employed with reference to one or other point in the credal story, from incarnation to parousia. Yet Justin is aware that the Christian attempt to integrate disparate scriptural material by means of the Christ-symbol is resisted. Thus, he anticipates the objections that Ps. 110 refers to Hezekiah and Pss. 72 and 24 to Solomon, and refutes them by claiming that the language of the texts exceeds what might properly be said about such figures. 'Not even you will venture to object that Hezekiah was either a priest, or is the everlasting priest of God; but this language shows that this is spoken of our Jesus' (*dial.* 33). 'I know that Solomon was a renowned and great king who built the temple at Jerusalem; but it is clear that none of the things mentioned in the psalm [Ps. 72] happened to him. For neither did all kings worship him; nor did he reign to the ends of the earth; nor did his enemies, falling before him, lick the dust' (*dial.* 34). The reading of such texts in terms of historical figures and events is associated with Trypho and with Jewish interpretation generally, and this embryonic historical interpretation is to be seen as a defensive strategy occasioned by the need to resist Christian claims. On the one hand, hyperbolic language that exceeds the limits of historical particularities reaches forward to attain its true goal and referent in Christ; on the other hand, hyperbole is referred backward to sharply-focused figures or events of the distant past, in order to prevent it straying from the limits assigned to it by the historicizing hermeneutic. A Christian hermeneutic that highlights and celebrates scriptural excess is opposed by a strategy of containment.[16]

Trypho is prepared to concede that the scriptural material identified by Christians may indeed refer to the history of the Christ, but he wishes to know on what grounds this history is identified with the history of *Jesus*: 'Now show if this man be the one to whom these prophecies refer' (*dial.* 36). It is noteworthy that Justin refuses to meet this request at this stage in the dialogue: 'I shall come to these proofs which you seek in the appropriate place; but now you will first permit me to recount the prophecies, which I wish to do in order to prove that Christ is called both God and Lord of hosts' (*dial.* 36). Justin's point is that the identification of the history of Jesus with the scriptural delineation of the history of the Christ cannot take place without a deeper understanding of what it means to identify Jesus as the Christ. Christ is the Lord of hosts spoken of in Ps. 24.10 (*dial.* 36); he it is who, in Ps. 45, is both addressed as God ('Thy throne, O God, is for ever and ever' [v. 6]) and differentiated from God ('Therefore God, your God, has anointed you' [v. 7]; *dial.* 38). All this seems blasphemous to Trypho, who now sees the point of the Jewish ban on contact with Christians (*dial.* 38). An Ebionite adoptionist christology would be tolerable (*dial.* 49), but not this. 'When you say that this Christ existed as God before the ages [*prouparchein theon onta pro aiōnōn*], then that he submitted to be born and become human . . . , this seems to me to be not merely paradoxical but simply absurd' (*dial.* 48). The Christian claims are grounded in scriptural texts which offer the most extreme cases conceivable of that language of excess on which the christological hermeneutic is dependent. They lead to the dangerous hypothesis of a twofoldness within the one God, clearly disclosed in the incarnation but foreshadowed in Old Testament references to the Logos who was with God and who was God.

Plurality within God is implied by the theophany of Gen. 18–19, discussed at some length in *dial.* 55–56. Of the three men who appear to Abraham and Sarah, two are identified as angels (Gen. 19.1, 15), while the third is identified as the Lord (Gen. 18.1, 10, 13, 17–33) who announces the imminent birth of the long-awaited son and who bargains with Abraham over the fate of Sodom and Gomorrah. The appearance of the Lord is in itself compatible with a modalistic explanation (later explicitly rejected by Justin, *dial.* 128), and need not imply plurality in God. Yet Justin is able to appeal to Gen. 19.24 ('Then the Lord rained on Sodom and Gomorrah brimstone and fire from the Lord out of heaven') in order to distinguish the Lord who remains inaccessible in the heavens from the Lord who appears in acts of covenant-faithfulness and judgment on earth. Texts such as Pss. 110.1 and 45.6–7 confirm this interpretation (*dial.* 56), as do later theophanies recounted in Gen. 32 and Exod. 3 (*dial.* 58–60). This plurality within God reaches back at least as far as creation, for Prov. 8 speaks of Wisdom as already present with God at creation (*dial.* 61), and in Gen. 1.26 we read that God said, 'Let us make man in our own image': this last text cannot be a reference to angels, for the creation accounts do not present human beings as the workmanship of angels (*dial.* 62). Only on the basis of this scriptural demonstration of the divinity of the Logos does Justin proceed to speak of his incarnation and death, by way of detailed expositions of Isa. 7.14 (*dial.* 66–78) and Ps. 22 (*dial.* 97–106) respectively.

The integration of this disparate material into a coherent whole again demonstrates the ability of the christological hermeneutic to discover illuminating significance in passages or ideas that might otherwise remain obscure or marginal. In addition, the citation of the various texts is supported by an underlying theory about the relationship between Father and Word in revelation:

> Wherever God says, 'God went up from Abraham', or 'the Lord spake to Moses', and 'The Lord came down to behold the tower which the sons of men had built', or when 'God shut Noah into the ark', you must not imagine that the unbegotten God himself [*ton agennēton theon*] came down or went up from any place. For the ineffable Father and Lord of all neither came to any place, nor walks, nor sleeps, nor rises up, but remains in his own place, wherever that is, quick to behold and quick to hear, not with eyes or ears but with indescribable power; and he sees all things and knows all things, and none of us escapes his observation; and he is not moved or confined to any particular place in the whole world, for he existed before the world was made. How then could he talk with anyone, or be seen by anyone, or appear on the smallest portion of earth, when the people at Sinai were not able to look on the glory of him who was sent from him . . . ? Therefore neither Abraham nor Isaac nor Jacob nor anyone else saw the Father and ineffable Lord of all (even of Christ); rather did they see the one who was according to his will his Son, being God [*ekeinon ton kata boulēn tēn ekeinou kai theon onta, huion autou*], and the Angel, because he ministered to his will. (*dial.* 127)

For Justin, Christian belief in the incarnation is rendered plausible not just by individual texts such as Isa. 7.14 but by its capacity to disclose a coherent view of God within this disparate scriptural material. The problem of scriptural anthropomorphisms which so exercised Alexandrian Jewish theology is here set in a new light.[17] Scriptural language speaks both of the transcendence of God and of his radical nearness to humankind as expressed in the concept of the covenant. To use Johannine language, it remains the case that 'no one has ever seen God'; but 'the only-begotten God [or Son], who is in the bosom of the Father, has made him known' – above all, in the event in which 'the Word became flesh and dwelt among us' (John 1.18, 14). The indirect disclosure of the invisible, transcendent Father through the incarnate Son is, for early Christian hermeneutics, the key to the Old Testament concept of God as well. While the Word has not yet become flesh, he already discloses the invisible Father and enacts the divine solidarity with humankind which will reach its logical conclusion in the incarnation. The incarnation demonstrates how it can be said of God both that he is 'the high and exalted one who inhabits eternity, whose name is holy' and that he dwells also upon earth 'with those who are contrite and humble in spirit, to revive the spirit of the humble and to revive the heart of the contrite' (Isa. 57.15). The transcendence of God does not imply a fastidious aloofness from merely human concerns; the nearness of God does not imply an all-too-human conception of a divinity subject to human control and manipulation.

In so far as Trypho has a doctrine of the Christ at all, it remains marginal to the scriptures, confined to texts such as Dan. 7 where the one like a son of man 'receives from the Ancient of Days the everlasting kingdom' (*dial.* 32). An Ebionite christology (cf. *dial.* 48–49) would presumably have to employ the distinctively Christian theory of the two advents, and would thus appeal to a richer diversity of scriptural material. But it is the 'orthodox' christology of Justin and others which is able to demonstrate the greatest coherence with Old Testament scripture, since it can appeal not only to traditional messianic proof-texts but also to the entire theology of the covenant and of the covenantal God who is both distant and near, holy and merciful. This suggests an unexpected and paradoxical conclusion: that *a 'high' christology has far deeper and more extensive Old Testament roots than a 'low' one.* Trypho's accusation of blasphemy as Justin begins to develop this christological theme recalls the Gospel of John, and confirms that high christology was a significant doctrinal issue in the 'parting of the ways'. Justin's defence of his incarnational christology on the basis of Jewish scripture suggests that we have here not a Gentile-Christian abandonment of the Jewish heritage but, on the contrary, a radical reinterpretation that creates a fundamental rift *within* that heritage.[18]

One reason why Christian theological exegesis of the Old Testament is thought to be so problematic is its tendency to overwhelm the particularity of Old Testament texts with a semantic content derived from the New

Testament, as though there were no difference between the two divisions of Christian scripture. The *Dialogue with Trypho* shows that early Christian scriptural interpretation can operate entirely on the basis of the Old Testament, with little explicit reference to the New. More importantly, the temporal particularity of individual elements is preserved. Not everything is appropriated by the dominant christological concern; or, better expressed, the incarnation of the Word is seen not as the total content of scripture but as the culmination of a long salvation-historical preparation reaching back to creation itself. The relation of the old to the new is construed in linear, narrative terms. The narrative has a beginning, universal in scope, which is gradually superseded by the time of the supplement during which the divine–human relationship is characterized by disciplines that shape the matrix within which the Word himself will be brought to birth, live, die and be raised. The theophanies too belong to the time of preparation. Yet this temporal particularity does not mean that the texts are closed in upon themselves. Thus, Moses is the lawgiver whose words are occasioned by a particular set of circumstances in the history of Israel; and yet he is also the prophet whose words transcend immediate particularities and point towards the qualitatively different future that they both reflect and shape. The teleological orientation of Old Testament narrative ensures that there is no pure, self-contained present that is not also open to the future. On the other hand, the gradual unfolding of the narrative ensures that the future remains the future and does not engulf the particularity of the individual moment in a timeless presence.

This discussion has sought to clarify the tacit understanding of the Christian Old Testament as a whole that underlies Justin's exegesis of individual passages. Close analysis of the interpretation of particular texts would in many cases confirm that, for all its difficulties, this radical rereading of Jewish scripture cannot easily be dismissed as the arbitrary imposition of an alien sense on texts whose real meaning lies elsewhere. At the very least, the interpretative tradition that is here in process of formation is an expression of a creative theological imagination that has learned to see the scriptural texts in the light of Christ, and Christ in the light of the scriptural texts.

NOTES

1. See, for example, W. G. Kümmel's *The New Testament: History of the Investigation of its Problems*, ET London: SCM Press, 1973, according to which investigation of the problems of the New Testament begins only in the eighteenth century: 'Earlier discussion of the New Testament can only be referred to as the prehistory of New Testament scholarship' (13).

2. Brevard S. Childs, *Exodus: A Commentary*, Old Testament Library, London: SCM Press, 1974; U. Luz, *Matthew 1–7: A Commentary*, ET Edinburgh: T. & T. Clark, 1990.

3. The *Dialogue with Trypho* was written later than the *First Apology*, which is referred to in *dial.* 120, and its dating is dependent on that of the earlier text. (On this issue, see E. R. Goodenough, *The Theology of Justin Martyr: An Investigation into the Conceptions of Early Christian Literature and its Hellenistic and Judaistic Influences* [1923], repr. Amsterdam: Philo Press, 1968, 80–81, 88, from which the following details are taken.) The *Apology* is addressed to the Emperor Antoninus Pius, to his son Verissimus the Philosopher and to Lucius the philosopher (*1 apol.* 1). Verissimus is Marcus Aurelius, whose reputation as a philosopher dates from around the beginning of his co-regency in 147; Lucius was an adopted son who first came to political prominence when he entered the Senate in 153. The reference in *1 apol.* 29 to 'Felix, the Prefect of Alexandria' (in office, 151–54) relates to an incident said to have taken place 'recently'. If the *Apology* belongs to this period, the *Dialogue* cannot have been written much before 155.

4. Although an actual encounter with a Jew named Trypho may have occurred, the fact that Justin took perhaps twenty years to fulfil his promise to write up this debate (*dial.* 80) suggests that the historical background to this text is to be found in Christian and Jewish debates in general, and not merely in a single encounter. To express admiration for Trypho's 'patience' in permitting Justin to lecture him at such length (W. H. C. Frend, 'The Old Testament in the Age of the Greek Apologists A.D. 130–80', *SJT* 26 [1973], 129–50, 145) is therefore beside the point. J. T. Sanders argues that the dialogue is a fiction, representing a christianizing of the Platonic genre, but that 'we are forced to conclude that Justin has some kind of first-hand awareness of the kinds of objections that knowledgeable Jews would bring to such Christian interpretation' (*Schismatics, Sectarians, Dissidents, Deviants: The First One Hundred Years of Jewish–Christian Relations*, Valley Forge, Pa.: Trinity Press International, 1993, 50).

5. Translation from *The Ante-Nicene Fathers*, IV (American edn.), repr. Grand Rapids: Eerdmans, 1976.

6. Translations are based on *The Ante-Nicene Fathers*, I (American edn.), repr. Grand Rapids: Eerdmans, 1975, altered in the light of the Greek text (using the edition of G. Archambault, *Textes et documents pour l'étude historique du Christianisme*, Paris: Picard, 1909). I have also referred to the translation in *The Fathers of the Church*, 6, Washington: Catholic University of America Press, 1948.

7. Justin was martyred in Rome *c.*165, and in the account of his martyrdom (*Ante-Nicene Fathers*, I, 305–6) he informs the prefect Rusticus that he is now living in Rome for the second time (*mart.* 2). The second *Apology* was certainly written in Rome (*2 apol.* 1–3), the first *Apology* probably so (cf. *1 apol.* 1, 26) if the second is to be understood as an appendix to it. Eusebius confirms that Justin 'lived at Rome' (*hist.eccl.* iv.11.10). As for Valentinus and Marcion, 'Valentinus came to Rome in the time of Hyginus [*c.*137–41], flourished under Pius [*c.*141–54], and remained under Anicetus [*c.*154–67]'; Marcion, succeeding Cerdon, 'flourished under Anicetus' (Irenaeus, *adv. haer.* iii.4.3). Justin wrote a work against Marcion (Irenaeus, *adv.haer.* iv.6.2) and a work 'against all the heresies that have existed', including, no doubt, the heresy of Valentinus (Justin, *1 apol.* 26). Even if the *Dialogue* was not written in Rome, it belongs to a period when Justin was already familiar with the Valentinian and Marcionite theologies developed there.

8. In his *The Partings of the Ways between Christianity and Judaism and their Significance for the Character of Christianity*, London: SCM Press, 1991, J. D. G. Dunn argues that it is now the task of both Jews and Christians 'to go behind the centuries of antagonism and to build on their common foundations' (250), acknowledging 'the essentially Jewish

character of Christian beginnings' (249), 'their *common* heritage from this earliest period' (250). Yet acknowledgment of Christianity's 'essentially Jewish character' has always been integral to catholic Christianity, which is why for Marcion (as later for Schleiermacher and Harnack) it is the product of illegitimate judaizing tendencies that defile an originally pure essence. The 'schism' occurs *within* Jewish tradition.

9. The fact that the pre-Mosaic patriarchs did not have the written law was already of interest to Hellenized Jews such as Philo. In his treatise on Abraham, Philo announces his intention to 'postpone consideration of particular laws, which are, so to speak, copies, and examine first those which are more general and may be called the originals of those copies' (*de Abr.* 3; *Philo*, VI, Loeb Classical Library, London: Heinemann; Cambridge, Mass.: Harvard University Press, 1935). These originals are the people who led blameless lives; Philo is thinking especially of two groups of three: Enosh, Enoch and Noah, and Abraham, Isaac and Jacob (48). Moses 'wished to show first that the enacted ordinances are not inconsistent with nature; and secondly that those who wish to live in accordance with the laws as they stand have no difficult task, seeing that the first generations before any of the particular statutes were set in writing followed the unwritten law with perfect ease . . .' (6). Like Moses himself, such people demonstrate that the written laws are 'likenesses and copies of the patterns enshrined in the soul' (*de vita Mos.* i.11; *Philo*, VI). Here, the authority of the written law is grounded in an original 'nature' which constitutes it as a secondary 'copy'. Justin too understands the law as secondary and appeals to the pre-Mosaic patriarchs, but the secondariness of the law is now an argument for its impermanence.

10. T. Stylianopoulos points out, however, that although for Justin the law was given because of the hard-heartedness of its recipients, it was 'remedial and beneficent', containing nothing 'irrational nor unworthy of God' (*Justin Martyr and the Mosaic Law*, Missoula: Scholars Press, 1975, 159). 'Otherwise, the goodness and perfection of God would remain open to attack by the Marcionites' (160).

11. W. Pannenberg has argued that it is 'the universal claim of the God of Israel', as depicted in the Old Testament, that legitimates the use by Justin and others of elements in the Greek philosophical conception of God ('The Appropriation of the Philosophical Concept of God as a Dogmatic Problem of Early Christian Theology', in *Basic Questions in Theology*, II, ET London: SCM Press, 1971, 119–83; 136). If the prophets answer the philosopher's question *peri archōn* (*dial.* 7), their answer can itself be rendered in philosophical language. Justin's emphasis on the universal dimension in the Old Testament may therefore be correlated with his application of philosophical conceptuality to the God of the Christians.

12. This is the programme of the 'parting of the ways' model of Jewish–Christian relations, acutely analysed and criticized by Judith Lieu ('"The Parting of the Ways": Theological Construct or Historical Reality?', *JSNT* 56 [1994], 101–19). According to this model, plurality within first-century Judaism issues in rabbinic Judaism and in Christianity in such a way that both can lay claim to continuity with their Jewish roots and thus to 'legitimacy' (106). Lieu argues that 'the relationship between Judaism and Christianity would have been differently perceived by the different participants, and in different contexts' (119), and that the apparent clarity of the apologetically-motivated 'parting' model is therefore historically suspect.

13. Something like this is apparently envisaged by J. D. G. Dunn when he speaks of 'a hope for a further leading and revelation of God which will be recognized *on both sides* as completing what has already been revealed in Torah, prophet, sage and . . . As Christians want to add – and not least in Jesus and through Paul. So Jews want to add – and also

through such great teachers as rabbi Akiba, rabbi Meir, etc. The test of genuinely open dialogue will be whether Jew and Christian can recognize the other's "and" without driving the debate to a mutually-exclusive "either-or" ' (*The Partings of the Ways*, 253). The hoped-for further revelation would appear to be the revelation to each side that the other is also right, that God (revealed in Torah, prophet and sage) is also revealed in Jesus, through Paul, and through Akiba, Meir, etc. The future revelation is the divinely-authorized removal of the all-too-human 'mutually-exclusive "either-or" '. If, however, the Christian dialogue-partner has already attenuated the substance of Christian truth-claims to the extent of 'want[ing] to add' (as though as a mere supplement to something else) that revelation occurs 'not least in Jesus' (as though apologizing for mentioning this contentious name at all), then the future revelation has clearly already occurred. One response to all this would be to commit the solecism of simply quoting a scriptural text: 'No other foundation can anyone lay than that which is laid, which is Jesus Christ' (1 Cor. 3.11).

14. The dialogue that takes as its premise the possibility of difference, and therefore of truth and falsehood, contrasts with the contemporary view of dialogue which 'assumes that many voices are coalescing around a single known object' and that 'the many different biographies (experiences) and traditions can be appropriated by all as angles upon the truth, which are themselves radiations from the truth' (John Milbank, 'The End of Dialogue', in G. d'Costa [ed.], *Christian Uniqueness Reconsidered: The Myth of a Pluralistic Theology of Religions*, Maryknoll: Orbis, 1990, 174–91; 177). Against this, Milbank argues that 'there is nothing in principle objectionable . . . in claiming that a particular culture is crucially in error at some point, even though this claim can only be made from the perspective of another, non-neutrally justifiable cultural reading' (183–84).

15. Thus the literary critic Northrop Frye can appeal to Augustine's maxim that the Old Testament is revealed in the New and the New is concealed in the Old, as the basis for 'a genuine higher criticism of the Bible' which would be 'a synthetizing process which would start with the assumption that the Bible is a definitive myth, a single archetypal structure extending from creation to apocalypse' (*Anatomy of Criticism: Four Essays*, Princeton: Princeton University Press, 1957, 315; compare Frye's *The Great Code: The Bible and Literature*, London: Routledge & Kegan Paul, 1982, xii–xiii).

16. To take another example, Justin is aware of a Jewish interpretation of Isa. 7.14 – obviously motivated by resistance to Christian claims – according to which the *parthenos* is simply a young woman (in accordance with the Hebrew term) and her child is Hezekiah (*dial.* 43). Essentially the same argument recurs in the work of the English Deist Anthony Collins, whose *Discourse of the Grounds and Reasons of the Christian Religion* (1724) seeks to destroy the credibility of Christian appeals to Old Testament prophecy. The words of Isa. 7.14 'do, in their obvious and literal sense, relate to a *young woman* in the days of Ahaz king of Judah', who 'in due time *conceiv'd and bare a son*, who was named Immanuel; after whose birth, the projects of Rezin and Pekah [cf. Isa. 7] were soon confounded . . .' (extracts in John Drury [ed.], *Critics of the Bible 1724–1873*, Cambridge English Prose Texts, Cambridge: Cambridge University Press, 1989, 21–45; 27). Excessive Christian confidence in the persuasive force of the argument from prophecy meets its nemesis in the equal and opposite one-sidedness of historical-critical arguments of this kind.

17. Justin's argument presupposes the early Christian appropriation of Hellenistic Jewish discussions of scriptural anthropomorphisms. In the case of Gen. 11.5, for example, Philo argues that to ascribe motion to God (as this text appears to do) is to be ignorant that God 'fills all things; he contains but is not contained; to be everywhere and nowhere is his property and his alone' (*de conf. ling.* 136; *Philo*, IV). Here and elsewhere, 'the lawgiver is applying human terms to the superhuman God [*tauta de anthrōpologeitai para*

tō nomothetē peri tou me anthrōpomorphou theou] to help us, his pupils, to learn our lesson'
(135). The Christian appropriation accepts the inapplicability of such scriptural assertions
to God the Father, but can nevertheless retain their literal sense by applying them to the
Son. Anthropomorphic language is an accommodation to human weakness in the sense
that it describes the Son's preparation for and orientation towards the true anthropomorphism of his own incarnation. The Old Testament shows how 'he was learning even
as God to converse with men upon earth, being no other than the Word which was to be
made flesh. But he was thus learning in order to level for us the way of faith, that we
might more readily believe that the Son of God had come down into the world if we
knew that also in times past something similar had been done' (Tertullian, *adv. Prax.* 16;
Ante-Nicene Fathers, III [American edn.], repr. Grand Rapids: Eerdmans, 1976).

18. According to J. D. G. Dunn, 'Christianity is only Christianity when it is
monotheistic. Only so can Christians remain true to their roots, to their heritage within
the religion of Israel. Only so can Christians continue to retain the Jewish scriptures
within their canon' (*The Partings of the Ways*, 247). If 'monotheism' here refers to a view
of God on which Jews and Christians agree, over against classical Christian trinitarianism,
these statements would have to be reversed. Christianity is only Christianity when it is
trinitarian. Only so can Christians remain true to their Jewish roots and to the Jewish
scriptures within their canon. A 'Christian' unitarianism is not a *Christian* faithfulness to
Jewish roots and scripture.

Index of Scriptural Texts

OLD TESTAMENT

Genesis

1.1	230, 253
1	256, 268, 269–70, 281
1–2	228–30, 232, 303
1.1–2.4	230–31
1–3	302
1–9	281
1–11	254
1.3	282
1.6–7	262
1.12	230
1.22	230
1.24–25	293
1.26	309, 323
1.26–27	16, 277–304
1.26–28	279
1.28	232
1.29	302
1.29–30	293
2.1	230
2.4	230, 253, 268
2.4b–25	230
2.7	253, 280
2.20	293
3.14	293
3.19	280
3.22	302

5.1	230, 282, 289, 293, 299
5.1–2	298–99
5.1–3	16, 279, 280, 288–89, 302
5.3	289
6.9	230
6.19	299
7.2–16	299
8.22	231
9.2–3	280, 294
9.3	302
9.6	280, 293, 299, 302
9.11–15	231
10.1	230
10.32	254
11.5	328
11.8	254
12.1	232
15.5	232
17.5	274
18	309
18–19	322–23
19.24	323
25.25–26	274
32	323
49.6	108

Exodus

3	233, 323
3.14	220

3.14–15	274
4.11	233
6.3	274
20	233
20.2–11	233
20.4	289
32	315
33.20	290
34.29–35	84
34.34–35	301

Leviticus
11	294

Numbers
33.52	288

Deuteronomy
4.32	282
5.8	289
6.13	240
12.9	200
32.8	254

Joshua
21.44–45	200

Judges
1	205

1 Samuel
6.5	288

2 Samuel
7.1, 11	200
16.1	296

1 Kings
8.56	200

2 Kings
11.36	200
16.10	288

Job
14	286
39.26–30	293

Psalms
8	16, 241, 286, 303
8.1	303
8.3–8	294–98
8.5–7	157
8.5–8	263
8.6	298
8.8–9	296
19	241
21.5	294
22	309, 317, 323
22.1	122, 240
22.22	122
24	321
24.10	322
33.9	282
41.6, 12	122
42	116–23
42.3–4	119
42.5	240
42.5–6	120, 122
42.11	120, 240
43.5	240
45.6–7	296, 309, 322, 323
49.12	298
49.20	298
50.12–13	253
51	240
72	321
72.7–8	294
76.3	107
82.1	294–95, 297
89.47	282
95	200
102.18	119
103	264, 265
103.1	265
103.2	265
103.2–5	265
103.4	265
103.8	265

103.11	265	147	265
103.17	265	147.3–4	266
103.19	265	147.5	266
103.20–21	265	147.8–9	266
103.22	265	147.12–17	266
104	241, 245, 262–66	147.16–17	266
104.1	263, 265, 266	147.18–20	266
104.2–3	262	148	241
104.2–4	265	150	241
104.5–6	262		
104.7–8	262	*Proverbs*	
104.10	262	8	309, 323
104.12	262		
104.13	266	*Ecclesiastes*	
104.14	262–63, 266	3.21	298
104.16	263	5.2	287
104.16–22	263	12.1	282
104.17–18	266	12.12	64
104.21	263		
104.24	263, 265, 266	*Isaiah*	
104.26	263	6	290–91
104.27	266	6.1	289
104.27–30	263	7.14	157–59, 309, 323–324, 328
104.29	265	9.2–6	159
104.31	263, 265	38.15	108
104.31–35	263	40.18	287
104.33–35	263, 265	40.25	287, 290
104.35	265	43.15–19	201
105	264, 266	43.18–19	229
105–107	265	52–55	321
106	264	53	317, 321
107	264	57.15	324
109	270	65.17	229
110	321	66.1–2	254
110.1	241, 296, 323		
110.4	321		
118.22–23	240	*Jeremiah*	
118.23	122	29.6–7	120
119	195–96	31.35–36	233–34
136	265–66, 269		
136.4–9	265	*Ezekiel*	
136.10–15	265–66	1.22–28	289–90
137	119–22	1.26	298
137.7–9	126	34.4	294
137.8–9	120–22		

Daniel
7   324
7.9   289
10.4–8   84

Joel
3.13   293

Amos
3.1   233
4.13   233
5.8–9   233
9.5–6   233

Micah
4.2   311

Malachi
1.11   309, 315
2.8   165
3.1   165
4.4–5   84
4.5–6   165

Wisdom of Solomon
2.23–24   300
7.26   301

Sirach
17.1–8   280–81

NEW TESTAMENT

Matthew
1.21   274
1.23   157
2.23   216
3.1–15   240
3.4   165
4.10   240
4.16   159
5–7   38–41
5.43–45   121
5.45   238

6.26   239, 241
6.28   241
6.28–29   238
7.6   239
8.20   239
10.16   239
10.29   239
10.31   239, 294
11.7–15   165
11.25–27   122
11.27   85, 148–49
12.11–12   239
12.12   294
13.1–30   238
13.16–17   150
13.32   239
16.17   85
17.10–13   165
19.4   236
19.8   314
19.24   236
20.12   238
21.5–7   216
21.42   122, 240
22.44   241
25.40   292
26.38   240
26.38–39   122
27.46   122, 240
27.52–53   61
28.18–20   237
28.20   53

Mark
1.1   83, 89, 105
1.2   165
1.1–8   75
1.7–8   87
1.9   103–6
1.11   60, 86
1.14–15   75–76
1.16–20   238, 239
1.32–35   237
2.1   237
2.27   239

3.11–12	86	*Luke*	
4.1	238	1.1–4	34–35
4.6	238	1.16–17	165
4.10–12	90	5.1–11	238
4.11	86	6	38–41
4.11–12	73, 78	6.13	182
4.21	88	9.28–36	149
4.21–22	74	9.52–55	121
4.22	77	10.29–37	287
6.14–15	86	10.22	148–49
6.41	238	10.23–24	150
7.10	84	11.11	238
8.1	237	13.15	239
8.14–21	86	13.21	238
8.17–18	78	15.3–7	239
8.27–28	86	15.11–20	287
8.27–38	92	23.33–34	121
8.29–30	77	23.34	270
8.35	76	24.44–45	123
9.1	86	24	2
9.2	237	24.42–43	238
9.2–3	83–84	24.45–49	237
9.7–8	84		
9.10–13	87–88	*John*	
9.11	84	1.14	86, 324
10.3–4	84	1.18	324
10.6	236	4.31	132
11.1–7	239	5.19	132, 291
11.12	237	5.27	303
12.26	84	5.30	132
13.10	76	6.1	238
13.19	236	6.38	132
13.24–25	238	7.6	20–21
14.9	76	10.6	78
14.12	237	12.15–16	182
14.34–36	122	12.41	291
14.51–52	79	12.45	85–86
15.42–16.2	237	14.9	291
16.1–20	90	14.26	182
16.8	60	15.2–11	132
16.15	76	16.13	182
16.15–16	106	16.21–22	123
16.15–18	237	16.25	78
16.19	77	16.29	78
16.20	76–77	17.1	21

20.21–23	237
20.30–31	36
21	35–36
21.9–13	238
21.15–17	237

Acts
1.4–5	87
1.6–8	237
1.8	250
1.11	284
1.21	182
2	182
7.48–50	254
12.1	20
17.16–34	244, 248–56, 273
17.16	255
17.17–18	252
17.18	250, 252, 256
17.18–20	249
17.19	250
17.20	250, 255
17.21	157
17.22	249, 252
17.23	249
17.24–25	253
17.25	254, 259
17.26	254
17.27	254, 255
17.27–28	273
17.28	250, 255, 256
17.29	255, 256
17.29–30	249–50
17.30	256, 257
17.30–31	256
22.8	284
26.13	283

Romans
1.1	260
1–2	245
1.6	260
1.8	260
1.14	260
1.16	260

1.18	257
1.18–23	244–45, 256–62, 273, 274
1.18–3.20	287
1.19	258, 261
1.19–20	256–57, 257, 258
1.20	257
1.21	259, 261
1.21–22	258
1.21–23	274
1.23	258
2.1	259, 273, 274
2.12	258
2.17–20	260, 273
3.11	258
3.18	258
3.19	257–58
3.22	261
3.23	273
3.27	176
4.2	176
4.9–12	314
4.17	236
5.1	261
5.8,10	121
7.10	261
7.24–25	261
8.18–23	242
8.18–27	229
8.29	292
9.14–29	287
10.12	286
11.17	160
12.2	292
15.13	229

1 Corinthians
1.17	104
1.18–25	23
1.23	159
2.2	244
9.9	216
15	23
15.3	159
15.12	105
15.25–27	298

2 Corinthians
1–7	302
3.7–18	216
3.10	84
3.16	301
3.16–17	302
3.18	282, 283, 292, 301
4.4	281, 282, 283, 292, 301
4.5	301
4.6	282, 283
5.17	236, 282

Galatians
1.7	146
2.14	146
3.16	216
3.28	303
4.4	159
4.21–31	216
6.15	236

Ephesians
2.10–15	236
2.17–18	165
4.11–12	106

Colossians
1.15	281, 282, 301
3.9–11	281
3.10	282, 301, 303

1 Timothy
4.3	236

Hebrews
1	296
1.1–2	203
1.3	281
2	16
2.5–9	295–98
2.6–8	157, 303
2.7	297
2.9	298, 303
2.10	297
2.11–12	122
2.14	297
2.15	298
4.9	200
5.8	298
12.2	298
13.8	53

1 Peter
1.1	120
1.5	21
1.17	120
2.11	120

2 Peter
1.18	85

Revelation
1.14–16	283
4.6	262
14–22	120
15.2	262

Index of Subjects

academic field 2–3
academy, theology in vii-viii, 2–9
accommodation 150–51, 313–17
anthropomorphism 324
Auschwitz 62–63, 120–21

Barmen, Synod of 202
biblical studies 2–6
biblical theology 8–9, 13; criticisms
of, 17–27, 209–11; descriptive,
28; as unifying theological
disciplines, 28

canonicity 49–50, 271–72
canonical context 90, 126, 159,
211–13, 266–67
capitalism 234–35, 269
causality 57–60, 68
classic, the 49–51, 66–67, 72–73
communities, interpretative 11,
95–97, 117–19
contradictions 38–41, 257
covenant 194–96, 220
creation 151–53, 161, 225–75;
eschatological orientation,
227–30, 267; in the beginning,
230–35; Jewish view of, 253–
54, 312; *creatio ex nihilo*, 268;
human dominion over, 293–96

deconstruction 10–11, 90, 91
deism 130, 169
demythologizing 156
dialogue 309–10, 316–17, 320,
326–28
directedness 72, 89
dogma 97

empathy 46–48
Enlightenment 46, 305

feminism 285–86

Geisteswissenschaften 45
gnosticism 80–82
gospels, historicity of 9–10, 33–37,
52–54, 65; as narrative, 33–37;
historical-critical approach to,
37–41; as gospel, 73–77, 105–6;
titles, 74–75, 89; as biography,
89

'Hebrew Bible' 5, 219
historic event 51–54, 66–67
historicism 45–49, 57–60, 191
historiography 41–45, 54–63, 64,
65
Holy Spirit 129, 268

indeterminacy 72

intention, authorial 11–12; 105, 112–113, 123, 125, 133–35

Jesus 'historical', 10, 38, 47, 64, 176; as the Christ, 36–37, 51, 64, 83–87, 92, 217; as a creature, 91, 236–41; identity of, 92–93
Jewishness of Christianity 17, 138, 158–59, 162, 310–11, 313, 324, 329

light 283–84
literal sense 11–12, 107–24, 125

narrative 15, 225–26; criticism, 63
Nazism 164, 175

objectivity 11–12, 43, 113–15, 124, 193
occasionality 49, 66
Old Testament, as Christian scripture 5–6, 13–17, 179–85, 197–219, 221, 286–88, 297, 310, 320–25; rejection of, 143–46, 150–51, 172; scholarship, 5–6, 184–85, 197, 207–8, 209, 218, 222–23, 305–6; as the Jewish 'letter', 137–41
'original context' 104–5, 125, 157–60

parables 73, 78–82, 88, 91
plot 55–57, 67
Platonism 310–13
pluralism 95–96
postmodernism 96, 111

prophecy 130, 139–40, 154, 157–60, 174–75, 201–2, 317–20, 328

radicalism 6–7, 24, 26, 29, 156
reason 170
religion 130–31, 141–42, 147–48, 152, 186–91, 274
revelation 85–86; in the Old Testament, 173–74; natural, 163–64, 242–48, 255–56, 259–60, 262, 263, 266–67, 271

speech-act theory 124
systematic theology 3–4, 171–72, 270
testaments relation of, 5–6, 13–17, 155, 165–68, 179–85, 213–18, 223, 286–88, 301
textuality 128, 135–37, 140
time 54–55; biblical words for, 20–22
transfiguration 82–88, 92, 149–50
translation 107–16
trinity 268, 299–300, 322–24, 329
truth textual mediation of, 1–2, 12–13; extra-textual, 9–12, 34–37, 64–65
typology 197–98, 200–1, 203–7

unitarianism 329

virgin birth 218

Wirkungsgeschichte 4, 49, 52
writing 35; and speech, 12–13, 28, 135, 171; as speech-act, 98–106; as communication, 98–106

Index of Names

Anderson, B. 219, 268
Aquinas 299, 303
Archambault, G. 326
Aristotle 15, 16, 54, 55, 225–26
Arius 174
Ateek, N. S. 176
Athanasius 174
Attridge, H. 303
Augustine 54, 55, 80, 141, 186,
    278, 305, 328
Aune, D. 89
Austin, J. L. 124

Barclay, J. 270
Barr, J. 15, 18–26, 29, 64, 223,
    243–48, 271–72, 273, 300, 303
Barrett, C. K. 245
Barth, K. 126, 154, 171–73, 175,
    188–91, 192, 220, 246–48, 268,
    271, 272, 273, 301
Barton, J. 172
Baumgärtel, F. 169
Baur, F. C. 147
Beethoven, L. van 49
Belleville, L. 302
Bonhoeffer, D. 92, 302
Bornkamm, G. 65
Bornkamm, H. 169
Brett, M. 223
Brueggemann, W. 124

Bright, J. 169
Brunner, E. 210, 248, 271
Buber, M. 220
Bultmann, R. 12, 13, 128, 153–69,
    174, 175, 176, 187, 188, 190,
    210, 220
Bunge, M. 169
Buren, P. van 210

Calvin, J. 38, 40–41, 63–64, 128–
    29, 135, 305
Carroll R. M. 269
Celsus 317–18
Childs, B. 14–15, 90, 125, 126,
    209–19, 223, 224, 269, 273,
    301, 306
Coleridge, S. T. 170
Clines, D. 124
Cochrane, A. 175, 221
Coggins, R. J. 172
Collins, A. 328
Conzelmann, H. 176
Cook, A. 41–45, 64
d'Costa, G. 328
Coverdale, M. 109, 110, 111
Cox, H. 210
Cranfield, C. E. B. 90, 245, 273
Crenshaw, J. 221
Crossan, J. D. 91
Cullmann, O. 19, 21–23

Cupitt, D. 91

Davies, P. 224
Delling, G. 20–21
Derrida, J. 13, 29, 171
Descartes, R. 129
Dibelius, M. 251–52, 272–73
Dilthey, W. 45–48, 66, 68
Dodd, C. H. 78, 270
Dray, W. 58–59
Drury, J. 328
Dunn, J. D. G. 326–28, 329

Ebeling, G. 28
Edwards, M. 64
Eichrodt, W. 14, 185–86, 192–97, 198, 219, 220, 274
Eissfeldt, O. 191–93
Eliot, G. 169–70
Ellingworth, P. 303
Engels, F. 269
Erasmus 188
Eusebius 326

Fiorenza, E. S. 124
Forsyth, P. T. 173
Fredriksen, P. 64
Frei, H. 63, 92–93, 125, 174–75, 220
Frend, W. H. C. 326
Foucault, M. 64–65, 272
Friedrich, G. 19–20
Frye, N. 64, 328
Furnish, V. 301

Gadamer, H.-G. 45–46, 49–51, 65, 66, 170
Gallie, W. B. 58
Gerrish, B. 128
Gese, H. 223
Gibbon, E. 42, 44
Goethe, J. W. von 144
Goldingay, J. 219
Gottwald, N. 213
Goodenough, E. R. 326

Goodspeed, E. J. 272
Goodwin, C. W. 269
Gossman, L. 42
de Gruchy, J. 175
Gunkel, H. 302
Gunton, C. 91, 270

Habermas, J. 67, 124
Harnack, A. von 12, 89, 128, 141–53, 172–73, 174, 186, 189–90, 220, 246, 327
Hauerwas, S. 66
Hayes, J. H. 219
Hays, R. 223
Headlam, A. C. 273
Hegel, G. 143, 171
Heidegger, M. 54
Hempel, K. 57, 58
Hengel, M. 89
Herder, J. G. 169
Herodotus 42
Herrmann, W. 186, 246
Hirsch, E. 169
Hirsch, E. D. 124, 125
Høgenhaven, J. 222
Holl, K. 187–88, 189
Hoskyns, E. 220
Hooker, M. 89
Houlden, J. L. 172
Humbert, P. 302
Hunsinger, G. 63, 92, 125, 220
Husserl, E. 54, 55

Ihde, D. 67
Irenaeus 74, 80, 173–74, 290–91, 305

Jaspert, B. 220
Jeanrond, W. 66
Jeremias, J. 78
Joyce, J. 79, 81
Juhl, P. D. 125
Jülicher, A. 78, 190, 220
Jüngel, E. 221
Justin Martyr 17, 307–29

Kafka, F. 81, 82
Kähler, M. 64
Kant, I. 54, 144, 172, 188, 271
Käsemann, E. 175
Kautzsch, E. 125
Keck, L. 272
Kermode, F. 10, 28, 67, 72–74,
    77–82, 88, 89, 90
Kierkegaard, S. 90
Kimmerle, H. 171
Kittel, G. 19–20, 21
Kittel, R. 125
Knight, D. 223
Köhler, L. 198, 302
Krauss, H.-J. 303
Kuhn, T. 272
Kümmel, W. G. 323

Lane, W. 303
Lemcio, E. 65
Lessing, G. E. 169
Levenson, J. 222
Levi, P. 62–63
Lieu, J. 327
Lightfoot, R. H. 92
Lindbeck, G. 274
Lohse, E. 301
Lowe, W. 90
Lücke, G. C. F. 130
Luther, M. 46–47, 76, 109, 110,
    143, 169, 186, 187–88, 219, 305
Luz, U. 304

McFadyen, A. 91, 303
Mack, B. 91–92
Mackintosh, H. R. 169
McLellan, D. 269
McNeill, J. 169
Mann, T. 55
Marcion 17, 127, 128, 141–53,
    172, 174, 269, 310–11, 313,
    326, 327
Martyn, J. L. 272
Marx, K. 269
Michaelis, J. D. 203

Milbank, J. 328
Moberly, W. 219
Moltmann, J. 15, 220, 227–32,
    236, 267, 268, 269, 270, 302–3,
    304
Moore, S. 28, 90–91
Morris, P. 302
Mozart, W. A. 49
Mudge, L. 68
Mueller-Vollmer, K. 66
Myers, C. 92

Niebuhr, R. 278
Nietzsche, F. 48–49, 66

Ogden, S. 175
Oman, J. 169
Otto, R. 188, 189, 190, 191

Pannenberg, W. 67, 221, 272,
    327
Perdue, L. 222
Phillips, G. 124
Philo 174, 277–78, 301, 312,
    327
Placher, W. C. 63, 92, 220
Plato 16, 311
Powell, M. A. 63
Pratt, M.-L. 124
Procksch, O. 192
Proust, M. 55
Provan, I. viii
Prussner, F. C. 219

Rad, G. von 14, 15, 176, 197–210,
    219, 221–22, 268, 269, 302
Reimarus, H. S. 169
Rendtorff, R. 175, 221–22, 268
Reventlow, H. Graf 29, 169, 221
Ricoeur, P. 28, 54–63, 67, 69, 125,
    171
Ritschl, A. 144, 246
Ritschl, D. 172
Rooke, B. 170
Rumscheidt, M. 173, 220

Sanday, W. 273
Sanders, J. A. 126, 222
Sanders, J. T. 326
Sawyer, D. 301
Sawyer, J. 302
Schleiermacher, F. 68, 128–41,
    143, 144, 170, 171, 172, 187,
    190, 271, 327
Scholder, K. 175
Schweitzer, A. 154, 270
Schwöbel, C. 270, 272
Searle, J. R. 124
Sellin, E. 198
Shaw, G. 273–74
Sherlock, T. 174
Simkins, R. 270–71
Smart, J. 29
Spinoza 46, 57, 65–66
Spriggs, D. 220
Stendahl, K. 28
Stewart, J. S. 169
Strauss, D. F. 38–41, 46, 64, 133,
    169–70
Stylianopoulos, T. 327
Sykes, S. 173

Tacitus 43
Talbert, C. 169
Taylor, M. 91
Tertullian 146–52, 329
Thiselton, A. 66, 67, 89, 124, 171
Thompson, J. 67, 68, 171

Thucydides 44
Thurneysen, E. 192
Tice, T. 170
Tillich, P. 210
Tolbert, M.-A. 90
Torrance, A. viii
Torrance, T. F. 92
Tracy, D. 66–67, 125
Trible, P. 303–4
Troeltsch, E. 57–58, 174, 203–4

Valentinus 17, 310–11, 326
Vanhoozer, K. 67, 68,
Veeser, H. A. 65
Vielhauer, P. 272, 273
Vischer, W. 202, 219, 221–22

Warner, M. 64
Weiser, A. 274–75
Weiss, J. 154, 173
Wellhausen, J. 213
Westermann, C. 174, 221, 302
White, H. 64
Wittgenstein, L. 58, 68
Wolff, H.-W. 221
Woolf, V. 55
Wrede, W. 154
Wright, G. E. 223
Wright, N. T. 301

Zahn, T. 89
Zimmerli, W. 125, 302